Artificial Africas

Reencounters with Colonialism: New Perspectives on the Americas

EDITORS
Mary C. Kelley, American History, Dartmouth College
Agnes Lugo-Ortiz, Latin American Studies, Dartmouth College
Donald Pease, American Literature, Dartmouth College
Ivy Schweitzer, American Literature, Dartmouth College
Diana Taylor, Latin American and Latino Studies, New York University

Frances R. Aparicio and Susana Chávez-Silverman, eds., *Tropicalizations: Transcultural Representations of Latinidad*

Michelle Burnham, *Captivity and Sentiment: Cultural Exchange in American Literature, 1682–1861*

Colin G. Calloway, ed., *After King Philip's War: Presence and Persistence in Indian New England*

Carla Gardina Pestana and Sharon V. Salinger, *Inequality in Early America*

Renée L. Bergland, *The National Uncanny: Indian Ghosts and American Subjects*

Susana Rotker, *The American Chronicles of José Martí: Journalism and Modernity in Spanish America*

Carlton Smith, *Coyote Kills John Wayne: Postmodernism and Contemporary Fictions of the Transcultural Frontier*

C. L. R. James, *Mariners, Renegades and Castaways: The Story of Herman Melville and the World We Live In,* with an introduction by Donald E. Pease

Irene Ramalho Santos, *Atlantic Poets: Fernando Pessoa's Turn in Anglo-American Modernism*

Ruth Mayer, *Artificial Africas: Colonial Images in the Times of Globalization*

Artificial Africas

COLONIAL IMAGES IN THE
TIMES OF GLOBALIZATION

Ruth Mayer

Dartmouth College
Published by University Press of New England
Hanover and London

Dartmouth College

Published by University Press of New England,

One Court Street, Lebanon, NH 03766

© 2002 by Ruth Mayer

All rights reserved

Printed in the United States of America

5 4 3 2 1

Library of Congress Cataloging-in-Publication Data

Mayer, Ruth.
  Artificial Africas : colonial images in the times of globalization /
Ruth Mayer.
      p. cm. — (Reencounters with colonialism—new perspectives on
the Americas)
Includes bibliographical references and index.
  ISBN 1–58465–191–1 (cloth : alk. paper) — ISBN 1–58465–192–X (pbk. :
alk. paper)
  1. Africa in popular culture—United States. 2. Africa—In motion
pictures. 3. Africa—In literature. I. Title. II. Series.
  E169.04 .M3694 2002
  960—dc21   2002006604

Photographs from *The End of the Game* by Peter Beard were reprinted with the
permission of the artist and Art + Commerce Anthology, Inc.
Details from *Vistavision. Landscapes of Desire* by Renée Green were reprinted
courtesy of Pat Hearn Gallery, New York.
Untitled (Went Looking for Africa) and *Untitled* (Ebo Landing) as well as
details from *Untitled* (Boone Plantation) by Carrie Mae Weems were reprinted
with the permission of the artist and P.P.O.W. Gallery, New York.
Details from *A Ship Called Jesus* by Keith Piper were reprinted courtesy of the
artist and Ikon Gallery, Birmingham, England.
Illustrations from *Captain Africa #3: Bite of the Scarab* (1994) by reprinted
courtesy of Dwayne J. Ferguson and Diehard Studio, Glen Ridge, New Jersey.

Contents

Acknowledgments

Writing a book can be an ordeal, as every so often writing is solitary work. If this book was a pleasure to write, it was due to my friends all over the world who made sure that loneliness was never part of it. They worked hard at keeping me happy, taking me out, taking me in, and taking me on whenever I showed up in need.

I started to do research for this study while still teaching at the University of Cologne in Germany. My friends and colleagues in Cologne have been part of the project from its very beginning. Thanks especially to Anke Bösel, Brigitte Weingart, Mark Terkessidis, and Stefan Römer for many suggestions, interventions, ideas, and distractions offered over the years.

The German Research Association be praised for granting one of the last two-year "Habilitationsstipendien," funding a wonderful and most productive period of research and writing in New York. Heinz Ickstadt, Don Pease, and Mike Rogin were immensely helpful in the application process for this grant. Without them, it would never have worked out. The sad news of Mike Rogin's untimely death some weeks ago affected me deeply. His interest in and support for my project meant much to me. I lost a wonderful adviser and a good friend.

The American Studies Program of the New York University kindly extended an affiliation. Special thanks to Andrew Ross for all the help there. Thanks to Maren Stange for providing shelter and much needed advice, to Ralph Obermauer, Gerald Echterhof, Andrea Dortmann, Zhang-Ga, and Claudia Klucaric for initiating me into the secrets of the city, and to many, many others for pointing me to material, sources, contacts, and connections in New York and elsewhere in the United States.

Many people have read parts of the manuscript; some have actually read all of it: thanks to Anke Bösel, Mark Terkessidis, Brigitte Weingart, Andrea Dortmann, Gesa Mackenthun, Gerald Echterhoff, Russ West, Lisa Lynch, Alex Weheliye, and Alondra Nelson for all the helpful remarks and for all the criticism, which I usually found tremendously annoying at first but quite insightful and to the point sometime later. Don Pease and J. Martin Favor, my readers for University Press of New England, took on the entire text, and so did the members of the committee of the University of Cologne, where the study was accepted as a Habilitationsschrift. All of these readers' suggestions were gratefully taken into account; many have made their way into the final version of the manuscript. Special thanks are due to Hanjo Berressem, who stepped in at a moment of dire need to head the Cologne committee, steer me through the strangely convoluted rituals of what we Germans call Habilitation, offered wagonloads of advice, and refused to get unnerved. Alex von Rönn, my research assistant at the University of Hanover, developed into a visual expert during the last phase of this project. Many thanks to her for picture work and image support of all sorts. The people at University Press of New England were a joy to work with.

Marcel Reginatto probably annoyed me most with all his critique and all his skepticism. His many interventions changed the book, and my life, most profoundly. Thanks for reading, thanks for insisting, and thanks for patiently holding out in all of these "I'm a genius / it's never going to work" times. And thanks, as always, to the people that shape my writing and my thinking in ways that are too intricate and too personal to disentangle here—my family.

Hanover, Germany
December 2001

Artificial Africas

Introduction

I.

Books about Africa are deceptive at best.

—Walter Abish, *Alphabetical Africa* (1974)[1]

This is not a book about Africa. It is a book about speculations, projections, fantasies, and fears—tracing the images of Africa in the
Western world. It is a book about the logic of cultural stereotyping,
a logic that seems to rely upon trite, narrow, and repetitive structures and
yet will turn out to be a complex technique of meaning making, constantly moving between the familiar and the new, and indefatigably adjusting the symbolic repertory of yesterday to the conceptual and ideological frameworks of today. And thus it is also a book about the
transformation of symbolic systems, tracing the transition from a colonial
rhetoric of conquest and discipline to a postcolonial[2] rhetoric of globalization,[3] communication, and control, a transition that is often enough
hard to pin down as it involves a repertory of images, tropes, and stock
figures that seems stable at first, disclosing its flexibility and precarious-
ness only at second sight.

Africa is an artificial entity, invented and conceived by colonialism.
There is no such thing as an underlying cultural heritage that would pertain equally to Egypt and Namibia, Kenya and the Congo.[4] Thus, the
very notion of Africa, or rather "Africanity," as I will call the artificial
concoctions of Africa, attests to the fact that at least in one respect the gigantic project of colonialism did work: forcing most diverse regions,
traditions, and cultures in Africa into one symbolic system, colonial
rule brought about an imperialist framework of representation that is
still effective today, even if the effects are not necessarily what they used
to be. Edward Said thus evoked "the residuum of a dense, interesting
history that is paradoxically global and local at the same time, and . . .
a sign of how the imperialist past lives on, arousing argument and

counter-argument with surprising intensity."[5] It is precisely on this basis—the succession of arguments and counterarguments—that the imperialist past both continues *and* undergoes transformations, living on in ever new guises and changing shape in the very process of being commemorated and preserved.

The rhetoric and imagery of colonialism, established in the heydays of imperial takeover, proved highly flexible and volatile, serving all kinds of purposes and interests after the demise of old-style colonial rule, when the incentives of unifying subjugation were challenged and new symbolic systems arose—not always and not necessarily in open contradiction to the old ones: "Representations of the African were, and are, evidently not 'fixed' but eminently recuperable and variable, depending on the political exigencies of any specific historical conjuncture," holds Annie E. Coombes. "As such, they tell us more about the nexus of European interests in African affairs and about the coloniser, than they do about Africa and the African over this period."[6]

Terence Ranger has delineated the same pattern of thought much earlier in his influential study on the British obsession with tradition and national identity, an obsession that left its traces in indigenous efforts at self-definition and independence, providing important patterns for talking about tradition: "the invented traditions of African societies—whether invented by the Europeans or by Africans themselves in response—distorted the past but became in themselves realities through which a good deal of colonial encounter was expressed."[7] And Kwame Anthony Appiah elaborated this idea of an invented tradition: "the very invention of Africa (as something more than a geographical entity) must be understood, ultimately, as an outgrowth of European racialism; the notion of Pan-Africanism was founded on the notion of the African, which was, in turn, founded not on any genuine cultural commonality but on the very European concept of the Negro."[8] Both Ranger's and Appiah's reflections, like V. Y. Mudimbe's work, show that a discussion of Africa should not run exclusively along the lines of categories like "genuine/faked" or "true/false," as emancipatory movements such as Pan-Africanism or négritude draw upon the very categories established by colonialism, so that the invented traditions and projections of the colonial regimes often enough can be seen to constitute the point of departure for radically oppositional projects of self-fashioning and critique.

II.

Reinterpretations and revisions do not take place only on the African continent in the reflections of postcolonial politics, art, and literature but all over the world—in the cultures of the African diaspora just as in Western mainstream culture, on movie screens, in pop songs, advertisements, and comic books. I will concentrate in this book on the context of the United States, where the imagery of colonialism has undergone a complex, if highly ambivalent, transformation within the last decades.

Hollywood, as perhaps the most influential producer of images in this century, has always loved colonialism. And a brief glance at the history of this love affair between American film and the British Empire might help to get a grip on the current state of affairs. After all, what we see in the movies is often enough not what the film claims to be about. Insofar, the filmic history of representing colonialism has been consistent since its outset in the late nineteenth century.[9] But of course, seen from a slightly different angle, the filmic traditions of representing colonialism and Africa have undergone tremendous changes, as there is no such thing as a timeless work of art. Thus, even where films pretend to be about another time and another space they invariably tell us also something about their time of production. And often, these hidden messages are more interesting than the explicit ones.

Let me elaborate this structure of indirection by way of an example: *Khartoum*, a Hollywood production of 1966,[10] at first glance seems to rewrite colonial history and its patterns of self-legitimation by presenting an episode of British colonial history in a light clearly sympathetic to the colonizers. The film is about a revolt in the 1880s against the Egyptian rulers of the Sudan, instigated by Al Mahdi, a charismatic spiritual and political leader. The historical uprisal culminated in the capture of Khartoum, the capital, by Al Mahdi's followers. As Egypt had been de facto under British control since 1882, the revolt was taken as an assault on the British Empire. In 1898, the Sudan was recaptured by British troops and turned in a British-Egyptian condominium one year later. In its Hollywood reiteration, however, this classical event of colonial history becomes a reflection of American cold war issues: When faced with the victorious ascent of the Mahdi (Laurence Olivier), the British prime minister Gladstone (Ralph Richardson) at first refuses to send troops, even in the face of appeals to Britain's "moral responsibility to Egypt." "I will not assume a British obligation to help the world," he declares unnerved. Instead of sending an army, he sends Charlton Heston to resolve the conflict covertly. Who does his best to avoid violence but, faced with African corruption and cruelty, most evident in the atrocious practices of the African slave trade, cannot help but fight.

What can of course be read as nostalgia for the British Empire in the face of its decline makes just as much sense as a "historical lap-dissolve by which British-dominated imperialism of the nineteenth century faded into the US-dominated imperialism of the twentieth," as Ella Shohat and Robert Stam pointed out.[11] Indeed, twentieth-century practices and rhetorics suffuse the film—Gladstone sounding like Lyndon B. Johnson, covert actions replacing open military aggression, spectacle diverting from politics, let alone the overall rhetoric of liberty, peace, justice, and responsibility, and the strategy of inverting the American history of race relations, projecting it onto another continent and thus absolving the West and blaming the rest (turning American slavery and violence into African slavery and cruelty).

Hence, this example of a twentieth-century revision of nineteenth-century history accentuates what Anne McClintock called the "*continuities* in international imbalances in imperial power,"[12] but even more important it points to the breaks between the colonial and the postcolonial situation, the unacknowledged and yet glaring transformation that the colonial rhetorics of legitimate rule underwent when translated into the more contemporary rhetorics of the "world police." Fashioning the Great Britain of the 1880s in the light of American cold war politics of the 1960s, yet simultaneously obfuscating this analogy, as it is not "about" the United States, the film reflects its contemporary political context precisely because it focuses on the far-away. *Khartoum* thus ends up neatly replicating the "cold war discourse, which defines American exceptionalism as inherently anti-imperialist, in opposition to the empire-building of either the Old World or of communism and fascism which collapse together into totalitarianism."[13]

And this is where Hollywood has remained true to itself over all these years. Today, as in the 1960s, colonialism is of interest to the movies because it is a foreign affair. While these days *Khartoum*'s open endorsement of colonialism would be inconceivable for a major picture, as box office hits from *Out of Africa* (1985) to *The English Patient* (1996), Clint Eastwood's *White Hunter, Black Heart* (1990) or Nicolas Roeg's TV movie *Heart of Darkness* (1994), take great pains to disavow colonial practices of subjugation and domination, such practices are nevertheless just as clearly demarcated as the sad side effects of a markedly bygone past, when stiff Brits and militaristic Germans ruled the world. And in line with such spectacles of distantiation, mainstream enactments of the history of US race relations such as Steven Spielberg's *Amistad* (1997) introduce a global context in order to deflect from a far from glorious national history.

Of course, such problematic oscillations between national and global matters are countered by just as many recent narratives that interlink the histories of Africa and America, and the contexts of slavery, colonialism, imperialism, and globalization, not in order to exculpate or aggrandize but to come to terms with a past and a present of race relations from the vantage point of international interests and global interrelations. This study deals with both kinds of links between Africa and America—acknowledged and obfuscated—and opens up a transhistorical perspective at that. This is not to say that I intend to compile an all-comprising catalogue of Africanist representations in the West. Instead, I will reread classical European texts on colonialism alongside American classics on Africa and its impact, and confront these readings with contemporary revisionary narratives and enactments of Africa. It will soon become obvious that all of these "artificial Africas" could not be farther away from the "lived reality," the *Lebenswirklichkeit,* of a geographical Africa. Once more, this is not a book about Africa. Neither is it exclusively a book about America, however. The Western fascination with artificial Africas calls for a wider perspective, for reflections that take into account the variegated and convoluted history of international efforts at interlinkage and distinction, unity and specificity.

I thus place my work into the context of a series of recent studies that have equally insisted upon the need to place the history of the United States back into a global context, forgoing American exceptionalism by giving scope to a wider view. The history of American literature, popular culture, politics, and academic debate has been read as intricately involved with more pervasive developments, interests, and incentives, a constant back-and-forth between the desire for expansion, the fascination with contact, and the fear of takeover, which infuses all kinds of cultural utterances and expressions.[14] In line with such reflections, Toni Morrison argued that Africanity has always functioned as a powerful subtext not only for black but also for white cultures in the United States, presenting highly ambivalent metaphors of authenticity, primitivity, difference, and otherness with alternately fascinating or frightening connotations. For Morrison, a "dark, abiding, signing Africanist presence" is situated at the core of American mainstream culture, a hidden and paradoxical system of reference for conceptualizing national identity: ". . . the process of organizing American coherence through a distancing Africanism became the operative mode of a new cultural hegemony."[15]

It is important to keep in mind, however, that such an "Africanist operative mode" should not be conceptualized as an all-conclusive and committing code or subtext but rather constitutes a fragmentary collection of images and styles, called up and acted out in ever varying ways and contexts. Africanity functions like a modern myth in the sense of Roland Barthes, who wrote about a photograph of a saluting black soldier underneath the French flag: "the negro who salutes is not the symbol of the French Empire: he has too much presence, he appears as a rich, fully experienced, spontaneous, innocent, *indisputable* image."[16] Modern myths are artificial, constructed and immediately accessible, as Roland Barthes maintained. And yet, as trite as such mythical concoctions doubtlessly are, they have far more sophisticated effects than we might first assume, and these effects are intimately conjoined with their very artificiality. To claim that a constellation is artificial or constructed—"mythical," in Barthes's terminology—is not to say, after all, that it may not have powerful ideological implications. To the contrary, it is precisely *because* of their artificiality and disposability that modern myths form the basis for ideological adaptations and transformations.

These aspects come to the fore in current African-American culture, where many Africanist images (from Kwanza celebrations to kente cloth) are doubtlessly artificial and often enough highly stereotypical. To judge these expressions on the basis of their lack of realism or historical accuracy alone, however, would be a fatal mistake. "[W]e labor / to make our getaway, into / the ancient image, into a new / correspondence with ourselves / and our black family," writes Amiri Baraka in his poem "Ka 'Ba" (1969) about the functions of "african imaginations"—and thus indicates that he cherishes the ancient not for its own sake but because it brings about the new, because it can be used to "raise up / return, destroy, and create."[17]

By dint of this approach, Africa indeed turns into a "getaway," not a geographical location or concrete cultural reference but a symbolic point of departure, a strategic signifier. The poem exemplarily expresses an insight that Paul Gilroy found to be central in black popular culture at large, where "the purist idea of one-way flow of African culture from east to west was . . . revealed to be absurd." Time and again, Gilroy argues, black cultural utterances simultaneously confirm and place into question "the principal symbol of racial authenticity,"[18] just as Baraka both draws upon the notion of an original (and highly exotic) African heritage and then turns it into a "new correspondence."

III.

Baraka's technique of inversion once more calls to mind the issues of subjugation and discipline—practices that lie at heart of race relations and of the systems of colonial rule and that rely very much on stereotypical discourse. As Homi Bhabha has shown, however, colonial discourse is not only restrictive but always also constructive, its very stereotypicality the basis for ideological reorientation and novelty: "My reading of colonial discourse suggests that the point of intervention should shift from the ready recognition of images as positive or negative, to an understanding of *processes of subjectivication* made possible (and plausible) through stereotypical discourse."[19] In this light, the stereotype becomes an ambivalent category that functions not only as an instrument of simplification and submission but contains much more productive potential, and thus may at times turn into a figure of empowerment and resistance. Hence it is not so much by way of dismantling the stereotype, always a hard thing to do, that colonial discourse is subverted, but by repeating it with a difference—turning the high drama into a farce, and the costume piece into a grotesque masquerade.

Michael Taussig invokes the terminology of "mimesis"—the process "wherein the replication, the copy, acquires the power of the represented"[20]—to delineate the subversion of preordained systems of signification, which are appropriated and transformed in the very act of repetition. As one example, Taussig discusses the practice of male Cuna Indians to adopt Western garb, while Cuna women stick to long-standing ethnic dress codes. While such shifts have traditionally been understood as indications of assimilation on the part of Cuna men, Taussig reads both male and female practices as instances of "mimetic labor," split up in a "male-female division."[21] Whether donning traditional or Western garb, Taussig argues, the Cuna practices have to be seen as efforts at making sense of the new, translating the foreign into the familiar, and changing both systems of knowledge in the course of this translation. The Cuna men thus put on Western clothes "like an actor donning another persona,"[22] refashioning the modern outfits in rituals of impersonation and magic, and what seems like a turn away from cultural difference, at first glance, soon appears as a much more complicated process of cultural meaning making: "What the alterizing Western eye tends not to see . . . in its infatuation with the Indian women's 'colorful' gear, is that its own, Western men's, clothes can have magical significance: that trousers and ties and derby hats create magic too. . . ."[23]

Let us neglect for the moment the tricky question of how the Western ethnographer is to perceive the Cuna world with anything but "Western eyes." What interests me in Taussig's anecdote is its insistence on practices of masquerade, impersonation, and imitation, practices that invariably figure forth sameness and difference, expressing the desire to become the other and still not lose oneself, or the logic of "almost the same but not quite," as Homi Bhabha had it.[24] By dint of such imageries, cultural contact may be conceptualized as the indirect and multilayered process it is, too complicated and too ambivalent to be explained along the lines of one-sided assimilation or subjugation alone. Whether such contact scenarios evolve in the context of colonial takeover or in the interactions of minorities and the mainstream in the West, they are never easily deducible from a systematic plan or a set of conscious strategies, as they are always caught in the pull of alogical forces and unacknowledged impulses, inflected with desire, fear, and the need to make sense of the new. Let me thus make totally clear that I consider such practices as neither intrinsically positive nor negative. The recognition that cultural contact brings about indeterminacy and ambivalence, that seemingly stable meanings may be subtly inverted in the very process of articulating them, does not imply a value judgment in itself. Concepts of cultural contact from mimicry to mimesis, from signifying to trickery, I argue, have to be implemented as purely descriptive categories, not as liberatory principles, even if the latter use seems to become increasingly popular these days.

This study thus definitely does not join into the current vogue of celebrating masquerade, impersonation, and parody as unfailing techniques of cultural subversion, and of reading any deviation from a code or norm in terms of resistance. Nor do I share the widespread enthusiasm for "cultural hybridity" as a blueprint for joyful resistance. As the mixed-up product of clashing symbolic systems and sociocultural tensions, hybridity will never resolve the problematic implications of uneven power conditions or exploitation, and while it may at times bring about carnivalesque pleasure, it can very well create frustration and fear once the circumstances have changed.[25]

IV.

Cultural contact is always messy. But rather than enthusing over this messiness, I intend to concentrate on its varying contexts and conditions and to investigate strategies of coping and containment, in order to come to terms with the ideological implications of the phenomena at hand. This is why I chose to focus on a relatively limited repertory of stereotypical images to enact difference, centered on the tropes of trickery and masquerade, and to pay close attention to the formal, structural, and stylistic conditions of these enactments. After all, the very same stereotype can adopt diametrically opposed functions depending on its historical and genre-specific context. Obviously Western representations of Africa and the African diaspora are determined to this day by an amazingly stable set of images, but less obviously these images have been invested with varying, often irreconcilable, connotations.

It is in popular cultural fictions and artistic representations that the intricacies of such enactments come to the fore, as here dominant conceptions and symbolic systems are both acted out and challenged, while alternative ideas are developed spontaneously, tentatively, and uncoordinately, thus often anticipating larger political and social transformations. Of course, these days more than ever before, the potential of popular culture to not only repeat but also rupture and transform dominant ideological stances is somewhat compromised, as popular culture appears to be deeply entrenched with commercial and political strategies of appropriation and co-optation. Since the 1960s, as Thomas Frank has shown, "hip is hegemon"—and long-standing binaries such as the "inflexible scheme of square and hip . . . , 'homogeneity' versus 'heterogeneity,' the 'power bloc' versus 'the people,' conformity versus individualism" have collapsed, as "hip became central to the way American capitalism understood itself and explained itself to the public."[26] But still—while popular fictions and narratives, street styles and fashion trends, may often reflect and express dominant ideological stances, they just as often indicate inconclusiveness or breaks within public discourses, and thus open up areas of cultural indeterminacy and change.[27]

V.

To talk about cultural contact and its changing forms and functions is to talk about acts of translation. And translation, this "somewhat provisional way of taking the foreignness of languages into account,"[28] is a complicated project. In his seminal reflections on the processes and problems of literary translation, Walter Benjamin argued that translations always cut both ways, as they are never neutral processes of information transmission. Depending on one's point of view, a surplus or deficit of meaning comes about when a text is transferred from one system of signification into another, and it is precisely this difference—the deviation of the "copy" from the original—that is of interest for the critic of comparative literature: "no translation would be possible if it were striving in its ultimate being for similarity with the original."[29]

Of course, such reflections gain even more weight once we turn to the field of cultural translation, where the differences between copy and original are more incisive still, as all kinds of additional disturbances arise next to the purely linguistic ones, all of them obfuscating the process of transmission further. And again, it is the translative deviations that are of interest here, the copy's status as "almost the same but not quite," as Homi Bhabha had it, and thus its propensity to change the status quo ever so slightly in the process of repetition.[30]

In the field of cultural contact, differences are closely enmeshed with value categories, so that the encounter of different symbolic systems time and again calls up questions of superiority and submission, specificity and assimilation. By consequence, translation almost invariably involves trickery—as each side tries to manipulate the other more or less subtly into complying with its own values and interests. After all, even where cultural contact is conceptualized as harmonious and benign (such as in representations of colonialism as a civilizing or Christianizing influence, or of globalization as a multicultural joint venture for the better of everybody involved), differences doubtlessly arise and need to be negotiated one way or another. More often than not such negotiations take place underneath the surface of what is said openly, and people resort to trickery in order to stabilize or improve power positions, or to carve out a sphere of social action and agency for themselves and their group. The systems of cultural communication can thus be said to oscillate between the need for understanding, the desire for control, and the fear of co-optation—a complicated balance of forces that easily runs out of hand, especially once established social hierarchies shift and cultural values change.

This is where what I will call "trick translation" sets in—modes of organizing cultural contact that seem to establish unobstructed circuits of communication but actually pursue unacknowledged interests and unvoiced plans. Such discursive manipulations take place on both sides of the colonial and postcolonial divide, as trick translators can be found among the colonizers and among the colonized, among the powerful and among the weak, their interference complicating the already complicated processes of cultural translation even more. Thus *the* colonial contact scenario—the colonizers' trading of cheap trinkets against the native treasures and goodwill—can very well be seen from two altogether different perspectives. Instead of envisioning the natives exclusively in terms of being tricked into compliance, as colonialism's naive and innocent victims, a slight shift of perspective suffices to imagine the native traders' point of view, who—relying upon a different framework of evaluation and values—have just as much reason to think that they are in charge: not the tricked ones, deplorable and ridiculous, but the tricksters. What both kinds of tricksters have in common is the insight that communication runs along crooked lines where power is involved. All of them know that the task of rendering difference manageable and making sense—and profit—of the other without getting lost oneself is not to be achieved by open talk alone. Thus the very scenario of cultural contact, as I conceive of it, calls for a reconsideration of the concept of communication along the lines sketched out by Fredric Jameson with reference to Jean-François Lyotard:

> . . . language itself [is] an unstable exchange between its speakers, whose utterances are now seen less as a process of the transmission of information or messages, or in terms of some network of signs or even signifying systems, than as (to use one of Lyotard's favorite figures) the "taking of tricks," the trumping of a communicational adversary, and essentially conflictual relationship between tricksters—and not as a well-regulated and noisefree "passing of tokens from hand to hand" (Mallarmé on denotative speech).[31]

The trickster figures of colonial and postcolonial contact narratives can be seen firmly entrenched in such conditions of uneven, disturbed, manipulated communication, and the very framework in which these tricksters move about epitomizes the shortcomings and potentials of this condition. The narratives of cultural contact themselves are, after all, invariably reflections on the powers and failures of communication. But then, to widen the perspective even further, storytelling in general could be conceived of as a perpetual acting out of communication, a never ending promotion and contestation of cultural values that to a large extent evolves indirectly, by way of formal manipulations of what Winfried Fluck has called a "cultural imaginary"—"a site of imagined meanings which struggle for articulation . . . and a repertory of images, affects, and yearnings which stimulate the individual imaginary ever newly and thus constantly challenge our understanding of reality."[32]

Again, it is the concept of translation that has been evoked in order to get a grip on the specific function and effect of fiction. Wolfgang Iser argued that fictional texts are both constituted by processes of translation and trigger them in turn, as producers of literature "translate" the imaginary into a concrete context or function and their recipients "translate" (literary) experience into understanding, actualizing it in the service of their own meaning making. Iser's "acts of fictionalizing" *(Akte des Fingierens)* are thus always also acts of translation.[33] While Iser cherishes the productive potential of these processes, however, once they are seen from the vantage point of ideological critique they may just as well appear as highly problematic.

Both the act of narrating and the act of reception, in their propensity to generate overarching meaning out of specific, disconnected, fragmentary elements of cognition and experience, have consequently been critized as projects of "totalization": "narrative strains to produce the effect of having filled in all the gaps, to put an image of continuity, coherency, and meaning in place of the fantasies of emptiness, need, and frustrated desire that inhabit our nightmares about the destructive power of time,"[34] as Hayden White describes this process, then proceeding to argue that all kinds of narratives, be they historiographical or literary, have a more or less acknowledged fictional dimension.

But of course, White's "anti-narrativist stance"[35] does not constitute the only model of reflecting upon possible ideological functions of narration, let alone fiction and storytelling. Writing about folktales, Michel de Certeau delineated the potential of narrative to put forth and circulate a markedly "irreal" view of the world and thus not only to create consensus and closure but to open up alternative perspectives or put existing ones into jeopardy:

The formality of everyday practices is indicated in these tales, which frequently reverse the relationships and, like the stories of miracles, ensure the victories of the unfortunate in a fabulous, utopian space. This space protects the weapons of the weak against the reality of the established order. It also hides them from the social categories which "make history" because they dominate it. And whereas historiography recounts in the past tense the strategies of instituted powers, these "fabulous" stories offer their audience a repertory of tactics for future use.[36]

Differentiating between instituted "strategies" and spontaneous "tactics"—the "art of the weak" and the maneuver "within enemy territory"[37]—de Certeau maps out a line of cultural action based upon narrative and trickery likewise, which manages to challenge an established repertory of signification precisely because it proceeds indirectly, experimentally, and unsystematically.

And yet, to split up the field of ideological criticism into the stances of pro- and anti-narrativism would be absurd, even if it makes sense to contrast narratives of totalization and narratives of subversion, as there are genres and discursive setups that clearly privilege certain aspects—so that both White and de Certeau have a point, if you will. Fiction, for one, derives its very fascination from the fact that these two aspects are usually not to be neatly separated, as processes of production and reception do not necessarily mirror each other, and as most fictional texts are much too indeterminate and open to lend themselves easily to readings along one line or the other.

VI.

Fiction, this practice of translating the imaginary into the concrete and experience into understanding, provides an exemplary realm for the practices of cultural meaning making discussed above. After all, Michael

Taussig's sense of wonder before "the capacity of the imagination to be lifted through representational media, such as marks on a page, into other worlds,"[38] and his consequent interest in the "magic of mimesis," which creates alternative realities paradoxically by imitating the existing ones, pinpoints precisely the workings of fiction, even if he makes it totally clear that his concept of mimesis pertains to more than just the representative arts. Fiction—in the sense of both an artistic practice of meaning making and a ritualistic act of make-believe—is of interest to him not because it might manage to solve the problems of politics and culture at large but because it brings them to the open, highlighting dead ends or inconsistencies, and time and again acting out and figuring forth the very act of translation. It was, not accidentally, with regard to a literary text, Joseph Conrad's novella *Heart of Darkness,* that Taussig first elaborated the techniques of what he later called "mimetic labor": In his *Shamanism, Colonialism, and the Wild Man,* he reads Conrad's efforts to come to terms with his experience of the cruel regime in the Belgian Congo at the turn of the last century as an exemplary case of indeterminacy. Conrad, he argues, managed to capture the horrors of colonialism precisely because he showed himself to be enmeshed in the system under investigation. Taussig takes his point of departure from the words of Conrad critic Frederick Karl, who wrote that *Heart of Darkness* "attempted to penetrate the veil and yet was anxious to retain its hallucinatory quality": "This formulation," writes Taussig, "evokes and combines a twofold movement of interpretation in a combined action of reduction and revelation . . .":

the mythic subversion of myth, in this case of the modern imperialist myth, requires leaving the ambiguities intact—the greatness of horror that is Kurtz, the mistiness of terror, the aesthetics of violence, and the complex of desire and repression that primitivism constantly arouses. Here the myth is not "explained" so that it can be "explained away," as in the forlorn attempts of social science. Instead it is held out as something you have to try out for yourself, feeling your way deeper and deeper into the heart of darkness until you do *feel* what is at stake, the madness of the passion.[39]

This conceptualization of myth as of something "you have to try out for yourself" calls to mind the Cuna practices of dressing up as white men in order to refashion indigenous rituals. Even though I read Conrad's text along altogether different lines than Taussig, as will become clear, this notion of myth—or fiction—as something that has to be worked through, tried out, put on, and that can be changed only in the process of reiteration, goes together well with my understanding of mythicizing and stereotyping acts of signification as part and parcel of a cultural imaginary that necessarily transcends individual control and consciousness and thus can be changed only from within and only gradually, in a complicated back-and-forth between repetition and inversion, between affirmation and critique, between totalization and the tactics of resistance.

Obviously, writing about the all-embracing workings of a cultural imaginary is problematic in the first place. After all, it is impossible to get an analytical grip on a framework that envelops the critic's world as much as it imbues the fictional worlds she writes about. This is why it is so important to pay close attention to a narrative's gaps and breaks, the text's "underside or impensé or non-dit," which Fredric Jameson called its "political unconscious." Focusing on this level of narrative, we might be able to get a grip on its unacknowledged and obfuscated inconsistencies, "the informing power of forces or contradictions which the text seeks in vain wholly to control or master."[40] A new historicist combination of contextualizations and close readings[41] might help to come to terms with the paranoiac tendency slumbering in the project of tracing a set of stereotypical patterns through time. That way, we might manage to view Africanity not as a unified discourse that remains "unchanging and consistent, both internally and across discourses," as Sara Mills remarked critically about Edward Said's concept of Orientalism, but as a constellation "made up of diverse elements which both contest and affirm the dominant discourse and other discourses of which it is composed."[42] For the purposes of the present study, such a historical perspective requires for once a careful examination of cultural tropes and images that have circulated for hundreds of years, and of the value systems behind these imageries. We cannot ignore the fact that the very rhetoric of difference has widely changed its face and function over the last years, as the categories of marginality and otherness, which have for a long time had largely negative connotations, now can very well be read positively in certain cultural contexts.[43]

VII.

While it is of vital importance to account for historical breaks and changes in a study like this, it is no less relevant to take into consideration groundbreaking discursive and genre-specific changes, especially when it comes to the field of fiction and the popular arts. It does matter, after all, whether a specific image is called up in the 1890s or the 1990s, and whether a specific concept is implemented in a novel, a film, or a study of the social sciences.

Moreover, to talk about fiction these days is not to talk exclusively— not even primarily—about literature. What Christian Metz noted in 1973 has acquired the status of a commonplace today: "the classical film has taken, relay fashion, the historical place of the grand-epoch, nineteenth-century novel (itself dependent on the ancient epic); it fills the same social function, a function which the twentieth-century novel, less and less diegetic and representational, tends partly to abandon."[44] In fact, since literature has passed on to film its status as *the* medium for "the changing manifestations of a cultural imaginary,"[45] a confrontation of popular colonial and postcolonial systems of signification cannot but take a comparative guise, focusing on literary and filmic approaches yet also taking into account other current forms of narrating, and contesting narratives—such as comic strips, installation art, photography, and pop music.

The bulk of my material stems from the realm that used to be called "mass culture" and mostly runs by the name of "mainstream culture" these days, a term that I employ with some reluctance, as I am well aware of its problematic implications. After all, the very concept of a cultural mainstream suggests that we can clearly distinguish between this mainstream and other—marginal—realms of cultural expression: subcultures, elite cultures. But as Pierre Bourdieu has shown, the categories of the mainstream and the margin, together with the complicated system of evaluations and hierarchies they call up, are quite precarious ideological constructions, highly susceptible to social rearrangements and manipulations, and thus far from reliable in their demarcation of cultural boundaries.[46] Moreover, in our times, staking off fields of cultural production along the familiar lines of distinction seems almost impossible, since by now the processes of cultural appropriation, adaptation, exchange, and co-optation take place with unprecedented velocity. "The mainstream presents itself as a minority" these days, Tom Holert and Mark Terkessidis sum up their analysis of the pop cultural status quo in 1996.[47]

The term "mainstream culture" consequently has to figure as an approximative term, more or less founded upon the aspect of commercial success, or at least big funding: best-sellers, potboilers, hits. When I confront such works with less commercially successful forms of expression—independent films, free art projects, novels with a low circulation—this is not to introduce a reverse evaluation through the back door. The "marginalized" is not per se good, and the "mainstream" is not invariably bad. It would be too easy to dismiss spectacular effects, big thrills, and a catchy structure as cheap attempts at ideological manipulation or stultification. After all, there is a lot of pleasure involved in good entertainment—many, myself included, get a kick out of the smooth functioning of special effects in action adventures and do cry happily along with Meryl Streep at her lover's grave in *Out of Africa*.

The pleasure of the spectacular, I thus argue, has to be taken seriously. But then again, this is not a new insight. In line with British cultural studies approaches, Stephen Heath has argued as early as 1976 that with regard to the Hollywood system, production *and* reception patterns have to be taken into account. In other words, films are not to be reduced to either their "content" or their "form":

films are industrial products, and they mean, and they sell not simply on the particular meaning but equally on the pleasure of cinema, this yielding the return that allows the perpetuation of the industry . . . ; a film is not reducible to its 'ideology' but is also the working over of that ideology in cinema, with the industry dependent on the pleasure of the operation. The problems for film theory today are those of an understanding of the fact of film in these terms.[48]

The "double determination"[49] of film—and all kinds of commercial art and mainstream expressions—thus prohibits a reading of such works exclusively along the lines of a master plan—the studios' attempt at ideological infiltration, or the market's effort at controlling public opinion.

And yet, to discard the notion of a central agency of manipulation— be it Hollywood or the market or the West or whatever other construct—is not to discard ideological criticism in general. Instead of trying to locate and lay bare bad intentions, however, it makes more sense to concentrate on structures of representation and the specific effects they have. And this is where we come upon the concept of narrative again, the fact that there are narratives that encourage critical engagement and others that do not. Hayden White's critique of narrative totalization thus surges up in Christian Metz's—doubtlessly somewhat sweeping—critique of "Hollywood Film," his claim that "any film based on narration and representation" actualizes a specific kind of discourse, which "obliterates all traces of the enunciation, and masquerades as story." For Metz, such films base their "narrative plenitude and transparency . . . on a refusal to admit that anything is lacking, or that anything has to be sought for,"[50] an illusion of narrative closure, which works perfectly—if paradoxically—hand in hand with the knowledge that it is "only a story," nothing but fiction.

While this insight into the ideological effects of narrative closure calls for close readings, it helps to confront these readings in turn with reflections on other texts, stemming from other cultural realms and from other areas of aesthetic expression. This is, after all, one way of coping with the fact that these days different modes and genres of representation interact intricately, as the boundaries between forms of aesthetic expression collapse. And while literature in its classical form has irretrievably lost ground against all sorts of representation and expression, this is not to say that written language has been replaced by images. Craig Owens spoke rightfully about an "eruption of language into the aesthetic field," setting in with the 1970s, and we can still feel the aftereffects of what he called the dispersal of literature "from the enclaves into which it had settled only to stagnate—poetry, the novel, the essay . . . — . . . across the entire spectrum of aesthetic activity."[51] It is against the backdrop of such developments that I chose to focus on all kinds of genres when talking about the late twentieth and early twenty-first century: after all, every fiction calls upon other fictions. And by venturing into this network of allusions, repercussions, and quotations one might manage to get a grip on the transformations at hand, transformations that are as much based upon social and political changes in the world at large as upon the strange momentum of their own that artistic discourses and aesthetic forms develop time and again. Hence, to cast a close look at how and where something is told often enough helps to approach its meaning.

VIII.

This study is divided into two parts—titled "African Adventures" and "Alternative Africas" respectively—and, given these two headings, one might be inclined to expect a report of progress, tracing a historical development from exoticizing adventure stories to "alternative" narratives that rupture the old clichés and open up more realistic perspectives. But the history of Africanist representations is more complicated than that, and the evidence here at hand, at least, does not suggest a structure of linear progression in the sense of a gradual overcoming of negative attitudes. Nor does it hint at the opposite model, however, figuring forth a slow deterioration or decline. The messy pattern coming into view instead attests to a multiplicity of forces and counterforces at work, reflecting the changing functions and the functional changes that the imagery of Africanity underwent throughout the last two centuries—from colonialism to globalization.

This is a study about the logic of stereotyping. And thus it has to deal with the disturbing fact that what is said openly in a text and what is uttered between the lines, communicated in allusions, quotations, and formal idiosyncrasies, do not always go together. The determination to break with the old and to implement a new unbiased view, for one, is definitely not enough to establish a different order. Stereotypes are not to be wiped out on the grounds of indignation alone. Alternative approaches, deviations from dated conventions and familiar patterns, can be just as problematic as long-standing habits, as will become clear. By the same token, however, these long-standing habits—the conventions and patterns of producing Africanity—need not be seen as exclusively negative.

Consequently, rather than organizing my material along chronological lines (from then to now, or from the present to the past) or within an evaluative grid (from good to bad, or the other way round), I decided to take the concept of alinearity seriously, and to proceed the same way, disclosing repercussions, contradictions, interlinkages in a continuous back-and-forth between colonial and postcolonial representations. The first part of my study, "African Adventures," investigates some classical genres and stock figures of colonial meaning making and their contemporary reiterations, from adventure fiction to colonial nostalgia, and delineates the contorted histories of some well-known characters of the colonial scene: the ape-man, the white hunter, the colonial lady. From a perspective of today these stock figures of cultural contact narratives often enough seem nothing but remnants of a hopelessly old-fashioned order, good only for the harmless pleasures of nostalgic commemoration or amused revision. But we shall see that there is more to them than the comic-strip charm of the slightly faded and clearly dated pop icon, that their specific enactments still reveal a lot about dominant conceptions of cultural contact and cultural difference, even if—or precisely because—the icons and tropes of yore have clearly lost their former cultural function, being ironized, criticized, or parodied in most of the revisionary representations of today.

There are multiple translations going on, after all, and not all of them are made explicit. Most obviously, the revision of European colonialism in big Hollywood productions and the transformation of H. Rider Haggard's adventure novels or Isak Dinesen's autobiographical reflections into the world of special effects and the spectacle are liable to affect more than just some plotlines or marginal characters. The unchanging settings of colonial contact narratives—the jungle, the safari, the farm in the Ngong hills—thus lend a deceptive closure to the ever changing masquerades and trickeries related. Tracing the enactments of today back to their sources, the material of yesterday, is thus to confront what John McClure called an "alternate trajectory" in American culture, in which "the manifest role of European writers such as Joseph Conrad in shaping contemporary American constructions of American imperialism" comes into view.[52]

Confrontational and comparative readings of texts, tropes, and patterns of representation across time help to conceptualize continuities and breaks—the surplus or lack generated by acts of translation. But so do synchronous cuts through periods. Therefore, I will not only compare colonial narratives and their contemporary repercussions but also confront the key narratives of European colonialism with some of their American equivalents, such as Edgar Rice Burroughs's *Tarzan of the Apes* (1914)—fashioned closely after Haggard's best-selling novels—or Hemingway's African stories, constituting a counterpoint in tone and subject matter to Isak Dinesen's autobiographical writing. Such synchronous or horizontal correlations also emphasize the fact that there is, of course, no absolutely closed "colonial period," just as there is no unified "global logic"; there are only analogies, variations, quotations, and deviations clustering around certain imageries and themes.

All of these classical texts belong to a liberal tradition, and all of them have at some point or other been celebrated as instances of colonial critique and antiracist commitment. Still, writers from Haggard to Burroughs, from Dinesen to Hemingway, are clearly involved in the very fabrication of what Edward Said called an "imperialist system of representation," even if all of them strained against this system at the same time: indubitably, these texts and their protagonists—Quatermain the adventurer, Tarzan the ape-man, Hemingway's white hunters, and Baroness von Blixen—shape what we think about when we think about colonial Africa. Moreover, all of them work within genres that constitute the very basis for popular enactments of colonialism and cultural contact: the adventure tale (this paradigmatic mode for exoticizing the other) and the autobiography (this paradigmatic mode for exploring the self).

And it is on these grounds that the narratives I investigate in the second part of my study—"Alternative Africas"—differ. Their "alternative" perspective, I argue, does not come about because their authors managed to extricate themselves from the ideological framework of their day and to steer clear of the problems at hand, but because they tackled the very foundations of this ideological framework—its representational and conceptual conventions. Two novellas, one English, one American, form the core of my reflections in this second part, both of them enthusiastically embraced by some critics for taking issue with imperialist practices of exploitation and subjugation, and both of them harshly criticized by others for falling back upon established patterns of stereotyping and mythicizing after all. I am referring to Joseph Conrad's *Heart of Darkness* (1902) and Herman Melville's *Benito Cereno* (1855), two very different texts that nevertheless have some interesting things in common. For one, both set out to display the structures of imperial meaning making, systematically dissecting the framework of exoticization and authentication. And both act out these strategies of dissemination with regard to the theme of trade—colonial trade in Conrad's case, the slave trade in Melville's.

What Michael Taussig wrote about Conrad's enactment of the colonial scene—his strategy of "leaving the ambiguities intact"—could be extended to Herman Melville's representation of the Middle Passage, this other framework of enforced contact that brings the perversities of imperial commerce to the fore: both narratives end upon a kind of impasse, a dead end. And this ambiguity is so disconcerting because the scenarios at hand are not cast as things of the past—a world in decline, "slowly and gravely withdrawing," as Isak Dinesen had it[53]—but as part of a new global order. Seen that way, "[t]he glamour's off,"[54] indeed—the imperial enterprise as represented by Conrad and Melville does not lend itself to nostalgic commemoration or critical retrospection at all. After all, it seems to be very much alive, if subject to continuous transformation: as the world has been mapped out and even the high seas have been charted, intricate commercial schemes replace step by step the larger projects of national expansion and imperial takeover. A new commercial world order comes into view, which then spawns a panoply of alternative narratives and reflections, all of them emphatically looking forward instead of looking back—turning away from the figures and tropes of old and adopting the perspective of the "unbiased glance," a perspective that has become a stereotypical formation in its own right by now, as we shall see.

All the texts under investigation in this study, be they retrospective or markedly futuristic, revolve around the concepts of contact, communication, and control. And all of them, especially the contemporary ones, struggle more or less openly with the insight that contact situations are always uneven, communication is never noise-free, and control is often too diffuse and too pervasive to become apparent. Individualistic concepts of action and resistance, as conveyed in the stock figures and scenarios of colonial narration, consequently meet with more and more skepticism, as they seem to be inadequate for coming to terms with the increasingly complex processes of interaction and exchange at hand. Hence the "alternative" narratives around trade and the Middle Passage time and again end upon the insight that new models of agency are needed to contest new forms of control. And this is where the concept of trickery enters the picture once more, this time setting the mode for indirect forms of action and depersonalized forms of agency.

At the very end of my study I will drop the pattern of a historicizing back-and-forth and turn to a trope for cultural contact that pertains very much to our own time and has come to provide a powerful new imagery for cultural contact, especially with respect to Africa: the trope of viral infection. Even if doubtlessly this trope goes back to older imageries of contact as contagion or disease, there is something structurally new to it that I mean to take seriously. The virus, I claim, is the ultimate trickster figure, and one that does not rely upon the modes of individualist action. It thus permits us to conceptualize cultural contact along different lines, not so much in terms of abandoning stereotypes but in terms of tactically "exploding" them. In the course of contemporary virus narratives, the fact that stereotypical discourse is never realistic, and thus not to be negated on the grounds of rational argumentation, good intentions, or open talk, is turned from a deficit into an asset. Of course, these narratives are highly fantastic. But so are the stereotypes of Africa. Seen that way, fantasy and fiction might turn out to constitute the only ground on which the fabrications of Africanity may be contested—its own ground.

I AFRICAN ADVENTURES

ONE

Special Effects: Encounters in Africa

The best point of departure for the exploration of artificial Africas is adventure fiction. After all, in this genre geographical locations are also artificial realms, spaces of fantasy and speculation cast in the guise of the far-away, so that the all-too-familiar may be overcome. Here, the transgression into unknown territory—the jungle, the desert, the magic castle—is a purely vicarious journey, which permits the audience "to explore in fantasy the boundary between the permitted and the forbidden and to experience in a carefully controlled way the possibility of stepping across this boundary," as John Cawelti noted in 1976, emphasizing the "escapist thrust" of adventures, mysteries, and thrillers.[1]

With the advent of postcolonial theory, the critique of adventure fiction's surrogate character was conjoined with a critique of its ideological work—the inherently legitimizing function of adventure scenarios for the politics of Western imperialism. Edward Said consequently came up with the term "adventure-imperialism" to demarcate a genre that for him works hand in hand with global power politics, acting out limited and easily solvable conflicts, while indefatigably glossing over the dirty reality of colonial power relations and distracting from the irresolvable incongruities between colonizer and colonized.[2] If adventure fiction thus proves to be intricately interlinked with a European history of colonization, it just as clearly attests to an American context, with regard to both production and narrative—fabricated largely in Hollywood, action adventures more often than not reiterate an imagery of invasion, survival, and self-assertion in the wilderness that is deeply ingrained in an American history of imperialist thought and politics, a history no less complicated and extensive than its European counterpart.

As I have already sketched out, American filmic and literary works may draw upon European settings, scenarios, and constellations, yet more often than not their enactment differs considerably from traditional colonialist forms of representation. Hence to conceive of imperial adventure fiction in terms of a "formula"—a structural blueprint more or less subtly organizing the narrative—is to grasp only half of its effectivity. After all, while the thrill of adventure fiction depends upon familiar and standardized scenarios—their reliable and reassuring sameness—ideological work calls for flexibility and variation. Both aspects, familiarity and variation, interact in a subtle and complicated way, as we shall see.

This interaction comes to the fore in the workings of trick translation, a trope that enacts cultural communication in terms of losing and regaining control, establishing understanding on the grounds of deception. Obviously, this is a pattern that lends itself exemplarily well to the imperial adventure genre, which also maps out the momentary loss of control on foreign ground, only to reaffirm the imperialists' superior wit eventually. The classical adventurer is a trickster and a translator—establishing contact and trying to maintain control over communication by all means possible. Like adventure fiction in general, the trope of trick translation can be seen to draw upon a standard setup that is put to radically different, even contradictory uses. Regardless of its relatively stable layout, the trope takes over most diverse ideological and conceptual functions, demarcating the versatility of the discourses involved precisely by way of its persistent reenactment. This is why it will serve as an organizing principle in this chapter, which moves from a reflection on the narrative enactment of early colonial contact in the Americas to the classical Africanist adventure narrative—H. Rider Haggard's novel *King Solomon's Mines* (1885). This novel will then present the point of departure for a reading of Hollywood action adventures of the 1980s, most notably the filmic remakes of Haggard's novels, which spectacularly recuperate the thrill of bygone conflicts. All of these texts map out trick translation in order to come to terms with the ambivalent implications of narrating cultural contact and the tensions inherent in adventure fiction itself. After all, the genre's very flexibility provides not only the basis for its ideological effectivity but also a constant source of ambivalence and insecurity. "The geography of adventure, despite its 'appearance of reality' and hence its fixity, is never static," claims Richard Phillips:

The world of adventure presents what Robert Louis Stevenson called a "kaleidoscopic dance of images". This is liminal terrain in which elements of the recognisable world appear in strange, ever-changing, sometimes disturbing configurations. It is a space in which to move, not to stop. Like all geography—all maps—it both constrains and enables. It constrains in the sense that it reproduces many values and assumptions, circumscribes some of the possibilities of geography and identity, and defines the terrain on which world views can be negotiated. It also enables in that it creates space in which writers and readers are able to rework and redefine values and assumptions and begin to transgress boundaries and categories. The geography of adventure is a point of departure.[3]

If formulaic colonial adventure narratives and the filmic genre of imperial action adventures lend themselves exemplarily well to the enactments of cultural contact, they may thus also prove adequate frameworks for revisionary projects. Such revisions need not imply an open and conscious challenge to the ideological status quo, as they are often enough expressed through narrative shifts, breaks, and inconsistencies. This comes to the fore in the aesthetics of technological excess suffusing 1980s Hollywood action adventures, an aesthetics that for once creates the effect of "narrative plenitude and transparency"[4] Christian Metz criticized in Hollywood cinema but that may at times flip over to suddenly disclose its own functioning—the self-contained logic of special effects.

Ambivalence, chaos, and confusion are vital elements for creating suspense in the adventure genre, even if these disturbing effects are usually taken back in harmonious endings and clear-cut solutions. This is why I will close this chapter by considering some enactments of trick translation that foreground the disruptive effect of adventure, and thus epitomize what we came to suspect before—that adventure is a tricky business, which may inadvertently lose its unidirectional thrust, from order to chaos to order, and slip from the reassuring display of controlled communication back into scenarios of misunderstanding and disorientation.

1.1 Manipulating the Savage Space: Trick Translation

Most things they saw with us, as mathematical instruments, sea compasses, the virtue of the loadstone in drawing iron, a perspective glass whereby was shown many strange sights, burning glasses, wildfire works, guns, books, writing and reading, spring clocks that seem to go of themselves, and many other things that we had, were so strange unto them, and so far exceeded their capacities to comprehend the reason and means how they should be made and done, that they thought they were rather the works of gods than of men, or at the leastwise they had been given and taught us of the gods.
—Thomas Harriot, A brief and true report of the new found land of Virginia (1588)[5]

Mary Pratt has differentiated two main stances in colonial self-stylizations, an imperial "rhetorics of conquest" suffusing the absolutist era and an ensuing rhetoric of "anti-conquest" demarcating the split consciousness of Westen travelers in the eighteenth and nineteenth centuries, their paradoxical desire "to secure their innocence in the same moment as they assert European hegemony."[6] Yet although this rhetoric of "anti-conquest" doubtlessly pertains mainly to modernity, the history of exploration and colonization has from its outset on been characterized by the awkward evidence of conflicting ideological stances: politico-economic interests were hard to identify with religious doctrine, and a practice of merciless and unconditional exploitation clashed with a theory of salvation and brotherly love. The reconciliation of these contradictory stances was a chief concern of colonial narratives—exploration reports, travel writing, autobiographies, and guidebooks. In these texts the evidence of violent takeover was either justified as a necessary sacrifice for the better of everybody involved or reformulated in terms of dialogic "persuasion" rather than enforced submission, so that from its very beginning colonialism has been involved in a rhetoric of anti-conquest.

To contain an imperialist system within a rhetoric of anti-conquest calls for confusion, however, and indeed a highly contradictory symbolical system resulted from the efforts to reconcile the irreconcilable. What I call "trick translation" is perhaps one of the most persistent tropes for casting colonial contact in terms of mutual understanding without abandoning the idea of a clear-cut hierarchy of communication and a European monopoly of meaning production. One early example is the much related anecdote of Columbus forecasting a partial eclipse of the moon to natives who had refused to provide his expedition with supplies. Casting the event as a sign of God's wrath, he allegedly frightened the natives enough to discipline them.[7] Similar accounts of tricking indigenous peoples into submission by profiting from superior skills or advanced information abound throughout the history of colonial contact and have become stock elements in adventure fiction. Next to amazingly many convenient eclipses of sun and moon, it was the technology of civilization that figured foremost in these scenarios of manipulated persuasion.[8]

As technology came to stand almost metonymically for the colonizers' worldview, it seemed to preclude the natives' understanding by definition. Thus another, less "advanced" discursive framework was required in order to enable communication. This is where a seemingly indigenous symbolical system comes in that seems to suggest itself as a native equivalent to European technology—magic: "European technology (especially of firearms)," as Peter Hulme remarked, "suddenly *became* magical when introduced into a less technologically developed society."[9]

Still, this transformation of technology into magic is more ambivalent than it might seem at first glance. In a close reading of colonial self-stylizations, Eric Cheyfitz came to the conclusion that the assumed analogy stretches out not so much between technology and magic but between magic and the colonizer's rhetoric, which after all brings about this transformation or translation of technology in the first place. Citing John Smith's account of a dazzling performance of European superiority in front of an Indian audience, Cheyfitz remarks: "Smith must have been quite an orator, quite a magician of persuasion, for, as we learn from his *True Relations,* he enchanted the Indians with only a compass and a pistol that broke during one of his demonstrations. . . ."[10] The colonizer's eloquence tricks the natives into submission, even as weapons misfire and the Europeans are hopelessly outnumbered. If we take further into consideration that Smith spoke hardly a word of the native language at that time, the performance becomes magical indeed, if not altogether in the intended sense. The actual encounter seems to have relied more heavily than acknowledged on the presence of the pistol after all.

But I am not interested here in the realistic dimensions of this account—in the natives' actual or feigned or ascribed admiration or in the likelihood of the scenario itself.[11] What interests me much more is the power of this and similar accounts to shape future fictions of cultural contact—the impact that these enactments of translation and trickery obviously had, erecting an imagery of an intercultural communication constructed on entirely fictional grounds. The trick translation seems to correlate different systems of thought—technology and magic—yet is based on the manipulative power of one side only, with the trick translator figuring as the ultimate master of the colonial game, who controls the colonial discourse both materially and rhetorically via technology, knowledge, and cunning. Thus travel reports and exploration accounts tend to turn the colonial space into the "stage" for a European performance, as Ulla Haselstein has shown:

The reason European authors have given for their successful use of ruses and tricks in their dealings with the Other is that the "savages" are unable to recognize the theatrical machinations as such: naive and superstitious, they are prone to fall prey to the illusions of their own forms of magic and hence their European counterfeits as well. For their own part, however, the Europeans interpret the successful creation of illusions as a confirmation of their presupposed cultural superiority. Thus linguistic colonialism with its "gift" of civilization addresses a domestic audience as well: by describing members of a different culture as "savages" and by subsequently representing these "savages" as fascinated watchers and helpless victims of dazzling performances, the Europeans are able to invent themselves as civilized and hence as joint authors and players in a theater of social power which learns to view and to describe itself only by way of its projection onto another culture.[12]

Confined to the "colonial stage," the trope of trick translation confirms the superiority of the European manipulators. Once it is seen detached from this context, however, it has to appear highly ambivalent.

Stephen Greenblatt commented upon this effect in his reading of another account of trick translation, Thomas Harriot's report of his dealings with the native Algonkians in Virginia in 1588, in which an asymmetry shows up similar to the one in Smith's account.[13] As Greenblatt pointed out, the colonial masquerade of the "great white gods" with "magical instruments" in front of a native audience would have gained quite disturbing implications if referred back to the European situation. After all, by dint of this logic, the entire system of Christianity could be conceived of as a volatile construction of clever rhetoricians and tricksters. Yet these implications were widely contained in the colonial period, as Greenblatt showed, and the containment was based upon two conditions: on the one hand the trick translator sides with a colonial readership, which is "in on the game" while the natives are "out of it"; on the other hand the colonial situation is rhetorically "bracketed" as altogether extraordinary, in no way comparable to the situation at home and thus calling for extraordinary strategies and patterns of behavior.[14]

If this containment seems inconsistent, we should bear in mind that so is the rhetoric of "anti-conquest" from which it derives or, even more broadly put, colonial discourse itself, in which a multiplicity of "interpretive possibilities" that are "logically exclusive, not only coexist but both equally and formally oppose each other," as Laura Chrisman has shown.[15] The trope of trick translation epitomizes such conflicting possibilities of interpreting colonialism, expressing the desire for communication *and* the fear of losing control. Thus the trick translator's insistence on the exceptionality of the act of trickery forecloses the idea of a pervasive political or religious manipulation of meanings, and at the same time ascertains the absolute value of the achievements of civilization.

1.2 Technologies of Culture: H. Rider Haggard's *King Solomon's Mines*

King Solomon's Mines might not be "THE MOST AMAZING BOOK EVER WRITTEN," as initially advertised,[16] but it was doubtlessly a tremendous success, creating a powerful imagery of Africanity for generations of adolescents to come and launching a vogue of African adventures in novels and films. One reason for this popularity throughout the twentieth century was most likely Haggard's adherence to the liberal rhetoric of "anti-conquest," his much acclaimed "admiration for natives in general."[17] In *King Solomon's Mines* (1885) colonial contact is enacted as a benign encounter, and violent conflicts are brought about only as inevitable reactions to native aggressions.

Thus the novel, which relates the quest of three gentlemen-adventurers into the wilderness, culminates in a confrontation of this group with attacking Africans. Quatermain, the narrator and leader figure, manages to stop them dead. Guess how:

"Stop!" I shouted boldly, though at the moment my heart was in my boots. "Stop! we, the white men from the stars, say that it shall not be. Come but one pace nearer, and we will put out the sun and plunge the land in darkness. Ye shall taste of our magic." (*KSM* 184)

Of course, conveniently enough, the eclipse of the sun, which Quatermain happened to have read about in his almanac, sets in at that very moment.

Using his superior knowledge to stupefy the natives, Quatermain, like countless other narrators of colonial encounters before him, draws upon the trope of trick translation as he casts Western knowledge in local terms and turns science into magic. And as before, these trick translations, which pretend to take the native point of view into account, are employed as gestures of goodwill, averting violent conflicts and protecting the Europeans on savage ground. Tricking the natives into consent thus figures as a—humane and liberal—alternative to the brutal techniques of imperialist subjugation or extermination, just as in John Smith's or Thomas Harriot's reports. And yet, the enactments of trick translation have changed since the early days of colonial contact. Although Haggard does implement the trope along the long-standing lines as in the "eclipse scene," a closer look at some other enactments of trick translation will reveal a significant shift in the trope's focus and function.

The novel has three white male protagonists, and each of them represents a specific stance of colonial history. While Quatermain is clearly the modern man, a trader who introduces himself as "a cautious man, indeed a timid one" (*KSM* 32) and a "bit of a coward" (*KSM* 155), his first companion, Sir Henry Curtis, is not accidentally compared time and again to the African warrior-chief Ignosi. Both are noble savages, admirable yet anachronistic.[18] The future belongs to men like Quatermain who negotiate their way through the wilderness rather than heroically fighting it out. In light of this dichotomy of the ancient and the modern, the third member of the expedition, Sir John Good, takes an interesting intermediate position, as he pertains to an older order morally yet testifies in his entire appearance to the advent of modernity.

While Sir Henry might make the most striking appearance of these three, it is not he that impresses the natives to no end, but Good. Ridiculously set on maintaining European standards of neatness in the jungle, Good, equipped with an eyeglass and false teeth, comes to incorporate European civilization in his very person. Quatermain keeps emphasizing the absurdity of this insistence on European norms in Africa:

There he sat upon a leather bag, looking just as though he had come in from a comfortable day's shooting in a civilised country, absolutely clean, tidy, and well dressed. . . . his eyeglass and his false teeth appeared to be in perfect order, and altogether he was the neatest man I ever had to do with in the wilderness. (*KSM* 54)

Yet Good's curious paraphernalia of modernity fail to make sense in the African context, and again trick translation serves as a means of ascribing new "local" meanings to them. In the first moment of contact with the Kukuana, a tribe living in total seclusion, Quatermain casts Good's pathetic appearance, which is doubly ridiculous at this time for his being only half-shaved and without his pants, in terms of magical intervention and primitive power:

"It is well," I said, carelessly, ". . . beware! Play us no tricks, make for us no snares, for before your brains of mud have thought of them, we shall know them and avenge them. The light from the transparent eye of him with the bare legs and the half-haired face (Good) shall destroy you, and go through your land: his vanishing teeth shall fix themselves fast into you and eat you up, you and your wives and children; the magic tubes shall talk with you loudly, and make you as sieves. Beware!" (*KSM* 118)

Africans, this logic runs, cannot grasp the new and unfamiliar unless it is "mythicized" and "primitivized," so that a glass eye figures as the "evil eye" and false teeth perform cannibalistic rites. And when Quatermain concludes that his "magnificent address did not fail of its effect" (*KSM* 118), trick translation appears as virtually the only way of gaining access to the savage mind, manipulation providing the only means of communication. And yet, it is interesting to see what precisely is being communicated here.

As I pointed out before, early trick translation celebrated the figure of the colonizer as the clever rhetorician and technological manipulator, casting European skills and instruments (the almanac, the gun, the compass) as elements of an elaborate machinery of deception. In *King Solomon's Mines,* however, what impresses the natives most deeply are everyday objects of use.[19] The eyeglass and the false teeth have nothing grandiose, sinister, or heroic about them, whatever way you try to read them. They become grandiose only by way of trick translation. Thus the trickery here comes across as more pervasive and more fundamental than its earlier versions. Not only does Quatermain translate between English civilization and African wilderness, but he moreover manages to transpose the mundane into the extraordinary, the ridiculous into the heroic. By consequence, a curious circle of projections evolves, in which the fascination about Western technology routinely ascribed to the natives echoes "the white man's fascination with the Other's fascination with white man's magic," as Michael Taussig wrote with reference to early anthropology and nineteenth-century travel writing, where the same pattern of representation can be traced.[20]

Projected upon the native mind, the sensation of fear and fascination vis-à-vis trite technologies of civilization elevates these achievements, while establishing a clear-cut hierarchy of meaning production and meaning reception. At the same time, Haggard's text relies upon a chuckling solidarity between narrator and reader that excludes the natives most efficiently—they figure only as the dupes, falling for the tricks played upon them. At any rate, the earlier incentive for trick translation has inadvertently changed. Now the foreigners are no longer out to promote the values of civilization but display its basic principles: the capacity to distinguish between true cultural achievements, such as science and art, and trite effects, such as the false body parts. In other words, Quatermain touts what Pierre Bourdieu called the symbolic capital of taste and distinction, and testifies to a bourgeois notion of culture as "not what one is, but what one has, or rather, what one has become."[21]

This notion of culture rests firmly on the grounds of subtle stratifications and fine-tuned distinctions. Africans might get the larger picture, but there is no way they will take in all of its facets anytime soon. This is why Quatermain's warning to the natives—"[p]lay us no tricks"—seems entirely superfluous. After all, the natives' tricks could never be as subtle and efficient as his own manipulations; they could never affect the European tricksters.

And yet there are some kinds of African "tricks" that seem very well capable of raising European apprehensions and fears. Paradoxically enough, African magic is evoked not only as a ridiculous superstition, rendering the natives prone to fall for European tricks, but also and simultaneously as a dangerous and sinister practice of resistance, embodied by the witch Gagool, who comes to represent everything Europe is not: primitivism, cruelty, perversity, and unmotivated hatred, making "the land evil in the sight of the heavens above" (*KSM* 245).[22] While Western systems of thought—technology and science—are shown to be rationally deducible and to serve always the right ends, African witchcraft is presented as weird and inexplicable.[23]

The curious fact that the Western system comes across just as inexplicable and weird to the Africans remains unacknowledged, although Gagool's invectives against the Europeans play upon this very reciprocity of projections. She calls them "magicians and evil-doers" (*KSM* 165), echoing their epithets against herself, and again—just as in the trickeries performed by Thomas Harriot, which Stephen Greenblatt related—the idea of a masquerade on both sides suggests itself. Briefly, in between, there is a moment of instability and ambivalence that is significant. Momentarily the colonial masquerade seems to be all-comprising, with everybody tricking everybody else and everybody believing to be in control. Yet again, to acknowledge this universality of masquerade would mean to question the underlying parameters for the colonial project at large—this time not in terms of questioning religion but in terms of questioning the distinctiveness of European cultural achievements: European values might not only be unfamiliar to Africans; they might just be irrelevant.

When the colonizers leave, however, Gagool is dead, and a hybrid English system of law and order has been established in Kukuanaland, so that this possible interpretation is effaced and the univocal hierarchy of manipulators and manipulated has been reasserted. The system the Britons leave behind constitutes a second-rate culture, a mock-modernity based upon primitive needs and customs, the paradigms of modernity (communication, technology, and transformation) subtly tuned down so that they comply with an "African" system of thought based upon silence, magic, and eternal sameness.[24]

This fake system of civilization works because the Africans take it for "the real thing." Again it is Good who involuntarily expresses this logic:

We were very sorry to part from him [Infadoos]; indeed, Good was so moved that he gave him as a souvenir—what do you think?—an *eye-glass*. (Afterwards we discovered that it was a spare one.) Infadoos was delighted, foreseeing that the possession of such an article would enormously increase his prestige, and after several vain attempts actually succeeded in screwing it into his own eye. Anything more incongruous than the old warrior looked with an eye-glass I never saw. Eye-glasses don't go well with leopard-skin cloaks and black ostrich plumes. (*KSM* 311)

The very idea of Kukuanaland, a sealed-off utopian island of savagery mocking civilization, is like this figure of Infadoos, in a leopard-skin cloak with an eyeglass. Civilization, once dissolved from its original setting (England), becomes a lifestyle to be donned and shed, to be given away and adopted at will, while the control over its images and meanings remains firmly in the hands of its originators, the Englishmen, who are consequently the only ones to detect this application's inherent absurdity, its incongruity, and its logical breaks: the eyeglass in the native eye.

1.3 From Kukuanaland to Disneyland: Imperial Action Adventures

Exotic cultures and colonial settings have always been popular in Hollywood, and an analysis of the countless film versions of Haggard's work alone would in itself present an interesting reflection of the varying colonialist imageries brought forth during this century.[25] In the 1980s, a series of adaptations starring Richard Chamberlain as Allan Quatermain refashioned Haggard's "adventure imperialism" in terms of the Hollywood "imperial action adventure" genre, which was so immensely popular in the wake of Steven Spielberg's *Raiders of the Lost Ark* (1981), the first Indiana Jones film. Thus J. Lee Thompson's film *King Solomon's Mines* (1985)[26] returns to Africa one hundred years after H. Rider Haggard published his first Quatermain novel and presents an Africa as cut off from the historical and political realities of imperialism as Haggard's Kukuanaland. By contrast to the novel, however, the film does not even pretend to historical plausibility, as the conventions of realistic representation are openly dismissed. Here Africa is staged as a timeless and familiarly exotic comic-book space with African warriors in leopard skins who carry spears, cook their enemies in huge pots, play drums, and—naturally—don masks whenever they get into a hostile mood. The Western adventurers, by contrast, are no longer British gentlemen set on establishing a benign and utopian empire in the wilderness but modern Americans who are perfectly satisfied to keep their civilization to themselves: while Quatermain drives a car through the desert, his African companion Umbopa (Ken Gampu), ridiculously afraid of Western technology, is seen running alongside it. And as the advent of modernity is not exactly a hot issue in a 1980s Hollywood production, Allan Quatermain's original self-fashioning as a trader rather than a hunter, a rhetorician rather than a fighter, is irrelevant for the film. This Quatermain is by no means "timid" nor a "coward" but a completely streamlined action adventure hero—a tough individualist, a "drifter" and "outsider" fighting nevertheless relentlessly to maintain the social status quo.[27] Likewise, in line with the Hollywood convention of combining love story and adventure plot, H. Rider Haggard's apologetic declaration "that there is no woman in [the story]"—meaning no white woman, of course[28]—does not apply to the film. Here, next to Quatermain, a no less stereotypical character of Hollywood adventures stumbles through the jungle: the white woman Jesse (Sharon Stone), who time and again endangers her own and her companions' lives by sheer naiveté, getting on the hunter's nerves in the first place and yet winning his heart eventually. Accompanied by the sheepish yet incredibly strong and absolutely devoted Umbopa, another stock character of adventure films, Quatermain and Jesse set out to look for King Solomon's Mines in an Africa that is as adventurous as an American theme park, and whose glaring irreality stands off against Haggard's technique of authentication by way of explanatory footnotes and asides. Moreover, Thompson's film does not enact an African "mock-civilization" but seems to insist upon African difference instead.

For Haggard, cultural contact served to further acculturation (on the native side) and distinction (on the English side), bringing both sides closer together without jeopardizing the existing hierarchies. In the

1980s, by contrast, as the world seems to grow smaller by the day, getting closer has lost much of its fascination and most of its thrill. Neither do the newly emergent scenarios of culture clashes and global conflicts fit the pattern of evening entertainment. As every possible adventure plot has been tried out and as excessive realism seems to be incompatible with the easy thrill of adventure, another mode of representation emerges that will carry the day: irony—the Indiana Jones phenomenon.

If Spielberg's Indiana Jones trilogy made one thing clear, it was that a 1980s audience did not mind seeing it all over again, as long as it was cleverly done. In fact, these films' radical break with all kinds of awkward questions around authenticity, historical correctness, and local specificity, with which the adventure genre had increasingly grappled,[29] came across as a liberation for both other filmmakers and a broad audience. The filmic universe of Indiana Jones, it seems, for once was precisely and exclusively that: a *filmic* universe, markedly unconcerned with the real world and its moral and political problems. To criticize these films, and the panoply of others that followed suit, on ideological grounds seems downright narrow-minded—after all, the films themselves constantly emphasize that they are nothing but fictions, mere fantasy, as Michael Rogin has pointed out:

When an imperial white male wins a white woman in violent combat with evil, dark tribes, as in the Indiana Jones movies, everyone knows that these surface cartoons are not meant to be taken seriously. So we don't have to feel implicated in their displays, can think they are send-ups of 1930s serials rather than precipitates of current covert operations, and forget what we have seen.[30]

What we also tend to forget is that it requires considerable knowledge to read these films—knowledge not about the histories involved but about the complex network of filmic quotations, genre codes, and plot conventions that is laid out in every single one of these action adventures. Moreover, both Indiana Jones and Quatermain—and countless others like them—derive their effect from being the prototypical adventurer with a metafictional edge, not only doing it all over again but being aware of it at the same time: "This is how Tarzan must have felt," quips Quatermain in Thompson's film, traveling through the treetops with the Obuqua, a native tribe that—for once—values peace and harmony over the strains of adventure.

Of course, this remark, just like many others, is not really directed at the silent natives. Quatermain's clever remarks address those who know to appreciate his wit and coolness: the adventure-proven audience. As for the natives, there is no need for verbal communication, as contact usually takes the guise of material exchanges—if exchange is the right word for these rather one-sided affairs: the Obuqua bring goods, the Kukuana throw spears. The witch Gagoola (June Buthelezi), Quatermain's most prominent opponent who had proven to be so uncannily "equal" to him in Haggard's book, does not even speak in the film; she screeches, groans, and croaks, so that any dissolution of the conflict by means of verbal communication, tricked or otherwise, is rendered virtually impossible.

For that matter, Haggard's verbal trick translation is replaced with visually much more impressive technological tricks: in the follow-up to *King Solomon's Mines, Allan Quatermain and the Lost City of Gold* (1986), this time directed by Gary Nelson,[31] Quatermain is forced to resort to cunning to save his and his friends' lives. A savage by the quite fitting name of Nasta (Doghmi Larbi) dares Quatermain to break a rock with his head. Now Richard Chamberlain's Quatermain may be all the muscular tough guy, but he still is not up to breaking rocks by head. Instead he secretively fastens a barrel of dynamite underneath a stone bench, mumbling with an almost unbearable wink to his American friends some "abracadabra," and blows the bench up. The natives are impressed, take him for a god, and once more trick translation, as in so many Hollywood films, has been replaced by special effects.

Indeed, in most action adventures of the 1980s and 1990s the coalition of understanding that Haggard established between narrator and readers finds its equivalent in a joint thrill in front of miraculously functioning technological, electronic, digital tricks that the hero plays upon his adversaries, the audience always merely half-initiated but only the more aware for that of the hero's brilliance, coolness, and expertise. Of course, this is the formula not only for colonial adventures but for thrillers from *Invasion USA* (1985) to *The Matrix* (1999), but foreign settings present especially adequate locations for such scenarios. The exotic background, be it African or Caribbean voodooism, the South American or the Indian jungle, provides not only a mass of easily impressible bystanders or easily dismissible victims but is eventually totally integrated into the logic of Western technology, or rather, special effects: technology *is* magic by dint of this turn. Thus, in *Live and Let Die*, a James Bond film of 1973,[32] set largely in Jamaica, a voodoo ritual set up to kill the Bond girl Solitaire is unmasked as the workings of a giant subterranean high-tech machinery controlled by the Harlem gangster boss Kananga. Where indigenous magic itself turns out to be nothing but technological hocus-pocus, remote controlled from underneath or behind, trick translation is no longer an isolated maneuver but the only discourse there is, a discourse, moreover, that does not even address the natives, who figure as nothing but a picturesque backdrop for a conflict between American gangsters and British secret agents. When James Bond discovers the machinery, he uses his own little tricks and devices to confront it while the natives stand by and are impressed, believing to the end in the power of voodoo where the power of special effects has long taken over.

This logic of special effects, however, functions on two levels: there is technological power on display (the bomb, the hand grenade, the fast car, the rocket, and—these days—cyberspace), and there are, analogous to these technological achievements, the workings of filmic technique and technology (the light and sound effects of the explosion, the high-speed montage and crosscuts of the car race, the digital simulation of virtual realities). Both aspects, although roughly subsumable to the different realms of content and form, are intricately laced up with each other, forming the two sides of what Stephen Heath has called the "cinema-machine." After all, as he elaborated,

[c]inema does not exist in the technological and then become this or that practice in the social; its history is a history of the technological and social together, a history in which the determinations are not simple but multiple, interacting, in which the ideological is there from the start—without this latter emphasis reducing the technological to the ideological or making it uniquely the term of an ideological determination.[33]

Action adventures are infused with an aesthetics of technological excess, working both on a symbolic and on a material level. But even if they are intricately enmeshed with each other, these two levels—represented technology and the technology of representation, as it were—should not be mixed up. There are significant divergences, after all: While on a diegetic level the display of technology is more often than not mapped out in terms of trickery and deception, when used on an extradiegetic level or on the level of film production, technological tricks lose this connotation of manipulation. In fact, to enjoy special effects is to defer the knowledge about their "deceptive" nature.

To defer, but not to forget. We are meant, after all, to appreciate the workings of special effects—the fact that we are being tricked. But the awareness of special effects and technological tricks need not bring about a disruption of illusion, as Edward Buscombe pointed out: "Not everything which is not realism is counter-cinema." His remarks about the effects of early color film can be easily extended to all kinds of new filmic technologies:

[C]olor in early Technicolor pictures operates as a celebration of technology: "look how marvellous the cinema is!" . . . Early Technicolor functions as a form of self-reflexiveness, which instead of deconstructing the film and destroying the illusion effects a kind of reification of technology. Other forms of film technology function in the same way: Cinerama, 3-D, even spectacular crane or helicopter shots all having the effect satirised in the Cole Porter song in Silk Stockings:

"glorious Technicolor, and breathtaking CinemaScope and stereophonic sound." So we might see color working to confirm Ernest Mandel's statement: "Belief in the omnipotence of technology is the specific form of Bourgeois ideology in late capitalism."[34]

Film audiences, even more than literary ones, develop a "double consciousness"—undergoing an ever more pervasive suspension of disbelief. Action adventures, in particular, come to rely upon this effect, as they easily adapt to a postmodern "cinema-machine," which works by way of allusions, repercussions, metafictional references, and pastiche: "The mixing of genres, with the mania for citation and self-referencing so typical of contemporary cinema, allows for a double inscription of audiences, with viewers simultaneously positioned as both naive and ironic, as both innocent and knowing subjects."[35]

And yet, this "double consciousness" characterizing the postmodern viewer becomes also the point of departure for sudden breaks and ruptures, time and again pulling the ideological framework around the genre inadvertently into view. This is what makes special effects such an interesting subject for adventure film analysis. After all, the insight that such effects are a form of trickery and manipulation may very well have consequences for our reading of the cultural contact scenarios on display. Often enough the problematic logic of imperial action adventures surfaces precisely in instances where special effects take over as the dominant mode of representation, on both a diegetic and an extradiegetic level. The conflict between undercover agents and underground gangsters in *Live and Let Die,* for example, which is acted out by way of technological trickery, at times appears as a self-referential activity, an overblown exhibition of technological skills and equipment for its own sake. By dint of that insight, the film not only cancels out native agency and self-determination, as I have noted before, but indirectly renders all kinds of action dubious—it is hard to ignore that both James Bond and his adversaries seem to take part in a complicated back-and-forth of trickery that has hardly any outside effect.

This strangely self-defeating logic becomes even more evident in another imperial action adventure—Lewis Teague's *The Jewel of the Nile* (1985),[36] the second film starring Michael Douglas and Kathleen Turner as an adventure couple in exotic countries all over the world. This film enacts cultural contact once more along the lines of special effects outdoing trick translation. Captured in the headquarters of the fanatic and power-hungry North African potentate Omar Khalifa (Spiros Focás), the American writer Joan Wilder (Kathleen Turner) overhears his admonition to an adviser: "This is not a cheap theatrical stunt. It's a miracle! My people have to believe it." "Omar, trust me," the adviser replies in a thick

Cockney accent, "Trust what I've got to say. Look, if I can make gods out of rock 'n' roll stars, imagine what I can do for you."

The adviser, an English "special effects wizard" (Daniel Peacock), is bound to go down, however, as he will be challenged on his own grounds by Joan, her man Jack Colton (Michael Douglas), and Nick Allder, the film's special effects supervisor. The English wizard tries to monitor a spectacular performance of Omar's from behind the scene but is replaced by Joan and Jack, who then set out to support their local hero, the holy man "Jewel" (Avner Eisenberg), who replaces Omar onstage. The ensuing display of special effects on all levels—diegetic and extradiegetic—involuntarily calls to mind Quatermain's confrontation with African witchcraft in Haggard's novel: briefly the entire scenario of cultural interaction appears as a giant machinery of manipulation, this time steered from behind the scene by outsiders and based upon the power of make-believe, which is the power of special effects. The old struggle of good and bad—here it suddenly appears to signify nothing but good special effects outdoing bad ones.

But just like Haggard's novel, Teague's film turns away from this momentary disclosure, containing the evidence of manipulation and restoring the clear-cut lines of good and evil eventually: the holy man is seen to perform a "real" miracle onstage, walking through flames, so that the machinery of special effects is once more closed off from view to become a purely extradiegetic means of representation. As the evil potentate is replaced by the harmless holy man and the calculating Brit gives way to the idealistic Americans, the evidence of special effects moves into the background. And yet, the restoration of the action adventure paradigm seems shallow, considerably less convincing than the games of manipulation and trickery displayed before. The suspicion of universal trickery has momentarily raised its ugly head, and it is hard to get rid of again.

1.4 Fake Communication: An Alphabetical Africa

The logic of anti-conquest rules virtually unchallenged in 1980s imperial action adventures, as Hollywood obviously considers the forceful subjugation of other cultures an inappropriate thing to do. Those who still pursue these evil goals are clearly characterized as fanatic and extremist others—be they Arab, African, or Nazi German—at any rate, not yet trained in the ways of the civilized West. The films' American protagonists, by contrast, prove to be in stark opposition to the wicked ways of tyranny and extremism, pitting the power of trickery against non-Western power politics, and countering the traditional tools of colonial interaction—rhetoric and violence—with the full force of their spectacular actions, the functionality of cultural contact swallowed up in the excessive aesthetics of special effects. As the exotic and the far-away have lost their exceptional quality—we've seen it once too often before—the thrill of novelty shifts almost imperceptibly from the foreign culture to the very phenomenon of contact, the spectacular mechanisms of trickery themselves taking center stage. We know that the savage tribe and the fanatic potentate will eventually give in; it is *how* they are made to comply that counts.

While *The Jewel of the Nile* briefly discloses this circular and self-centered logic, only to take back the disclosure eventually and to return to the conventions of adventure narration, Elaine May's *Ishtar* (1987),[37] an adventure film that carries the established patterns of action at times to hilarious extremes, renders the tautological dimension of trickery pivotal. Here, the changed situation of cultural contact is tackled much more directly than in most other action adventures of the day, and it is a very specific implementation of the trope of trick translation that serves to drive the point home.

Ishtar presents a world in which communication is not so much manipulated but abandoned altogether. Which is not to say that the film celebrates silence—to the contrary. It relates the fate of two American showmen, Lyle Rogers (Warren Beatty) and Chuck Clarke (Dustin Hoffman), in North Africa, where they get entangled against their will in large-scale political conflicts. At the height of their plight we see them in the desert, having run out of their water supplies. This is when they come across a group of very different people involved in some kind of sales negotiation. Two British arms dealers and their Arab accomplice, who brought a truckload of weapons into the desert, try to make a deal with delegates of various North African tribes, and they take Lyle for the auctioneer and interpreter they have been waiting for—a dangerous mix-up, given the Americans' precarious situation. Once more, trick translation sets in, and once more, it becomes a matter of Western interaction instead of intercultural exchange. Chuck, wrapped in the local garb, mingles with the native clients; Lyle sets out to interpret for the dealers—not knowing any of the languages involved apart from English.

He succeeds, needless to say, yet not because he establishes some kind of nonverbal understanding with the Africans but because he is a performer—he just makes up the entire exchange. Screaming hysterically at the tribesmen while waving his hands fanatically, he simulates the stereotype of the Oriental first and then sets out to "interpret" his audiences' gestures of confusion and incomprehension: "They say they could hardly believe their ears . . . ," while Chuck steers the situation from the other side. Thus they keep a conversation going that is entirely devoid of information or meaning in any traditional sense of the words. And yet, the deal is made and weapons are sold. Lyle's spectacular show of translation works because he takes over all parts involved, figuring simultaneously as the translator figure and the exotic other, from the vantage point of the Westerner. This kind of communication serves not so much to effect some hidden manipulation but to hide the fact that verbal exchange is no longer necessary, as material exchanges like the arms deal have long gained a momentum of their own. Mediation, translation, interpretation become ends in themselves, while signification turns into the pure act of speaking.

But May's film is not the first text to trace this process of displacement. In his 1974 novel *Alphabetical Africa,* Walter Abish charted the same phenomenon much more radically than any action adventure ever would. Here another trite adventure story is told, revolving around a white male protagonist on a quest, a beautiful white woman, a perverted dictator, and some black and white villains, coming complete with lustful black men and erotic black women and a panoply of magic rituals and exotic customs. But the story line is definitely not the point of this narrative. While fulfilling the plot criteria of a classical adventure, *Alphabetical Africa* by no means complies with the requirements of structural simplicity. Indeed Abish is quite hard to read.

Alphabetical Africa sets out with the chapter heading "A" and runs through all the letters of the alphabet to "Z" and then back again to "A." In the first chapter every word starts with the letter *a,* and in the following chapters step by step the other letters of the alphabet are included and then discarded again as the headings run back to "A." As the letters are "collected," the plot of the novel slowly crystallizes: An "author" who only later becomes an "I" relates his adventurous quest for a beautiful blonde, Alva, throughout the African continent. In the course of this quest he discovers the quite frightful fact that Africa is shrinking (of course this is not revealed until chapter "S"). In the beginning, however, we are faced with almost meaningless, fragmentary sentences due to the fact that alliteration rules mercilessly. Yet while in Abish's presentation Africa has become a purely semiotic space, "[h]idden somewhere within the mind-numbing, machine-gun-like rapidity of the alliterative absurdities of this chapter is a politically oriented course. . . ."[38] Heaping cliché upon cliché—linking "African amulets" with "amorous Angolan abductions," "abhorrent acts" with "anachronistic assaults"[39]—Abish from the very beginning leaves no doubt about the fictionality of his Africa yet manages to render this fictionality, this constructedness its most central feature—an "alphabetical" Africa indeed.

In this respect Abish's Africa resembles the absurd comic-strip Africa in the Quatermain films, although Abish insists upon the problematic and paradoxical implications of this "Disneylandization" of Africa. His narrator, the "author" and "I" of the novel, involuntarily epitomizes precisely this absurdity when emphasizing his need for authenticity and truth by way of a highly stereotypical imagery of Africanity:

I came here at a moment's notice because my book defied completion. It needed local color. Authentic African cries. I measure my deliberate advance into Africa. I measure my concern, my difficulties, my long horseback journeys. I came here carrying a duffel bag containing a compass, a handgun, a few books, a large map, a dictionary, handkerchiefs, condoms, a classical assortment, also an itinerary. I'm in a black country, everything is dark, everything, even all sounds, heavy, dark, beating drums, in my ears even African joyous dancing appears dark and mysterious. Because I am insecure, I'm always looking at my map and checking my compass. (*AA* 34–35)

Even if the author's "classical assortment" contains the stock instruments of the explorer and adventurer—the compass, the map, the handgun—he is more of a tourist, equipped with every possible item to facilitate his "deliberate advance into Africa." And the advance is not as innocent as it may appear—the author twists and distorts the evidence at hand according to his own interests and needs, "an unreliable reporter" who cannot be "depended upon for exact descriptions and details" (*AA* 56), as he believes that "facts can always be changed, can always be adjusted, can always be altered" (*AA* 125). What could be taken as a pledge to artistic freedom, however, quickly turns out to be a much more ambivalent insight, as the volatility of facts and reality is seen to cut both ways—affecting the author himself as much as his subject matter.

After all, not only Africa is vanishing but also the alphabet. After having been laboriously assembled, the very material for writing a novel disappears again, until the book's initial stage of stammering alliterations is reestablished. Seen that way, *Alphabetical Africa* is a novel about losing control on all kinds of levels—control over a continent, control over one's language, and, by consequence, control over cultural communication.

There is no agent behind this deprivation, however, no identifiable individual or community to be held responsible for the pervasive corrosion of power we witness. Significantly enough, the guerrilla troop that relentlessly undermines the state of things in Africa is represented as ants, faceless and deindividualized forces of disruption. Likewise, none of the African characters gain a personality; most of them remaining nameless. But then again, the Europeans, who are named, do not come across as deep characters either; the entire novel is pure surface, as the author makes unmistakably clear: "I don't dig into ground because everything, but everything is above, and by digging I am falsely implying an interior, a depth beneath" (*AA* 129). Thus every kind of action in this novel resembles an empty ritual, devoid of intention or volition, while communication turns out to be nothing but a farce.

This comes to the fore in the attempts of a central character, the "French Consul," to solidify cultural contact. Leading a group of expatriates, "[a]ccompanied by a few hundred carriers," through the continent, although he has long lost any sense of orientation, the French Consul tirelessly pursues his project of gaining access to the native mind:

... after a few months, certain linguistic difficulties arise as both ends, having developed different dialects, can no longer communicate. It is most distressing. Lacking a compass, a dictionary and now, also a common memory, both ends are apprehensive about future contacts. Despondently, each morning French Consul holds a conference. Every inch a diplomat, he addresses his end, but he also is addressing a communal conscience of East and Central Africa. He keeps explaining in his aristocratic French how much he loves Africa. He knows Africans are easily moved by an emotional appeal. Africans, it appears, are moved less by explanations and more by eloquent facial expressions. French Consul, after all, is a master at conveying his distress by lifting an eyebrow. How delightful, how exquisite. African drums immediately describe facial expression. Consul is a consummate artist. Nobody can forget his fantastic expression. Everyone is lifting an eyebrow, enraptured at finding a new feat in communication. Arched eyebrows are included in a cuneiform code. I may be lost forever, comments French Consul, but I feel happy at having fathered a cultural explosion. (*AA* 117)

Indeed, the French Consul manages to accomplish what long generations of explorers, travelers, and adventure heroes have not brought about: true and univocal intercultural communication, a cultural explosion indeed. The fact that, just as in *Ishtar,* nothing is communicated cannot diminish this achievement. It is no accident that it is the imitation of a facial expression that facilitates the complicated process of translation here, as time and again in this novel people resort to imitation, mimicry, and masquerade to establish contact, if contact is the right word for this perpetual projection and reflection of expressions.

While the French Consul proves to be pretty good at the games of imitation, it is another potentate who seems literally to incorporate the principle of fake and make-believe. Queen Quat, a person of unclear gender and unclear origin—both male and female, African and European—makes mimicry the basis of imperial power, ordering his/her subjects to paint entire countries orange, blue, or green in order to match their representation on Western maps, and finally disturbing the author deeply by "impersonat[ing] Africans in the bush, and me, mimicking my accent, my awkward embraces, my hesitations" (*AA* 45). The fact that Queen Quat makes a fortune out of a "cosmetic empire" does not surprise.

In this novel, colonialism and imperialism figure as stock elements in an all-comprising masquerade, a global drag show in which "[a]ll foreigners are actors for an African continent" (*AA* 132), while "Africans are applying American cosmetics" (*AA* 19). Once more, just as in 1980s action adventures, cultural contact becomes a matter of universal make-believe and manipulation, a game whose goals and incentives are unclear and might be long forgotten by the individual players. If this game seems highly arbitrary and artificial, it is nevertheless all there is—"a delicate balance exists between crumbling continent, curious African audience and an ant colony gnawing away . . . " (*AA* 134). Stepping outside the prefabricated imagery of Africanity seems out of the question in Abish's narrative universe.

This insight discloses itself not only on the plot level, however, but in the very structure of Abish's text, which loses itself time and again in endless lists and enumerations, inventories and assemblages, giving vent to the desire for all-inclusive representation and order and still achieving precisely the opposite effect—confusion and discontinuity. At one point, Queen Quat makes up a list that starts with "same shit," then slowly finds its way into an alphabetical order by way of lining up the nouns: "same safaris same safeguards same saffron . . . same sporadic sprees same staples same steatopygia same sterilyzed syringes same surprise" (*AA* 100–101). The oxymoronic ending—"same surprise"—disrupts the alphabetical logic, but its effect can hardly be called spectacular—the surprise remains vicarious, the thrill of the new irretrievably entangled in the old, stereotypical systems of meaning making.

The novel ends upon "another" seemingly meaningless and almost endless list of repetitive constructs: "Another abbreviation another abdomen another abduction another aberration another abhorrent ass another abnormal act another aboriginal another approach . . . ," which for a last time runs through the alphabet. After several run-throughs the alphabetical order is disrupted here, too, as the novel's "protagonists" are lined up: " . . . another Alva another Alex another Allen another Alfred another Africa another alphabet." "Another"—it could mean a true alternative, but most likely it announces just "another" version of the well-known, a repetition without a difference—"same surprise" or, more appropriately, "same shit."

Both *Alphabetical Africa* and *Ishtar*, as radically different as these texts are, make out communication and cultural contact as purely performative events, self-serving and strangely afunctional, their course more or less well rehearsed, their outcome unsurprising and predictable. By consequence, the formulaic character of the adventure genre is radically foregrounded—in line with 1980s action adventure trends toward metatextuality and irony as in *Ishtar*, or in line with avant-garde techniques of parodic reiteration as in *Alphabetical Africa*. In both cases the effect is largely comic, the emphasis on textuality and formula preventing the accentuation of darker aspects of the theme of fake communication. The very same semantic field of trickery and deception, misleading communication and cultural manipulation, does present itself in a radically different light, however, once it is approached from a less formalistic angle, as another narrative exemplifies, one that focuses not so much on the structural unfolding of trickery but on its conceptual consequences—presenting a world in which trick translation has invaded the very last resorts of selfhood.

John Edgar Wideman's novel *The Cattle Killing* (1996) approaches the theme of global contact and cultural translation from a variety of perspectives, moving between Africa, England, and the United States, not to mention the imaginary realms and mindscapes interlinking these geographical locations for Wideman's protagonists—most of them travelers, outcasts, diasporic subjects. The novel's title refers to an episode in South African history, taking place during the so-called Kaffir Wars between Dutch and English colonizers and Xhosa colonized, among others. In 1857 the Xhosa experienced a self-inflicted backlash that led to their eventual defeat: responding to a prophecy they killed their own cattle, thus depriving themselves of meat and milk and triggering a period of widespread starvation.

In Wideman's novel this episode is told as a dream vision, the Xhosa girl who will come to initiate the cattle killing invading the dream of an African-American preacher during the yellow fever epidemics in Philadelphia in the late eighteenth century. In his dream she narrates her encounter with strangers who turn out to be spirits—her father's dead brothers. One of them then instructs the girl that "the cattle must be killed" in order to bring about a "new world," in which the "ancestors . . . return and dwell again on the earth, bringing with them endless herds of cattle to fill our kraals."[40]

The Xhosa girl is so much taken in by the encounter that she manages to convince her tribe. The cattle are killed, but of course the promised turn of events does not come about. Like so many colonized peoples before them, the Xhosa have been tricked into acting against their own interest:

We'd been deceived. It was not the shade of my father's brother who spoke through me that day beside the pool. No. It was a spirit of despair grown strong inside our breasts, as the whites had grown strong in our land, during years of fighting and plague and hate. A spirit who whispered the lies of the invaders in our ears. Who tricked us into toiling for our foes. Taught us to kill our cattle, murder ourselves. (*CK* 147)

Like Haggard, Wideman describes the invasion and appropriation of an indigenous system of belief to achieve subjugation and defeat. But in contrast to countless earlier enactments of trick translation, here trickery does not originate from the Western intruders but emanates from the native mind. Communication is not centrally controlled and willfully contorted in Wideman's novel but literally hollowed out from within; there is nothing left over to posit a counterweight to the invasive forces, as the seemingly most inalienable and immaculate realm of spiritual certainty has been taken over—the "great white god" *is* the African spirit here.

Needless to say, this is a nightmare for the African-American dreamer, even though his visitor ends upon a note of reconciliation:

Sleep, my child, my pumpkin, and I will come to you in another dream. This one is too old and sad, she said. I will return in a happier dream in a new land where the cattle are not dying, the children not dying. Only our enemies dead in the new dream, the slaughter of our cattle, the slaughter of our children not dyeing our hands blood red with guilt. A love dream. Yours. Mine. (*CK* 148)

The Xhosa girl's last words of encouragement, hinting at an ideal state of diasporic, transcultural solidarity, do not bear a lot of effect in *The Cattle Killing,* though, as a large-scale scenario of infiltration and involuntary compliance with the enemy evolves, which seems to reach out from the days of slavery to the present time. Like *Alphabetical Africa,* Wideman's novel envisions trickery as a dangerous and powerful device, a means of manipulation and misguidance that seems to have gained a momentum of its own, independent of personal will and individual interests and almost impossible to overcome by way of individual action or resistance.

If both Abish's and Wideman's novels stop short at such scenarios of individual irrelevance and inertia, both of them painting vastly negative pictures of losing control over one's own affairs, it is on the same ground that other narratives set out to revise the scenarios at hand, approximating the tropes of deception and trickery once more under changed insignia and using them for markedly different purposes. Before turning to these revisionary accounts, however, I will cast a closer look at some enactments of cultural communication that map out imaginary Africas not so much to break with the established order but to reassess the old convictions so that they fit the requirements of a global system. In the course of these narratives, the practices of trickery and mimicry turn out to be quite powerful means of cultural and national self-fashioning. And again, the notion of translation proves vital. The idea of cultural communication, however, will be seen to undergo a remarkable transformation.

TWO

Monkey Business: Of Ape-Men and Man-Apes

olonialism has always been a business of power and exploitation, and this ugly fact has made many of its advocates uneasy. This is why the rhetoric of anti-conquest evolved, which busily translated the evidence of takeover and subjugation into narratives of benign, if clearly uneven, encounters in the wilderness. The trope of trick translation plays a major role within such enactments of anti-conquest, as it allows for a conception of colonial contact in terms of communication rather than battle, while simultaneously retaining the notion of distinct parties organized along clear-cut hierarchical lines—tricksters and tricked ones.

This is, of course, a far from uncomplicated maneuver. After all, to claim univocality and distinction on the basis of a trope that proceeds via obfuscation and confusion must needs turn out a tricky thing in its own right. And indeed, the goal of indubitable lines of differentiation and stable systems of stratification is often to be achieved only at the cost of momentary instabilities and uncertainties, as we have seen: time and again, narratives of cultural contact, be they literary or filmic, call up ambivalences, which might be contained and downplayed eventually but are still there, somewhere in the textual background—its political unconscious, if you will.

Yet if even texts that set out with clear-cut binary distinctions—the colonized/the colonizers, Africa/the West, black/white—tend to lose grip on their repertory of differentiation, how are we to read texts that collapse such binaries in the first place? What happens when the very protagonists of colonial contact narratives become dubious characters of unclear cultural background? What if the two sides of the colonial divide are mixed-up? This is the situation given in many recent narratives around diasporic "contact zones," as we shall see later on in this book—

narratives that deliberately undermine the categories of differentiation and classification at large, and thus "deploy the cultural hybridity of their borderline conditions to 'translate,' and therefore reinscribe, the social imaginary of both metropolis and modernity."[1] But diasporic narratives are not the only texts enacting a liminal state in-between cultures—there are other, earlier, enactments of the concept of cultural hybridity that prove succinctly that this concept need not necessarily imply a liberatory or counterhegemonic move. To the contrary, hybrid constellations may very well serve to stabilize hegemonic systems of signification, as old dichotomies and hierarchies are often not discarded but welded together—translated to fit the frames of newly emergent symbolic systems. This is the development I will trace in this chapter, setting out with a text that exemplarily performs the maneuver of disrupting a set of binary distinctions to implement a new framework of signification.

A mere plot summary of this text could very well be read exclusively in terms of ideological subversiveness: A white man grows up primitive in the jungle, unaware of the implications of whiteness and masculinity. He develops a sense of identity by negotiating various options of selfhood—apeness, humanness, wildness, civilizedness—as he comes across numerous other displaced and disoriented persons, among them a black American woman who has to confront Africa as an unfamiliar terrain. You should have recognized the story by now, and you might be aware of the fact that the novel that first laid out this plotline is much less disruptive than my description suggests. I am, of course, talking about Tarzan, or, to be more precise, about Edgar Rice Burroughs's *Tarzan of the Apes* (1914), a novel that risks playing around with the dichotomies of colonial reasoning on the basis of a no less stable, if differently organized, system of cultural hierarchies.[2]

The novel gives evidence of the conceptual framework of twentieth-century American imperialism, a framework that reflects *and* ruptures the logic and rhetoric of colonialism.[3] While the proponents of American imperialism around the turn of the century did call upon a central tenet of colonial legitimation—the notion that in the colonial venture the rest of the world is awarded the gift of one's own culture—it is interesting to see how this tenet gradually dissolves to give way to a diametrically opposed stance: once the imperial project is associated not so much with permanent rule abroad but with momentary interventions and provisional maneuvers on foreign territory, culture tends to be conceived not as a gift to give away but as an endangered good, easily corrupted by outside influences and by too close contact—an imagery that was of course just as popular in early-twentieth-century debates around immigration and migration in the United States.[4] In line with such reconceptualizations, the notion that other cultures should ideally become "mock-civilizations" is step by step modified, eventually giving scope to a model of cultural contact as functional interaction or technical compatibility, a model that will culminate in the contemporary concept of globalization, as we shall see. It is against this backdrop that the figure of the ape-man, this epitome of hybridity, appears fraught with consolidating rather than disruptive functions. After all, Burroughs's notion of the aristocratic jungle man, veering between nature and culture, owes much to nonfictional approaches of the day to the concepts of primitivity and acculturation.

Not surprisingly, it was the scientific discipline of primatology that played a major role in such reflections upon the transition from nature to culture, from bestiality to sociality. For centuries, primate apes have been studied in order to come to conclusions about human beings—usually not to question the borderline between the animal and the human realm but to specify it.[5] And the transition between scientific and fictional approaches has always been somewhat obscure. In her seminal study on the cultural history of primatology, Donna Haraway coined the term "simian orientalism" to demarcate the continuities between scientific and aesthetic projections. She argued that, like so many other discourses concerned with exotic difference and its familiar strangeness, primatology revolved around the issues of selfhood and otherness, time and again tracing the question of (natural) origin in order to tackle the structure of (cultural) refinement. After all, the ideological construction of selfhood always already involves a differentiating move:

Simian orientalism means that western primatology has been about the construction of the self from the raw material of the other, the appropriation of nature in the production of culture, the ripening of the human from the soil of the animal, the clarity of white from the obscurity of color, the issue of man from the body of woman, the elaboration of gender from the resource of sex, the emergence of mind by the activation of body. . . . Primatology is western discourse, and it is sexualized discourse.[6]

In the course of the twentieth century, when identity increasingly came to be explained in terms of culture instead of race or blood, subtle distinctions and gradual differentiations became ever more important. Consequently, whiteness and masculinity were conceptualized in terms of a refinement of biological "material," emanations from essential categories like animality, femininity, blackness. But to conceive of white male identity in such terms is also to turn it into a precarious quality, an accomplishment that can get lost, a complexity that can collapse.

This chapter will explore some fictional speculations around men and apes to inquire once more about a changing imagery of contact and communication. Enactments of encounters between humans and primates have always been charged with the symbolics of cultural contact and race relations, even in fictions where apes clearly do *not* figure forth Africans. Seen that way, my focus has not changed. But we shall soon see that ape-man narratives and their counterparts—man-ape stories—cast the contact zone in a different light than the tales of trick translation investigated before. There is more at stake for the protagonists of the ape-man story— the ape-man does not transgress boundaries to find out about the world but can be seen (re)drawing boundaries to safeguard his self. Tarzan may opt for manhood or apeness, or remain precariously poised between both states—but he can never step as completely outside the jungle as Haggard's Quatermain, who leaves Kukuanaland behind at the end of *King Solomon's Mines* to experience "real" civilization for a change. Whereas colonial adventures speculate about first contact from a safe distance, for ape-man stories contact has always already taken place: there seems to be no way back and no way out.

Every so often, the fictions of American imperialism, mapping out scenarios abroad, can also be read as fictions of national race relations. And certainly, to write about Africa in the United States was always also to write about African-Americans. This comes exemplarily well to the fore in countless *Tarzan* narratives throughout the twentieth century, narratives that can in many respects be read as a counterpoint to narratives of the Middle Passage, that other obvious point of convergence between international and national concerns, to be investigated at a later point in this study. Where contemporary fictions of the Middle Passage will be seen to sketch alternative histories, however, ape-man stories, just like colonial adventures, set out to reenact and solidify more or less successfully a hegemonic history, according to which the potential "contagion" of contact calls for all kinds of regulatory practices and safeguarding measures.

2.1 Tarzan and Tautology: Work Your Body, Work Your Mind

Even if Edgar Rice Burroughs's hero is as different as can be from the "cautious" and "timid" trader figure Quatermain, the similarities in the plotlines of *Tarzan of the Apes* and *King Solomon's Mines* are hard to miss: Apart from diligently replicating the adventure formula devised by Kipling, Haggard, and others, Burroughs installs an exotic environment clearly reminiscent of Haggard's work. Like *King Solomon's Mines*, *Tarzan of the Apes* investigates the contact zone, and like the earlier novel it seeks alternatives to the imagery of unfriendly takeover and violent aggression associated with colonial rule. Moreover, Burroughs follows in the footsteps of his much admired predecessor Haggard by enacting the first encounter between the civilized (men) and the (simian) savages around the technology of firearms. Burroughs's apes can be seen reacting like Haggard's natives to the gun, the report of which triggers a "story of the thunder-stick" that "surrounded the white man's deserted abode with an atmosphere of weirdness and terror for the simians."[7] And again as in Haggard, the gun is eventually made out as an instrument unfit for gaining and maintaining control. Yet this is where the analogies end. In *King Solomon's Mines,* the gun was rejected in favor of more sophisticated testimonials of civilization—the glass eye and the false teeth—which permitted the clear-cut differentiation between English refinement and African primitivity on the grounds of wrong and right "use." In *Tarzan,* the "imperialist" novel[8] written almost thirty years after the "colonialist" *King Solomon's Mines,* the gun is rejected not because it is too blunt and explicit but because it is already too refined. The gun, we learn very early in the novel, might very well be the epitome of civilized culture. Yet in order to survive in the jungle, civilized culture is not enough.[9]

Two central scenes in *Tarzan,* one of them forming the dramatic exposition in Africa, are centered on firearms, and both show women handling them. When Lady Greystoke, Tarzan's mother-to-be, intervenes with a gun to save her husband from an assaulting ape, she manages to kill the ape, but more or less accidentally. For a precarious moment before the ape collapses, the horrified Lord Greystoke sees him turning around and charging at "the terrified girl vainly trying to fire another bullet into the animal's body; but she did not understand the mechanism of the firearm, and the hammer fell futilely upon an empty cartridge" (*TA* 39). Later on, a similar scenario of physical helplessness and technical futility evolves around Jane Porter, who, when confronted with an assaulting lion, can think of no better use of the pistol in her hand but to kill her servant and herself to avoid the terrible fate—and even there she fails. Putting the pistols in the hands of women who do not know how to use them properly points to a trenchant skepticism in this novel against the achievements of civilization, a proviso equally illustrated by the intellectual figures, Jane's father, the Professor, and his assistant—"impractical theorists" (*TA* 134).[10] It is no surprise that Tarzan, this "personification . . . of the primitive man, the hunter, the warrior" (*TA* 122), prefers the knife or bow and arrow to the mechanical weapons the Europeans and Americans brought along.

This preference for more "physical" weapons goes along with a focalization on the male body, which becomes Tarzan's ultimate weapon in the course of the novel. By dint of this process it might seem that eventually *Tarzan* recuperates another stock figure of nineteenth-century adventure fiction—the "white warrior," exemplarily embodied by Haggard's Sir

Henry Curtis. But Tarzan's strength is not a product of archaic masculinity, even if it is time and again described in terms of classical heroism and ancient grandeur. Significantly enough, Edgar Rice Burroughs criticized the makers of the early Tarzan films for casting Elmo Lincoln, the hulky muscle man, for the part:

> Tarzan was not beefy but was light and graceful and well-muscled. . . . Tarzan must be young and handsome with an extremely masculine face and manner. . . . It may be difficult to get such a man but please do not try to get a giant or a man with over-developed muscles. It is true that in the stories I often speak of Tarzan as the "giant Apeman" but that is because I am rather prone to use superlatives.[11]

The Tarzan of the novels is not a freak of nature; his body is the result of highly modern planning, not biologically but culturally extraordinary.

Reflecting on the imagery of the "white man's muscles," Richard Dyer differentiated between the "natural" and the "trained" body along the lines of biological disposition and cultural work. Reading the *Tarzan* films in their obsessive enactment of the perfect body, he concludes that, within the figure of the built body, tradition and modernity interfuse. The bodybuilder draws upon allegedly long-standing aesthetic principles and techniques, yet the product of this work is markedly up-to-date:

> The built white body is not the body that white men are born with, it is the body made possible by their natural mental superiority. The point after all is that it is built, a product of the application of thought and planning, an achievement. It is the sense of the mind at work behind the production of this body that most defines its whiteness.[12]

The very same reconceptualization of body/mind constellations suffuses *Tarzan of the Apes*. The novel's ideological framework could be said to rest upon Tarzan's well-trained shoulders: his built body makes him equal to the apes and the natives, without qualifying his difference.

Situating this display of work and discipline in the African jungle, Burroughs manages to reenact the lines of differentiation between Europe, Africa, and America: the English lord who grows up wild in the African wilderness manages to find himself by way of training, or rather, bodybuilding. And while the self Tarzan eventually finds for once clearly attests to his "aristocratic birth" and "many generations of fine breeding" (*TA* 202)—and thus to the "old world" of Anglo-Saxon tradition—his disregard for status and overrefinement, the traditional markers of prestige in the old world, clearly discloses a new frame of reference for this particular self-fashioning: Tarzan the bodybuilder is Tarzan the new (world) man.

Yet rendering bodybuilding the epitome of cultural self-fashioning is not unproblematic, as there is a structural deficit inscribed into the practice itself: its "uselessness." The implication of self-referentiality, of a lack of purpose, has haunted modern sport from its beginnings in the nineteenth century. Both the new sport clubs established around the turn of the century and the paramilitary youth groups of the time could not altogether deny their "lack of any clear goals. Activity was an end in itself; the only commitment was to the idea of commitment," as T. J. Jackson Lears pointed out. "Formed in opposition to modern moral flaccidity," he concludes, "paramilitary youth groups unknowingly exacerbated it."[13] The very rhetoric of cultural masculinization and reinvigoration that these organizations enthusiastically embraced, alongside the Rooseveltian notion of a "strenuous life," thus always ran the risk of flipping over into its counterpart, the endorsement of decadent self-indulgence.

At first glance, Tarzan's bodybuilding seems to be unaffected by the stigma of unpractical narcissism, as it is justified time and again in countless fights against various beasts of the jungle. And yet, at a closer look it turns out that Tarzan's lifestyle is altogether far from practical—his special status as a "white ape" can be seen to depend upon this very quality of bodybuilding, which its American proponents around the turn of the century were so anxious to downplay: tautology. After all, apart from demarcating his equality with the "fierce brutes of the jungle" (TA 62), Tarzan's body always also demarcates his fundamental difference, his exceptionality. Let me give an example: At one point in the novel, Tarzan escapes from his archenemy, Sabor the lioness, at almost the last moment. He reacts on the grounds of his "quickness of mental action" (TA 55), jumps into the river, and then works out how to swim, thus giving one more proof of his superior intellect and his bodily fitness (the ape on his side is killed). Yet at the same time Tarzan also discovers the "feeling of freshness and exhilaration which the cool waters had imparted to him" and discovers sport as a leisure activity: "ever after he lost no opportunity to take a daily plunge in lake or stream or ocean when it was possible to do so" (TA 56). Here, both the concept of work (training) and the concomitant concept of "workout" (leisure) delineate the borderlines of Tarzan's exceptional situation in the jungle, setting him off from the apes who "did not like to enter water, and never did so voluntarily" (TA 56).

Not accidentally, it is after his first longer contact with civilized life that Tarzan experiences a similarly pleasurable "time-out": "it was with a feeling of exultant freedom that he swung once more through the forest branches. . . . Civilization held nothing like this in its narrow and circumscribed sphere, hemmed in by restrictions and conventionalities" (TA 259). Even when presented in this contrastive way, the confinements of civilization and the pleasures of physical exercise seem to strangely rely upon each other—so that work and leisure, confinement and momentary escape appear in dialectical interdependence, forming a close alliance after all, which in turn stands off against the apes' monotonous lifestyle, this "dull round of searching for food, eating and sleeping" (*TA* 56).

To indulge in the pleasures of recreation is to step momentarily outside of the routines of work and training without challenging these routines' priority. The implications of this logic for the mechanisms of cultural contact come to the fore when physical workout turns into mental work, when Africans instead of apes are confronted, and when training becomes trickery. The theme of playing tricks comes up first in Tarzan's handling of his wicked "foster father," the ape Tublat, and there it is already tightly conjoined with the notion of a tautological performance, an action for its own sake:

His superior intelligence and cunning permitted him to invent a thousand diabolical tricks to add to the burdens of Tublat's life.

Early in his boyhood he had learned to form ropes by twisting and tying long grasses together, and with these he was forever tripping Tublat or attempting to hang him from some overhanging branch.

By constant playing and experimenting with these he learned to tie rude knots, and make sliding nooses; and with these he and the younger apes amused themselves. What Tarzan did they tried to do also, but he alone originated and became proficient. (*TA* 57)

If the tricks played on Tublat do not exactly testify to a clear-cut pragmatic goal on Tarzan's side—especially when compared with the strategies of trick translation in *King Solomon's Mines*—the self-referential quality of such instances of self-assertion is even more trenchant when Tarzan comes across the African natives.

Having killed a black warrior, Kulonga, Tarzan uses the confusion in the African village and the absence of the villagers to enter a hut filled with spears and human skulls:

One by one, as he took each article from the walls, he placed them in a pile in the center of the room, and on top of all he placed the cooking pot, inverted, and on top of this he laid one of the grinning skulls, upon which he fastened the headdress of the dead Kulonga.

Then he stood back and surveyed his work, and grinned. Tarzan of the Apes was a joker. (*TA* 98)

At no other point in the book before or after does Tarzan reveal this inclination to joke; indeed his lack of humor elsewhere seems remarkable. As Walt Morton summed up his analysis of Tarzan films, "Tarzan is a serious fellow," his very masculinity apparently in contrast to the frivolous behavior and silly conduct of civilization.[14] Why then here suddenly this humoristic trait? It is definitely not meant to establish some kind of contact reminiscent of Quatermain's trickery—Tarzan never seeks to communicate

with the natives. Even if the effect is the classical effect of trick translation—the natives take Tarzan for some "jungle god"—it takes quite some
time for Tarzan to notice and to profit from this reaction, that is, to take
the weapons and food the natives put out for him. Yet, if the action in the
hut was indeed intended as nothing but a joke, then it is a poor one—
when faced with the fear and superstitious awe of the natives upon discovery of his weird prank, Tarzan is not amused, but confused: "There was
much in their demeanor which he could not understand, for of superstition
he was ignorant, and of fear of any kind he had but a vague conception"
(*TA* 100). What kind of joker is that, who does not even get the joke?

If bodybuilding acquired somewhat tautological connotations earlier
in the novel, the same connotations are hard to miss when it comes to
trickery. Although the first encounter with the natives ended up with confusion on both sides, Tarzan seeks the same experience time and again afterward: "He looked about for some hint of a wild prank to play upon
these strange, grotesque creatures that they might be again aware of his
presence among them" (*TA* 105). Apparently, the practice of trickery is
an end in itself here, devoid of the strategic use value and devoid of the ra-
tionalistic implications emphasized in *King Solomon's Mines*. Like bodybuilding, Tarzan's trickery takes the guise of a ritualistic performance,
acted out without any clear idea about its purpose and its consequences.
Trickery, like nobility, seems to run in the blood.

Indeed, Tarzan's entire behavior is made out as instinctive, determined
by both his highly trained body and a highbred ancestry, which can be actualized whenever needed with "utter unconsciousness of self," constituting a "hereditary instinct of graciousness" (*TA* 202). Insofar heredity and
training function as equivalents, even if they are put into explicit opposition—"heredity spoke louder than training" (*TA* 202). Throughout the
novel the two extremes in Tarzan's personality, his aristocratic blood and
his primeval training, seem to confirm rather than contradict each other,
suggesting a concept of identity as procedural quality—the instinctive
body knowledge and the genealogical archive, which form the backdrop
for never ending processes of self-fashioning in the wilderness—which
becomes in turn the blueprint for any new and alienating environment.[15]

Eric Cheyfitz has reflected upon the "irony of redundancy" in *Tarzan*,
coming to the fore in the notion "that a man must be civilized in order to
be civilized."[16] And indeed, while H. Rider Haggard stylized civilization
as a gift to be handed over to the unknowing natives, Edgar Rice Burroughs makes it out as a complicated mixture of heredity and training
that has to be protected and cultivated, and is much too unique to be
passed on. Walter Benn Michaels has shown how such a notion of civilization as precarious heritage rather than disposable achievement goes

very well together with the "culturalization" of identity in the twentieth century: "Culture, put forward as a way of preserving the primacy of identity while avoiding the embarrassments of blood, would turn out to be much more effective . . . as a way of reconceptualizing and thereby preserving the essential contours of racial identity."[17]

Tarzan of the Apes can be seen as located at the outset of this development: obviously, the rhetoric of race and blood still prevails, yet it is increasingly by way of cultural practices—training and trickery—that it comes to be expressed. In the course of this subtle substitution—or hybridization—categories like race are not discarded but translated into the vocabulary of modernity, while cultural practices of training and trickery are drained of any clear functionality or reference and thus essentialized in turn. Both the trained white body and white trickery document superiority (actively overcoming the animalesque and primitive) and demarcate difference. In the course of this development, identity comes to be conceptualized as a highly performative quality, suggesting an underlying matrix that has to be acted out time and again in order to be sustained. If instincts, intimations, and unconscious reflexes bring about the true self, then the traditional means of self-reflection—meditation and communication—have to figure as detours and deflections at best. To paraphrase Walter Benn Michaels: To be a white male you have to do white male things, but you can't really count on doing white male things unless you are already a white male.[18]

Hence, Tarzan's obsessive enactments of white male identity are necessarily as self-referential as they are: instead of imposing himself on others like Haggard's bearers of civilization, he fences himself markedly off from his environment—be that primitive wildlife or effeminate civilization. As this differentiation is an end in itself, tautology becomes the trope of the day.

2.2 "A Mimic of Uncanny Ability": *Greystoke*

Tarzan of the Apes had a man's figure and a man's brain, but he was an ape by training and environment. His brain told him that the chest contained something valuable, or the men would not have hidden it; his training had told him to imitate whatever was new and unusual, and now the natural curiosity, which is as common to men as to apes, prompted him to open the chest and to examine its contents.

—Edgar Rice Burroughs, Tarzan of the Apes (1914)

Compared with Burroughs's "adventure imperialism" in *Tarzan of the Apes,* the 1984 film *Greystoke,*[19] based upon Burroughs's first two Tarzan volumes, is an epitome of political correctness. The first Tarzan film that forgoes the adventure genre, *Greystoke* seems to have been produced in an effort to do nothing but the right thing. Marianna Torgovnick consequently compared the film favorably with all of its predecessors and praised it for presenting "ultimate harmony between humans and animals, humans and nature, without troubling relations of hierarchy and Otherness."[20] Indeed, this British take on the Tarzan story, directed by Hugh Hudson, not only adheres to an agenda of animal rights and ecological preservation but moreover misses no chance to point out the evils of colonialism, relocating the focus from American imperialism to the history of the British Empire. The film thus performs a significant shift of the entire scenario—figuring forth a contemporary reflection on masculinity and race (or species, to stay within the filmic terminology) that is eventually as ambivalent as its preceding versions.

Celebrating his hero as "the hunter, the warrior," and dwelling on his physical presence time and again, Burroughs made it totally clear that Tarzan's superiority derived from his toughness and strenuousity, qualities associated with both his training and his heritage, and thus celebrated as the consequences of his upbringing as an aristocrat in the jungle, a human being among beasts of prey. In the 1980s film, the novel's celebratory tone is clearly abandoned. The film's grid of evaluations and conceptions, for that matter, is much more difficult to determine.

The film's model male is not the hunter or sportsman, to be sure. After all, the paradigmatic "white hunter" figure is implemented in the film and does not seem to function as a role model. Major Jack Downing (Nigel Davenport), part of an expedition of the English Museum for National History, is a wild game hunter and taxidermist, a cold and cruel man, who shoots a gorilla mother carrying her baby without hesitation and then makes out to kill the baby too. His credo of roughness—"sport and blood . . . stuff of life"—indubitably deviates from the overall tone of the film. Yet his opponent on the expedition, Sir Evelyn Blount (John Wells), who eventually keeps him from shooting the baby ape, is significantly enough hardly more likable, his entire appearance—carefully trimmed mustache, glasses, and safari hat—indicating the pomposity and weakness he is later seen to act out. While we are not led to sympathize with the hunter here, we are neither invited to identify with his counterpart, whose squeamish intervention appears inappropriate given his central involvement with the project of the expedition and given the tough and dangerous jungle setting at large: in the very next scene the expedition's camp will be attacked by natives, the hunter being killed while posing for a photographer next to the carcass of the ape he shot.

It is, of course, Tarzan, or rather Lord Greystoke or "Johnnie" as he is called throughout the film, who comes to provide the ideal middle ground between these equally unsatisfactory extremes of cruel hunter and effeminate museologist. Played by the French actor Christopher Lambert, this Tarzan's entire appearance seems at least in one respect to comply with Edgar Rice Burroughs's initial conception of the character—his idea of a "light and graceful and well-muscled" person. Where actors from Elmo Lincoln to Ron Ely always seemed somewhat maladroit in the civilized dress they invariably donned at some point, Lambert casts a good figure either way—as apish jungle man and as cultivated lord. Thus Warner Bros.' press releases, celebrating *Greystoke* as the "authentic Tarzan legend," "filmed as Burroughs originally conceived it,"[21] seem to have had a point: Christopher Lambert's Greystoke comes closer to the creature moving between two worlds than any of the earlier impersonators.

Greystoke is neither a tough guy nor a refined intellectual, or rather, he is both of these—a sensitive savage if you will. This neither/nor or both/and option is typical for the entire film. Although *Greystoke,* just like *Tarzan of the Apes* and more than any other film version, traces the theme of difference—between African nature and European civilization, between man and beast, between the laws of the jungle and the artistocratic codes of England at the turn of the century—its conclusions differ dramatically from the novel's. And the figure of Greystoke epitomizes the film's specific concern: this Tarzan is an ambivalent figure in every respect—not a hero but a victim, not an adventurer but a creature tragically torn between glaringly different options. In Burroughs's novel Tarzan is a very active character, for action, be it bodybuilding or self-assertive trickery, sets the boundary between the white male subject and passive apes or natives. The Lord Greystoke in Hudson's film is everything but active, not a self-fashioning action hero but a pure recipient, shaped by whatever or whoever comes along. At an early point in the film we see the young Greystoke sneaking up on an ape, half-asleep on a tree limb. He scares the ape off by roaring like a wild animal into his ear, thus playing one of the typical Tarzan tricks. And yet, trickery undergoes a significant twist here: this Tarzan is a mimic rather than a trickster, an imitator rather than a perpetrator. He is, in other words, a true ape-man—at times calling to mind not so much Burroughs's Tarzan but rather his apes: "What Tarzan did [the apes] tried to do also, but he alone originated and became proficient" (*TA* 57).

This strange deviation from the novel's logic is made explicit only much later by Greystoke's teacher and mentor, Phillippe D'Arnot (Ian Holm), a Belgian who accompanied the British expedition to Africa and got lost, wounded and helpless, after the attack on their camp. D'Arnot figures as the film's anti-imperialist consciousness, commentator, and off-screen narrator. He identifies his rescuer as John Clayton, Lord Greystoke, and proceeds to teach him not only English but apparently also the basics of anthropology, history, and philosophy: "Jean is a mimic of uncanny ability," we hear him comment after the first attempts at communication between the two: "Words became like magic tricks to him and in six months he has managed to grasp the rudiments of language. And now I have to convince him of who he is. And what he is."

During these offscreen comments we see Greystoke, this well-trained and strong young savage, half leading, half dragging a still weakened D'Arnot through the jungle, a strange scene calling to mind countless other filmic scenes of male bonding in which the men seem just as intimate yet are further differentiated by their skin color.[22] But then, racial difference generally seems to take far from center stage in this film. Apart from the natives who kill Greystoke's ape-mother Kala and attack the camp later on, Africans take no part in the action. This is not to say, however, that the victims of colonization do not come into view—only that their part is transferred to somebody else: Greystoke. In a subtle shift of emphasis, by no means unusual in the 1980s, Tarzan, the British aristocrat in the jungle, is transformed from model imperialist to model victim. While in the novel Tarzan functioned as a focalizer for the imperial project, suggestive of a sort of natural imperialism, in this film he comes to be cast as the representative of the colonized, a highly volatile group made up of apes, natives, wildlife—anything African, in short.[23]

This transformation from agent to victim, trickster to imitator, has a lot to do with changing systems of cultural evaluation and classification. Thus not only the colonialist venture itself but also the traditional institutions for evaluating cultural difference—the museum of natural history and the sciences of life—meet with much criticism these days, on the grounds of their complicity with the imperial projects of subjugation. Greystoke clearly endorses today's critique of traditional techniques for "displaying" and "dissecting" cultural difference, and D'Arnot figures as this critique's spokesman throughout the film. "Science? Whose science? Your science? The imperial science?" we once hear him challenge Sir Evelyn, the priggish museologist, thus epitomizing the film's moral stance.

Yet ironically, Hudson's film itself replicates precisely the representational strategies of the traditional museum of natural history, depicting an Africa as detached and timeless as the dioramic scenarios on display in the glass cases of the Museum for Natural History in London, in which a central scene of the film takes place.[24] Like Burroughs, Hudson casts Africa as everything the West is not, but Hudson clearly inverts the hierarchy at work in Burroughs's novels. In *Greystoke,* Africa figures as the true if sometimes cruel space of origin, by contrast to a deceitful, alienating, class-divided England/Scotland. By extension of this logic, Africa is presented as the realm of stable meanings in *Greystoke;* it is here where Greystoke is taught to relate words to objects by imitating his teacher, D'Arnot. In England, by contrast, the behavioral code established in Africa does not work any longer, and it is precisely Greystoke's "uncanny" gift of imitation, his determination to repeat rather than to interpret and his inclination to take everything at face value, that will obstruct his socialization there: the British aristocrats do not mean what they say.[25]

Greystoke's mimicry and its effects call to mind Homi Bhabha's model of colonial mimicry. Bhabha described mimicry as the ambivalent outcome of colonialism's "reforming, civilizing mission," a practice of imitation that brings about a disconcerting "excess" or "slippage" of meaning, as the imitation is never perfect, the repetition never complete. Colonial mimicry, Bhabha concludes, produces "almost the same, but not quite," a slight variation of the original, caused by the mimic's (racial) difference—"almost the same, but not white":

In the ambivalent world of the 'almost quite/not white' . . . the *founding objects* of the Western world become the erratic eccentric, accidental *objets trouvés* of the colonial discourse—the part-objects of presence.[26]

However, if Greystoke's mimicry of the Western world seems at some point to accomplish a similar "rupturing" of the original text, we should bear in mind that what is unmasked and exposed here is not a dominant symbolic system but a simulation of hegemony at best. After all, Greystoke's deviations from the filmic status quo, constituted by the clearly outdated elaborate codes of the British fin de siècle and the indubitably bygone practices of colonialist rule, can hardly be considered provocative to a 1980s audience. By contrast to these purely performative gestures at disruption, however, Greystoke's earlier mimicking of the apes and then of D'Arnot does not imply rupture at all, but sovereign takeover and refinement.

Where Tarzan the trickster fashioned himself by obsessively acting out his white male identity, Greystoke the mimic acts out other identities, posing alternately as ape or aristocrat, in performances that are never entirely convincing, indeed "not quite" *it.* Thus, just like colonial practices of mimicry, Greystoke's imitation accentuates the originals' shortcomings, yet obviously not in the sense of contesting an overarching system of signification. Fashioning the white man as a mock-African and as an imitation ape, *Greystoke* creates a white male identity relieved of the awkward burden of guilt without ever jeopardizing its protagonist's pivotal position in the games of appropriation and signification.

When Greystoke opts against the "fake" mimicry of British aristocracy and for the "true" mimicry of the jungle, he opts for the only kind of self-assertion still left to the politically correct white male in a period in which "[i]t is no longer possible simply to declare one's manhood as a form of identity politics":[27] self-assertion by way of identification with (or impersonation of) the other. In Africa, the realm of the truthful mimics, the nonironic and unambiguous imitators, a white man may finally be nothing but a white man.

2.3 Africa without Africans: Tarzan Goes Disney

When Greystoke returns to the jungle at the end of Hudson's film, it is to leave the inauthentic and ambiguous world of the British aristocracy behind and to live where there are no elaborate social codes: pure nature, real life. Seen that way, Hudson pits Africa firmly against turn-of-the-century England—evoking two mutually exclusive symbolic orders. But at the same time, the filmic spaces of old-fashioned England and timeless Africa have to be seen as closely connected. *Greystoke* presents a case study of what Fredric Jameson called the "nostalgia film," a genre that entangles the far-away and the long-ago into smooth, superficial, and completely self-referential imageries:[28] after all, *Greystoke*'s Britain is hardly less exotic than its Africa.

This is where Hudson's film differs most dramatically from the most recent version of the Tarzan story, the animated Disney film *Tarzan* released in 1999.[29] Although the Disney Tarzan eventually takes the same decision as Greystoke, opting for the jungle instead of England, and for apeness rather than lordship, this step is taken under remarkably different circumstances. The animated Tarzan does not choose Africa over England because European modernity and its codes are too much for him but because European modernity is not advanced enough. Where most of Disney's Brits are amiable but doubtlessly a little old-fashioned, the African apes are as contemporary as it gets. Just like all the other recent Disney animations mapping out ethnic histories on foreign or ancient ground—from *The Lion King* (1994) to *Pocahontas* (1995) to *Mulan* (1998)—*Tarzan* derives its entertainment effect from glossing over the far-away and long-ago with the all-too-familiar. By consequence, this Tarzan's jungle is not exotic at all—unless you happen to find American suburbs exotic.

Given this initial layout, little Tarzan should not have much problem adapting to the jungle. And indeed, from the very first scenes onward the film stresses the message that Africa really is not that hard to get used to. Scenes of Tarzan's parents coming to Africa, their baby in tow, are montaged with pictures of his foster parents-to-be playing with their little ape baby, soon to fall prey to the leopard Sabor, and for the ones who still do not get it, Phil Collins spells it all out in the musical score: "Two worlds—one family." Once adopted by the apes, Tarzan assimilates easily and quickly to life in the jungle and soon swings through the trees as fast as computer-generated motion allows. His ape-mother Kala (spoken by Glenn Close) is motherly, his ape-buddy Terk (spoken by Rosie O'Donnell) supportive, and there are enough occasions for Tarzan to prove his courage, commitment, and comradery in turn. From this vantage point, Tarzan's desperate outburst early in the film—"why am I so different?"—has to appear unmotivated, to say the least.

But there is more to a family than mother and son, and once the father enters the picture, problems arise. All the chauvinistic male, Tarzan's ape-father Kerchak (spoken by Lance Henriksen) is definitely unenthusiastic about the addition to his family: "I said he could stay," he grimly grunts at the film's outset, only to qualify this concession in the same breath: "That doesn't make him my son." Kerchak's reluctance to accept the human baby and to ignore that "it's not our kind" will inform the entire film. As different as this animated *Tarzan* may be from *Greystoke*, in one respect the two films are in keeping with each other: In both cases the story of the outsider, the underdog, the marginalized is played out under the insignia of whiteness. It is the white male who figures as victim of colonialism in Hudson's film, and it is the little white boy who comes to carry all the burdens of social segregation in the Disney film. But still, the films steer different courses. Where *Greystoke* maps out ways for finding oneself by way of impersonating difference, the animation shows how to become just like everybody else. And such assimilation is clearly not a matter of learning. Seen that way, Tarzan's ape-father does have a point: "You can't learn to be one of us," he holds.

Yet that is not to say that the film casts identity as a matter of blood, as Kerchak would like to believe. Where Burroughs verged between the logics of race and culture to map out the quest for identity, the animation opts firmly for the latter—in 1999, the "embarrassments of blood," as Walter Benn Michaels had it, are no longer to be ignored. The film, as its preproduction debates already made clear, is determined to do the right thing. And the right thing, in a 1990s Hollywood production, cannot possibly be killing Africans and speaking French: "We would never dream of doing anything that would offend anyone. . . . It's going to be PC, of course. It's a family picture," a Disney spokesman announced as

early as 1995, thus legitimizing the company's decision to "sidestep the racial issue by not including blacks at all."[30] Avoiding the embarrassments
of blood, indeed. This Tarzan is not to take over the burdens of colonialism, because in Disney's Africa colonialism never took place, not to mention American imperialism. Moreover, apart from disturbing characters
such as Kerchak and an evil British white hunter—figures that appear
ideologically outdated rather than culturally different—everybody in this
film fits into a multicultural harmony that is as uniform as a Benetton advertisement of the 1980s—many colors, one knit.

This might be the reason why enthusiastic critics praised the film's
"overall sensibility,"[31] claimed that it "teaches diversity" and shows "that
we can all inhabit this planet together"[32]—in short, why they read it as
figuring forth "the latest version of democratic multiculturalism."[33] Obviously, the film's strategies of obfuscation work. Where Burroughs
mapped out white male self-fashioning in terms of a gradual surmounting
of the influences of bestiality and Africanity, Disney depicts a world already in compliance with Burroughs's utopia—a "native white Protestant
dream of a world without blacks or immigrants."[34]

Consequently, in this Tarzan's jungle difference has already been refashioned into sameness, so that his problem is not how to come to a
sense of selfhood in an alienated and alienating environment but how
best to fit into a homogeneous world order. And while, just as in *Greystoke*, imitation and mimicry play a focal role for finding one's self, here
these techniques are clearly not enough. "Can't you imitate any quieter
animals?" Kala once complains to the young Tarzan when he—in true
Tarzan fashion—roars like a lion to scare her: "Why don't you just come
up with your own sound?" Searching for his own sound, Tarzan will continue to imitate, but his mimicry will prove strangely self-centered. The
characteristic Tarzan yell, for one, with which countless filmic and TV
Tarzans gave proof of their animalesque vigor, is doubtlessly only a step
on the way of this Tarzan's self-discovery. Meeting Jane, who makes her
appearance as the scientifically minded daughter of a British primatologist, the grown-up Tarzan can be seen diligently mimicking her every
word and gesture at first. But the result of this mimicry is truly amazing:
imitating Jane, spoken by Minnie Driver with a markedly British accent,
Tarzan, now spoken by Tony Goldwyn, miraculously produces flawless
American English. Of course, this does not come as a surprise by the logic
of the film, because this is the accent Tarzan has had from his childhood
days onward: the apes and young Tarzan spoke, after all, with unmistakably American accents.[35] His acculturation thus ends where it began. You
are what you are, because you do what you do—Disney's film is not second to Burroughs's novel when it comes to the enactment of tautology.

Just like the original story, the animated version embraces tautology to safeguard and stabilize selfhood against all odds. Americanness, or, to be more precise, white male American identity, seems to be what comes naturally, an "unmarked" state of being. Where Burroughs thus enacted white male identity as a mixture between heredity and training, a precarious refinement sharply set off from "inferior"—black, female, animal—selves, the Disney film turns it into a gift. Burroughs's Tarzan had to pull himself together; the animated Tarzan just lets go. Again, just as in *Greystoke,* the white male is characterized in terms of passivity rather than action. In line with this logic, the Disney Tarzan's socialization (or junglization) is not represented in terms of training or discipline but as a process of playful adaptation. The much praised animation technique, which calls to mind sophisticated video games in its 3-D effects and free-wheeling computer-generated camera movements, turns Tarzan into a smoothly functioning part of his environment. Even when he takes to action eventually, saving the apes from the evil doings of the white hunter and assuming his ape-father's position in turn, he seems to react rather than act, to tune in rather than set the tone.

Let me cast light on this imagery and its implications by changing focus one last time: Another recent adaptation of the Tarzan theme, this one from the early 1990s, presents an interesting variation of the quest for a new man, and again the notion of leadership and domination is discarded in favor of less aggressive qualities like flexibility and adaptation. Moreover, just like the Disney animation, the Canadian TV production *Tarzan,* which ran from 1991 to 1993, abandons the awkward backdrop of colonial history, this time by transferring the action to the present time. Tarzan's jungle existence is explained with a plane crash that killed his parents and left him on his own. Like his contemporaries in film and animation, this Tarzan can be seen to adhere to a code of honor that would be worthy of a Greenpeace activist, coming complete with an ecological research station, headed by another scientifically minded woman called, little surprisingly, Jane (Lydie Denier). In the course of the TV series, Tarzan is implemented as the epitome of what Andrew Ross called "eco-man"—"men who are scheduled to speak alongside native peoples who alone can grant them salvation for their settler ancestors' sins. . . . Their fierce individualism alludes to a culture of free association identified with the Western states that preexists the culture of social security identified with East Coast liberalism."[36]

The logic of "white guilt" underlying the eco-man concept calls to mind *Greystoke* rather than the happy-go-lucky Disney world, and indeed the TV *Tarzan* could be considered the missing link between *Greystoke*'s political correctness and the Disney film's family values. While depicting an African jungle as fantastic as the animated one of 1999, the series never tires to obsess about "African specificity"—or what is made out to be specific about Africa here. The TV Tarzan (Wolf Larson) seems just as determined as his filmic predecessor in *Greystoke* to keep Africa pure, alternately destroying photographic material of the wilderness, rescuing artifacts from greedy art dealers, preventing trophy hunters from trophy hunting, and hiding treasures so they won't attract visitors. But that is not to say that he lives in isolation among apes: in fact, there is quite a lot of coming and going in this African jungle resort, and the TV Tarzan has as much occasion as will the animated one to rescue visitors from attacking animals and animals from attacking visitors.

Burroughs's Tarzan introduced the imagery of leisure to the wilderness, turning the jungle into a huge gym, which figured not so much as a contrast to the disciplined order of Western civilization but as its annex. The new Tarzans in animation and TV seem to totalize this imagery of the workout, so that it completely displaces the notion of work or training: the animated Tarzan does nothing but ride the jungle, his moves allegedly fashioned after the skateboarding teenage son of animator Glen Keane, and the eco-Tarzan swings between the treetops or crawls through the lake in a style fit for the Olympics. "No traffic, no noise, no responsibility," one visitor in the TV Tarzan's jungle, an American businessman, can be heard pinpointing this logic.[37] But the TV Tarzan objects: "There is much responsibility." And he has a point: the eternal vacation that the Tarzans of the 1990s seem to live might just as well be described as never ending work.

In the late twentieth century, writes Gilles Deleuze, the societies of discipline are being replaced with "control" societies, in which "nothing's left alone for long."[38] In current social formations, the actual and the symbolic order of the factory is abandoned in favor of the order of the business, while workers and employees are reconceptualized as independent entrepreneurs with personal commitment and personal risks. The hero of the age, Deleuze's "control-man," figures forth individualist action in a system that has been running along far from individualist lines for quite some time. Apart from maintaining the illusion of personal control, the order of the business suspends the very boundary between responsibility and recreation, realigning work along the lines of entertainment, and entertainment along the lines of work: "In the society of discipline, labor and leisure were strictly separated, today labor looks like leisure and leisure like labor," write Mark Terkessidis and Tom Holert.[39]

Control-men and eco-men go very well together, and the 1990s ape-men fit right in—flexible figures, smooth operators. In a certain sense, this reconfiguration of the ape-man in fictions of the 1990s indicates the takeover of a new group of cultural agents—specialists and expert figures. The expert, this very particular kind of "interpreter and translator of his competence for other fields," as Michel de Certeau had it,[40] is by definition a transcultural (or acultural) persona, an "unmarked" being like the subtly Americanized Disney Tarzan or the TV hero, a white man who speaks (broken) English. The transition from adventure hero to expert figure, however, involves an evaluative shift that is not to be underestimated: experts, we shall see, may be detached, but they are rarely independent. It is, after all, significant that cooperation, interactivity, and communication are the buzzwords of the day. Today's translator figures—the experts and specialists of a global system—work best in a team.

I will ponder the effects of such a conceptual shift for the imagery of masculinity, especially the image of the white male hero in the wilderness, in the next chapter. Before I return to the issues of masculinity, performance, and whiteness, however, I would like to cast a closer look at the implications of a current reconceptualization of cultural contact and communication in terms of expertise rather than exchange. We have seen in the last chapter that in contemporary narratives cultural contact scenarios are increasingly—if often unintentionally—enacted as quasi-mechanical processes, which are then seen to gain a momentum of their own. By consequence, cultural communication presents itself as a precarious activity, which more often than not threatens to undermine stable systems of order and established structures of control. Now, the Tarzan plot always capitalized on the notion of contact as contagion, back-grounding the aspects of exchange and reciprocity to the point of disappearance. The recent trend to write Africans out of the picture altogether could almost be read as an awkward acknowledgment of this underlying phobia, figuring forth a world conveniently rid of cultural diversity—a fantasy space.

I will close upon a narrative that stages an Africa no less artificial than Tarzan's jungle yet capitalizes at the same time on the effect of realism, stemming from an author famous for his skill in converting the most fantastic scenarios into realistic accounts by means of the jargons of science, technology, and economics. Michael Crichton's novel *Congo* (1980) is of interest to me because it conceives of contact and communication once more in terms of biology rather than culture, while clearly addressing cultural issues in turn. Moreover, Crichton's text inverts the imagery investigated up to now, turning from ape-men to man-apes, and thus introduces a new, if by no means altogether original, angle to the concept at hand.

His reflections on apes acting like men reiterate many of the patterns we came across before, in narratives around men acting like apes. But eventually Crichton's text moves beyond a mere reiteration. Interlinking the rhetoric of biology and technology, *Congo* pinpoints a break in the conventions of Africanist representation—from the (imperialist) logic of Africa as primitive otherness to the (global) concept of Africa as the total interface—impenetrable, but absolutely compatible.

2.4 Understanding Is Everything: Michael Crichton's *Congo*

Like so many ape-man narratives, Michael Crichton's *Congo* describes a venture in the African jungle that brings apes and humans closer together than they want. And like the tale of Tarzan in its many variations, *Congo* fantasizes about an intermediate figure pertaining to both worlds. But where fictions from Burroughs's novel onward focused on a man going ape, Crichton introduces apes going human. That is, as long as we conceive of language and militant violence as specifically human characteristics.

At first sight, however, the novel's protagonists are not concerned with contact—cultural or biological—at all. Instead, *Congo*'s set of protagonists seems to replicate the stock characters who have invaded Tarzan's realm time and again in classical and contemporary fictions: the white hunter, the scientist, and—lately—the businessperson. There is Captain Charles Munro, the white hunter who knows everything about African regimes and upheavals. There is Peter Elliot, the biologist who knows everything about primate apes and nothing about the jungle and would not stand a chance in the Congo without Munro. And there is Karen Ross, the aggressively ambitious young computer specialist who seems to be another scientifically minded female at first glance and yet turns out to stand rather for postmodern business politics—she works for the US corporation that financed the expedition in the first place. None of these figures offers much ground for sympathetic identification. Hence, the 1995 film version of Crichton's novel, directed by Frank Marshall, returns little surprisingly to characterizations much more in accordance with (adventure) filmic conventions—an African-Americanized "Monroe" becomes the widely unfractured adventure hero (a politically correct twist of the "white hunter" formula), flanked by a sympathetic young scientist and a charmingly streamlined Karen Ross.[41]

By contrast to the film, all of the novel's protagonists are definitely somewhat unsavory characters, and none of them seems fit to act as a translator figure between Africa and the West. However, initially there is no need for human translation or "cultural meddling" in the novel, because a huge arsenal of intricate communication tools, global transmission gear, and—not least—ultramodern defense weapons performs these functions better than any single person could. By thus replacing the human translator figure with a technological apparatus of translation, Crichton disavows the entire concept of unmediated contact and opts for the total (technological) interface instead: if you'll never get to the heart of darkness anyway, this logic runs, you might as well stay at a safe distance.

But then again: *Congo* is an adventure novel, and it does derive its thrill from the breakdown rather than smooth functioning of systems. Thus the satellite links between the rain forest and the corporate headquarters in the United States are eventually severed, and the expedition runs out of ammunition. As technology malfunctions, crashes, or is just no longer available, the expedition's precarious situation—"a handful of frightened people deep in the Congo rain forest" (C 239)—is no longer to be ignored. Now the jungle calls for a confrontation "on its own terms" (C 253).

This is where a translator figure is direly needed, and as there is no ape-man around, a man-ape has to do: Amy steps in, the gorilla Elliot brought along from the United States. As a horde of highly aggressive apes of unknown origin threatens to do away with the expedition, Amy's intermediation between humans and apes seems to offer the only way out. After all, Amy is not only capable of communicating with the scientists in sign language but also understands the aggressive killer apes: *"Amy understand thing talk"* (C 271).

On first sight, the fact that an ape replaces the impersonal machineries of translation seems to endorse a critique of streamlining global technologies of communication and a plea for direct contact with local conditions, a critique apparently shared by the novel's narrative voice—at some point the animal behaviorist Frederick Pearl is quoted approvingly: "We can imagine language-skilled primates acting as interpreters or perhaps even as ambassadors for mankind, in contact with wild creatures" (C 65). But Crichton is not Hugh Hudson, or Walt Disney at that: he neither envisions primitivity as salvation, nor does he preach universal harmony and understanding. A closer look at the encounter of killer apes and translation gorilla evinces consequently that the technological machineries of communication are eventually reimplemented rather than unhinged. By dint of an almost imperceptible shift of metaphors, the jungle will become an interface, and the apes will turn into cyborgs—and the different realms of Africa and America, nature and culture, technology and biology will be refashioned in terms of contiguity rather than opposition—one world, different functions.

Donna Haraway has provided the analytical tools to reflect upon this pattern of thought. For her the very concept of a "primate ambassador" or "translation ape" entails a breakdown of established lines of thought, introducing a category between apeness and humanness: hybrid beings, cyborgs. Her reading of the "space apes," who were sent into outer space at the beginning of the space research era, calls to mind Amy's in-between position:

The line between natural organisms and constructed technical systems was redrawn in a radical way, so as to produce the cyborg as the central natural-technical object of knowledge in the last half of the twentieth century. Both organism and technology were theorized and encountered in practice as communications engineering problems, where the ontological distinction between the natural and the artificial lost meaning. The naturalistic primate studies in the ethnologically constructed field intersected the extraterrestrial primate studies of the space program in the electronically recorded and telemetrically implanted simians beaming information to listening scientists in the field, laboratory, and command center.[42]

While this seems to be a perfect description of the "translation ape" Amy, on another, less obvious level, Haraway's concept also applies to Amy's negative counterparts in the novel: the killer apes. After all, their background is strikingly similar to Amy's—all of them being products of human training for specific purposes.

The American scientists find out that the killer apes stem from a gorilla species bred centuries ago by the inhabitants of the prehistoric city Zinj to function as guards and a defense troop—"an animal elite, ruthless and incorruptible" (C 249). This troop, we further learn, seems to have run out of control eventually; apes turned against humans, and in a gruesome massacre the legendary city was obliterated. Yet the training the apes underwent was quite effective, as they never stopped defending their territory against anybody threatening to invade it.

Not accidentally this imagery of uncontrollable fighting machines calls to mind endless debates around military technologies of "prevention" in the 1970s, debates in which the fear that an elaborate nuclear weaponry might run out of control held center stage. These debates figure quite prominently on the novel's plot level, after all, as everybody but Elliot knows from the beginning that Amy's repatriation is only a cover for the expedition, which actually is funded by Karen Ross's employers to locate a new mineral source for the arms and information industry—industrial-grade diamonds with semiconductive properties to run a new laser-based data system. When Karen Ross tries to legitimate the fact that the new computer networks are primarily to be put to military use, the same predicament shines up that faced the inhabitants of Zinj ages ago:

Since human beings responded too slowly, it was necessary for them to relinquish decision-making control of the war to the faster intelligence of computers. "In the coming war, we must abandon any hope of regulating the course of the conflict. If we decide to 'run' the war at human speed, we will almost surely lose. Our only hope is to put our trust in machines. This makes human judgment, human values, human thinking utterly superfluous. World War III will be war by proxy: a pure war of machines, over which we dare exert no influence for fear of so slowing the decision-making mechanism as to cause our defeat." (*C* 294)

Elliot's horrified response—"But you can't give up control"—characterizes the novel's cause: maintaining control. Yet by dint of Ross's logic the transition from the old electronic to the new laser-based data transmission systems is really not the point, as she does not fail to clarify:

We've been doing it for centuries. . . . What's a domesticated animal—or a pocket calculator—except an attempt to give up control? We don't want to plow fields or do square roots so we turn the job over to some other intelligence, which we've trained or bred or created. (*C* 294)

Yet of course Ross's implicit conflation of plow horse and pocket calculator on the one hand, and killer apes and war technologies on the other, is too simplistic. As we shall see shortly, there is a difference between domestic animal and war machines, or communication ape and killer apes at that: biological, mechanical, electronic, or laser-driven technologies, the novel shows, become destructive at precisely the point when they start to run on their own.

At heart, it is true, all of these complexes function along the same lines, be they man-made or merely man-trained. Significantly enough, Peter Elliot describes Amy's very intelligence in terms of response rather than originality: "When Amy was given a human IQ test, she scored ninety-two. For all practical purposes, Amy is as smart as a human being, and in many ways she is smarter—more perceptive and sensitive" (*C* 252). Amy's real talent is imitation—she is the perfect mediator. But then again, it is due to the same disposition that the killer apes managed to establish their gruesome rule in the first place, as Elliot very well knows:

[Amy] can manipulate us at least as skillfully as we can manipulate her. These gray gorillas possess that same intelligence, yet may have been single-mindedly bred to be the primate equivalent of Doberman pinschers—guard animals, attack animals, trained for cunning and viciousness. But they are much brighter and resourceful than dogs. And they will continue their attack until they succeed in killing us all, as they have killed everyone who has come here ever before. (*C* 252)

Once imitation is practiced by gorillas instead of white men, it gains a series of dangerous implications. As the experts in aping that they are, gorillas tend to overdo it, turning from excellent tools into destructive weapons, from translator figures into killers. And this is where the white man enters the picture once more, this time not as a mimic and not as a trick translator but as an expert—supervising and monitoring the contact zone. If Elliot, Crichton's scientist figure, is definitely not a hero, he makes an excellent expert when put to the task—ensuring that individual specificity or local differences do not step in the way of overarching interests.

Read along these lines, in terms of biological interaction going global, Amy's lack of concentration, her unreliability, and her childish distractedness are not as negative as they might seem: after all, these features prevent her from running out of control, accentuating the secondary status of her work. The results of her somewhat erratic screening of killer ape language have to be laboriously reviewed and "reinterpreted" by Peter Elliot before they make sense. He distills fragments of meaning out of Amy's babble, which are then broadcast to the killer apes on their next attack. And indeed, the apes hardly come to hear the subtle messages GO AWAY, NO COME, and BAD HERE in their own language before they give up their attack. Fighting machines that they are, you just have to find the off button, the right code to formulate the order STOP, and immediately the univocal hierarchy is reestablished, control reasserted. This solution epitomizes the strategic montage of technologies in Crichton's novel: communication means compatibility, and compatibility means control. Seen that way, training apes ideally functions just like the implementation of semiconductive material (which is what the expedition is all about): both procedures "intensify distribution flows while at the same time imposing intricate circuitries of control,"[43] as Jonathan Crary noted about optically active semiconductors and other means of visual communication in the 1980s. And Michel Serres, reflecting upon what could be called a "parasitic" turn in contact and communication narratives, demarcates the same pattern of thought by dint of reconceptualizing reciprocity as compatibility: "The flow goes one way, never the other. I call this semiconduction, this valve, this single arrow, this relation without a reversal of direction, 'parasitic.'"[44]

In the late twentieth century the disciplinarian structures of imperialism and Fordian industrialism have clearly come under suspicion. This came to the fore in Hugh Hudson's apprehensions of "imperial science" and the museum of natural history in Greystoke, and it also suffuses Crichton's evaluation of primatology as "industrialization" of apes. But strategies of streamlining and supervision are by no means abandoned altogether—they only shift their ground. Eventually, not only Hudson secretly restores the criticized practice of musealization, when he enacts his filmic Africa like an exhibit under glass—Crichton does the same, replicating the very techniques of abstraction and utilization that he seems fiercely to contest in the first place. Again, Donna Haraway's analysis of popular thought casts light on such a pervasive rearrangement of control. In *Primate Visions* she analyzes a 1984 advertisement of Gulf Oil Corporation in *Natural History Magazine,* which describes the work of primate researcher Jane Goodall underneath the headline "Understanding is everything" in terms of a process of sympathetic approximation and translation:

The post–World War II threat is not decay, but the failure of communication, the malfunction of stressed systems. The fantasy is about language, about the immediate sharing of meanings. Gulf Oil Corporation explains: "Our goal is to provoke curiosity about the world and the fragile complexity of the natural order; to satisfy that curiosity through observation and learning; to create an understanding of man's place in the ecological structure, and his responsibility to it—on the simple theory that no thinking person can share in the destruction of anything whose value he understands."[45]

Science, Haraway concludes, is made out as the means of facilitating contact and universalizing access, in stark opposition to older, "imperialist" techniques of subjugation and obfuscation. But of course, for all the explicit enthusiasm about "shared meanings," the new networks of communication just like the old ones function on the basis of suppressing noise, noise that time and again comes to be tacitly associated with resistant or discordant voices, blurring and obstructing the desired effect of understanding. Today, control is enacted not by way of prohibiting communication but by subtly channeling it. Haraway's analysis resonates with Deleuze's insight that the cybernetic and computerized societies of our day "no longer operate by confining people, but through continuous control and instant communication."[46]

This development comes to bear strongly on fictional texts, be they filmic or literary, which are, after all, communication machines in their own right. The arguably most obvious fictional version of the ideology of unobstructed, universal communication is given in Disney's utopias of understanding, the visions of a world where everybody speaks the same language. But we have seen that Crichton's novel gives scope to the same ideal—if adopting a much more realistic frame than Disney's fairy-tale scenarios: he envisions a highly flexible linguistic or symbolic code, which allows for a transfer of basic information while safeguarding distance and discretion. This is when the semiotic rhetoric of communication reveals its complicity with the technological rhetoric of compatibility: apes appear indeed as the ideal translator figures and go-betweens—machines that smoothen communication where human interaction threatens to run out of hand. It is precisely in this conjunction of communication and compatibility—or in the silent replacement of human go-betweens by cyborg translators—that the novel comes to exemplify the transition between the logic of imperialism and the logic of globalization, a transition that I will map out in greater detail later.

The film, so much more formulaic than the novel, pins the predominance of compatibility down when equipping Amy with a technoglove transferring her gestures into words, which then come out in a little girl's voice—the ape is a cyborg, the cyborg a little girl. But then this is also where verbal communication starts and ends in *Congo* the film. The killer apes experience another kind of contact altogether: "What's that?" asks Monroe in a seemingly desperate confrontation, the expedition surrounded with attacking apes. "The latest thing in communication," quips Laura before she blasts the apes away with the laser gun fueled with the diamonds of Zinj.

This is not a good time for heroes. The African jungle, for one, which used to weld the aristocratic white man into an epitome of primitivity redeemed, seems to have lost its effect on today's white men. But then, exotic environments have come down in the last decades, as the difference between jungle, adventure park, and suburban backyard seems to decrease rapidly. Not even apes are too good anymore at telling one environment apart from the other. "It's a meticulously re-created complex ecosystem, not an amusement park," claimed a 1999 advertisement, on display all over New York City, for the "Congo Gorilla Forest" in the Bronx Zoo. A photograph on the ad showed a gorilla's face, and the text continued: "But just try telling him that." The ape on the picture looked stunned. But perhaps that is only my projection. After all, in the 1990s an environment that feels more like an amusement park than like an ecosystem may very well be considered "home." The happiness of hybridity.

If the homesteads of apes and ape-men—the zoo, the game park, or the jungle—turn out to be as artificial as it gets, this is not to say that disorientation or alienation obviously suffuse contemporary ape-man narratives. Ape-men have a long tradition of fencing themselves off from corrupting and confusing influences. The model male of the moment, it seems, may not be as heroic and as self-possessed as Burroughs's Tarzan used to be. Yet when it comes to this strange mixture of flexibility and self-assurance—constant change that still brings about nothing but what was there all along—today's men are by no means second to the ape-men of yore. Not only the animated ape-man remorphs with admirable ease—remorphing is what keeps gender going, it seems.

Yet once one turns away from the ape-man, that fantastic creature between worlds, and focuses on images of ordinary white men in the jungle, this malleability proves to be far from unproblematic. Peter Elliot, Crichton's scientist in the jungle, may be superior to the white hunter Munro when it comes to flexibility, as he ceaselessly develops and applies new concepts of communication, but that does not make him less of a coward. Thus *Congo* releases a tension that was present but contained in recent enactments of the Tarzan tale: the fact that the stock figure of the heroic individualist is step by step replaced with a much less impressive character these days—the expert, a man who knows how to act but never really does much. As we shall see in the next chapter, countless narratives running parallel to ape-man stories put white men in Africa much more markedly to the test, and even where the tasks at hand are solved and the difficulties overcome the results often enough leave a lot to be wished for.

THREE

Being Game: The White Hunter and the Crisis of Masculinity

Shortly after the turn of century, the white male became an endangered species in the United States. Endangered, that is, if one is to believe popular magazines, pamphlets, and a huge machinery of political propaganda reveling as never before in horror scenarios of a country inundated by a flood of foreigners and smothered in the sticky sweetness of a "feminized" culture of sentimentality. And as different as the individual approaches and agendas were, in one respect everybody seemed to agree: it was time to act. And acting—in both senses of the word—became indeed a means of dealing with the alleged crisis. *Tarzan of the Apes,* we saw, turned white male identity into a performance piece, thus drawing indirectly—and certainly unintentionally—upon contemporary models of ethnicity in order to conceptualize whiteness and masculinity. But of course, Burroughs's most spectacular move vis-à-vis an ethnified and feminized modern American culture consists in his choice of location: to become truly white and truly male, his novel argues, you have to go to Africa and become an ape.

Then again, this is an extreme move with extreme implications. Not to forget its comic appeal. After all, the Tarzan figure has quickly gained a dubious reputation—there is undeniably something embarrassing about a man yodeling in the treetops. By contrast, Burroughs's big idol, Theodore Roosevelt, found a mode of endorsing wildness and animality without the extreme implication of turning into a wild man, or an ape. Associating wildness with Native Americans and animality with big game, Roosevelt promoted fighting and hunting as means of acquiring the attributes of masculinity, without losing the refined status of whiteness. As Gail Bederman noted about Roosevelt's careful self-stylization in the frontispiece of his *Hunting Trips of a Ranchman* (1885): "Sans eyeglasses, . . . TR stands in a woodland setting, wearing a fringed buckskin suit. . . . although he bears the weapons, and manly demeanor of civilized man, he wears the clothing of savages. . . . he is at once like the Indians and superior to them."[1] In a way, Roosevelt anticipates the moves of mimicry so popular in contemporary enactments of white men—his ranchman is, after all, almost, but not quite, like an Indian. If this Western frontier act was successful, Roosevelt would later become even more famous for another white hunter performance—this one set in East Africa.

The gestures of masquerade and mimicry permeate twentieth-century white hunter narratives, and even if most of them are less open about their performative agenda than Burroughs's *Tarzan,* enacting ranchmen, cowboys, and white hunters instead of an ape-man, they conceive of white male identity along exactly the same lines as Burroughs: as a category that has to be acted out incessantly in order to be maintained. While ape-man stories (with the possible exception of *Greystoke*) were getting more and more fantastic throughout this century, white hunter stories were becoming more and more nostalgic. This development is already pertinent in the work of a writer who would literally come to embody the white hunter figure, following hard on Roosevelt's heels in his performative interlinkage of life and work. Ernest Hemingway's "public image . . . as the white hunter of the safari, overtook and, some would argue, overshadowed the private artist," as Paul Smith pointed out in a reflection on the intersecting functions of self-stylization and writing in Hemingway's life.[2]

Even if, as we shall see, Hemingway's project differs considerably from Roosevelt's—or Burroughs's at that—there are some commonalities between these Americans' approaches to Africa that should be briefly considered. From Roosevelt's *African Game Trails* (1910) to Burroughs's *Tarzan of the Apes* and Hemingway's *Green Hills of Africa,* the experience of Africa is time and again enacted via a strange oscillation between an almost aggressive claim for authenticity ("this is what life is really like") and an emphasis on the experience's fantastic exceptionality ("this is in no way like ordinary life"). Africa, as Toni Morrison put it with reference to Hemingway's posthumously published *The Garden of Eden,* figures as "a blank, empty space into which [the writer] asserts himself, an uncreated void ready, waiting, and offering itself up for his artistic imagination, his work, his fiction."[3] By this token, Africa becomes the epitome of authenticity—the uninscribed, primeval continent—*and* at the same time a fantasy space. The perfect setting for a daydream.

Of course, on a basic level every adventure narrative revolves around just that—daydreams. Not accidentally the genre has been described as giving vent to a very specific kind of identification: "Its purpose is not to confront motives and experiences in myself that I might prefer to ignore but to take me out of myself by confirming an idealized self-image."⁴ And indeed, even more than Roosevelt or Burroughs, Hemingway seems to be obsessed with leaving the mundane routines of modern urban life behind, so much so that his African writing at times involuntarily calls to mind the vagaries of one of the most proficient daydreamers ever—James Thurber's Walter Mitty. This character, so popular in the United States of the 1940s, could be seen to dream himself time and again out of his middle-class urban white male existence into stereotypical setups that paradoxically promised agency and authenticity by way of blotting out everyday experiences, most notably the experience of an overpowering wife, cast as a "predatory female, spawned—like the perplexing machines around her—by an industrialized and advanced culture."⁵

But as striking as the analogies between Walter Mitty, on the one hand, and Hemingway's protagonists in "The Short Happy Life of Francis Macomber" and "The Snows of Kilimanjaro," on the other, might be—all of these men desperately striving to escape the stranglehold of modernity and femininity—Hemingway's implementation of the daydream mode is too complex to be explained in terms of escapism. Or rather, it is too complex to be explained in terms of escaping Western modernity alone. In a way, as we shall see, Hemingway's protagonists try to get away not only from the West; eventually they will escape from Africa as well, and in that respect they certainly top both Roosevelt's white hunter and Burroughs's ape-man, not to mention James Thurber's Walter Mitty. Totalizing the very aspects of withdrawal and isolation that his predecessors took such great pain to downplay, Hemingway manages to contain the paradoxical insight that the notion of authenticity—being a true man—came to be intricately conjoined with the logic of escapism and the daydream—leaving the real world behind.

What Hemingway kept at bay, however, takes center stage in contemporary white hunter narratives. It seems that for several years now, popular narratives could not stress enough that authenticity is a mere construct, and the quest for self-authentication a fantasy. Yet that is not to say that the white hunter is finished. We shall see with respect to current filmic, literary, TV, and comic-strip versions of the white hunter narrative that this cultural icon is tougher than it seems. But then, as my reading of *Tarzan* and its reenactments in the present time should have shown already, while "male identity" has become ever more difficult to stake out in universal and unilinear terms—"always ambivalent, always dependent on the exigencies of personal and institutional power"⁶—the very flexibility and ambivalence of this category forms the core of its ongoing efficacy. Andrew Ross has commented upon this interlinkage:

Patriarchy is constantly reforming masculinity, minute by minute, day by day. Indeed, the reason why patriarchy remains so powerful is due less to its entrenched traditions than to its versatile capacity to shape-change and morph the contours of masculinity to fit with shifts in the social climate; in this it shares with capitalism a modernizing hunger to seize the present and dictate the future. Sometimes we feel that the new man, even when he is PC, is much less palatable than the incorrect guy he displaced.[7]

Still, even if the quandaries of the white hunter in the late twentieth century need not mean his demise, the current processes of reconceptualization should not be cast as a "return of the repressed" or as a conspirational plot to reinvigorate outdated concepts of power and control. Instead, the very breaks and incongruities between a long-standing (imperial) imagery and a newly evolving (global) context testify to a significantly changed framework and changing functions of concepts such as masculinity and whiteness, which in turn link up with new imageries of contact and communication. In the course of such larger conceptual shifts and changes, however, Africa may inadvertently turn from a dreamland into a nightmare space, no longer the last resort for acting out control but the ultimate setting for experiences of loss and deprivation.

3.1 Taking It All In: Hemingway's Hunt

Large parts of early-twentieth-century cultural history could be written in terms of a desperate struggle for authenticity and truth in the face of technological overrefinement and alienation. Donna Haraway has shown how in the course of this struggle African "unspoiled nature" came to function as the counterpart for notions of civilization as a "germ."[8] While the desires for an unchanged and unchanging order were to some extent projected onto African natives, the full force of the Western desire came to bear on another object: big game. Big game hunting presented itself as the cure for the diseases of civilization and, by extension, as the reinvigorating potion for white men.

As we have seen with regard to Burroughs's *Tarzan*, the imperialist formula of true manhood drew on the components of hunting and sportsmanship likewise, figuring forth the white man's being equal to but never identical with the jungle population. Reflecting upon Ernest Hemingway's African writing, Peter Messent paraphrases Donna Haraway's description of Rooseveltian sportsmanship to suggest Hemingway's adherence to the selfsame imagery: "Africa functions as an unspoiled territory where 'decadence . . . decay's contagion, the germ of civilization' can be combated by a narrator who 'restor[es] manhood in the healthy activity of sportsmanlike hunting.'"[9]

Yet while for Theodore Roosevelt and Edgar Rice Burroughs sportsmanship and hunting were indeed tightly conjoined, matters are different with Hemingway, let alone with later writers, filmmakers, and artists grappling with the icon of the white hunter. If in *Tarzan* sport, training, and bodybuilding figured as the civilizing elements in a savage setting, in Hemingway's "The Short Happy Life of Francis Macomber" (1936), published more than twenty years after Burroughs's first *Tarzan* volume, it is precisely by way of the differentiation between the sportsman and big game hunter that masculinity will be mapped out. This shift goes along with another, no less consequential, reevaluation: where *Tarzan of the Apes* focused on the spectacularly trained white male body, Hemingway's short story seems curiously unimpressed with the trained, well-muscled, built body and its display:

Francis Macomber was very tall, very well built if you did not mind that length of bone, dark, his hair cropped like an oarsman, rather thin-lipped, and was considered handsome. He was dressed in the same sort of safari clothes that Wilson wore except that his were new, he was thirty-five years old, kept himself very fit, was good at court games, had a number of big-game fishing records, and had just shown himself, very publicly, to be a coward.[10]

Francis Macomber, the man whose cathartic "coming of age" we witness in Hemingway's short story, is indubitably a sportsman, a member of the "international, fast, sporting set" ("M" 26). But sportsmanship is no proof of manhood here. While Macomber's entire appearance calls to mind Tarzan's well-muscled but not disproportionate body, it is Robert Wilson, the white hunter, who comes to demarcate the model here. And Wilson is not "handsome":

He was about middle height, with sandy hair, a stubby mustache, a very red face and extremely cold eyes, with faint white wrinkles at the corners that grooved merrily when he smiled. . . . she looked away from his face at the way his shoulders sloped in the loose tunic he wore with the four big cartridges held in loops where the left breast pocket should have been, at his big brown hands, his old slacks, his very dirty boots and back to his red face again. . . . the baked red of his face stopped in a white line that marked the circle left by his Stetson hat that hung now from one of the pegs of the tent pole. ("M" 4)

Wilson is dirty, ungroomed, weatherworn, a far cry from Macomber's neat and fit appearance. Both descriptions are given from the point of view of a woman, Macomber's wife, Margot, who looks the men over, "as though she had never seen them before" ("M" 4), and in the following tries to come to terms with the fact that it is not the handsome sportsman she is attracted to: "Wilson, the white hunter, she knew she had never truly seen before" ("M" 4).

This experience of the suddenly changed perspective, the "never before seen," will inform the entire story, a story that has after all been canonized for its intricate techniques of focalization, continually switching points of view, so that we obtain a multitude of insights into what is going on—and a highly fractured picture. If Margot is introduced in the process of reorientation, it is her husband's much more pervasive transformation that forms the core of the narrative. The story builds up slowly to relate the circumstances of his embarrassment, his cowardice at a lion hunt, and then reiterates and refashions this experience in positive terms, tracing the sportsman's transformation into a white hunter. This process takes the guise of replacing one framework with another, the frameworks themselves being described in terms of useful and useless knowledge. Macomber came to Africa knowing a lot of useless things:

He knew about . . . motor cycles—that was earliest—about motor cars, about duck-shooting, about fishing, trout, salmon and big-sea, about sex in books, many books, too many books, about all court games, about dogs, not much about horses, about hanging on to his money, about most of the other things his world dealt in, and about his wife not leaving him. ("M" 21)

Macomber's American "knowledge" comprises a well-balanced mixture of athletic (sports and hunting), educational (books), business (money), and social skills, in which the wife figures as just another calculable asset—in other words, this knowledge demarcates the framework of modern upper-class masculinity. The monotonous list of banal entertainments and skills emphasizes the predictability of this framework, in which sport functions as a regular and superficial practice among others, a leisure activity that is very much part of the workday.

Africa, however, appears to call for a completely different kind of knowledge, if knowledge is the right word for what is needed here. In a recapitulation of the lion hunt, Macomber's predicament is summed up as a lack of "knowing":

Macomber did not know how the lion had felt before he started his rush, nor during it when the unbelievable smash of the .505 with a muzzle velocity of two tons had hit him in the mouth, nor what kept him coming after that, when the second ripping crash had smashed his hind quarters and he had come crawling on toward the crashing, blasting thing that had destroyed him. Wilson knew something about it and only expressed it by saying, "Damned fine lion," but Macomber did not know how Wilson felt about things either. He did not know how his wife felt except that she was through with him. ("M" 21)

What Macomber does not know is precisely what gets the narrative going—an insight into other beings' innermost life, their feeling. The fantasy of knowing what others feel seems to infuse the very narrative strategy of multiple focalization, which is after all just another way of getting in on other modes of perception in order to relate the "never before seen." And on the plot level it is this kind of knowledge, or rather "knowingness" as Hugh Kenner called it,[11] that will turn Macomber from a member of the "international sporting set" into an African white hunter. "Knowingness," the mindframe of the bullfighter and the white hunter, entails a peculiar mode of action, not rationalized, regular and standardized as in the American way of life but deeply corporeal, instinctive, animalesque: "action in which you had something to do, in which you can kill and come out of it, doing something you are ignorant about and so not scared, no one to worry about and no responsibility except to perform something you feel sure you can perform," as Hemingway described the same phenomenon in *Green Hills of Africa*.[12]

Seen that way, knowing comes to merge with this other key term of Hemingway's story: feeling. However, the skill of entering the other mindframe is not to be confused with compassion: getting a feel for the lion's predicament does not bring about communion but ensures "the compressed act of shooting a lion."[13] This kind of identification eschews communication or exchange; the contact imagined is strictly unidirectional, demarcating an extreme form of takeover or intake, and thus an endeavor much less self-transcending and expansive than it might seem at first glance.

The impression of withdrawal or isolation is further enhanced by what Walter Benn Michaels called Hemingway's "aesthetics of untranslatability,"[14] the insistence that what Macomber experiences is beyond words, pure feeling, to be cast in negative terms, vague allusions or tautologies at best: "For the first time in his life he really felt wholly without fear. Instead of fear he had a feeling of definite elation" ("M" 31). "I've never felt any such feeling," "I feel absolutely different" ("M" 32). Talking about this feeling will not do, not even among the initiates, between white hunters:

"Do you have that feeling of happiness about what's going to happen?" Macomber asked, still exploring his new wealth. "You're not supposed to mention it," Wilson said, looking in the other's face. ". . . Doesn't do to talk too much about all this. Talk the whole thing away. No pleasure in anything if you mouth it up too much. ("M" 33)

Talking about an extraordinary experience means getting a grip on it or holding it at bay, and this is the last thing Hemingway means to achieve in this story. The strange must never be familiarized, difference never collapsed into sameness—a logic that pertains to the very effort at translation, as Michaels has shown, and that pertains to the convention of omniscient narration just as well. The practice of multiple focalization, by contrast, allows for momentary glimpses at the "never before seen" without compromising its difference, the very transgression of boundaries bringing about their stabilization. By the same token, the white hunter's transgression into the animal world ultimately reinforces the autonomous male subject, precisely because it elides communication and reflection, as Macomber's very last confrontation with this different realm underscores:

> . . . they saw . . . the bull coming, nose out, mouth tight closed, blood dripping, massive head straight out, coming in a charge, his little pig eyes bloodshot as he looked at them. . . . Macomber, as he fired, unhearing his shot in the roaring of Wilson's gun, saw fragments like slate burst from the huge boss of the horns, and the head jerked, he shot again at the wide nostrils and saw the horns jolt again and fragments fly, and he did not see Wilson now and, aiming carefully, shot again with the buffalo's huge bulk almost on him and his rifle almost level with the oncoming head, nose out, and he could see the wicked little eyes and the head started to lower and he felt a sudden white-hot, blinding flash explode inside his head and that is all he ever felt. ("M" 36)

This passage conveys an impression of utter concentration or focalization, a narrowing down of vision (from "they" to "he," from an overall view to chaotic details) suggestive of a series of extreme close-ups or the fragmented density of a cubist painting: the nose, the mouth, the horns, the head, the nostrils, the horns, the huge bulk, head, nose, eyes, the head. The delineation of short descriptive nouns and concise paratactical sentence structures communicates a breathtaking closeness but forgoes contact—both in the sense of a devastating clash and in the form of merging. Instead, the intense awareness of the other's presence brings about an extraordinary self-awareness or self-feeling, further accentuated in the ulterior transmutation of vision into feeling: the "sudden white-hot, blinding flash" is felt, not seen. This last turn culminates the story's strange logic of internalization, its privileging of daydreamlike seclusion,[15] as it demarcates that most precarious, most private and uncommunicating of moments: dying—it is, after all, the moment when the bullet, not the bull, hits home; his wife having shot Macomber from behind.

If "Macomber" seems to eschew the rhetoric of control and distantiation dominating so many Africa narratives from *Tarzan of the Apes* to *Congo*, it eventually proves to be no less entrenched in a logic of isolation and withdrawal, since the real adventure does not take place on African ground but deep within the white male psyche. Seen that way, Hemingway's enactments of African adventures could be said to demarcate the extreme other end of a genre first mapped out in detail by H. Rider Haggard. Moreover, in its marked disregard for contact or exchange, "Macomber" at times comes across like an inverted version of *Tarzan of the Apes,* the celebration of masculine body-feeling replacing and aggrandizing the earlier celebration of the trained male body. In their dismissal of the appearances and exteriorities of American middle-class life, Hemingway's heroes figure forth another stage for performing masculinity: the male psyche.

3.2 *White Hunter, Black Heart,* or, Elephantasias

> You ask how this was discussed, worked out and understood with the bar of language, and I say it was as freely discussed and clearly understood as though we were a cavalry patrol all speaking the same language. We were all hunters . . . and the whole thing could be worked out, understood and agreed to without using anything but a forefinger to signal and a hand to caution.   —Ernest Hemingway, *Green Hills of Africa* (1935)

In Africa, Hemingway suggests time and again, instinctive and immediate insights supersede calculation, reflection, and ultimately language itself. What has rightfully been called an "aesthetics of untranslatability" is intricately entwined with an "aesthetics of action"—both systems eliding communication and exchange and both indulging in the isolated and totalized experience of selfhood, an experience best brought about by hunting.

   Yet the aesthetics of action and the theme of hunting present themselves in stark contrast to this other big project of representing "Africa" in the first half of our century: primitivism. In Hemingway's autobiographical reflections, *Green Hills of Africa,* this opposition is brought to the fore when he relates an absurd encounter in the wilderness: the semicelebrity Ernest Hemingway coming across the semicelebrity Wassily Kandinsky, a European who evidently adheres to an entirely different set of values than his American peers:

> "I kill nothing, you understand," Kandinsky told us. "Why are you not more interested in the natives?"
> "We are," my wife assured him.
> "They are really interesting. Listen—" Kandinsky said, and he spoke on to her.

Hemingway would rather discuss the results of the outing of the day with his white hunter and leaves Kandinsky to his wife, the latters' remarks then forming the comical backdrop to the manly debates around tracking, shooting, and skinning wild game: "'So,' Kandinsky was saying to my wife. 'That is what you should see. The big ngomas. The big native dance festivals. The real ones.'"[16] If the Hemingways did ever go to see one of these dance events, it certainly did not make its way into *Green Hills*. Kandinsky, however, would himself make good use of the "real" Africa that he encountered. But that is another story.

In *Green Hills*, the anecdotal encounter is meant to differentiate Hemingway's project unequivocally from what is presented as a sentimental fantasy: while Kandinsky's "interest for the natives" appears as trite exoticism, hunting is made to demarcate a much more concrete, realistic, and direct approach to the foreign space. Instead of seeking contact with the natives, Hemingway chooses to go native himself, mapping out a quest not for knowledge but for knowing, not for cultural inspiration but for sensual focalization—self-feeling.[17] At the same time, his plea for sincerity against trite clichés inaugurated the dichotomy of the sentimental glance and the unflinching gaze, which was to experience a dramatic revival in the rhetorics of travel writing, journalism, and their fictional outcrops from the 1980s onward, as we shall see.

Yet if Hemingway's rhetorical tirade against sentimentalists and romantics in Africa became a standard device, the conceptual grounds for his distantiation to Kandinsky did not hold out for long. Being interested in the natives and being interested in wild game turned out to be very compatible concerns, as white hunters and African natives came to be paired in countless narratives of hunting and traveling in the following decades, and the more the figure of the white tough guy was discredited, the more credit the African native (or, to be precise, the symbolic systems of blackness and Africanity) gained. We have seen that countless contemporary Tarzan narratives invert whiteness and Africanity, turning the white man into the exemplary African while bringing the old paradigms of white huntership up to date with current cultural values and incentives. The compensatory function of many such inversions comes exemplarily to the fore in the film version of *Congo*, when the African-American guide on African ground introduces himself as "Monroe Kelly. I'm your great white hunter for this trip. Though I happen to be black," thereby minutely demarcating the only difference there is—his color obviously a bow, and nothing more, toward political correctness.

In *White Hunter, Black Heart*[18] finally, Clint Eastwood's 1990 return to the theme of the white man, the wild animal, and the failure at killing it, it is the very contact with the African native that brings about the demise of the white hunter. Or so it seems. At any rate, Clint Eastwood's white hunter will never kill big game. Instead, he will come to face the fact that the classical white hunter model has outlived itself, and the film will eventually vehemently disclaim Hemingway's collation of the white hunter with the realistic perspective and consign the figure to the realm of fantasy. But then reality and fantasy have always been hard to separate when it comes to Africa, so that this relegation demarcates not so much the final disassembly of the established imagery as its reconfiguration in the face of different circumstances.

From its outset on, *White Hunter, Black Heart* is stranded between the real and the fictional—the film relates the familiar story of coming to terms with the self on foreign ground, which is stratified on two levels here: First, there is the traditional—Hemingwayesque—plotline of self-authentication by way of shooting wild game. And then there is another plotline of self-authentication by way of shooting a film. Negotiating these two narrative realms involves the inevitable insight that the very boundaries of reality and fiction are hard to make out these days, as they are certainly no longer to be equated linearly with the practices of hunting and filmmaking. In a thinly veiled allusion to the events around John Huston's making of *The African Queen* in 1952, Eastwood's film traces the trials of an American director in Africa, who instead of concentrating on the film to be shot works himself into an obsession about hunting an elephant. Hence for the most part of *White Hunter, Black Heart* the film project is used as a cover for the "real" project of elephant hunting. It is only at the end that the error of this preference for hunting over filmmaking becomes evident. The times of hunting, this self-fashioning by violence, are over. Now self-fashioning is to be achieved by representation. The camera has replaced the gun as the main instrument of control.

In line with this reconfiguration, the dichotomy of hunter and sportsman seems to undergo a profound reevaluation in *White Hunter, Black Heart*. While filmmaker John Wilson (Clint Eastwood) clearly represents the hunter, his best friend, scriptwriter Pete Varrell (Jeff Fahey), just as clearly stands for the sportsman. At the beginning of the film Varrell has just arrived from a skiing trip; in Africa he plays tennis in an immaculate white outfit and soon joins the local soccer team. Representing the voice of reason and moderation as opposed to Wilson's egomania, Varrell is, not surprisingly, vehemently opposed to the project of shooting an elephant, endorsing Kandinsky's objections when he calls elephant hunting a "crime" against a species that is "part of a world which no longer exists." This kind of logic is lost on his friend though, who, Ahab-like, seeks the absolute encounter and victorious conquest. When Wilson finally confronts the elephant, an extreme close-up of the animal's eye quotes an earlier, much similar shot: the vicious eye of the white whale in John Huston's *Moby Dick*, produced four years after *The African Queen*.[19] The outcome of the 1990 confrontation with the wild beast deviates from the established pattern, however. Wilson refrains from his destructive quest and lowers his gun.

But his conversion comes too late; the elephant charges after all, and the white man's life is saved only because the African guide Kivu (Boy Mathias Chuma) steps in and dies in his stead. This turn of events is even more devastating, as Kivu came to represent everything truly important to Wilson before: the epitome of silent, dignified, authentic manhood. Kivu figured forth the ideal partner, so much more attractive than the foolish and self-centered blonde women the film lined up in unabashed misogyny and so much more authentic than the white men behaving like "dames" and "old ladies." The fact that this partnership precluded communication—none of them spoke the other's language—only enhanced the impression of "an instant bond that transcends language and culture,"[20] as one reviewer put it.

The film's last scene seems to give the lie to this idyll, though. Tough masculinity, we are told, brings about death, as the quest for the primeval confrontation ends up revealing nothing but its futility and meaninglessness. Eventually, Wilson returns to Kivu's village, the place where his film is to be shot, and sits down to do what he is there for. *White Hunter, Black Heart* ends upon a close-up of his tired face; his voice cracks: "Action." Fade to African landscapes, the drums mourning Kivu's death merging with the Africanized musical score.

"The ending turns the entire film upside down, or rather, right side up," enthused film critic Verena Lueken:

For Eastwood up to then enacted at length more than familiar rituals of masculinity, in the course of which John Wilson may come across somewhat exaggeratedly at times, yet remains "intact" as a sympathetic figure despite some flaws . . . , but after this, the same John Wilson is mercilessly dismantled in the last scenes and together with him all the rituals he and the film celebrated before.[21]

But can an ending turn an entire film around? Can images be taken back? Impressions simply blotted out? While it is certainly interesting to note that the film's ending seems to see a need to distance itself from the preceding action, to turn around and disclaim everything that has been presented up to then, I doubt whether this deconstruction works. Or whether it was meant to work in the first place. Thus, Susan Jeffords's reflections on another Eastwood film, the western *Unforgiven* (1992), seem much more to the point here: "it simultaneously presents and critiques a version of hard-bodied masculinity that verges on machismo, while debunking the myth of Hollywood westerns."[22] Of course, Clint Eastwood's work lends itself exemplarily well to such "renarrations," as it was he himself who once set the status quo now to be revised and reassembled: "What . . . is most fascinating about . . . *White Hunter, Black Heart* is that Eastwood still seems to be working through a self-critical agenda: about himself, about performing, about the egoism and vulnerability of the artist," another critic noted.[23] Eastwood is a master at the game of self-reflection and self-referentiality, a game that is also played in virtually all action adventure films of the period, as we have seen—variously inflected with irony or skepticism. But Eastwood adds a characteristic note to the generic trend. His film transmutes the symbolic system of action into the symbolic system of acting. In *White Hunter, Black Heart* the quest for truth and authenticity entails masquerade and make-believe, until these strategies finally take over.

Seen that way, the film does not question Wilson's belief that filmmaking and life are basically conjoined and subject to the same laws but rather his definition of these basic laws: sincerity and simplicity. When discussing the screenplay with Pete Verrill in Africa, he rejects an episode on the grounds of its being too complicated. In one of his many pompous monologues he then continues to lay out his concept of art:

That's what creates truly important art. It's simplicity. . . . Hemingway understood that. That's why he always reduced life to its simplest terms. Whether it's courage, fear, impotence, death. People's lives just sort of unfolded, things just happened to them, one thing after another. They were never bogged down with that nonsense of subplot that we sweated over in the past.

He gives this speech first reclining in a chair in the open air, in safari gear, balancing his gun, and then posing on the edge of a terrace, aiming his gun at obviously no particular goal. This strangely out-of-place white hunter act—this is a script session after all—makes the passionate plea for simplicity and sincerity ring false. But then Wilson's entire lifestyle deviates radically from his own maxims—he lives a masquerade of masculinity. Thus his outings in African safari gear echo the scenes in England with which the film began: the American on horseback clothed in a classy red coat—fox hunting—and then made up in aristocratic garb in the impressive mansion he got to live in during the production phase. He played the aristocrat just as he will play the white hunter, a filmmaker having thoroughly, but also quite self-defeatingly, absorbed the principles of his profession. Hence the unnerved request that his producer Paul Landers (George Dzundza) voices in Africa seems very well to the point: "Can you dip that phony English accent and, for God's sake, abandon your role of the great white hunter and become a movie director again?" But Wilson can't and won't at this point, getting sharply back at Landers to the embarrassment of the dinner company around:

My role of the great hunter, as you put it, is strictly my own business. It has nothing to do with you. It's a sacred subject. . . . Why, I'd have to explain to you the sound of the wind and the smell of the woods. I'd have to create you all over again and stamp out all those years you spend on the dirty pavement in cramped shoes.

This arrogant retort contains a logical twist that is crucial for the entire logic of the film: if Wilson can embrace a "role" as his true identity, turning the masquerade into the epitome of self-fashioning, why shouldn't the same logic work for Paul Landers? Why indeed can he not be "created all over again"? The answer, of course, is that such self-fashioning from scratch is a precarious undertaking in the first place, always at the risk of clashing with the harsh facts of everyday life, the cramped shoes, if you will. This is what Farrell tries to tell Wilson when his aged body gives out during one of the safari outings: "Come on, let's face it, this country is too tough for us. . . . We're not two heroes out of one of your films." Just like Hemingway's "Macomber," it seems, Eastwood's film turns against Burroughs's myth of the well-trained body. But where Hemingway turned to body-feeling, Eastwood stays firmly on the grounds of looks, or rather, images.

It takes some time, but eventually Wilson will accept that the white hunter is a creature not of real life but of fiction, an artificial image.[24] And still, his final turn away from hunting and back to his film project comes across less as an act of fundamental reorientation—Wilson's finally being "able to sit down and be himself"[25]—than as a continuation of his former masquerades by other, more appropriate means. Where Macomber's defeat, his failure to shoot the lion, called for a cathartic re-iteration of the hunt, now in daydreamlike control, Wilson's defeat, his failure to shoot the elephant and to save Kivu's life, brings about the white hunter's transformation into the filmmaker. And indeed, having control over images seems to be so much more crucial than having control over wild game in the late twentieth century, in a time that has discovered the "joy of receiving from the external world images that are usually internal, images that are familiar or not very far from familiar, of seeing them inscribed in a physical location (the screen)," as Christian Metz defined the age of the cinema, in which "fiction film enters into a functional competition with the daydream."[26]

Turning the white hunter figure into nothing but an act, the film takes a peculiar stance vis-à-vis established concepts of masculinity and whiteness, a stance reminiscent of Greystoke's techniques of imitation (of apes and aristocrats) to come to a sense of selfhood. Where Greystoke mimicked others, however, Eastwood's persona mimics other, earlier versions of itself. With this the film seems to visualize what Eric Lott called practices of "self-mimicry" in white male self-fashioning, giving evidence of the fact that "whiteness itself ultimately becomes an impersonation,"[27] or, to cite Judith Butler, that gender is "a *corporeal style*, an 'act,' as it were, which is both intentional and performative."[28] In the representational framework of our day, the act is all there is—there is nothing underneath it any longer but other images, different acts. Thus just like Hugh Hudson's *Greystoke,* the Disney *Tarzan,* and Michael Crichton's *Congo, White Hunter, Black Heart* evokes a concept of self-fashioning that almost unnoticeably moves away from long-standing notions of originality, independence, and autonomy toward the idea of life as mimicry. By this token, to turn from actor to director might be the best you can achieve in terms of individual agency.

3.3 Display Cases: Peter Beard and Renée Green Exhibit Africa

Eastwood's film manages to render the white hunter problematic and still sustain his iconic image, as it hovers between critique and celebration, revision and repetition, time and again setting the image against explicit statements, without acknowledging the contradiction on the level of diegesis. Of course, it is precisely this capacity at doubling that renders film, especially fiction film, such a powerful instrument for shaping, circulating, and transforming stereotypical setups. This capacity pertains not only to film but also, perhaps even more pointedly, to photography, this visual medium that exemplarily combines the indexical and the iconic, statements about reality and stylizations of reality, and thus "has become a principal agent and conduit of culture and ideology."[29]

Photography promises accuracy and authenticity, an "emanation of the referent," as Roland Barthes pointed out, and even if things have changed considerably with the advent of digital media, the "credibility factor" activated by photography is far from defunct: "in Photography I can never deny that *the thing has been there.*"[30] This is of course what makes photography such an interesting medium for the depictions of cultural contact, or rather cultural observation, as it exemplarily achieves the effect of pulling the far-away into sharp focus without the risk of interaction and the troubles of communication. In the work of Leni Riefenstahl and other producers of alien and exotic difference, these dimensions of photography (the promise of authenticity and the stylistics of distantiation) were enacted time and again, to both display the unknown and keep it that way—at bay: "Menschen wie von einem anderen Stern" (People as from another planet), ran the German subtitle to Riefenstahl's 1974 photo documentation of the Nuba.[31] Given the spectacular quality of such quasi-anthropological projects, it may not come as a surprise that fashion and society photographers have taken over the project of searching the remotest nooks and corners of the globe, producing time and again the selfsame repertories of exotic difference in unchanging sameness. Guy Trebay's sardonic comments on one such project, Hibiki

Kobayashi's photo book *Tribe,* pin down the mechanisms at work not only in Kobayashi but in his forerunners Irving Penn, Herb Ritts, or Riefenstahl just as well:

Toothless, or wearing penis sheaths or neck rings, or daubed with mud, and with affectless expressions (don't Yanomamis smile?), Kobayashi's subjects might be models for a desperate edition of *Third World Vogue.* "The people in [his] images are presented quietly, self-contained in their outside body-shells," writes photographer Peter Beard, himself no stranger to exoticizing peoples' outside body shells. (Remember when Beard touted Somali model Iman as the child of a goatherd? Her father was, in fact, a diplomat.) "You see in their eyes a far-off connection," continues Beard's introduction, "a consciousness of something very important and elusive." What in the (shrinking) world could that be? one wonders. Lunch?[32]

While this sadly enough does sum up the overall logic of the genre, there is more to Peter Beard than his undeniable propensity for exoticism and benign racism. While indubitably moving between fashion photography and wildlife documentation, African ethno-kitsch and Western myths of masculinity, he tends to combine these imageries in striking and strange tableaux, designating a sphere truly in-between, weirdly mixed up. Again, the white hunter theme crops up, both in allusions to long-standing imageries and in artistic self-stylizations (Beard comes across at least as narcissistic as Hemingway or Eastwood in his intermixture of life and work), and again, as in Eastwood's film, it undergoes a fundamental transformation as the icon of authenticity is univocally demolished and the artist, the producer of images, takes the place of the image. In the course of this substitution the external referent might get lost, but the myth of autonomy and self-authentication in the wilderness is salvaged against all odds, while the logic of the daydream is totalized.

Where Eastwood maps his quest for the white hunter around the obsession of shooting an elephant, Peter Beard became famous not for killing a living elephant but for shooting dead ones. His photo book *The End of the Game* (1965), which came out in a revised and enlarged edition in 1977, traces the disappearance of the elephant in East Africa (fig. 1). The 1977 edition ends upon page after page of elephant corpses, decaying, skeletonized, most of them photographed from the air: at one point we see a plane's shadow in immaculate outline next to the clear-cut, if grotesquely flattened, form of an elephant body in decay (fig. 2).

There is a story behind these displays of death—the story of urbanization and industrial spread in East Africa, which brought about the elephants' confinement in the narrow spaces of East African national parks and the starvation documented by Beard—but the pictures themselves do not relate it, as they beautify and monumentalize the dead

Fig. 1. Peter Beard, *The End of the Game* (detail).

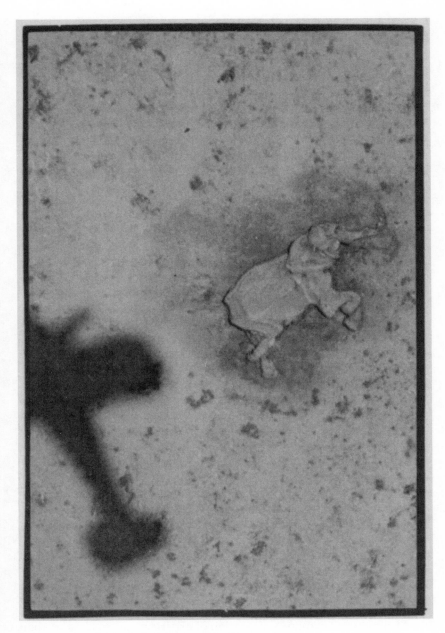

Fig. 2. Peter Beard, *The End of the Game* (detail).

bodies, turning the atrocity of starvation into a spectacle of abstract form and surreal grace. In a paradoxical contestation of Barthes's insight that every photograph stages "the return of the dead,"[33] these photographs blot out death by totalizing it: figuring forth the sealed-off perfection of *nature morte*.

If Beard's early work resonates with a certain self-referential grandeur, reveling in form and structure, this aspect takes center stage in *the* 1990s exhibition of his work: "Carnets Africains," shown from 1996 to 1997 in Paris and from 1997 onward in a permanent exhibition in New York. Beard always oscillated between photography and bricolage, as his diaries proved before: elaborate collages of mixed media—photographs, press clippings, drawings, and all kinds of souvenirs glued in, next to his looping scribbles in colored ink—which have been aptly described as "a combination of adolescent daydreaming, fiendish detritus, cosmic dandruff, frantic tangible psychotherapy, and visual novas page after exhausting page."[34] But these days the bricoleur seems to have won the game, as Beard frantically dismantles, reviews, and reassembles his earlier work together with other material, and thus seems to turn everything he does into an extension of his diaries.

"Carnets Africains" is shown in New York in Peter Beard's own SoHo gallery called, quite appropriately, The Time Is Always Now. But then, the show's geographical location seems irrelevant: if there ever was an artificial Africa, "Carnets Africains" maps it out. Huge photographs and posters are mounted in seeming disarray on the walls, and glass cases in the middle of the room display Beard's diaries together with African trinkets, artifacts, and souvenirs, while potted plants and stones in the corners further "Africanize" the space. The photographs themselves, huge gelatin silver prints, have been considerably edited by Beard, who painted them with colorful "ethno-style" frames of insects, plants, or just "primitive" ornaments, added handwritten quotes of the famous from Leonardo da Vinci to T. S. Eliot reflecting upon the grand themes of mankind, and often pasted other material onto the photographs—newspaper clippings, snapshots, African souvenirs. One of these collages contains a cutout from a 1950s comic book showing a "white hunter" with bare upper body, shaving, and his black servant in the background. Below, a snapshot of Peter Beard shows him similarly bared in a similar posture, a repetition that suggests parodic fracturing.

And yet, Beard's project should not be hastily conflated with a postmodern aesthetics of parody or pastiche, as Beard's fragmentation resembles Hemingway's extreme focalization of experience so much more than, say, Andy Warhol's leveling of past and present in his pastiche technique. This is paradoxically epitomized in Beard's very collaborations with

Andy Warhol, which do attest strongly to the latter's aesthetics. "Carnets Africains" shows a little collage called *From the Jungle to the Jungle*, a flattened package of Sunshine's Animal Crackers pasted onto one of Beard's dead elephant photographs, the dark stylized outlines of wild and domestic animals on the package reverberating the outline of the dead animal in the photograph, and thoroughly undermining its spectacular effect in turn. Another collaboration with Warhol, a series of collages called "Things of Life," registers the paraphernalia of exoticization and male individuation, as in the advertising display of a Camel Cigarettes package pasted on paper. The scribbled comment underneath: "homage to wild animals."

These collaborations stand in stark contrast to Beard's work on his own, although he very well takes recourse to similar techniques of representation. If he, just like Eastwood, leaves no doubt that the days of colonialism and the times of the white hunter are over, his entire perspective on this period is inflected with nostalgia. In introduction after introduction to his photo books, Beard deplores the demise of the old order and the takeover of "paradise" by "power," while painting increasingly more apocalyptic scenarios of cultural contact and international interference.

But then, if Beard seems to pit nature against culture at first glance, he actually collapses cultural and biological concepts into the same apocalyptic scenario of irreversible global destruction. His description of the processes of colonization in his 1965 introduction to *The End of the Game* is an early case in point:

To understand this final era in Africa we must first speak of the white man—his coming and his conquering. In the old days he was either an amiable eccentric or an explorer. Against enormous odds, equipped with a child's dreams and a man's courage, he opened up a new continent. The European missionary and the white hunter were the advance scouts of the Western World. When the game control officer J. A. Hunter worked on the Mombasa Railroad in 1908, they were already finishing up. They had filed their romantic reports, and the vanguard moved in. Railroad tracks were laid, steel shafts through the shadows. . . . What now of the white hunter? He is still with us, though heavily compromised. Once an explorer, he is now a licensed hired hand. . . . [35]

Here the white hunter, just like this other icon of colonization, the missionary, comes to figure not as a perpetrator in the colonialist scheme but as its most prominent victim, blotting out in his misery the actual African victims. This calls to mind the representational strategies in Hugh Hudson's *Greystoke*, and indeed Beard's turn from documentary photography to collage echoes Hudson's musealization of Africa, if on a larger scale. In Beard's current work the referent is no longer "the essence of African life, the animal,"[36] but his very own depiction of this African life—

the photographs of the dead animals effacing the continent and its ongoing history altogether.

In one of the revised elephant photographs, Beard tugged a crushed Pepsi can in the lower corner of a print much larger than the tiny one used in the collaboration with Warhol. The effect is definitely not one of persiflage or parody but a further aggrandizement of the subject of death, the dead animal monumentalized in its very opposition to the trite object of civilization, emphasizing its perfection and controlled containment by contrast to the unruly and insignificant piece of trash. The effect calls to mind Roland Barthes's remarks about photographed corpses: "if the photograph then becomes horrible, it is because it certifies, so to speak, that the corpse is alive, as *corpse:* it is the living image of a dead thing."[37] Yet the bringing to life of the dead thing, underscored here by the presence of the actual "dead thing"—the can—also entails its totalization. These photographs are not meant to "restore what has been abolished"; they are not even meant to "attest that what I see has indeed existed."[38] They are completely self-contained and utterly self-referential.

In his 1997 introduction to an Italian exhibition catalogue, Beard reveals the conceptual framework motivating this withdrawal:

It took millions of years for humans to reach a population of one billion (circa 1850). Now, we add a billion people to our planet every ten years—every four days a million of us die from starvation and density-related diseases. The glacier of human flesh presses on, squeezing almost all of natural history into museums, zoos, fun parks and shopping malls. Like elephants, we cunningly adapt to the damage we cause.

Like elephants, we suffer the consequences. Density and stress, aid and AIDS, deep blue computers and Nintendo robots, heart disease and cancer, liposuction and rhinoplasty, digital pets and Tamaguchi [sic] toys have delivered us into the brave new world. . . . What better time to settle down on my retirement mat and paste up all the pettiness and futility, all "the daily news," all the tacky fragments, stuffed into life-thickening daybooks.[39]

Once more cultural contact is turned into a contaminating disease, as the striking interpolation of aid and AIDS makes dramatically clear. Sexual intercourse, transnational interference, and cultural interaction are leveled off to figure forth the unchanging spectacle of global decay—a spectacle that turns everybody into a victim, as helpless and inert as the East African elephants over twenty years ago. In the face of the "glacier of human flesh" pressing on and the masses of industrial waste in its wake, the 1960s photographs of decaying animal bodies paradoxically demarcate the relief of arrested development—an uncanny "revival" of H. Rider Haggard's Kukuanaland, this African utopia perfectly sealed off from the rest of the world.

If Beard proves to be in accordance with a pervasive populist tendency of "scapegoating natural limits rather than the internal contradictions of capitalism" for the devastating situation at hand,[40] his work inadvertently epitomizes the shortcomings of this logic, registering the fact that it precludes virtually any concept of human agency or social change. The photographer, having replaced Hemingway's white hunter and Hemingway's aesthetics of action likewise, does not even document death any longer; he tautologically confines himself to review the fading documents of death, desperately trying to revive what gains its perfection from being dead.

Beard's obsessive circulation around images of the past curiously calls up Hemingway's logic of the daydream, as Beard's work, too, revels in ever more escapist gestures of retreat, a retreat that once more is paradoxically enacted in the aggressive style of self-assertion. Relocating the white male's project in the wilderness even more markedly than Eastwood onto the level of representation, Beard declares the classical white hunter—this "amiable eccentric"—dead and gone. Where Eastwood obsesses about the hunter, Beard monumentalizes the prey.

While Beard's introductions spawn an aura of disillusionment, skepticism, and resignation, calling to mind the negative ending of Eastwood's film, this negativitity bears little effect for the contemporary collages. Just like Eastwood, Beard fails to dismantle the myths of Africanity. In both cases, the very repertory of Africanity can be seen to envelop and obfuscate any project of demystification, effectively canceling out the gestures of distantiation and critique brought forth time and again. By consequence, the techniques of montage, masquerade, and parody are by no means as subversive as they are made out to be: the effect of Beard's collages and Eastwood's performance is not the collapse but the stabilization of Africanist imageries against all odds.

Images are liable to gain a momentum of their own, it seems, as they often work almost unnoticeably against the statements of intention accompanying them and as they tend to naturalize and reify their subject matter. Which is why the concept artist Renée Green took great care to emphasize the frames around the images she exhibited. In fact, her 1991 installation *Vistavision: Landscapes of Desire* (Pat Hearn Gallery, New York), which I will juxtapose to Beard's enactments of Africanity, could be said to be *about* framing devices and forms of enactment. First and foremost, however, the installation is about images of Africa. Again, Africa is approached indirectly and ironically, and again Africa is enacted as a space of projections and desire: mostly the projections and desires of white men—white hunters, explorers, and artists. Yet *Vistavision* seems not so much intent on dismantling the artificial Africa it brings into view

Fig. 3. Renée Green, *Vistavision. Landscapes of Desire* (detail). (Pat Hearn Gallery, New York.)

as concerned with its reproduction in vitro: Green erects a laboratory of Africanity—exoticism under glass.

This stance of scientific detachment curiously reflects the projects investigated in *Vistavision,* stemming from fields such as biology or anthropology, which traditionally professed to precisely such a spirit of disinterested disclosure, culminating in the dioramic displays of exotic cultures in the classical museum of natural history. *Vistavision* was, after all, motivated by a discovery in its own right—Green's "discovery" of Theodore Roosevelt's safari souvenirs in the American Museum of Natural History in New York. But of course, Green's installation inflects the traditional projects of exhibiting culture and difference, as it is the scientific procedures and conventions themselves that are investigated now. Insofar, *Vistavision* calls to mind the critique of imperial science brought forth in Hugh Hudson's *Greystoke.* And yet we shall see that Green's project in its entirety takes an altogether different course.

The installation extends over three rooms, each of them staking out a different aspect of Africanist representations in the sciences and the arts. A first room holds a telescope on a stepladder, two rows of files that contain boards with the Latin names of African wildlife, and framed pages of Haggard's *King Solomon's Mines,* Roosevelt's *African Game Trails,* and Somerset Maugham's *The Explorers* on the wall. The files lead up to a tent with a treasure chest and more boards with the titles of both science books and adventure fiction (fig. 3).

The middle room displays documentary films on ethnographers and explorers on two video screens, next to a collection of Ph.D. papers on African culture and a documentation of Green's own sources, while the last room finally reenacts a colonialist study and white hunter's resort— stuffed animals and exotic souvenirs, pipes, and guns. A shelf holds framed photographs of hats and arms—stetsons, safari hats, pistols (figs. 4 and 5).

Folding the gaze back on the instruments of cultural contact and its representation—the gun, the compass, the telescope next to the stuffed animals and trophies—Green not only points out the constructedness of Africanity but insists simultaneously on this construct's ideological impact: its paralyzing—or deadening—effect. By this token, the installation does repeat the critique expressed in Beard's collages or in Hudson's film. Yet where Hudson eventually turned Africa into something like a filmic diorama, and Beard ended up hypertrophying the very practice of taxidermy, Green manages to avoid such totalizing effects, because she maintains her distance. Neither perpetrators nor victims of the colonial venture come into view, and Green also takes pains to keep its effects at bay. Calling to

Fig. 4. Renée Green, *Vistavision. Landscapes of Desire* (detail). (Pat Hearn Gallery, New York.)

Fig. 5. Renée Green, *Vistavision. Landscapes of Desire* (detail). (Pat Hearn Gallery, New York.)

mind Walter Abish's *Alphabetical Africa,* the novel that dismantles the logic of adventure narration by displaying its material base, its "alphabet," Green's installation forces the gaze on the museum glass cases themselves—the frameworks and conditions for colonial representation.

The questions Renée Green asked her audience to keep in mind while

watching the exhibition—"How is Africa (or how are Africas) constructed in our minds? What sort of projects and desires do we bring to
the landscape?"[41]—point to the phantasmic quality of sight and the self-
perpetuating power of the imageries of Africanity, a power "related to
seeing and vision"[42] that *Vistavision* takes very seriously in its determination not to come too close. This is exemplarily brought to the fore in the
installation's last room, which undermines the aura of the white hunter
so much more effectively than either Eastwood or Beard, precisely because Green does *not* enact the icon itself but only its paraphernalia—the
stage props that keep the masquerades of masculinity and whiteness in
the wilderness going. Where Eastwood turned the white hunter from an
actor into a director, thus leading him offstage and assigning him the responsibility for the symbolic system at work, and where Beard monumentalized the aura of loss and longing he associates with this vanishing
act, Green turns the tables on the figure—showing it to be nothing but an
effect of circumstances, if a highly consequential effect.

3.4 Big Games: Indiana Jones, Jr., T. C. Boyle, and the Virtual Safari

The Civilized Way to Answer The Call of the Wild. . . .
   On Safari in Africa
   By Private Luxury Jet and the Legendary Blue Train. . . .
   Stay at the very best, like Cape Town's Mount Nelson Hotel and La Mamounia in
Marrakech. Game lodges such as Botswana's Chobe Game Lodge and Tanzania's
Ngorongoro Serena Lodge. And several nights in classic tented camp. The exclusively
reserved Kichwa Tembo in Kenya's magnificent Masai Mara. . . .
   All-Inclusive Price $36,800 per person. . . .
   Intrav Private Jet Adventures
   Beyond First Class.   —Advertisement, *New York Times* (July 12, 1998)

Hemingway presented Africa as an ideal backdrop for envisioning the
"never before seen." Today, by contrast, going on safari is not meant to
bring about revelations but to confirm set expectations. If the very idea of
hunting in Africa has always been tinged with the desire for an experience
of a different kind, these days this desire often seems to focus not on the
primitive but on other, earlier approaches to primitivity. The imageries of
African wildlife and British colonialism have merged into one big concoction signifying "adventure," regardless of whether the quest for the authentic experience takes the guise of nostalgia film or tourist routine—
neither of these modes of framing experience is liable to dismantle
established habits or even trigger epiphanous insights.

One master figure for this paradigm of "adventure without risk" is certainly Indiana Jones, this 1980s icon of the postmodern traveler, who encounters familiar scenarios of difference everywhere and still manages to get something out of them. Instead of envisioning the "never before seen," in the Indiana Jones trilogy we encounter long-standing stereotypes in markedly ironic detachment, thus seeing and not seeing at the same time, or "forgetting what we have seen," as Michael Rogin put it.[43]

While Steven Spielberg's Indiana Jones trilogy worked out a powerful paradigm for action adventures of the eighties and nineties, the logic of a reliably exotic world suffusing the films was also to inhabit a popular TV series of the early nineties, clearly cashing in on the films' blockbuster success: *The Young Indiana Jones Chronicles*.[44] Catering to a teenage audience, the series fleshes out the childhood, adolescence, and young manhood of Indiana Jones, following the successful pattern of Spielberg's *Indiana Jones and the Last Crusade* (1989). And if the filmic Indiana Jones was already involved in events of global historical relevance, his kid version on TV seems to be at the very heart of world history, running into somebody of world fame every other minute, and thus working hard at getting the playful historical education across that the series is meant to provide.

One episode shows Indiana (Corey Carrier) with his parents on safari in East Africa, and here it is Theodore Roosevelt, the great white hunter personified, who lends historical weight to the African experience, quickly inciting the boy with breathless admiration for his tough talk and paternalistic benevolence. The episode emphasizes Roosevelt's scientific project, his dedicated and manly quest for specimen to be analyzed and displayed by American scientific institutions—the very material and project Renée Green came to reflect upon, if in a markedly different vein. On TV, we see Roosevelt concerned with a particularly elusive animal, the oryx, which little Indiana will manage to track down against all odds, having consulted a native tribe first. A herd of oryx is finally stalked by Roosevelt and his hunters; two of them are shot, but then Indiana interferes and scares the other animals off—in compliance with what we learn to be the "native view." In line with the logic of the series, Theodore Roosevelt does not bear a grudge for long about this, nor about being lectured by the kid on how to do the right thing. Instead, the former president and "Rough Rider" accepts gracefully the premature demise of his entire worldview and its replacement by a 1990s rhetoric of animal rights and global responsibility. After all, not only this series but also countless others from *Star Trek: The Next Generation* to *Sliders* never tire of touting the belief that you can transpose any maxim accepted as correct in the United States today to any (historically or culturally different) context, if you only talk long enough about it. The imagery of communication provides, as we have seen before, the most powerful means of establishing and obfuscating control these days. Where colonial literature proudly displayed the machinery of manipulating other peoples into compliance, today they are convinced or just left behind.[45]

Even when there is nothing much for Indiana to teach, he leaves an impression—as in another African episode, set in 1917 in the Congo, where an older Indiana (Sean Patrick Flanery) meets Albert Schweitzer (Friedrich von Thun), who promptly reels off phrase after phrase of profound insights, none of them by any means refutable—or new. But this does not mean that he will be left unaffected—after short exposure to the American we see him giving up Bach to play boogie. And he provides young Indie with a line of wisdom that could be turned into the credo not only of this series: "A little subversion is good for the soul." Just don't overdo it, or it might actually have an outside effect.

All of this is, of course, also very much the material of satire. And while the series does take its protagonist dead seriously, another contemporary fictional refashioning of the (post)modern quest for adventure revels in precisely the absurd dimensions of "the civilized way to answer the call of the wild"—T. Coraghessan Boyle's story "Big Game" (1994). The story reverberates with Hemingway's quest for the perfect experience in Africa and revises it drastically, unhinging its very foundations in its manipulation of setting, setup, and, most important, characters: the figure of the white hunter, for one, won't survive this cruel game.

Just like the *Indiana Jones Chronicles,* which more often than not used a kid character to spread the wisdom of the present all over the globe, "Big Game" dislodges the paradigms of male toughness and white hunter bravado by endorsing the voice of the "next generation." Teenage Jasmine reprimands her father, real estate tycoon Mike Bender, sharply for his safari plans: "And so you go and kill some poor lion that isn't hurting anybody, and what's that supposed to prove?"[46] True, the father tries to counter by playing the card of experience, strongly backed up by his white hunter Bernard Puff:

"All of this hippie-dippy save-the-environment crap might be alright if you're twelve, but you've got to realize hunting is as natural a part to man as, as—"
    "Eating or drinking," Puff put in. . . ." ("BG" 10–11)

But both of them should have known that in the 1990s kids tend to have the last word:

"*Right!*" Jasmine cried, on her feet now, her eyes like sinkholes, her mouth twitching at the corners. "And so's shitting, farting and, and *fucking!*" And then she was gone, stamping down the trophy-hung hallway to her room, where she flung the door with a thunderous crash. ("BG" 11)

Then again, by stark contrast to little Indiana, this is not a likable kid. Nor are we likely to build up sympathy for her father, or her stepmother or the white hunter at that. The entire scenario of this safari does not leave the reader a lot of options apart from ironic distantiation. After all, the Benders did not set out for Africa in the first place but to Puff's African Game Ranch in Bakersfield, USA, to experience the thrill of adventure without all its tedious and dangerous side effects. Jasmine's verdict, snorted out at the very outset of the story, does indeed ring true: "'I mean like shooting lions in Bakersfield? Tacky city. Tacky, tacky, tacky'" ("BG" 5). More than that, however, Bender's very incentives for hunting are quite "tacky," a far cry from the Hemingwayesque desire for the truly unsettling:

He'd had an itch to hunt lion and elephant and rhino since he was a kid and first read *Confessions of a White Hunter* and the Classic Comics version of *King Solomon's Mines*. And this was his chance. So maybe it wasn't Africa, but who had the time to go on safari. If he could spare three days he was lucky. ("BG" 5)

Boyle's fictional universe could very well have accommodated Intrav Private Jet Adventures, along with a lot of other outgrowths of the contemporary adventure industry, which has, after all, transformed the classical terrain of East African wildlife into huge game parks, as Bender contends: " . . . you couldn't shoot anything over there anyway. Not anymore. Everything was a preserve now, a game park, a conservancy. There were no more white hunters. Just photographers" ("BG" 5).

And indeed, in a certain sense the artificial Africa in Bakersfield turns out to be as real as it gets, as Bender, like Francis Macomber before him, will encounter deepgoing defeat and destruction there. Frightened stiff at his first encounter with a lion, Bender fails to shoot, and Puff has to intervene, shooting the lion's head off and winning the admiration of the beautiful wife—Hemingway's "Macomber" looming large in the background. But then Boyle's deviations from the classical patterns are more significant than his repetitions: this story is not about action or agency but about loss of control and the reversal of the established pattern. When Bender declares himself ready for hunting—"I'm game" ("BG" 9)—he does not know how right he will be. "Big Game" casts the white hunter in the role of prey and lets the big game win the day. In a gory showdown at the end of the story, the elephant Bender plans to kill in order to make up for his former lack of courage strikes back, killing Bender, his wife, and his white hunter.

Where Eastwood's *White Hunter, Black Heart* exposed the white hunter act as a masquerade, Boyle turns it into a farce. His white hunter, aptly called Bernard Puff, is as phony as the "Britishisms" he is so fond of and the fake Africa he has established around himself, yet his delusion is never tragic. Nor is Bender's failure to live up to the myth of male supremacy, as this character never acquires depth either. Underneath his business persona is just another stereotypical setup: "the tennis pro and backyard swimmer climbed out from behind the mask of the petulant real estate wonder boy" ("BG" 17). And when Puff at one point senses something "beating hot and hard beneath [Mrs. Bender's] mask of blusher and eyeliner and the puffed-up lips" ("BG" 13), it is certainly not unquenched sexual passion, as he likes to think, but the superficial and unthinking drive for money and success that indeed forms her very core. If these lives are trite and meaningless, so are the deaths, brought about moreover by an animal, which does not stand for instinct, natural force, or authenticity either but which is just another playactor—"a veteran of thirty-eight years with the Ringling Bros. and Barnum & Bailey Circus who'd performed under the name 'Bessie Bee.'" Earlier on, Puff was pleased to note that the old animal "still had a bit of showmanship in her" ("BG" 6), and it is precisely this performative spirit that eventually leads to his death— Bessie Bee playing her part only too well.

But then everything in this story evolves like a circus performance, the characters mechanically acting out their routines like trained animals, and not even the catastrophe at the end comes across as a breakthrough. Narrated from Puff's perspective—"[h]e was in shock, he told himself, repeating it aloud, over and over" ("BG" 21)—the events seem utterly artificial, showpieces gone awry: "He looked up at the noise, a shriek of great conviction, and saw Bessie Bee rubbing her foot thoughtfully, almost tenderly, over Mike Bender's prostrate form" ("BG" 21), "Mrs. Bender, the wife, Nicole, one of the finest expressions of her species, . . . was running from the Jeep and exercising her lungs" ("BG" 22), "[a]nd then all at once, strange phenomenon, the sun was gone, and the vultures, and a great black shadow fell over him" ("BG" 22).

"Boyle's frenetic style erases, suspends, and fragments the violence so that it is denied the force of realism," wrote Michael Walker about an earlier short story, "Greasy Lake": "the narrative style—humorous to brutal—relieves both narrator and audience of any terror, suspense, or moral responsibility."[47] Although by contrast to Walker I do not consider this lack of moral commitment to be typical for postmodern literature at large, with respect to Boyle's short stories and his later writing he certainly has a point.[48] Boyle's use of multiple focalization could not differ more from Hemingway's logic of the daydream in "The Short Happy Life," as Boyle's narrative seems to refocus whenever it comes too close or pushes too deep, discouraging identification and eliding sympathy.[49]

As "Big Game" is not about the quest for a deepgoing revelation but about the desire to get one's money's worth, the gory ending is enacted as nothing but a nasty and unpleasant surprise, if with fatal consequences. And it is not the sudden upsurge of violence that is shocking at the end of "Big Game" but the fact that it does not matter—nothing whatsoever comes of it. Boyle may manage to turn the tables, and to display the hunter as the prey, calling to mind Renée Green's subversion of the very imagery of individual self-assertion at the heart of the classical white hunter narrative. But in contrast to Green's *Vistavision,* Boyle's "Big Game" does not bring about an effect of critical distance but rather a feeling of futility. The masquerade of money and power, which has long extinguished any trace of deep feeling and authenticity, will go on, not despite but *because* of the fact that it is tacky:

Half a mile away, . . . Jasmine Honeysuckle Rose Bender . . . opened her eyes. She was, in that waking moment, sole inheritor of the Bender real estate empire, and all the monies and houses and stocks and bonds and properties that accrued to it, not to mention the beach house and the Ferrari Testarossa, but she wasn't yet aware of it. Something had awakened her, some ripple on the great pond of life. For just a moment there, over the drone of the air conditioner, she thought she'd heard a scream.

But no, it was probably just some peacock or baboon or whatever. Or that pitiful excuse for an elephant. She sat up, reached into her cooler for a root beer and shook her head. Tacky, she thought. Tacky, tacky, tacky. ("BG" 23)

Where Peter Beard withdrew into self-referentiality, Boyle—perhaps out of a similar pessimism about the global situation—distances himself completely from the scenario he sets up, seemingly unperturbed in his depiction of "a self-perpetuating machinery geared toward the haves rather than the have-nots," as Theo D'haen wrote of Boyle's 1987 novel *World's End.*[50] In a world that is nothing but a huge business venture, a highly predictable and regularized global game, the individual players are as insignificant as any local specificities or deviations. By dint of this logic, Bakersfield *is* Africa.

3.5 The Wild East of Africa: *The Ghost and the Darkness*

White hunters are not very popular these days. As audiences are prone to side with the animal—"actually, I felt sorry for the lion," Nina Baym sums up one typical response to "Macomber"—the act of tough guy versus nature, which fueled not only Hemingway's machismo, threatens to wear thin. This is not to say, however, that popular culture discarded the white male hero on foreign ground, just that certain classical manifestations fell into disrepute and certain stances are now hard to pull through without risking ridicule. This is why Clint Eastwood, ceaselessly working through a repertory formerly established not least by himself, *has* to turn to self-reflexivity and masquerade in the 1990s, performing masculinity more than embodying it. And this is why Peter Beard might seem ironic and distanced, although he could not take his retrofitted white hunter act more seriously.

But masquerade and irony constitute only one facet of a more pervasive configuration. Other, less distanced reenactments of the white hunter under the insignia of the present bring about revisionary scenarios as entangled in fantasies of agency and control, of self-authentication and male bonding on foreign ground, as Hemingway's stories used to be. Most of the current enactments of the white hunter theme tend to fall into the pattern of Jamesonian "nostalgia narratives"—if not explicitly set in the past, they are tinged with the aura of "pastness"—and this kind of approximation calls up a concrete context of race, gender, or cultural conditions only to dismiss it in the same breath: this is not about politics but about duty. This is not about ideology but about a specific task to be performed, a deed to be done.

This logic of deferral suffuses the early 1990s DC comic *Congorilla,* which stages the resuscitation of the great white hunter in almost paradigmatic terms, inadvertently bringing out the absurd dimensions of the quest for authenticity and self-reliance in view of its countless earlier enactments. In issue 4, *Ape Fear!*[51] the comic's protagonist, Congo Bill, is called back to duty after having retired to the mountains outside Kinshasa, where *Congorilla* is set. With his longish hair, his unkempt beard, his eye patch, and his military gear, Congo Bill covers a lot of stereotypical ground, calling up all kinds of male icons from white hunter to lone ranger to pirate to Rambo-style mercenary. At fifty-six, he's past his prime fighting age, and seems to have settled down for the quiet country life together with his companion, Nuli, an African woman who is made out as his partner, not his playmate. This is, of course, the standard outset for "hard body" narratives of the 1990s, as Susan Jeffords pointed out with regard to westerns from Eastwood's *The Unforgiven* to *Diggstown* (both 1992), which time and again line up the aged male hero "voicing the essential cry of the 1980s hard bodies: that they are authentic, that they have not disappeared, and that they can still win the important fights and defeat the important villains, if only the country as a whole will support and believe in them."[52]

If Congo Bill decides to go hunting once more, it is to confront a prey that he alone can master. To make a complicated and rather silly story short: his former protégé, "Janu the Jungle Boy," has had enough of the white system dominating the country, a system that is clearly characterized as racist and corrupt. He becomes "Congorilla"—a creature between superman and ape, complete with a series of ghetto allusions and racial codifications, on a brutish rebellion that does not offer any ground for identification. Still Congo Bill feels some kind of bond, which he manages to overcome, however, killing off Congorilla: "He was like my son. . . . And the body was like my own!" (*AF* 28), he commemorates, somewhat belatedly, next to the ape-man's dead body.

Yet if hunter and prey are quite close, the monumentalized wildness and conscious malevolence of the latter also draw a clear-cut line between them, aggrandizing the hunter's quest in turn and legitimating his manic self-absorption. Thus the most pressing question—why should Congo Bill side with the corrupt system in the first place?—is blotted out by the scenarios of immediate duty, instant action. This is especially evident as the entire hunt does not take place in a timeless jungle setting but in an urban environment (vaguely fiftyish, in accordance with the comic's "classical" aesthetics), with Congo Bill alternately swinging on vines or elevator cords and with the last scene set in an ultramodern hall with a simulated jungle in its midst. This is where Bill's companion, Nuli, enters again, tries to approach him, and is pushed away by one of the guards standing around: "No Kafirs [*sic*] allowed!" (*AF* 28). Congo Bill is briefly enraged but quickly resigns. "Africa!" sighs Nuli in the last panel. "Everywhere, Nuli!" replies Congo Bill: "Everywhere except where we live!" "Let's go home . . . !" (*AF* 28). In the background we do not see the domesticated jungle now but a wall with a frieze showing vaguely antique scenes of love and battle.

Of course, Congo Bill's very involvement with the system gives the lie to the comic's logic of the white hunter as a mythical creature fighting the eternally evil. In fact, Congo Bill proves to be as independent and as authentic as the artificial jungle in the city hall. When he replaces Congorilla in his intermediate position between wilderness and civilization, a constellation comes about that calls to mind the 1990s ape-man narratives I investigated before, most notably the TV series in which Tarzan came to be cast in terms of acultural expertise—in line with modernity without ever having to don a suit and tie. The global system does, after all, encourage fantasies of individual specificity and personal responsibility, as long as cooperation and compatibility are granted—"a little subversion is good for the soul." Likewise, the comic-book hunter is cast as an outsider within the system: a hired hand, a mercenary, employed temporarily to sort out other people's dirty business—another expert, if a markedly unintellectual one.

Congorilla, this hodgepodge of pop cultural clichés in often unintentionally comic combination, gives scope to all kinds of standard imageries of white masculinity. Interlacing the ape-man and the white hunter figure with the imagery of the Wild West hero, the comic writers replace the messy issue of cultural contact with a neat scenario of "natural" conflict. But enacting this "natural" contact scenario within the city and within a political system of control and subjugation, the writers end up just like Peter Beard, struggling with the insight that nature is not as natural as it used to be and that not even white men are totally in control of their lives any longer. The same predicament inflects Stephen Hopkins's film *The Ghost and the Darkness* (1996),[53] another wholehearted 1990s revival of the white hunter figure under the sign of modernity and expertise, which moreover manages to interlink the representation of colonialism with the rhetoric of globalization.

Much more aware than the comic of the problematical implications a modernized white hunter figure invariably calls up, the film once more opts for colonial nostalgia to bypass some tricky aspects of the theme of white male self-assertion. *The Ghost and the Darkness* is based on the autobiography of John Henry Patterson, a British army major and engineer in charge of a bridge-building project in British East Africa in 1889. From the very beginning of the film this project is subjected to different interpretations: For one, Beaumont (Tom Wilkinson), Patterson's self-centered and mean superior, explains it in terms of the "glorious purpose of saving Africa from the Africans," thus neatly subsuming the bridge building to the colonialist enterprise. Patterson (Val Kilmer) himself, on the other hand, seems to have a much more idealistic—and less dated—aim in mind: "What better job in all the world than build a bridge? Bring land over water. Bring worlds together." Although this is, at a closer look, just another way of describing the colonialist endeavor, Patterson's rationalization will come to figure as a counterpoint to Beaumont's and demarcate the logic the film will stick to eventually. But before it comes to that, the construction project will drop out of sight completely, and another, more pressing, concern will take its place. Two lions start to stalk the railway camp, killing off worker after worker, while Patterson, who easily shot another lion when first coming to Africa (at the same time introducing his standard line—"I'll sort it out"), cannot gain control of them.

With all its emphasis on historical credibility and overall plausibility, the film never even tries to offer a rational explanation for the lions' strange behavior—hunting in a pair, attacking in plain daylight, concentrating on human prey. "These lions are no lions," Patterson ventures at some point, leaving open what precisely he believes the animals to be instead. For this is what they truly are—"different." Consequently all the attempts at explaining their behavior dwell upon an "African" system of signification, as summarized by the railway camp's African majordomo Samuel (John Kani), who also functions as the film's offscreen narrator:

The men called them the Ghost and the Darkness. There were two of them. And that had never happened before. Because maneaters are always alone. They owned the night. But they also attacked in daylight. Alone or together. Some thought they were not lions at all, but the spirits of dead medicine men come back to spread madness. For others they were the devil sent to stop the white men from owning the world.

I believe this: that they were evil. And what better ground for evil to walk than Tsavo? Because this is what the word Tsavo means: a place of slaughter.

No single one of these explanations is ever openly endorsed by the film, but none is disparaged either. And while the varying "belief systems" called upon mix together mysticism, colonial critique, and tidbits of horror fiction, they add up to convey the impression of an extraordinary, unnatural threat emanating from the lions, which once more calls for spectacular action, not reflection—thus reverberating the tautological logic of "a man's gotta do what a man's gotta do" that also organized *Congorilla*.

When Patterson first arrived in Africa, however, it seemed as if he was bound to fight a battle on an altogether different field. On a first tour through the camp he compliments Samuel, who is soon to become his friend, on its orderliness—"everything seems to be under control"—only to learn about the truth beneath the calm surface: "If it is, it's a miracle. The truth is the workers don't like each other at all. Obviously the Africans hate the Indians, but the Indians also hate other Indians. The Hindus believe cows are sacred, while the Muslims eat cows." Well versed in the colonial enterprise, Patterson does not seem too troubled, referring to his experiences with a similar project in India: "I've worked with both Hindus and Muslims. Maybe I can help." Indeed, he could face worse problems than the workers' conflicts among themselves. And, of course, eventually he will.

While the African Samuel is just too good to be true, a perfect gentleman and good-natured buddy, his tribal scars and native gear notwithstanding, the camp's Indian foreman, Abdullah (Om Puri), is another story altogether. The moment the lion problem arises, he starts making trouble. And where Patterson endorses the logic of the essential, primeval conflict, Abdullah racializes. "I'll sort this out," Patterson assures at an early point. "I will kill the lion and I will built the bridge." "Of course you will," Abdullah replies meekly, only to add under his breath: "You're white. You can do anything," when Patterson turns away. Patterson overhears and is furious: "It would be a mistake not to work together on this thing, Abdullah." In Patterson's world, which is a world of cooperation and compatibility, whiteness is just no issue. We will see that he is mistaken, but not because whiteness—or race at that—should prove to be relevant by the film's logic but because he forgot about the third *c* completing the agenda of global interaction: control.

Abdullah may subside after this first clash, but as the conflict with the lions reaches its climax he abandons the course of "working together" once more, openly confronting Patterson in what threatens to turn into an insurrection. But if this is the moment where Patterson clearly does lose control, the camp's order is never seriously endangered, because it is also the moment when the film's true hero takes over. Abdullah gains the upper hand only to find himself at gunpoint: Charles Remington, the man of whom "every man who's ever hunted has heard," has made his entrance. And Michael Douglas, who plays Charles Remington *and* happens to be the film's coproducer, has made sure that it is an impressive one.

Patterson, for one, is obviously fascinated, quickly relating to the older man in a pattern familiar from many other father-and-son-like relationships in Hollywood film. And Remington teaches him so much more than only hunting tricks. In the second half of the film, Patterson learns a lesson, which the film itself propagates on another scale: how to translate the political into the mythical, commemorate it nostalgically, and weld a global enterprise on the side.

If Remington is the great white hunter par excellence, he is also very much a 1990s Hollywood hero, which means that the joy of killing wild game that Hemingway thrived on is not for him. Patterson, all the sensitive soul mate, recognizes this instinctively: "You don't like killing," he ascertains at the first occasion they have to really talk. Dr. Hawthorne, the camp's cynical doctor, always late at getting what is going on, chimes in: "Then why do it?" "Because I got the gift," answers Remington to no one in particular, getting up and joining the Masai hunters he brought along in their tribal dance—in a scene that would perhaps be a little less embarrassing if it didn't call up Michael Douglas's earlier campfire hopping in *The Jewel of the Nile* (1986), where the act was clearly meant to prepare not for killing but for sex. While Remington is seen with the warriors, doing all the appropriate things such as drinking blood and chanting chants, Samuel relates his story to Patterson:

Samuel: "Two great tribes of his country fought a terrible civil war for many years."
Patterson: "His side lost."
Samuel: "Everything. Land and family. Very young ones and the very old ones. All lost. He buried his family and left his country forever. Now he hunts all over the world. But he always returns here. He says Africa is the last good place."

This depoliticized understanding of the Civil War calls to mind the "unhistoricized" and decontextualized setting of popular frontier narratives and westerns in the late nineteenth century in the United States, which equally referred to concrete national history only in personalizing and mythicizing asides, as Lee Mitchell has shown with reference to Albert Bierstadt and Zane Grey.[54] Moreover, Samuel's tale of Remington's plight resonates the curious double function of frontier fiction, as not only the political causes of the Civil War but also the political conditions of the frontier are obliterated in the course of their mythification. Transposed into Africa, the Civil War veteran discovers a new and ultimate frontier, so much better than the American one because it is even less entrenched with a cumbersome social reality. And cultural conflicts drop completely out of sight, as the film mythicizes the monumental hunt rather than relating the building of a railroad to conquer the land—a theme that would have been so much more appropriate, if somewhat less glorious, for a narrative that analogizes American and colonial African history.

In line with the tribalization of history, the techniques and technologies of conquest are naturalized, cultural achievements and skills turning into inexplicable "gifts." Remington, the great white hunter, has the gift for killing and—by implication—the duty to act it out, just as his family had the gift for building firearms and Patterson has the gift for building bridges. In turn, almost unnoticeably, the dirty business of colonialism turns into the noble business of fighting evil and "bringing people together"—creating cultural contact and global harmony. Beaumont's powerful position at the heart of this project, as Patterson's superior, is never dismantled—it just drops out of sight. As Remington appears, Beaumont disappears and with him his racist scheme of "saving Africa from the Africans," while Patterson's harmonic image of the bridge as cultural link takes center stage. *The Ghost and the Darkness* thus manages to map out an economic venture in the spirit of colonialism without ever acknowledging this continuity, which is obfuscated by the display of the main characters' goodwill, practicality, and modernity.

The film ends upon a black-and-white still of the finished bridge with a train crossing, its sepia tones signifying the authenticity and historicity of an old photograph, and evoking nostalgic remembrance—Patterson's perspective and the ideal viewing position. "You know, I just keep wondering if we're gonna remember all this," muses Remington in the last conversation he will ever have with Patterson. "I love Africa. I could never forget her," Patterson replies. The film makes sure that the memories are nice ones.

3.6 Dream On! Irvine Welsh's *Marabou Stork Nightmares*

Giving scope to daydreams, fantasies, projections, and desires, the icon of the white hunter characterizes exemplarily the workings of nostalgia, a representational mode that glosses over the awkward evidence of an ambivalent, contradictory past with the aesthetics and ideologies of the present. Thus *The Ghost and the Darkness* dismisses the embarrassing truth that the "good" rugged individualist was an intricate part of the "bad" colonialist project by eventually blotting out colonialism altogether, replacing the past rhetoric of takeover ("saving Africa from the Africans") with the present rhetoric of global culture (cooperation, communication, bridge building) and thus tingeing both past and present in the sepia tones of universal goodwill and understanding—a technique that adds another twist to Peter Beard's aesthetics of conservation: where Beard nostalgically chose a good past over a bad present, Hopkins's film effaces a bad past in the very process of nostalgic revision, totalizing the African daydream at the cost of African (and American) history, while simultaneously suggesting an authentic and accurate representation of the past.

This interfusion of fact and fantasy under the insignia of historical fiction is, of course, far from uncommon in contemporary filmic, literary, and other narratives. And as I have mentioned before, this technique is in turn intricately interlaced with the logic of the daydream, which reconciles "a bit of the wish . . . with a bit of reality thanks to a bit of magic," thus establishing the "divided regime" of the "conscious phantasy," as Christian Metz has pointed out.[55] This "conscious phantasy" merges the most personal with the most mundane; private life and intimate feeling on the one hand with popular imageries and template scenarios on the other. Either way, the daydream allows one to face the most dangerous and extreme circumstances and still to maintain absolute control.

This logic motivates the denouement of Hemingway's "Macomber," where the protagonist's "coming of age" is enacted as a highly private process that cannot and must not be communicated or "mouthed up" as the white hunter Wilson puts it, an exhilarating experience of absolute self-feeling and absolute control, culminating in the utter internalization and withdrawal of dying. The pleasurable dimension of the daydream consists in precisely its precarious poise between self-awareness and exterior impulses, the fact that reality is not suspended altogether but subtly edited in line with the desire for control and concentration.

If the logic of daydreaming is but implicit in Hemingway's text, it organizes more recent enactments of the hunting theme much more openly, motivating the striking reorientation from elephant hunter to filmmaker in Eastwood's *White Hunter, Black Heart,* and thus indirectly and probably unwittingly staking out the real site for the contemporary enactment of daydreams, which is, after all, not East Africa but Hollywood, USA. And even if such daydreams are unmasked as hopelessly "tacky"— as in T. C. Boyle's "Big Game"—colonial nostalgia and white hunter fantasies are not liable to fade away but are most likely to continue smoothly integrating any critical intervention and easily appropriating the gestures of ironic distantiation. The figure of the white hunter might be dated, but it still works, as we have seen.

This insight forms the core of Irvine Welsh's recuperation of the white hunter myth in another narrative obviously intent on dismantling the image. At first sight Welsh, like Boyle before, seems to take recourse to irony to undermine the imagery of the white male on foreign ground in his 1995 reiteration of the theme, *Marabou Stork Nightmares*. No less self-important and pompous than Boyle's Bernard Puff, Welsh's white hunters in Africa, Roy Strang and Sandy Jamieson, come across as bad actors at best, uninspiredly reeling off the routines of wild game hunting. Their quest is for an almost supernatural beast of prey, the "scavenger-predator bird known as the Marabou Stork," an "evil and ugly creature" that habitually mangles and feasts on flamingos, and that the two Scottish hunters intend to "drive . . . from the African continent."[56] Yet their determination rings false from the very beginning, as time and again the hunting plot is ruptured by strange lapses, slips, and aberrations, and as another, more realistic plotline keeps filtering in, which will eventually expose this artificial Africa and these artificial adventurers as nothing but daydream material. The daydream will, moreover, quickly turn into a nightmare, running out of control and bringing about a deconstruction of the white hunter myth considerably more radical than all the other revisionary narratives we have looked at up to now. The stance of detached irony is quickly abandoned when a narrative of brutality, abuse, and grotesque melodrama sets in.

This African "daydream" is the product of a young man, Roy Strang, who was hospitalized after a suicide attempt that left him in a coma. His white hunter fantasies alternate with flashbacks to his childhood and youth and with brief impressions of the actual outside world, bits and pieces of overheard conversations of visitors and their attempts to break through to Roy, represented in typographically different passages. Roy is a highly unreliable I-narrator, ever attempting to keep information in and to avoid facing the facts. The hunt is his big alternative project, and yet it is nothing but a weak barrier against the inexorable return of the repressed. If this white hunter comes to identify with his prey, it is not to get the better of it eventually but to learn the ugly fact that they are one and the same: Roy Strang *is* the Marabou Stork, this creature "detested and despised by human beings" (*MSN* 55).

In line with the logic of the daydream it is not the artificiality and staginess of his Africa that proves problematic for Roy but the fact that the dreamscape's boundaries keep caving in: "It hasn't been so easy recently.

Characters and events have been intruding into my mind, psychic gate-crashers breaking in on my private party" (*MSN* 17). The solipsistic dreamer's early reassurance that it is irrelevant "whether it's produced by my senses or my memory or my imagination" (*MSN* 16) shatters as he loses control over all of these features, sense impressions, memory, and imagination interlacing to reveal what he does not want to see and to tear down what he established instead.

Both the biographical and the mythical strand of the narrative in *Marabou Stork Nightmares* are replete with subtexts always liable to gain the upper hand. And there is a lot to repress in Roy's case, as we gradually learn. This protagonist is Scottish, not American, and he is poor, an eternal underdog, which is why Africa, especially apartheid South Africa, opens up such exhilarating possibilities to him: "Edinburgh had the same politics as Johannesburg: it had the same politics as any city. Only we were on the other side" (*MSN* 80).

In line with the conventions of New British Cinema, Welsh depicts the dreary Edinburgh housing schemes of Roy's childhood and youth simultaneously in terms of authentic familiarity and exotic strangeness, depicting a background both mundane and grotesque, familiar and utterly strange. Growing up "in what was not so much a family as a genetic disaster" (*MSN* 19), Roy spends a miserable youth between scheme and street, football terrace and pub, finally finding a dull job as a computer programmer, significantly enough in a department called "Systems Control." Only in South Africa is this miserable existence briefly interrupted; Roy detects "a sort of paradise," where he develops an interest in ornithology and even starts to do well in school. For once, a system seems to work in favor of Roy and not against him:

Back in Edinburgh, we would be Kaffirs; condemned to live our lives in townships like Muirhouse or So-Wester-Hailes-To or Niddrie, self-contained camps with fuck all in them, miles fae the toon. Brought in tae dae the crap jobs that nae other cunt wanted tae dae, then hassled by the polis if we hung around at night in groups. (*MSN* 80)

If this passage collapses race and class into an inescapable worldwide system of subjugation and control, the categories themselves soon prove to be arbitrary. While race does not figure prominently as a category of differentiation at all in the novel, class and regional difference are foregrounded, yet function as symbolic systems rather than social categories. Thus the Scottish dialect signifies the intrusion of alien, repressed material into the sealed-off world of the dream. All of these demarcations of difference can be subsumed underneath the novel's central overarching category: masculinity. In *Marabou Stork Nightmares* the myth of male toughness and autonomy, epitomized in the white hunter, is cast as the most powerful and most fatal of all the mythical categories of differentiation at work in the late twentieth century.

The product of a rigid system of control and constraint, Roy comes to figure forth the stereotypical male per se, "a subjectivity that is organized within structures of control and authority,"[57] having thoroughly imbibed the logic of repression and disavowal. Indeed, this is the only reason he can talk about his actual African experiences in terms of paradisiacal pleasure in the first place: after all, Africa was also the place where Roy's misery reached a peak, as his uncle Gordon set out to regularly abuse him sexually. This experience forms the unacknowledged backdrop of Roy's memories and fantasies, and it will come to shape his further life, culminating, true to the perverse logic of systematic give-and-take haunting his life, in a gang rape he initiates and leads on. While he talks about his own abuse only in asides, playing it down against the "good time" he had—"[t]he funny thing is that it didn't really feel like abuse at the time, it felt mildly funny and amusing watching Gordon making a drooling tit of himself over me" (MSN 72)—the gang rape is described in all its gruesome details, although Roy, very much in keeping with the narrative perspective of another—filmic—manifesto of guilt-ridden masculinity, Fight Club (1999), has repressed his central role and relates everything from the perspective of a horrified bystander hardly taking part at all. Even if Roy and his friends are never convicted of this crime, it will destroy his life—he will never manage to deny these memories completely, as he has done with every other bad experience before.

Throughout his life Roy strives for control, to be on top of things, to gain respect and raise fear, only to discover in the end that the very categories of control, agency, and autonomy are untenable, chimeras for the likes of him who refuse to face the truth: that everybody is a victim—some know it, some don't. Seen that way, the novel could be read as a fatalistic bildungsroman in reverse, in the course of which Roy is made to become aware of his own victimhood, forced to take into account that the tough guy in Africa is a mere figment of his imagination and to face the fact that he is really nothing but a "vegetable" (MSN 31) in a hospital bed, unable to move, to talk, to communicate. And in line with this logic the gory denouement in the hospital, when Roy's rape victim, Kirsty Chambers, takes horrible revenge on the inert body in the bed, is not to be read as a last turn of the tables but rather as final evidence that nobody is ever in control:

I understand her.

I understand her hurt, her pain, how it all just has to come out. It just goes round and round, the hurt. It takes an exceptionally strong person to just say: no

more. It takes a weak one to just keep it all to themselves, let it tear them apart
without hurting anyone else.
  I'm not an exceptionally strong person.
  Nor is Kirsty.
  We're just ordinary and this is shite.
  We both understand everything. (*MSN* 264)

Roy's death vehemently contests John Major's infamous claim, quoted as
an epigraph to the novel: "We should understand less and condemn
more." But of course, the logic of "understanding" that the novel endorses by letting us in on Roy's final revelation is a markedly private one,
by no means liable to present a point of departure for change or critique,
not even for communication—there is, after all, nobody to blame here, or
to talk to at that. The novel's "understanding" is thus no less solipsistic
than Hemingway's notion of "knowledge"—both experiences are entirely self-contained, and neither one aims at contact, exchange, or outside impact. No wonder both Hemingway's "knowledge" and Welsh's
"understanding" reach their peak with their protagonists' dying.
  The novel's obsessive quest to kill the Marabou Stork is accomplished
in the end, as Roy discovers himself to be the prey—or the victim. More
important, however, the novel's true monster—the white hunter himself—comes to be exterminated. By extension, *Marabou Stork Nightmares* relentlessly wipes out any trace of colonial nostalgia: where other
white hunter narratives turned to an idealized past to forget about the
ugly facts of the present, this novel collapses past and present into a
nightmarish continuity; here the days of colonialism do not lend themselves to nostalgic commemoration, because they have never ended.
  However, while totalizing the colonial condition and detecting it
everywhere, in South Africa just as in Scotland, Welsh also naturalizes it,
implementing a conceptual framework of drives and passions, destructive
impulses and instincts, that turns any kind of action into an emanation of
the unconscious. In line with this logic, the very differentiation between
"Western" sportsman and "African" hunter, which proved so central to
Hemingway's, Eastwood's, and Boyle's narratives, comes to be effaced:
For Welsh, sport is far from a superficial and alienated activity. On the
contrary, it demarcates modern life's unacknowledged raison d'être, a
colonizing force in its own right, as Roy's white hunter alter ego remarks
at one point: "Perhaps sport has colonised capitalism rather than the
other way around. . . . sport and the sporting instinct are sovereign and
. . . capitalism is just a branch of sport, a warped, inferior branch of sport,
sport with money . . . " (*MSN* 46). Much later in the novel this detached
observation will be dramatically concretized, when Roy remembers his
days of hooliganism in terms of sportsmanship and extreme sensual

elation: "I steamed in swinging, kicking and biting. This cunt I was hitting was hitting me back, but it was like I couldn't feel a thing and I knew that he could because his eyes were filling up with fear and it was the best feeling on earth" (*MSN* 134). The sportsman, the hunter, the killer, the rapist—driven creatures pursuing the entirely self-serving quest for control.

Briefly, however, there is a time in Roy's life when he abandons this quest and for once loosens up: After the rape, Roy leaves Edinburgh to settle down in Manchester, and here he discovers the rave scene and the drug ecstasy, experiencing a curious "time out," for eventually his guilt will catch up with him, and he will return to Edinburgh. His first ecstasy trip is exceptional in more than one sense:

It was an incredible experience, beyond anything I'd known. I could never dance, but all self-consciouness left me as the drug and music put me in touch with an undiscovered part of myself, one that I had always somehow suppressed. The muscles in my body seemed in harmony with each other. My body's internal rhythms were pounding. I could hear them for the first time: they were singing to me. They were singing: you're alright Roy Strang. You're alright, we're alright. People, strangers, were coming up to me and hugging me. Birds, nice-looking lassies n that. Guys n aw; some ay them cunts that looked wide and whom I would have just panelled in the past. I just wanted to hug them all, to shake them by the hand. Something special was happening and we were all in this together. (*MSN* 237)

Time and again Roy emphasizes the openness and intimacy of the Manchester rave crowd, the feeling of ease and security in an environment that seems truly to cancel out the rigidly stratified order of his life up to then. And yet, the passage relating his Manchester experience does end upon an all too familiar note: "I felt totally in control. I'd never felt so much in control" (*MSN* 239).

A strange and unacknowledged analogy emerges between the rave scene, with all its celebration of peace and understanding, and the hooligan episodes earlier on. As different as the circumstances and implications are, both scenes come across as highly exceptional, bracketed off from the ordinary world, retreats for some chosen few who are "different": "We were big news because we were different; stylish, into the violence just for itself, and in possession of decent IQs" (*MSN* 137), as Roy sums up the gang's effect, while his enthusiasm for the rave scene testifies to a similarly escapist elitism, drawing its self-esteem entirely from a sense of difference and distance from the rest of the world:

I saw them all in our offices, the poor sad fools, I saw them in their suburbs, their schemes, their dole queues and their careers, their bookies shops and their yacht clubs . . . it didn't matter a fuck. I saw their limitations, the sheer vacuity of what

they had on offer against this alternative. There would, I knew, be risks. Nothing
this good came without risks. I couldn't go back though. No way. There was
nothing to go back to. . . .
  . . . like now there's nothing to come up for. . . . (*MSN* 237)

"Coming up" refers to the brief moments of half-consciousness during
the coma, and inadvertently both hooliganism and rave call to mind the
comatose fantasies in turn, the football casual and the raver strangely
equivalent to the white hunter in the African dreamscape. By that token
Welsh's rave utopianism turns out to be just another daydream, pitted not
so much against reality but against other, less agreeable daydreams.
Above all these dreams, desires, and projections a depersonalized logic of
control rules uncontested, motivating political, economic, sexual, and racial schemes of suppression and takeover that seem to run on their own,
to be countered with escapist fantasies at best and suicide at worst.

Withdrawing to ever more evanescent spheres—from African grassland
to the film screen, to the simulated African ranch in the United States, and
to fantastic mindscapes—the white hunter seems to have become an endangered species indeed these days. Yet to foreground fictionality and
fantasy need not mean to accept resignation and defeat, as we have seen,
as more often than not new realms of meaning production are established
in the course of such relocations, which are hardly less pervasive than the
old ones used to be, if organized along different lines and accounting for
different exigencies. As Hemingway's aesthetics of action moves into the
background, an aesthetics of acting, masquerade, and make-believe takes
over, which paradoxically enough does not do away with the white
hunter figure, this epitome of sincerity, but manages to consolidate and
stabilize the imagery of white male self-authentication on foreign ground
once more, and seemingly against all odds. This is what Renée Green's installation epitomized in its exposure and exhibition of the mechanisms of
colonial authentication and self-fashioning, mechanisms that seem to
work because of—rather than despite—their blatant theatricality.
  The efficacy of this turn to masquerade and make-believe comes to the
fore in the efforts to dismantle it in turn, which grapple with established
notions of agency and resistance without ultimately coming to terms with
them or mapping out any possible stance for alternative action. Thus
both T. C. Boyle and Irvine Welsh insist upon the imaginary, ludicrous,
and aberrational status of the white hunter figure, but both end upon
notes of fatalism: in Boyle's narrative the death of the white hunter proves
to be irrelevant, as the masquerade will go on with other actors, and in
Welsh's novel the myth of the white hunter is at best replaced by other

daydreams and fantasies, none of them liable to establish a ground for cultural reorientation. The scenario of the helpless victim in a chaotic dreamscape—so vehemently opposed to the earlier scenario of an autonomous hero in the wholesome wilderness—rules out any idea of individual resistance or self-help.

After all, like Boyle, Welsh insinuates that the notion of individual control is an oxymoron, as control and agency have long been absorbed by larger, impersonal forces—Boyle's "real estate empire" or the global politico-economic forces dimly and darkly evoked in *Marabou Stork Nightmares*. The insight that what is going on is not to be countered on the level of individual reflection or activity calls for concepts of cultural representation and global interaction that are located on another scale altogether. In other words, the problems of the white hunter may be faced in the white hunter narrative, but they are not to be solved here, as other narrative modes and new concepts of representation are required to truly come to grips with the problem—a different stage with another setting, to take recourse to Renée Green's imagery.

As the symbolic system of globalization gradually replaces the symbolic system of colonialism, new models of action and of agency come up that are less conscious, less strategic, and less static than the old ideals of heroic individualism. Seen that way, it does not come as a surprise that the rugged white individualists of yore are increasingly replaced with the smoother and smarter figures of today—experts, specialists, globetrotters. While these figures may very well go together with the white hunter model, as we have seen, they come in all kinds of shapes and guises these days. After all, they are not gender specific. They might be male, but they can just as well be female. In fact, we shall see that often enough women do better in these parts. Two other icons of Africanity will consequently prove to be much better equipped to face the exigencies of global interaction and cosmopolitan life: the colonial lady and her modern offspring, the global girl.

FOUR

Colonial Ladies, Global Girls

Since *Tarzan of the Apes* we know that women handling weapons are to be watched carefully. Even with the best of intentions, they tend to do more harm than good in their incapability to "understand the mechanism of the firearm" (*TA* 39). Thus, faced with an attacking lion, Jane Porter sees no way out but killing her servant Esmeralda and herself with the two bullets left in her revolver. Fortunately, even when pressing "the muzzle of the revolver against that devoted heart" of her servant, she miraculously manages to miss, so that Tarzan can step in and save the women's life by the power of his "steel forearms" (*TA* 150) alone—indeed "the last word in heroism" (*TA* 149), as a breathless bystander concludes.

If Jane Porter plain fails to accomplish what she set out to do, matters are more complicated with that other white lady on African ground, Margot Macomber. When she interferes with the manly business of the hunt, her bullet does hit home, with devastating effects: "Mrs. Macomber, in the car, had shot at the buffalo with the 6.5 Mannlicher as it seemed about to gore Macomber and had hit her husband about two inches up and a little to one side of the base of his skull" ("M" 36). Even if one ignores the highly ambivalent circumstances of the shot—the fact that the alleged accident conveniently rids Mrs. Macomber of a newly self-confident husband—it is impossible to miss the overall impression of failure and malfunction in this episode, an impression clearly associated with the woman's hysterical takeover of technology and plunge into action[1]—"Women *are* a nuisance on safari" ("M" 25).

In classical colonial fiction, women, or to be precise white women, are better left out of the picture, as H. Rider Haggard knew only too well. They just complicate the plot unduly, deflecting from the central conflict between man and nature, or civilization and wilderness. "They—the women I mean—are out of it—should be out of it. We must help them to stay in that beautiful world of their own, lest ours gets worse," Joseph

Conrad writes a little later in *Heart of Darkness,* this text revolving around the white woman left in the dark about what is really going on. But of course, like so many other tenets of colonial meaning making, this rule of exclusion no longer applies. In present-day action adventures and nostalgia films white women, and strong and active white women at that, abound. And as we have seen with regard to Irvine Welsh's revisionary white hunter narrative, the ongoing project of all-male adventure itself gains highly ambivalent connotations in the 1990s, evoking repression, disavowal, and fear.

One powerful subtext to all kinds of current narratives focusing on the white woman in Africa is, of course, Isak Dinesen's autobiographical re-appraisal of her African sojourn from 1914 to 1931: *Out of Africa* (1938). But then the point of reference itself is blurred, as it was Sydney Pollack's film version of Dinesen's novel, released in 1985, that triggered this hype about Dinesen, subtly infusing the 1930s narrative with preoc-cupations and fantasies of the 1980s.[2] At any rate, both Dinesen's text and Pollack's film insist that the white woman can survive on her own on African ground, and that she may very well handle firearms without doing harm to herself or other humans: in fact, Pollack's film seems to ad-vise white women on how to look good with a gun.

Dinesen is less obsessed with looks and relies much more on the clas-sical tropes of hunting than the later film. Yet by contrast to her contem-porary Hemingway, who evoked the fusion of man and world in terms of a powerful incorporation, Dinesen's hunt reaches out. In a much commented-on passage in *Out of Africa* she describes an outing with her friend and lover Denys Finch-Hatton, who shoots a lioness feeding on a dead giraffe. Returning to the scene later on, they come across a lion— the animal's mate—whose killing is then made out as an almost mythical event:

I rose up in the car, so strong was the impression that he made, and Denys at that said: "You shoot this time." I was never keen to shoot with his rifle, which was too long and heavy for me, and gave me a bad shock; still here the shot was a dec-laration of love, should the rifle not then be of the biggest caliber? As I shot it seemed to me that the lion jumped straight up in the air, and came down with his legs gathered under him. I stood, panting, in the grass, aglow with the plenipo-tence that a shot gives you, because you take effect at a distance.[3]

Commenting on this passage's sexualized subtext, Sidonie Smith comes to the conclusion that "in this imaginary Africa, Dinesen finds the op-portunity to . . . refigure herself against the conventional cultural assign-ments of gender, and to celebrate a unification that collapses the binary oppositions of male and female into silence. . . ."[4] But if such an aura of unification and ecstasy is definitely given in the episode, it is mitigated, and not accidentally, by the fact that explicitly the scene is one of hunting, not of love—Dinesen both evokes and evades the subtext of desire, carefully translating it into the imagery of female self-assertion and autonomy. After all, even if a big rifle may mean more than a big rifle here, the episode's most spectacular effect may very well be found in its most literal dimension: the point that for once a woman uses a gun and does not miss.[5]

By extension, the feeling of "plenipotence" Dinesen conjures up—the pleasure deriving from the fact that effect is taken "at a distance"—is significant in more than one respect. As we shall see, Dinesen time and again evokes the utopia of establishing contact and yet staying detached, or of being in charge yet not altogether in control, thus lending a remarkably different scope to the classical contact narrative and its obsession with control and distance likewise. Since narratives around single white women in Africa are invariably also narratives around female emancipation, the logic of empowerment "at a distance" is not to be conflated with the white hunter's daydream of control, although it clearly is not altogether unrelated to this fantasy either. The intersecting rhetorics of gender, race, and class, cultural, ethnic, and economic difference, run along twisted lines and establish by no means univocal categories of differentiation and stratification, not reproducing the dominant discourses of power linearly yet neither presenting a clear-cut alternative, as Sara Mills has shown with respect to nineteenth-century female travel writers:

The work of women travel writers cannot be fitted neatly within the Orientalist framework, and seems to constitute an alternative and undermining voice because of the conflicting discourses at work in their texts. They cannot be said to speak from outside colonial discourse, but their relation to the dominant discourse is problematic because of its conflict with the discourses of "femininity," which were operating on them in equal, and sometimes stronger, measure. Because of these discursive pressures, their work exhibits contradictory elements which may act as a critique of some of the components of other colonial writings.[6]

Yet if such "discursive pressures" brought about more or less verbalized breaks with the dominant logic at some times, often enough patriarchal and colonial oppression were not tackled alongside, but in mutual exclusion. After all, many white women's relative freedom and self-reliance in the colonies was based upon the colonial order, so that on a most obvious level to bond with the colonized would have meant to threaten a privileged and precarious position. By consequence, narratives around the white woman in Africa relentlessly trace her relations both to figures of power (usually white men) and to subaltern figures (often black women), relations that are heavily inflected with the impulse of desire. Given this scope, the unbroken interest in the figure of the colonial lady should not come as a surprise; indeed she has become as much of a popular icon as the white hunter, if with different implications.

On the other hand, there have been variations to the image of the white woman in Africa that seem hard to subsume underneath the category of the colonial lady, a category that does, after all, depend upon the historical dimension and a nostalgic or revisionist mode of narration. Another figure of white femininity on foreign ground has crystallized in the last decades, demarcating a pointedly modern girl, a cosmopolitan traveler at home all over the world, although clearly socialized in a Western framework in the first place—a figure I will call the global girl. Where the colonial lady is ideally blonde and very white—Meryl Streep in *Out of Africa,* Greta Scacchi in *White Mischief,* or Kristin Scott-Thomas in *The English Patient* come to mind—the global girl can very well be black or Asian, although usually she is not.

Both figures have appeared in all kinds of popular discourses of the last twenty years, but there is one powerful symbolic system interlinking the different areas of enactment: fashion. For that matter, the most impressive enactments of the colonial lady and the global girl arguably did not take place on the film screen but on the runway, in the pages of stylish fashion magazines and—not least—on the street. It is in this context that the power of style to register larger ideological shifts and transformations comes most spectacularly to the fore.[7] And as these figures' spectacular appearance often reveals more about them than the explicit messages they propound, it is worthwhile to pay close attention to what they wear and how they live.

4.1 Goddess in Khaki: Isak Dinesen's *Out of Africa*

Experiencing first contact with a white woman, Tarzan has no doubt whatsoever about the function of this strange creature: "He knew that she was created to be protected, and that he was created to protect her" (*TA* 164). This line of logic is exactly what Karen Blixen[8] comes to fear most in Africa. She can handle the plight of everyday life without the help of a husband (Bror Blixen hardly enters the picture), she can handle the dangers of African wildlife, and she can certainly handle the management of the coffee plantation and the supervision of its many workers—it is male protection that she is afraid of. When the First World War hits East Africa, pitting Kenya against the German territory in the South, her worst nightmares seem to come true:

. . . shortly afterwards there began to be talk of a Concentration Camp for the white women of the country; they were believed to be exposed to danger from the Natives. I was thoroughly frightened then, and thought: If I am to go into a ladies' Concentration Camp in this country for months,—and who knows how long the war is going to last?—I shall die. (*OA* 255)

In this version it is hard to miss the repressive nature of the gentleman's code of protection. Yet while the idea of a "ladies' Concentration Camp" insinuates a rigid hierarchy of gender, this is not to say that the overall situation for white women in the colonies comes across as more repressive than in Europe. The extraordinary circumstances in Africa may call for extreme measures of confinement and repression, but they just as well open up extreme possibilities and chances. After all, where else would a white woman come to head a military expedition at that time?

And this is what Karen Blixen ends up doing instead of going to the camp. Bror Blixen, who joined the army at the southern border, writes back for supplies and ammunition to be sent on four oxcarts with "a white man in charge of them" (*OA* 256). The man Karen Blixen selected is arrested as a German spy at the last moment, and suddenly a completely new and profoundly exhilarating possibility opens up: ". . . at that hour I saw in his arrestation, the finger of God, for now there was nobody but me to take the waggons through the country" (*OA* 256).

Of course the fact that such possibilities present themselves does not mean that the colonial system outrules itself, or that existing hierarchies are altogether undermined or even collapsed. Both options, concentration camp and expedition, come to pass, after all, as reactions to a native presence—so that the white woman's position may change from victim to agent precisely because the natives are always cast as dangerous and unreliable. As Anne McClintock has shown in her delineation of nineteenth-century England and South Africa, in the colonies established European categories of differentiation such as class and gender came to be interlaced with the category of race in a series of complicated and utterly uneven analogies and references.[9] In the course of this development, areas of indeterminacy disclosed themselves for white women and white working-class men at the expense of the colonized population. Emancipation, especially emancipation of white colonial women, often enough entailed racial subjugation, and time and again the logic of feminism ran counter to the logic of anti-imperialism.

Even if Isak Dinesen, reiterating a late stage of the colonialist project, showed herself deeply aware of many of the ideological incongruities at hand and thus took a stance so much more reflective than, say, the Victorian South African feminist Olive Schreiner, or her contemporaries Beryl

Markham and Joyce Cary, she could not possibly step completely outside of the complicated system determining her very situation, where her gains almost invariably turned out to be other people's losses. As Abdul Jan-Mohamed has shown without playing down Dinesen's indubitable anti-colonial attitude, *Out of Africa* stakes out a utopian space informed by the very logic of colonialism, albeit a colonialism markedly "edited and revised." Africa figures as a bracketed sphere for Dinesen where the lacks and shortcomings of twentieth-century Europe can be ignored, if not suspended altogether: "the point is that the models used to structure this secular utopia are not indigenous to Kenya but are brought from aristocratic Europe. [Dinesen's characters] attempt in vain to isolate and preserve some of the European social models while leaving behind those they consider odious. . . ."[10] Dinesen's very critique of colonialism thus can be seen to rest upon long-standing European categories of evaluation and segregation, most notably the category of class evoked time and again to pit Dinesen and her aristocratic friends firmly against the new white middle-class settlers. The fact that colonialism in Kenya—as opposed to West Africa—took the guise of a newly emergent "feudal culture," with the white settler in the role of the "Lord of the Manor and the agent of the colonial government,"[11] helped to further this system of thought: Dinesen's "timeless" African utopia is, in fact, quite dated.

The volatile and exceptional quality of this colonial system—a liminal space, far away and self-contained, figuring forth another order, itself long past—constitutes both its most trenchant deficit and its positive potential for Dinesen. Just as the terrifying prospect of a "ladies' Concentration Camp" can inadvertently flip over into the opportunity of a "Wartime Safari," so the repressive order of feudalism contains at its core the possibility of a preindustrial utopian enclave. Significantly enough Dinesen compares the bliss of being in Africa to the logic of dreaming:

People who dream when they sleep at night know of a special kind of happiness which the world of the day holds not, a placid ecstasy, and ease of heart, that are like honey on the tongue. They also know that the real glory of dreams lies in their atmosphere of unlimited freedom. It is not the freedom of the dictator, who enforces his own will on the world, but the freedom of the artist, who has no will, who is free of will. The pleasure of the true dreamer does not lie in the substance of the dream, but in this: that there things happen without any interference from his side, and altogether outside his control. . . . All the time the feeling of immense freedom is surrounding him and running from him like air and light, and unearthly bliss. He is a privileged person, the one who has got nothing to do, but for whose enrichment and pleasure all things are brought together; the Kings of Tarshish shall bring gifts. He takes part in a great battle or ball, and wonders the while that he should be, in the midst of those events, so far privileged as to be lying down. (*OA* 83–84)

Where white hunter narratives from Hemingway onward chose time and again the daydream as their model of thought, Dinesen embraces the dream itself and thus turns away from the idea of absolute control over one's fantasies—the "freedom of the dictator"—to give scope to a pleasurable sense of losing control, if at no risk at all. The abandonment envisioned here is not frightening, because it takes place within a framework that is absolutely reliable—the dream will never turn into a nightmare, as the dreamer indirectly and unwittingly does control its proceedings, not by force of her will but by force of her desire.

This is precisely the logic ruling the "War-time Safari," which in many respects forms a *mise en abyme* within the *mise en abyme* of the colonial order. Both situations are bracketed off from a larger context whose structure they reflect, exemplify, and render perfect.[12] While being in charge officially, Dinesen clearly casts herself as part of a team, working together with her African companions. When she describes her privileged position in the group—"[t]hey carried bath water for me on their heads a long way across the plain, and when we outspanned at noon, they constructed a canopy against the sun, made out of spears and blankets, for me to rest under" (*OA* 260)—it is not to underline her power but to emphasize further an atmosphere of dreamlike control without force. Her exceptional position is miraculous, magical, and, most important, not so much assumed as assigned: "Under the circumstances I was to the expedition, I believe, a kind of Guardian Angel, or mascot" (*OA* 260). The effect of this experience of being in control without having to act out control calls to mind the feeling of "plenipotence" evoked before. In retrospect, Dinesen envisions the expedition in terms of inebriation—a pleasant suspension of control: "The air of the African highlands went to my head like wine, I was all the time slightly drunk with it, and the joy of these months was indescribable. I had been out on a shooting Safari before, but I had not till now been out alone with Africans" (*OA* 257).

Like Dinesen's ideal African system, the "War-time Safari" recurs to older models of social order; no wonder "[t]hose who had been with me came to look upon themselves as a Safari-aristocracy." But like the larger *mise en abyme* of "African feudalism," the safari is a highly precarious undertaking, as pleasurable as a dream but also as fleeting: "After three months I was suddenly ordered home. As things began to be systematically organized and regular troops came out from Europe, my expedition, I believe, was found to be somewhat irregular. We went back, passing our old camping-places with heavy hearts" (*OA* 261).

Dinesen's Africa is carefully bracketed off from Europe, even if she draws upon long-standing European cultural categories to map it out. Unlike Haggard, whose sealed-off Kukuanaland evokes a "mock-modernity" in the midst of African primitivity, Dinesen objects to the very project of putting "the Natives into European clothes, which, I thought, did them no good from any point of view" (OA 28). No wonder Peter Beard, this other enthusiast for self-contained and ahistorical "noble savages" all over the world, came to celebrate Dinesen's work and seek her friendship. Yet Dinesen's concept of difference is more complicated than Beard's, who produced the bulk of his work from the 1970s onward, as for her the very effort of coming to terms with the African conditions and the natives, especially the native women, figures forth a need to come to terms with her own situation, her own difference. After all, from the vantage point of the European system, Blixen's existence as white woman farmer in Africa is hardly less exotic than the lives of native Africans.

This twofold approach, stranded between exoticization and identification, is epitomized in Dinesen's description of a group of Somali women on her farm, whose position of utter dependence proves to be so much more powerful at second glance. The women, who "cannot own themselves but must needs belong to some male, to a father, a brother or a husband . . . " (OA 175), turn out to be "ferocious young she-wolves in sheep's clothing" (OA 174), secretly in charge after all—"conquering the conqueror, and extortionating the extortioner" (OA 176). It is on these grounds that mythification sets in. Dinesen envisions a Somali matriarch "enthroned as a massive dark symbol of that mighty female deity who had existed in old ages" and conjures up "the idea of a Millennium when women were to reign supreme in the world" (OA 175).

And yet, she ends her reflections on an altogether different note, abandoning her attempts at bonding and adopting a stance of general observation and comparison:

. . . they so strongly reminded me of the ladies of a former generation in my own country, that in my mind I saw them in bustles and long narrow trains. Not otherwise did the Scandinavian women of the day of my Mothers, and Grandmothers,—the civilized slaves of good-natured barbarians—do the honours at those tremendous sacred masculine festivals: the pheasant-shoots and great battues of the autumn season. (OA 177)[13]

The strange back-and-forth of these reflections epitomizes Dinesen's unease with the very notions of secrecy and subversion. Where this other modernist narrator of Africa, Joseph Conrad, time and again envisions Africa as Europe's inverted image, subverting the established order via its distorted repetition, Dinesen touts exceptionalism. She abandons her attempts at identification not because the Somali women are too different but because they are all too familiar, and thus not liable to present an alternative to the dreaded European system of gender hierarchies, economic constraints, and cultural corruption.

By this token, it is not subversion from within the system but its momentary suspension that Dinesen comes to endorse. And while the Somali stood for the former model of thought, it is another white woman who will figure forth the latter—Karen Blixen's Swedish friend Ingrid Lindstrom. Having followed her husband to Kenya on what seemed to be but "a joyous adventure, a picnic," Ingrid, just like Karen, got hooked, putting in "all her strength to save the farm for her family [and] working like a slave." If this sounds like the epitome of self-sacrificing womanhood, the next sentence sets us straight: "In the course of that strife she fell deeply in love with the country . . . in such a great desperate passion that she would have sold both husband and children to keep it" (*OA* 201–202). Approaching the figure of this woman friend, Dinesen will come to stress the empowering implications of work over the enslaving implications of the established system. The established system of gender relations, that is, as Dinesen—again in marked contrast to Joseph Conrad—takes great pains not to apply the imagery of master and slave to the colonial order itself.

Later on, the imagery of slavery and bondage reappears when Dinesen relates that Ingrid's husband, "to make money to pay off their Njojo land, had taken a job with a big Sisal company at Tanganyika, . . . just as if Ingrid had been leasing him out in the quality of a slave, for the sake of the farm" (*OA* 355). Inadvertently, the white woman's position has radically shifted—no longer a "civilized slave of a good-natured barbarian," she is now installed in the master's position herself, taking charge of the matters at hand, without any need for camouflage or masquerade. Focusing on the notion of a clear-cut power relation, however, Dinesen elides the negative implications of the imagery of slavery, its implications of subjugation and brutality—Ingrid's "rule" is made out as the powerful aftereffect of a "love affair," her passion for the country. Once more, the "force of the dictator" is replaced with the "force of desire," an instinctive, immediate, dreamlike line of action.

In close analogy to the mythification of the Somali matriarch, Dinesen then mythicizes the white woman farmer in Africa, equally envisioning figures of distanced dignity and spiritual power: "In spite of our old khaki coats and trousers, we were in reality a pair of mythical women, shrouded respectively in white and black, a unity, the Genii of the farmer's life in Africa" (*OA* 357). In contrast to the Somali women, however, Ingrid Lindstrom and Karen Blixen gain this status not on the grounds of maneuvers and ploys against an overarching patriarchal order but by dint of their already exceptional and extraordinary situation— white women in the wilderness. Seen that way, the khaki clothes are in perfect accordance with the myth: these women have no need to hide behind "masses of stuff" (*OA* 172) like the Somali women or behind "bustles and long narrow trains" like their European ancestors. The extremely limited and highly precarious setting of the African farm allows for a momentary break with the masquerades of gender, paradoxically expressed by the takeover of male roles and garments: giving scope to the freedom of desire, the goddess in khaki.

4.2 Dress to Excess: The Colonial Lady and Pollack's *Out of Africa*

We sat by the fireplace in the huge living room and Jason slipped the *Out of Africa* tape into the VCR.
"Oh please," I said. "Let's watch something else."
"I just want us to get ideas for sets and costumes, in case we end up getting the Smirnoff job."
"All right then." I sat next to him, pad and pen in hand.
I tried to watch the film with a professional eye, but by the time Meryl reads the poem on Finch-Hatton's grave in the Ngong hills, whispers *"He wasn't mine"* with a dead stare and walks away in the grass, Jason and I—the deserted souls—had used half a roll of loo paper to wipe away our tears.   —Francesca Marciano, *Rules of the Wild* (1998)

Isak Dinesen stylizes her African farm as a mythical place, far away from the conventions and constraints of modern-day Europe and Africa likewise, although drawing upon a panoply of selected traditions from both sides, mixing up feudal culture and primitivism into a strange concoction—another artificial idyll, not altogether Europe, not altogether Africa. The precarious poise of this exemplary and exceptional site is further accentuated by Dinesen's narrative perspective—looking back on a situation irretrievably lost, a bygone period of perfection and grandeur.

Given its autobiographical scope, Dinesen's text takes a peculiar stance, forgoing both the grand narrative of major historical events or large-scale developments *and* the small narrative of the personal and private laid bare—we learn little about Kenya's history and almost nothing about Dinesen's love life in *Out of Africa,* apart from allusions, hints, and asides. And even these may have been considerably "edited," as Judith Lee has pointed out with regard to the many discrepancies between Dinesen's letters from Africa to European friends and relatives and her later autobiography. While contending that the letters "accommodate different audiences and thus [are] in a sense no more 'true'" than the autobiography, Lee nevertheless finds a logic in Dinesen's omissions and rewritings, a logic especially pertinent in view of the author's love life, which takes center stage in many of her letters and in Sidney Pollack's film version of the book. Editing out the "emotional ups and downs of the private relationship" to Denys Finch-Hatton and portraying instead "a relationship . . . in which she and her mate are interdependent and enjoy an ideal reciprocity,"[14] Dinesen's technique of "taking effect from a distance" can be said to inflect the very setup of her narrative. In *Out of Africa*, she lends some kind of closure to the story of her life precisely by keeping it open and indeterminate, thus calling to mind Paul de Man's remarks about the autobiographical mode: "[t]he interest of autobiography . . . is not that it reveals reliable self-knowledge—it does not—but that it demonstrates in a striking way the impossibility of closure and of totalization (that is the impossibility of coming into being) of all textual systems made up of tropological substitutions."[15]

Dinesen's famous opening line—"I had a farm in Africa, at the foot of the Ngong Hills" (*OA* 3)—pins down this aura of a lack, demarcating a concrete space that is irretrievably lost but perfect for that very reason—translated into pure language and thus perfectly contained and preserved. Seen that way, the autobiographical mode, which "deprives and disfigures to the precise extent that it restores," as Paul de Man had it, collates with the nostalgia mode, this retrospection on a past made perfect by its very pastness. Significantly enough, Sidney Pollack's film version of *Out of Africa* capitalizes on Dinesen's opening line, turning it into the frame for the African events: "I had a farm in Africa," we hear Meryl Streep's Danish-accented voice-over at the film's outset and at its end, when it returns once more to the Danish setting of the beginning. While this technique reverberates with Dinesen's incessant attempts at bracketing, her strategy of the *mise en abyme,* it is hard to tell what precisely is bracketed out in Pollack's version, as the frame seems to envelop all there is. After all, the film's inner narrative does not set out in Africa but in Denmark, showing "Baroness Blixen" in elegant hunting gear and as a perfect shot, and thus prefiguring similar scenes later on in Africa. At second glance, the film thus performs the very totalization that Dinesen was so anxious to avoid—evoking sameness instead of difference, analogy rather than exceptionalism.

This is not to say, however, that difference is not celebrated in this film, only that it is located on an altogether different level—on the level of reception instead of diegesis. Made for a 1980s audience, the film tinges early-twentieth-century Africa and Europe likewise with nostalgic longing. While explicitly disclaiming colonialism, *Out of Africa* endows the colonialist framework both in Europe and in Africa with the glamour of an exotic order of the past, as Renato Rosaldo has pointed out when criticizing the spirit of "imperialist nostalgia" in 1980s cinema:

The white colonial societies portrayed in these films appear decorous and orderly, as if constructed in accord with the norms of classic ethnography. Hints of these societies' coming to collapse only appear at the margins where they create not moral indignation but an elegiac mode of perception. . . . Evidently, a mode of nostalgia makes racial domination seem innocent and pure.[16]

Where *Greystoke,* this other nostalgia film, pitted a decorously vicious colonialist England against a primeval and timeless Africa, and where *The Ghost and the Darkness* blotted out British rule to recast colonial Africa as an Americanized global venture, Pollack's *Out of Africa* stages Europe in Africa, focusing on colonialism at work. Yet in contrast to Dinesen, Pollack is not interested in the indeterminate sphere between official "grand" history and private "small" narratives; his *Out of Africa* is all about private matters and personal relations—pure melodrama. By the same token, history gains the status of a style, and again Fredric Jameson's definition of the nostalgia film comes to mind: like *Greystoke* and *The Ghost and the Darkness, Out of Africa* approaches "the 'past' through stylistic connotations, conveying 'pastness' by the glossy qualities of the image, and '1930s-ness' or '1950s-ness' by the attributes of fashion."[17] Within the nostalgia mode, spatial and temporal distance, historicisms and exoticisms, have exactly the same function, both of them providing the gloss that seals off and glamorizes the object at hand, without rendering it disturbingly foreign or strange.

Hence, to read Sidney Pollack's *Out of Africa* within the logic and rhetoric of colonialism would be to miss its point. This film is thoroughly entrenched in the zeitgeist of the 1980s. Laura Kipnis has rightfully argued that "Dinesen's writings (along with her heavily revised biography) are the upmarket raw materials [for Pollack's film] reworked and recoded into representations of the past that make sense only as an attitude or necessity of the present: the production of a first world discourse of postcolonialism."[18] While such a contextualization in terms of present-day discourses of globalization and postcolonial reformation definitely makes sense, it is just as important to locate the film within the context of current gender images. After all, *Out of Africa* clearly draws upon the filmic stereotype of the "independent heroine" implemented by Hollywood films and TV serials of the 1970s:

Such films centred around the stories of women who are independent of men, who are sexually free and who, to an extent, determine their own lives. Forming a recognisable sub-genre these films are also primarily concerned with detailing the problems faced by the independent woman in achieving her independence. . . . These fictions offer, that is, a new, or at least revised stereotype. . . . In responding to feminism, image-makers sought to present women as active and as powerful, mobilising already-existing types and conventions, images that were an established part of popular culture. . . .[19]

Meryl Streep's performance in *Out of Africa* as a tough but caring, cool but passionate woman on foreign ground testifies to this new repertory of female images in Hollywood cinema, which was by the 1980s firmly established. For that matter, I do not read the film, as various other critics do, in terms of a misogynist Hollywood code of representation, which "scapegoats the female protagonist as the carrier of colonialist ideology and makes her lover . . . the bearer of the liberal 'norms of the text.'"[20] Instead, I argue that Streep's Karen Blixen may very well be made out as more entangled in the social and cultural conventions of the day than her white hunter counterpart, but simultaneously her naiveté and commitment are contrasted favorably with his ironic detachment, which does border on cynicism, after all. Blixen is clearly the film's central character, destined to engender sympathetic identification.

What is even more important, however, is that while Robert Redford's Finch-Hatton may very well get all the good lines, it is Meryl Streep who gets all the good images. With this I do not mean to implement Laura Mulvey's well-known differentiation between the active male Hollywood hero and the spectacular heroine, at least not in its assumption of female marginalization:[21] Streep might stand for image rather than action in *Out of Africa*, but in a film that capitalizes on the spectacularity of style, image easily supersedes action. "[W]ithin melodrama, and within popular cinema more generally, meaning is generated through *mise en scène* (through costume, setting and so on)," writes Yvonne Tasker,[22] and in many respects Pollack's *Out of Africa* could be said to replace Dinesen's technique of *mise en abyme* with a very specific technique of *mise en scène*, embracing the mode of the spectacle.

Karen Blixen's very unfolding as a strong woman is cast as a spectacular process. And initially, it does seem as if spectacularity is associated with female inferiority: Making her first appearance in Africa, Blixen looks both transfixed and out of place, wearing an all-white frilly nightgown on a train ride through the country. This is how she meets Finch-Hatton, who watches amusedly as she tries to "shoo" some natives away from boxes containing her china, of all things. Their next encounter is no less embarrassing: Finch-Hatton comes across Blixen as she is stalked by a lion, gives instructions that show him to be completely in control, and once more turns the force of his irony against her: "Doesn't this outfit come with a gun?"

But Karen Blixen learns incredibly fast to don the right outfits with all the appropriate accessories. Style is, after all, her domain. Moreover, while Finch-Hatton's skepticism about Blixen's many possessions is never contradicted openly, the film comes to revel in their display: the camera dwelling at length on the beautiful furniture, the old books, the elegant finery Blixen brought to Africa. In the end even Finch-Hatton gets what is going on: "I was beginning to like your things," he remarks as Blixen is about to leave for Denmark again, her possessions packed away, the rooms empty. But then, by this time the things have long taken over the film's symbolic center, demarcating not only the colonial lady's domain but the white hunter's space just as well: or how else should we read a safari that includes elegant dinner parties à deux and romantic dances?

Of course this very correlation of exoticism and luxury goes back to Dinesen's text, where the imagery of civilization in the wilderness came to signify the logic of the *mise en abyme,* the wholesome enclave of nobility and aristocracy in Africa set against not only the wilderness around but most of all against the corruption and cultural leveling emanating from Europe. However, Dinesen clearly differentiated between a European and an African order of things, time and again invoking culture gaps brought about by the encounter of the "ancient" with the "modern." Pollack's film, conversely, makes no difference whatsoever between old-fashioned cars and horseback riding, between colorful native costumes and khaki outfits—it's all old, it's all exotic, and it all looks good. In that respect, the colonial lady seems to totalize the masquerades of her white male counterpart. Where the white hunter is propped up by an artificial environment, a stage set, the white lady comes to find expression in it. Renée Green's *Vistavisions* project, which managed so succinctly to dismantle the white hunter by laying bare the scenarios around the figure, would fail once applied to the colonial lady, who is pure style.

In a reflection upon the "colonial safari look" of the 1980s, Judith Williamson implicitly interlinked the logic of fashion with the logic of imperial nostalgia. She pointed out the "function of difference" within modern advertising, a logic of quotation that has "fashion photographers . . . re-placing models in the original locations of the styles they wear":

[Y]ou see glamorous, leggy women posing in denim shirts in gas stations, pouting women in boiler-suits and cloth caps perched on factory equipment . . . , or women in khaki draped across camels or Land Rovers in deserts—the colonial safari look. In these concoctions . . . , the borrowing of the exotic is very much in evidence. Yet the clothes manage to suggest both colonized and colonizer together with their mixture of sari-style wrap and military khaki—"safari dress," to quote the catalogue—blended with "punjabi trousers" and topped by a choice of army cap or turban. This proximity of army gear to the "exotic" is very revealing: the entire colonial relation can be expressed in one outfit. . . . The *meaning* of British colonization in India is eclipsed as the two sides of a real conflict are rolled into one and come to stand for an "otherness" and "exoticism" that have no content, merely a style.[23]

This highly artificial aesthetic pertains to the imagery of the imperial nostalgia film just as well. Here, too, style—the outfits and hairdos of the wilderness—functions as a central means of symbolic organization. The female characters' downdressing in khaki shirts and safari pants is clearly stylized as a means of true self-fashioning, of natural and highly erotic self-expression. Not accidentally, the public craze around *The English Patient* (1996),[24] this repercussion of the *Out of Africa* pattern ten years later, focused on the female protagonist's oscillation between the native and the colonial order, both systems made out to be utterly foreign and fascinatingly exotic. And not accidentally, it is Kristin Scott-Thomas's outfits that signify this oscillation, an oscillation between desert gear, native wraps, and elegant gowns that brings into relief the white woman's spectacular difference. No wonder one of the many Oscars for the film went to the costume designer Ann Roth.[25]

The same effect of spectacular difference is achieved in a key scene in *Out of Africa*, when the "War-time Safari," this episode of dreamlike control and exceptionality in Dinesen's text, gains an entirely different status: After witnessing Blixen's trials in the countryside, we finally see her on horseback riding into the army camp she was headed for all along. Rows of British and African soldiers line her way. Her hair is loose and wild, her clothes dirty; the camera tilts from her tired but happy face to the staring white and black men. This woman clearly sticks out, spectacularly different from Europeans and Africans, white and black likewise. Her husband's first remark, however, sets the record straight: "You wear your hair different." She laughs, we laugh, because the remark seems so inappropriate. And yet it is precisely to the point. Just like countless other postcolonial colonial ladies, Karen Blixen manages by the sheer force of her appearance to absorb all the contradictions, conflicts, and hierarchies of the colonial situation, to be neither colonizer nor colonized—or rather, both of them at once. At a time when fashion and society magazines from *Cosmopolitan* to *Harper's Bazaar* cast the career woman in terms of appropriately "practical" outfits and an intricate system of styles to be mastered, the independent white woman in the wilderness becomes just another challenge, met brilliantly by Streep and Milena Canonero, this film's costume designer.

Seen that way, it is not African culture that is fetishized in *Out of Africa*, as Ioan Davies argued,[26] but the white woman, whose performance in the setting of colonialism eventually manages to blur the very distinction between Africa and Europe, as the film meticulously reinstalls the regime of dress codes Dinesen defied so vehemently. In the course of this masquerade, Africa is not so much taken over as swiped away, buried under the mass of Blixen's possessions and outfits, the excessive display of things. "I'd like to run my own show some day the way you do," Blixen's young admirer, Felicity, says early in the film. And indeed, Karen

Blixen runs a perfect show, up to the end, when she elegantly kneels in front of the new governor, Sir Joseph Byrne (Leslie Phillips), to make a plea for "her" Gikuyu. As Sir Joseph hesitates, his wife (Annabel Maule) intervenes and promises to take care of the matter. But then she is a woman. She must have seen how beautifully Blixen knows to kneel.

4.3 Gender Blenders, or, the Bluest Eyes

Tanzania is celebrating the anniversary of Quat's arrival. Everyone is rehearsing for the gigantic tableau. Since Quat's coronation, no one can quite trust or accept another person's gender. The customs officials have learned to ask: are all airplane pilots airmale. They're always compulsively touching all those control knobs. . . . Queen Quat of Tanzania personally sat in the airplane tower, and taking control of our landing, talked the plane down. Is that a guy or a fucking dame, asked the pilot after he had received his click instructions.   —Walter Abish, *Alphabetical Africa* (1974)

Around the turn of the century in Europe, dressing in male attire was considered to "unsex" the female body, making it "rough, coarse, clumsy, masculine"[27]—attributes that were, not accidentally, time and again associated with working-class women and single women in the colonies likewise. The same notion of "unsexing" seems to be at heart of Dinesen's turn to a male set of clothes in order to do away with a female code of behavior, her paradoxical determination to end the masquerade of gender by playing it to the full. In our day, such practices have gained radically new connotations, as "androgynous" styles pervade the fashion magazines and runways and cross-dressing has seemingly turned from deviant behavior to a mainstream practice. Produced three years after *Tootsie*, Pollack's other film about "running one's own show" by means of all the right accessories, *Out of Africa,* depicts Karen Blixen's sojourn in Kenya largely in terms of donning the right clothes in order to fit in *and* stick out—accommodate to the local situation and yet not become a uniform part of it, being the same *and* different, or the same in a different way.

If the white woman is fetishized in the course of this reconceptualization, so is colonialism, which turns into a spectacle, a huge masquerade of outfits, styles, and gestures against the backdrop of an exotic environment. This logic comes to the fore most glaringly in a film that has often been praised for its ruthless break with the colonial nostalgia mode and its depiction of colonialism's ugly underside, figuring forth "a subjugated country hardly noticed by the perfumed women and cynical men" profiting from the subjugation.[28] Michael Radford's *White Mischief* (1987)[29] presents Kenya in 1940, a country in the ultimate stages of its colonial rule, as a last resort for European decadents who play their wicked games while Europe is torn asunder by the Second World War. Given the film's scope, however, the aura of apocalypse merges with an impression of timelessness: it is hard to imagine what should come after the current regime; the land seems thoroughly emptied of a culture of its own, nothing but the colonialist order coming into view. Seen that way, the film's German title, *Die letzten Tage von Kenia* (the last days of Kenya), seems so much more appropriate, as the end of colonialism is indeed envisioned as the end of the country itself.

A central scene of the film is set at a costume ball—the theme: crossdressing. It is here that the heroine, Diana Broughton (Greta Scacchi) finally gives over to the entreaties of her lover, Josslyn Hay (Charles Dance), while her aged husband (Joss Ackland) watches jealously, dressed in a woman's robe. Although Diana's marriage agreement with her husband included her right to leave whenever she meets someone she loves more, her decision to follow this through will prove fatal—her husband eventually killing both her lover and himself. Contracts and agreements like this, trying to regulate or replace passion, do not work, as we have already learned in Pollack's *Out of Africa*, when Karen Blixen proposed to a man in the form of a business agreement. "You don't think you're being too romantic?" was Bror Blixen's ironic comment then, and he should have known that women cannot possibly be too romantic in contemporary Hollywood cinema.

In fact, if the classical narrative around the colonial lady testified to the need or urge to leave the most personal aspects out of the picture—be it to write an alternative life story as in Dinesen, be it because "it would have been considered improper for a woman writer even to consider sexual matters"[30]—today this convention has flipped over into its opposite mode: the colonial nostalgia stories of our day are stories of love and desire, great feelings and uncontrolled passions. And it is the white woman, the colonial lady, who comes to bear the full weight of this emotional excess. All of these stories relate a woman's unconditional love pitted against a man's (initial) unwillingness to commit: Karen Blixen confronting the lone white hunter Finch-Hatton, Katharine Clifton (Kristin Scott-Thomas) in *The English Patient* winning over Laszlo de Almásy (Ralph Fiennes), who declares that what he hates most is "ownership, being owned," and Diana Broughton, who apparently transforms Josslyn Hay from notorious womanizer to dedicated lover.

These love stories are enacted in stark contrast to the films' conventional relationships—the women's marriages. As the regularized and ordinary relationships are swept away by so much more glamorous *amours foux*, the notion of Africa as a terminal space is foregrounded; indeed

"The Last Days of Africa" would be a perfect title for all of these films. Thus, a sense of imminent apocalypse informs the costume ball scene in *White Mischief,* a poignantly artificial setup around the classic tune of exoticization, "Begin the Beguine." Cross-dressing is not to obfuscate gender differences here but to highlight them. Greta Scacchi is dressed up in a low-cut tuxedo, her long hair elegantly pulled back, and Charles Dance wears a garment that looks at first sight less like a woman's dress than like a tunic or caftan, calling to mind this earlier epitome of "passionate eroticism"—"the spectacular success of an Italian-born actor, dressed in Arab robes, on the Hollywood screen": Rudolph Valentino. Indeed, the intricate concatenations of "gender- and wardrobe-switching" suffusing twentieth-century popular culture may to a great extent be deduced to this figure and the vogue of the Sheik films.[31]

Tightly conjoining the exotic and the erotic, Valentino's Sheik films spawned the formula of "erotic ethnicity," drawing upon Orientalist and American identity markers likewise and playing the gendered connotations of all symbolic systems involved to the full, as Miriam Hansen has argued: "As could be seen in the nativist-racist slurs [against Valentino], the opposition of male and female was overlaid with an equally rigid opposition of American and un-American, which in turn was coupled with binary terms such as natural versus artificial, authentic self versus mask. . . ."[32] To this day, colonial nostalgia fictions revolve around these binaries, alternately blurring and accentuating established differentiations, while rarely leaving the familiar scenarios. Most significantly, it is white men who come to figure forth racial difference in these films: once more, Denys Finch-Hatton's bonding with his "half-Masai" servant Kanuthia (Job Seda) clearly "Africanizes" the white hunter; Almásy, the "desert lover," is time and again stylized as more African than British; and Josslyn Hay dresses up as an Arab to seduce his white lady. No wonder Africans are markedly absent in these films—Kanuthia, for once, dies off without ever having spoken a word—their impersonation by white men renders them utterly superfluous. By the same token, the white woman's going native in colonial nostalgia films means falling in love with a white man.

The colonial lady is a melodramatic figure, firmly entrenched in an aesthetics of excessive display and grand gestures, a pathos that this other stock figure of white womanhood in Africa, the global girl, seems designed to disrupt. *The Sheltering Sky* (1990),[33] Bernardo Bertolucci's film following Paul Bowles's novel, veers between both stereotypes—colonial lady and global girl—as the female lead, Debra Winger, impersonates both the passionate and nonconformist woman of colonial nostalgia narratives and the boyish girl on her own in the wilderness, the heroine of global travel fantasies.

On first glance, the film seems to comply neatly with the pattern of colonial nostalgia: "Reduced to the plot essentials, *The Sheltering Sky* is a sort of essential update of Rudolph Valentino's old chestnut 'The Sheik,'" wrote Vincent Canby in his *New York Times* review of the film,[34] only to take the comparison right back with reference to Bertolucci's much more intricate aesthetics. But actually the comparison is very adequate, as Bertolucci too enacts a journey through North Africa in terms of a highly sexualized masquerade of gender and race, although in this case a woman's body becomes the screen for most of these projections.

The film's narrative sets in with the arrival of three Americans in Tangier in the 1940s. They step into view one after another, followed by an endless bustle of carriers piling up crates, boxes, bags, and trunks, a bulk of things that will then be lugged along through the country by a never ending series of other native servant figures. Although not implicated in a clear-cut colonialist scheme, the Americans profit from a seemingly absolutely stable hierarchy, defined by money: "C'est pas possible," protests a Moroccan ticket seller (Kamel Cherif) when they want to board a bus that is already full. "C'est possible.—C'est possible.—C'est possible," says Port Moresby (John Malkovich), the group's leader, all the while throwing money at the Moroccan until he, too, chimes in: "C'est possible.—Américain?"

The Americans seem not so much on a journey as on the run: "We're not tourists, we're travelers," declares Port right at the beginning, although this description fits mostly his own person—as his restless wandering seems to be exclusively driven by the desire to be on the move. His companions, though—his wife, Kit (Debra Winger), and their friend George Tunner (Campbell Scott)—are much more sedentary, seeking stability rather than the constant thrill of change. While Tunner leans toward Kit, Kit leans toward Port, who seems unwilling to commit, or incapable of committing, as much as she wants him to. "I wish I could be like you, but I can't," Kit tells Port and continues along familiar lines: "You're not afraid to be alone. You don't need anything. You don't need anyone. You could live without me." If this calls to mind Karen Blixen's endless complaints in *Out of Africa* ("I'm not allowed to need you. Or rely on you. Or expect anything from you. I'm free to leave. But I do need you."), *The Sheltering Sky* eventually deviates from this set pattern and steers a new course. Tunner is left behind, Port dies, and instead of ending at this tragic point the film strangely sets out to relate an altogether different story—Kit's story.

Where films from *Out of Africa* onward associated the white woman's presence in Africa with an excess of things, here the outset of the woman's story entails loss of luggage. When Port falls ill, Kit discards everything, leaving behind step by step all of their possessions. As she abandons their things, she gives up on established forms of traveling, going native and going all the way. Or so it seems.

Early in the film, Port visits a prostitute in the outskirts of Tangier. He keeps her from stealing his money and is beaten up by her companions in turn. It is hard to tell what thrills him more, making love or being beaten, both experiences demarcating his way of going native: approximating the utterly strange without establishing communication—the white hunter pattern. Kit, by contrast, will go native in a different way. Wandering off into the desert after her husband's death, she is picked up by a caravan of Tuaregs, whose leader, Belqassim (Eric Vu-An), eventually takes her along to his household, dressed up in the same clothes he wears—the voluminous bluish robes of Tuareg men, including a headdress that reveals only the eyes. Where Port sought self-authentication wherever he went, Kit seems to lose herself completely in this experience: at one point we see two giggling Tuareg boys watching her, as she imitates Belqassim's every movement, his mirror image. One of the little boys wears her sunglasses, the other her safari hat—and again the accessories seem to have strangely "made" the white woman. Without them, she is nothing.

Kit is clearly going crazy. But then she always was a little weird, a person hovering between established categories, her boyish haircut and slender figure just like her strange moods clearly setting her off from the film's other white women—Mrs. Lyle (Jill Bennett), an overpowering matron domineering both her effeminate son and the Africans, and an equally unattractive and controlled elderly US-government official (Carolyn de Fonseca) who makes a short appearance at the film's closure. Seen that way, Kit indeed seems to personify what Marjorie Garber, reflecting upon the logic of cross-dressing, called a "third term" that is "*not a term*. Much less is it a sex, certainly not an instantiated 'blurred' sex as signified by a term like 'androgyne' or 'hermaphrodite'. . . ." Intervening between the binary categories, this "third" disrupts their very setup, as it "reconfigures the relationships between the original pair, and puts into question identities previously conceived as stable, unchallengeable, grounded, and 'known.'"[35]

Garber reads *The Sheltering Sky* along these lines as an attempt at going native by way of cross-dressing, an endeavor that fails, and has to fail, as the self's desire to merge with the other is not to be fulfilled, but that nevertheless accomplishes "the fantasy of otherness as an achievable goal within the self," a reading that for Garber resonates in the film's context, Debra Winger's reputation as a "'fast-living, chain-smoking, harddrinking' woman"—"the ennui and rootlessness of the Hollywood star displacing and replacing the quests of European romantic dreamers and postwar American intellectuals."[36] The fact that Eric Vu-An, the actor playing Belqassim, is of French and Vietnamese parentage, a well-known ballet dancer in France with a boyish figure, seems to contribute further to this blurring of gender and race categories the film endorses. Although Belqassim's face is not seen for most of the film, his eyes convey a sense of nonthreatening openness, girlish fascination.

Yet although the movie indubitably achieves a certain suspension of differences—between American and African, between woman and man—it strikes me as so much more significant that ultimately the disruptive power of the "third" takes effect not because of Kit's desire or failure to go native (as in Bowles's existentialist novel) but because of her incapability to go all the way. In Bowles's novel, Kit is finally expelled from the Tuareg home by Belqassim's other wives. In Bertolucci's film, this expulsion takes the guise of a self-chosen retreat—it is almost as if Kit has discovered that she cannot possibly ever fit in. Although she comes to this conclusion only gradually, we have known it all along: After all, the elaborate headdress and the Tuareg garments may have hidden her female figure, but her race was always glaringly and unmistakingly present, as the blue robe only further accentuates Debra Winger's startlingly blue eyes. Alone in her room in Belqassim's household, we see her frantically writing in her diary and then tearing it up to decorate her room with slips of paper. One such scribble, echoing a jazz song, reads: "AM I blue, AM I BLUE?" And briefly before she confronts the Tuareg women, she is seen looking long and hard into her little mirror, covering her nose with her hand and concentrating on her eyes. If blue is the color of the gear of Tuareg men, it is also the sign of Kit's difference. She is not altogether like the other white women, but she is certainly not black either—truly in-between, if with less liberating implications than Garber's reading suggests.

Time and again, this film reduces its protagonists to facial features, most notably eyes. After all, it sets in with an extreme close-up of John Malkovich's eyes filmed upside down, a focal shot to be taken up again later on. And the transition from "his" to "her" story is visualized in terms of eyes closing and opening—the camera panning from Port's closed eyes as he is dying to Kit's opening eyes next to him. The Tuareg men, finally, seem to be only eyes, as the film's second half proceeds largely without language. The film's privileging of the extreme close-up corroborates an overall tendency at fragmentization and decontextualization—after all, such shots are most often not revealing but confusing, making sense only as the camera pulls back to reveal a context and to grant a sense of space. On top of that, the "eye shots" promise an intimacy that they can never bring about, offering the closest possible view and yet revealing absolutely nothing. Kit's blue eyes signify a difference that is both utterly arbitrary and absolutely insurmountable; they set her off from the others without providing any ground for constructive self-fashioning along the lines of masquerade or cross-dressing. The film ends upon Kit entering the bar in Tangier where she used to go with her husband, passing a row of mirrors. As the camera focuses on her mirrored face in profile, the film's narrator, Paul Bowles, is heard asking, "Are you lost?" The camera pans along the line of mirrors to his unmoving face as she answers, "Yes."[37]

Abandoning one's things is a precarious undertaking for a white woman in Africa, it seems. Chances are that she is going to lose her self along with her dresses and accessories. In a world in which self-fashioning is nothing but a masquerade, donning the wrong outfit can have a fatal effect indeed—pulling into view a state of being in which all established identity markers have lost their meaning, absolutely accidental, absolutely empty. In films from *Out of Africa* to *The English Patient* and *The Sheltering Sky* the rituals of self-fashioning in a terminal space and under markedly artificial conditions are always tinged in the sepia tones of nostalgia—spectacular and spectacularly dated. The white woman and her things remain precariously poised in the wilderness, as she derives her very effect from her position on the verge, her difference. Addressed under the conditions of melodrama, this constellation must needs appear fatal.

Yet the material of melodrama has always lent itself exemplarily well to rewritings under the mode of the burlesque. What appears tragic in the melodramatic mode comes across as hilarious if seen from this different vantage point: costume drama turns into a comedy of manners, as it were. Thus *Ishtar*, Elaine May's 1987 film, equally enacts North Africa as a stage for all kinds of masquerades of gender and race, pivoting around a woman who dresses as a man. Yet here the insight that there is nothing underneath the masks does not give vent to anxiety but to comic relief. As mentioned before, the film traces the plight of two American showmen, Lyle Rogers and Chuck Clarke, in North Africa. They come across Shirra Assel (Isabelle Adjani), the cross-dressed leader of a local resistance group that fights the totalitarian regime in a ficticious neighboring country, Ishtar, and set out supporting her out of some kind of romantic love interest. Chuck, however, is soon also enlisted by a local CIA agent, Jim Harrison (Charles Grodin), who convinces him in no time at all that Assel is about to unleash a conflict that would "destabilize the entire Middle East." Clearly at a loss about the significance of any of the events they witness, the Americans constantly rearrange their sympathies, oscillating between the parties involved in their clumsy efforts to come to grips on a personal level with the situation at hand.

Politics is a confusing matter in this film, and political conflicts are invariably waged as secret affairs, undercover agents clashing with underground organizations and conspirational groups, giving scope to Michael Rogin's claim that the spectacular and the clandestine are no longer at odds these days, that "[c]overt operations actually function as spectacle."[38] In the frantic attempts to personalize politics in *Ishtar,* political conflicts and political issues turn into a farce, drained of any larger significance and tinged with the glamour of mass spectacle instead.

At one point the Americans are seen at a bazaar in Marrakech, both of them aware about the other's affiliations but not admitting to it, so that their conversation takes the guise of obscure hints and allegations. They are followed by a panoply of secret agents and undercover activists, all of them behaving spectacularly unobtrusive and dressed markedly unremarkable. Thus two CIA agents, obviously American in their entire demeanor, although dressed up in Turkish caftans with fezzes, comment upon the layout: "The KGB is here. I recognized two agents." "The ones dressed as Texans?" "No, the ones dressed as Arabs. The ones dressed as Texans are Arab agents." The film promptly shows the Russians dressed up as Arabs, who are talking in Russian, the words "CIA" clearly understandable, as we see the "Turkish" Americans reflected in a mirror in the background. As the conversation goes on, the mirrors on the stalls around the agents illustrate their efforts to make out other visitors' possible affiliations. Eventually, however, the only people taken to be outsiders—"The ones in the Hawaiian shirts are tourists"—take over, threatening to abduct Rogers and Clarke and triggering a shoot-out in which the two of them manage to escape, dressed up as Arabs in long robes.

Yet where the men's masquerade remains clumsy to the end, the white woman once more is seen to run the best show in Africa. Although Shirra Assel is made out as a native of Ishtar, Isabelle Adjani's star personality, just like the fantasy status of the country, clearly demarcates this figure as "white," as is then further accentuated by her bonding with the Americans. Due to the very flatness of the narrative, this figure exemplifies the logic of the global girl—boyish and erotic, cool and controlled, tough and versatile, a professional everywhere at home in the world, who easily switches from military garb to Arab robes to the nice summer dress she wears at the end. "For God's sake forget my body. I am begging you to give me the chance to overthrow a tyrant," she hisses at Lyle Rogers when he, having just discovered that she is a girl, does not stop feeling her up. Her request to forget the body is more justified than it might seem at first glance: After all, whoever tries to look for some essential truth, some genuine incentive, behind the masks and outfits of this film—the body and the true self underneath—misses its point. There is nothing underneath, the spectacular surface just as all-pervading as is Shirra's line of performances.

"Let's work together as agents," suggests Marty Freed, the singers' agent (Jack Weston), to Jim Harrison, the CIA agent, at the end of the film. And indeed, show business and politics seem to be too tightly conjoined to tell the difference these days, both areas best handled by people who know to manipulate others into trusting—if not believing—their performance. Seen that way, Shirra Assel, the woman who poses as a man, and Isabelle Adjani, the European star posing as an African rebel, set the tone for up-to-date action: model figures.

4.4 Model Cases: Colonial Fashion, Global Chic

If the colonial lady is good at one thing it is at getting dressed. Khaki for the safari, off-white linen for the club dance, and elegant long skirts for in-between—Meryl Streep set the mode in 1985, and countless others followed suit. Entire fashion concepts from the retail chain Banana Republic to designer Ralph Lauren's advertising campaigns have been inspired by this pattern, and to this day outfits that used to be more appropriate for a day in the veldt than for an urban outing are a most common feature in the streets of New York and Berlin, Tokyo and Milan. Khaki shirts and baggy trousers have become an integral part of Western women's fashion. While the colonial-lady style seems to have altogether blended in, however, fashion designers and promoters are moving on to different novelty effects. And this is where the global girl comes in, this icon of mobility, at home and at ease all over the world, regardless of the most dangerous and disconcerting circumstances, precisely because she does not even try to fit in but stays on top of everything. After all, sticking out has always been so much more exciting for fashion purposes than blending in.

"Jerry Hall's swimwear may have raised a few eyebrows in Morocco. But no one's really sure," we read in an advertisement of 1989 underneath a photograph of the famous long-legged blonde towering over a group of crouching women in heavy dark veils, revealing only their eyes. Hall's posture calls to mind Botticelli's *Birth of Venus*, her bright red bikini, light green see-through veil, and many bracelets coming across both vaguely antique and vaguely oriental. The advertisement, however, does not mean to sell Jerry Hall's line of swimwear but the very concept of Western lifestyle on foreign ground. Or, to be more precise, the Western lifestyle *of* the foreign ground. The ad is for *Condé Nast Traveler,* a magazine promoted as "[t]he insider's guide to the outside world."

The copy goes on to explain that "[e]leven years ago, Jerry Hall and Mick Jagger took their first vacation as a couple in Morocco," at which occasion Hall introduced her collection "inspired by the glamour of old Hollywood." It was, little surprisingly, *Condé Nast Traveler* that "recorded the unveiling of Hall," in a "travel story with an unusual perspective." The ad's unusual perspective, however, derives exclusively from the contrast between local women and global star, between a hardly spectacular outfit and a context in which this outfit is thought to have some kind of provocative effect. A provocation that remains entirely vicarious, of course, as both symbolic systems involved—Islam and "old Hollywood"—appear tinged in nostalgia, the veiled women as dated as Hall's style. While the various Orientalisms in the picture out-exoticize each other, the global girl takes over—it is after all Jerry Hall, the famous model, we see, and she is the same wherever she appears, immediately recognizable, familiarly spectacular. Thus the global girl herself is now associated with the effect of novelty and spectacular difference, which used to pertain to the foreign ground. By extension, the travelers, the "insiders" *Condé Nast Traveler* caters to, are seen to thrive on *other* people's surprise and bewilderment—the position of the insider and the voyeur merging indissolubly in the days of globalization.

Unless, that is, you happen to be on the "local" side. The ad's entire setup clearly presumes a Western viewer, and a quite uniform audience in terms of religious and cultural backgrounds at that. In the changed fashion scene of the late 1990s and early 2000s, such preconceptions seem less adequate, just as the fetishization of the white woman is liable to raise more objections today than it did ten years ago. In a reflection on the increasing debates around such issues within the fashion scene, Amy Spindler characterized the problem as a problem of representation in every sense of the word:

For the last year designers have drawn overwhelmingly from African and Asian cultures on their runways. That in turn has presented a problem for the editors who eventually choose the clothes to be photographed. Either they can cast models to somehow indicate their understanding of the clothes—black models in Masai-inspired looks, for instance (no matter from what country the black models hail), or Asian models in kimonos or chinoiserie (no matter from what country the Asian models hail). Or they can ignore the collection's message at the risk of incongruities—or insensitivity—and show a white model in them instead.[39]

White goddess or black warrior princess—none of these alternatives seem too enticing, and their effects are strikingly similar eventually. The stylization of black women into savage desert creatures, as most famously performed by Peter Beard with his "discovery" Iman and topped off in the 1997 Ralph Lauren campaign featuring Naomi Campbell in full

Masai regalia, reverberates the move of the *Condé Nast Traveler* ad, as the utterly foreign merges indissolubly with the utterly familiar, the supermodel functioning as a template figure for spectacular difference. Iman, for one, made a career out of this appeal, appearing in films from *Out of Africa* to Nicolas Roeg's version of *Heart of Darkness* as the model-savage—silent, solemn, and sexy.

While such images are still in use, they are by no means univocally embraced any longer: as the "fashion system" goes global, fashion magazines and advertising agencies cannot but acknowledge the somewhat problematical implications of blatantly exoticizing representations. After all, "fashion images now go around the world. What made Mr. Gautier's Hasidic-inspired collection so controversial four years ago was that the culture that was pillaged was watching, and was offended. With satellites today, every culture is watching," Amy Spindler concluded.

As the idea of "pillaging" other cultures falls into disrepute and as "other cultures" increasingly take part in the fashion system, the representational mode of exotic distantiation loses its grip, and the term "hybridity," this big buzzword of the academic scene, increasingly crops up in the editorials of trendy fashion magazines and on-the-edge lifestyle features. The logic of contact, merging, and mixture rules the day, as even Iman found out, who promotes her new makeup line with reference to the "Tiger Woods generation," casting the golf star of Thai and Native American parentage—a "hybrid rose" as *Sports Illustrated* once called him—as the new model hero.[40] As film stars from Isabelle Adjani to Debra Winger go native and cross the gender line, and as "new" supermodels and public personae like Kiara Kabukuru and Vanessa Williams emphasize their "mixed heritage," fashion magazines too discover the fascination of the "third," to evoke Marjorie Garber's terms once more. Posited between male and female, between cultures, this "third" seems to open up an entire new prospect for fashion—not only a new aesthetic but moreover a new notion of fashion's function. Thus trends like the much criticized "third world aesthetics" and the "ugly chic" in the wake of 1980s British and Japanese fashion design reflect an emergent reconceptualization of fashion that turns from a mere embellishment or decoration into an index of culture:

Ugly style . . . reflects not only the style of a group of people, but their living conditions as well. Ugly fashion, this conglomeration of retro looks and rejected fabrics and colors, is the look seen on the streets of African nations. It is also the style worn by immigrants for whom money is scarce. It is a look that reflects straitened circumstances.[41]

However it is to be judged, the new aesthetics of the twenty-first century clearly testifies to a move from pleasurable distance to provocation and mixture, as fashion's cultural significance is increasingly foregrounded and fashion magazines are eager to redefine their role: "We always aim at disclosing a world, drawing links which document how much our fashion style depends upon a certain life feeling and vice versa. . . . COSMOPOLITAN typically sets out to look for connections, the roots of the trend, the associations to our everyday life," is how the editorial director of the German *Cosmopolitan*, Lisa Feldmann, pins down this new understanding of fashion.[42]

In line with this reconceptualization of fashion, German *Cosmopolitan* featured its section "Cosmos Mode" ("Fashion Cosmos"), in which such an intermixture of fashion and real life, of the familiar and the faraway, was enacted time and again.[43] One such series, titled "Cosmos Orient" (May 1997) and shot by fashion photographer Michel Haddi, is set in Yemen, depicting a white model in colonial-style blouses, shirts, and pants and, alternately, ethno-style dresses, tunics, scarves, and veils,[44] and adding arbitrarily selected passages of the novel *The English Patient* as captions to the images, cashing in on the film's success and testifying to the fact that it was received at least as much as a fashion system as *Out of Africa* over ten years before.

Although at first glance the feature seems to neatly replicate the standard repertory of depicting the Middle East and Northern Africa—Orientalism unleashed[45]—the photographs themselves disclose a focus that calls to mind *The Sheltering Sky* rather than *The English Patient*, the global girl rather than the colonial lady. For one, the model herself, with short dark hair and a boyish figure, does not fit the pattern of the white lady. And then the photographs seem to envision cultural contact rather than exotic difference, immersion rather than voyeuristic distance.

A central picture in the series shows the model on the arm of a Yemeni man: she is dressed in a suit looking vaguely military in cut and color; he wears the traditional garb of Arab men, a long robe. Set in a public space, a marketplace with cars in the background, the context is clearly demarcated as contemporary, modern—an impression further emphasized by the woman's strong position in the scenario, her white garment highlit, her posture proud and self-confident, especially given the vaguely menacing situation, as two other "oriental" men approach with raised knifes.

Figuring forth an interracial relationship and a break with established gender hierarchies, and drawing upon a logic of immersion and contact (the white woman as part of the "oriental" environment), the image seems to subvert the conventions of fashion photography in exotic spaces that Judith Williamson pointed out. But there is more to the image than this "narrative" lets on, as the indexical level of representations is intricately wound up with an iconic dimension of signification that raises altogether different associations. After all, the constellation in the image's center, the "mixed" couple, calls to mind the images of countless proud white men in military garb with exotic women at their side, safeguarding them against their own dangerous culture. The strength and independence of this white woman seems iconically linked to the familiar scenario of the colonial order, called up in the image's structure, dress code, and lighting. A photo-realist element of representation in turn mitigates the nostalgic aura of such colonial connotations, bringing the image up to date: on the extreme left margin we see a hand holding not a knife but a camera, thus epitomizing the enactedness of the scene, but at the same time communicating the impression of an actual, unstaged event—a glimpse at real life.

A variety of incompatible codes (photo-realism, authenticity, and everyday life, just like exotic difference and colonial nostalgia) and incongruent systems of signification (the strong white woman, the colonial hierarchy, the exotic-erotic *and* the Arab macho) interact in this image, cleverly canceling out each other's problematic or discordant connotations rather than foregrounding them. "We stood among them" ("Wir standen mittendrin") begins the line of *The English Patient* underneath the image. And the desire to be "among them" or "in the midst," which would be the literal translation of the German phrase, could indeed be called the most basic motive of a fashion aesthetics for the global girl, an aesthetics of the mix, which thrives on the excitement of immersion at a distance, contact via contrast.

4.5 Another Mimic of Uncanny Ability: The Gorilla Girl

"Can you teach me? Speak Gorilla?"   —Jane to Tarzan in *Tarzan* (Disney 1999)

Dressing up is vital for the global girl, but it is not necessarily about looking good. Both cross-dressing and going native are time and again envisioned in terms of practical requirements or specific circumstances—in *Ishtar* Isabelle Adjani dons military-style clothes because she plays a guerrilla fighter, not because khaki becomes her, although the latter aspect clearly informs the film on an extradiegetic level. The same dichotomy is even more evident in contemporary fashion photography, where toughness and no-nonsense practicality are stylish features and looking disheveled, or even looking ugly, can very well "mean" looking good. Suggesting ambivalence and hybridity, the global girl is time and again associated with the aura of qualified transgression—going native, but not going all the way.

In many respects the white woman's intrusion into the wilderness can be seen as a Tarzan story in reverse. The self-fashioning of Greystoke, who mimics a French scientist in the jungle to become a man, strangely reverberates in the self-fashioning of Kit Moresby, who mimics a Tuareg chief to become a (fake) native. The scenario of man aping man to distinguish himself from a bunch of gorillas resonates most strikingly, however, in another film about mimicry: Michael Apted's *Gorillas in the Mist* (1988),[46] which enacts a white woman in the jungle going—not native but gorilla, in a process of imitation and intimation that leaves not only the gorillas "quite confused as to [her] species." Where Greystoke learned to talk French and eat with knife and fork, primatologist Dian Fossey (Sigourney Weaver) is seen gradually losing her social skills, turning into what she once calls a "gorilla girl, . . . a real weirdo"—a hybrid, in other words. The gorillas, by the way, are of the same kind in both films— Apted employed the much praised ape impersonators of *Greystoke*.

Reduced to its plotline, *Gorillas in the Mist,* this "true-life story" around Fossey's biography, sounds even more fantastic than *Greystoke,* this fairy tale of jungle life. After all, Greystoke falls in love with a woman, and when he returns to the jungle there is no ape-lady waiting in the treetops for him. Fossey, by contrast, forgoes marriage not only in order to stay with "her gorillas" but also because there is one among them that is special to her—Digit, the ape she comes to hold hands with, whose photograph she is seen kissing shortly before she dies, and with whom she shall be united in death, sharing one grave like a married couple. If this scenario sounds grotesque, Apted manages to present it as altogether unspectacular—or should I say, natural? "[T]he most remarkable aspect of the film is the way in which it manages to make its psychosexual dynamics seem innocent," wrote Tania Modleski in her analysis of *Gorillas in the Mist.*[47]

The film might present a woman's love for an ape as a quite innocent thing, but that is not to say that it condones her decision to stay on in Africa against all odds. Gradually and almost imperceptibly, this global girl loses her most admirable quality—the flexibility, the ease with which she quickly makes room for herself in a foreign environment. When first arriving in Africa, Fossey is seen worrying about one of her bags, which contains "my hairdryer, my make-up, my underwear, and my brassieres," and which is about to be left behind. "If they don't go . . . , I don't go," she declares, as if talking about her family—not an altogether inappropriate analogy for the white woman's things in the wilderness, as we know by now.

The bag is taken along, and later on, when she is expelled from her research camp by Congolese guerrilla fighters, "hairdryer and nail polish" are the "necessities" she acquires first to reestablish herself—along with a gun. During her relationship with Bob Campbell (Bryan Brown) this mixture between toughness and chic is constantly foregrounded; in the love scenes Fossey appears impeccably groomed, with lipstick, painted toenails, and shaved legs, the perfect global girl. Yet the relationship is not going to last: Bob tells her about a new assignment in Borneo and asks her to come along, as she is trying out a piece of brightly colored material against her body at the local marketplace. She cannot bring herself to join him, and she will not buy the cloth. Once more, a global girl is about to lose her balance.

And once more, the lapse into the extreme is associated with a change of style. Appropriating the superstition the local Batwa have about her, Fossey dons a Halloween mask to frighten a little boy into revealing what he knows about a poacher organization going after the gorillas: "If they want a witch, I give them a witch." She does not know how right she will be. Fossey does here what male adventurers and explorers on African ground have allegedly been doing for centuries—tricking the natives into compliance by manipulating their symbolic system.[48] But she will fare much worse than her male colleagues. Female trick translators, it seems, easily get entangled in their own manipulations. What is more, Fossey's trick translation takes the guise of a masquerade, and we have seen before that wardrobe switchings have quite deepgoing effects for white women in Africa. The witch act in this film will eventually affect the "witch" as much as the "bewitched." And while Fossey believes herself in control of the images and projections around her to her very end, soon her manipulations and masquerades gain a momentum of their own—this woman does not run her own show for long.

She also clearly loses the aura of the detached scientist. If she ever had it. The film makes a great deal out of the fact that Fossey was not a trained primatologist when she first came to Africa, "'deprofessionalizing' Fossey, neglecting to mention her growth as a scientist who in the course of her research in the mountains of Rwanda earned a Ph.D. from Harvard,"[49] as Modleski pointed out. The enactment of the woman scientist in terms of intuition rather than analysis is, of course, nothing new, and especially women doing anthropological fieldwork and engaged in primatologist research have been traditionally associated with extrascientific qualities. In such circumstances "(white) woman" seems exemplarily equipped to "represent (species) man," as Donna Haraway has shown: "The body is nature to the mind of culture; in primate narratives, white women negotiate the chasm."[50] In her comments on the 1965 *National Geographic* documentary *Miss Goodall and the Wild Chimpanzees* about that other glamour girl of primatology, Jane Goodall, Haraway elaborated a set of implications for enacting the white woman scientist in Africa that strikes me as relevant for the fiction film *Gorillas in the Mist* just as well:

Goodall's coming formal scientific credentials are carefully framed in this film's narrative of good science. In the first scenes of the film, the viewer learned that Louis Leakey sent "Jane" to the field to explore the origins of man because she was a "girl with no special training, but a natural aptitude, . . . with no preconceived ideas." In the course of the film, Goodall "overlooks no detail" that might shed light on man's mystery and the chimpanzee's secret. She is less a twentieth-century scientist than a girl guide. The discoveries she makes . . . all were coded into the narrative of western origin stories. . . . These discoveries were not like engineering new macromolecules for biotechnology-based corporations or cracking the atom for nuclear energy and weapons; they were rather at the level of unlocking the secret of the "human nature" that brought these other ambiguous objects into the world.[51]

This image of the female scientist, emotionally rather than analytically in touch with the secret of nature, forms a marked contrast to the image of the expert as constructed in a novel like Michael Crichton's *Congo*. Both of the book's two expert figures, Peter Elliot, the biologist, and Karen Ross, the systems analyzer, approach the world from an angle that differs radically from the one taken by women scientists in popular "primate narratives."

Neither Elliot nor Ross are translator figures in the traditional sense, as we have seen—their attempts at communication with the creatures of the wild aim not at exchange but at control, since the notion of compatibility replaces the idea of communication as a two-sided dynamics. This substitution goes along with Michel de Certeau's definition of the modern expert as a very special kind of "interpreter and translator," monitoring cultural communication from a distance rather than taking part in it.

By contrast to the expert figures in Crichton's text, Apted's Fossey and *National Geographic*'s Goodall come across as intricately involved with the local conditions. While such unmediated contact ideally brings about unmediated insight and direct communication, at worst it ends up in a pervasive loss of control. And this is what *Gorillas in the Mist* traces in its second part. As distanced observation is replaced with the spirit of intimacy and immersion, the gorilla girl's desire for sameness cancels out the expert's investigation of difference.

When first coming to Africa, Fossey tries to compensate for her lack of experience in primate research by diligently adhering to George Schaller's *The Mountain Gorilla,* the seminal work of the field at the time. But as soon as she makes contact with the gorillas she stops imitating Schaller and starts imitating the apes instead. "I've got them accustomed to me by mimicking them, and they're fascinated by my facial grimaces and other actions that I wouldn't be caught dead doing in front of any one. I feel like a complete fool but this technique seems to be working," we hear Weaver's offscreen comment, citing a letter to Fossey's mentor Louis Leakey. On-screen we see precisely what the woman does not want us to see: her aping of the apes. Yet Fossey's reluctance to be seen imitating is soon enough overcome on a diegetic level, too. Shortly, she is doing her ape show in front of the man she will come to love, photographer Bob Campbell, only to totalize the act further after he is gone. Forgetting her social skills and hysterically overreacting to the people around her, Fossey withdraws more and more into the company of apes: only here, as an ape among apes, does she seem altogether herself.

If that development calls to mind Hugh Hudson's *Greystoke,* Apted's animal kingdom turns out far less isolated than Hudson's jungle. Time and again, Fossey's utopian enclave clashes violently with a dark African social reality of civil wars, poacher organizations, corruption, and poverty. Her efforts to protect herself, and the apes around her, from the big bad world are bound to fail eventually, and her resistance against the outside intruders soon takes the guise of monomania—"This is not your private kingdom," a young male American research student chides her after witnessing one of her masquerades of witchcraft vis-à-vis the Batwa, this time a fake lynching. The gorilla girl's self-fashioning might be a tempting move, and it certainly comes across as spectacular and thrilling in this film—but all its ecologically correct connotations notwithstanding, going gorilla clearly does not present a viable alternative to the logic of global expertise. Where Hugh Hudson's film maps out white male self-fashioning by way of mimicry and imitation, Apted's film leaves no doubt that white women in the wilderness should steer a different course. Imitating African witches and apes turns out to be a dangerous project here.

The autonomy of the gorilla girl seems to rest upon her distantiation, her in-between position at the film's outset, which demarcates the stance of the global girl—in the midst of, yet at a remove. In that respect, these figures call to mind Dinesen's African dreamscape, her logic of the *mise en abyme.* But where Dinesen envisions an exemplarily different "African" order of things, the global girl seems to run into trouble the moment she settles down. That may sound like a deficit, as time and again the global girl is seen to fail where her male equivalents—the white hunter, the adventurer, and the explorer—excel: going native is not her thing. And yet—approached from a slightly different angle, the white woman's precarious poise between self-realization and self-loss will turn out to be an asset. Every so often, the white hunter appears as a figure of the past. The global girl, by contrast, comes to demarcate the stance of the future, or rather, the cutting edge of present fantasies: the cosmopolitan existence.

4.6 Cosmopolitan Cool: Francesca Marciano's *Rules of the Wild*

Isak Dinesen cast the white woman in Africa as the epitome of exceptionality, spectacularly different from both the white men running the country and the African women around. It is on the grounds of this difference that white women gain their almost mythical power for Dinesen—goddesses in khaki.

By now, however, the figure of the white woman in Africa, and most notably the white lady in Kenya, has lost much of her provocative appeal, not only because Meryl Streep has wandered in and out of Africa in the meantime, but also because so many other documents have cropped up since then that record foreign and female experiences of Africa. Tourists, travelers, scientists, peace corps workers, and seekers of an alternative lifestyle have invaded the wilderness, more often than not taking great pains to make their experiences known to the world by way of travelogues and journals, essay collections and documentaries. Most of these writings are heavily inflected with autobiographical concerns, and in this respect too Dinesen's example looms large. Thus a book such as *I Dreamed of Africa* (1991), the best-selling autobiography of an Italian, Kuki Gallmann, about her days in Kenya from the 1960s onward, echoes Dinesen's writing not only in its very title and a highly poetic—if not always highly original—language but also in countless other features, from the cast of characters and relationships up to general reflections on the European presence in Africa.

Of course, this analogy does not imply a case of plagiarism or dishonesty but simply brings to the fore a powerful intertextual framework: a repertory of long-standing narrative conventions and of plot configurations and models of thought that organizes and motivates the representation of white women in the wilderness to the present day. The fact that the film version of Gallmann's book, starring Kim Basinger and directed by Hugh Hudson, was celebrated as one of "10 very fashionable films" in the magazine *Movieline* before it even opened,[52] and sticks close to the plotline of the colonial-lady narrative, proves that the style of the colonial lady is far from defunct within this repertory, even if the global girl tends to take over.

"At times the writing bears so much: emotions at a husband's grave, and a son's. But at other times, the writing leaves loose threads or raises unsettling questions. . . . At moments in this narration, aesthetic perceptions undercut emotional truth,"[53] writes Marianna Torgovnick about Gallmann's autobiography. Yet of course the very differentiation between "aesthetic perception" and "emotional truth," narrative pattern and authentic experience, is a doubtful one in the context of African representations—as the rhetoric of authenticity, depth, and unmediated contact has itself clearly become a convention, an aesthetic formula that used to convey "emotional truth" yet does wax thin these days. This is the problem not only with Gallmann's writing but with a lot of similar approaches to Africa, such as Peter Beard's photography or a film like *Gorillas in the Mist*—all of them pitting African unspoiled nature and innocent indigenous cultures against modernity and cultural contact, and mourning the demise of a perfection that is shown to be already irretrievably lost.

But Dinesen's legacy stands far from unchallenged today, as the work of another Italian living in Kenya exemplifies: Francesca Marciano's novel *Rules of the Wild* (1998) seems to be written in defiance of the convention of celebrating African authenticity. At one point in the novel, a journalist by the telling name of Hunter Reed vehemently confronts the beautiful Swedish author Iris Sorensen, who has spent most of her life with the Samburu tribe and made a living documenting their traditions and lifestyle:

"I can't bear another minute of these clichés. . . . It's time your beautiful Samburu peacocks leave their beads and spears behind, join the rest of the world and learn how to operate a computer if they don't want to be seriously taken advantage of! . . . Maybe it's time you . . . start reading the *Economist* instead, if you care to have a larger picture of the future in the third world. Which I am sure is the last thing you'd want to do. Much more fun running around wearing beads with good-looking warriors and cashing in on their wild looks. One thing's for sure: the minute they cut their hair and get a job, you are out of yours. So I'm not surprised you want them to stay where they are."[54]

If Iris indubitably propounds clichés, however, Hunter, this journalist turned cynic over the depressing experience of central African poverty, corruption, and warfare, is not really as groundbreakingly unconventional as might seem at first glance. In fact, he can be seen neatly replicating the symbolic repertory of the close look and unbiased confrontation, a repertory that has in the meantime spawned a "school" of African representation in its own right, as I will show in the next chapter.

But then, this novel seems to strongly discourage the quest for originality and newness in the first place. *Rules of the Wild* depicts an Africa that has been inscribed with so many stories that it is impossible to push through to some authentic level of experience, let alone "emotional truth." Marciano's protagonist, the Italian socialite Esmé, who left Italy for good to stay with her lover Adam in Kenya and falls in love with Hunter the cynic in turn, may love to analyze herself and others, but the results are momentary glimpses at best, liable to be blurred at the next rearrangement of the local scene, which is bound to happen shortly. In that respect, Esmé's Kenya calls to mind the decadent scenery of *White Mischief* rather than the grand feelings of *Out of Africa,* to which the novel alludes time and again. The imagery of *Rules of the Wild* draws heavily upon the symbolic systems of film and theater, as the situation in contemporary Nairobi is constantly compared to a huge play, a "crazy film without an ending, where new characters kept popping up nonstop just when you thought you'd reached the climax" (*RW* 256). And ironically enough it is Iris, this worshiper of authenticity and the simple life, who comes to represent this logic of the masquerade best, working relentlessly at fashioning a perfect image of the colonial lady for herself—only to be cruelly cut short by an utterly banal death in a car accident in Nairobi. Esmé objects when a screenwriter plans to turn Iris's biography into a script, only to be set straight by her clear-sighted friend Nicole:

"Iris is a Hollywood script. She worked *all her life* at it, it was such a perfectly rehearsed screenplay. Finally this successful writer comes along, happens to see a book of hers at the hotel shop, reads it and dreams of turning her into the Karen Blixen of the year two thousand, and *you don't want to help?* She's probably cursing you from Heaven, my dear." (*RW* 212)

Yet if Iris, veering between authenticity and masquerade, safari outings and society events, is revealed as "another hybrid" (*RW* 155), it is Esmé herself who figures as the point of reference for this comparison, personifying the creature in-between, "an outcast, some kind of monster" (*RW* 135), as she calls herself in a moment of despair. "I was a stranger and would always be" (*RW* 94), as she recapitulates her first months in the country, an insight that is soon to express self-confidence rather than insecurity. After growing up in New York and Naples, she comes to Nairobi not so much to finally settle down but paradoxically to stabilize the instability of her lifestyle, to integrate her outside position. It is consequently not the specific location of Kenya, or Nairobi, that constitutes the fascination of Africa for Esmé but the notion of an indeterminate space, a neutral ground, as she makes clear when first arriving in Africa:

. . . by the time I was sitting in the transit area in Cairo, waiting for the Nairobi connection, the panic dissolved like smoke in the wind. I looked at the other passengers half asleep so typical of every third-world airport. American missionary priests, Nigerian dudes in baseball caps, heavily veiled Yemenite girls, Indian families with incredibly noisy children, German backpackers immersed in the Lonely Planet guide.

The transit area: I had reached the neutral zone inhabited only by dispossessed beings—in purgatory en route to final destination—and our common position made me feel much calmer.

There seemed to be room for a lot of different people. I figured that, in the end, if there was room for the Yemenite girls, the missionaries, the Nigerian dudes and the screaming Asian children, I didn't see any reason why there shouldn't be room for someone like me. (*RW* 59)

The transnational community of travelers—tourists, expatriates, migrants—in perpetual "transit" seems to correspond perfectly with the utopian concept of cosmopolitanism as elaborated exemplarily by Anthony Appiah: "In a world of cosmopolitan patriots . . . [m]any would, no doubt spend their lives in the places that shaped them. . . . But many would move, and that would mean that cultural practices would travel also." For Appiah such "traveling cultures," and the intermixture of local and foreign practices in their wake, would ensue in "a world in which each local form of life is the result of long-term and persistent processes of cultural hybridization—a world, in that respect, much like the world we live in now."[55] Esmé, the American-Italian-Kenyan, the "eternal stranger," seems to demarcate the cosmopolitan experience exemplarily.

But as Esmé's cosmopolitan lifestyle is mapped out in greater detail, the utopia of a totalized "transit area," or cultural contact zone, is considerably qualified. The notion of a cosmopolitan community that involves "not only cultural tourism . . . , but migration, nomadism, diaspora,"[56] or, in Marciano's words, makes room for all kinds of "dispossessed beings," soon gives way to a much narrower concept of solidarity and bonding, a concept that tacitly replaces the transnational community with another, more homogeneous group. The "common position" in the airport, uniting the Italian socialite with the "heavily veiled Yemenite girls" among others, proves just as ephemeral as the link Isak Dinesen tried to establish with the Somali women on her farm, and, just as Dinesen did sixty years earlier, Esmé turns to other white women for "future role models" (*RW* 76). Casting herself as a member of the "tribe of women who have come to live in Africa merely by coincidence" (*RW* 77), Esmé replaces the notion of cosmopolitan bonding with the notion of white female friendship, while the concept of the "transit area" turns almost imperceptibly into a metaphor for a place with markedly complex rules of its own, the place of the global girl. Amanda Anderson has argued that "the articulations of cosmopolitanism often occur not within a philosophic or high theoretical mode, but rather within genres more classically literary or eclectic: the essay, the autobiography, travel writing, and works of literature generally."[57] And indeed, this novel's unacknowledged displacement of the transnational community in the airport by a small group of white women on foreign ground, and its tacit "gendering" of cosmopolitanism, might be indicative of a trend exceeding its confines.

Esmé's first encounter with Nicole and Nena, her best-friends-to-be, pulls into view the by now familiar pattern of the woman "in the midst" of things who manages the situation at hand with spectacular expertise:

They were incredibly attractive, wore Ethiopian silver bangles, old-fashioned silk dresses and sandals, had a throaty laugh and a dry sense of humour. These women spoke to Adam about drainage and electric fences, while firmly rejecting wrong-size nails and carefully selecting wood planks in fluent Swahili. They were hardware shopping with the attitude they might have had having lunch with a rock star in a trendy restaurant. I found them terribly sexy and wished to learn their language. (*RW* 77)

These women have clearly left the beaten track of Dinesen's self-fashioning behind; khaki, it seems, is definitely out, as is the "dry dykey look" of the "tough Kenya cowgirls"—"all baggy shorts, strong calves and no make-up" (*RW* 76). Their self-fashioning is on the other hand not based on nostalgia or escapism either: after all, the dowdy "diplomats' wives" (*RW* 42), who desperately try to replicate some middle-class European lifestyle in Nairobi, meet with even more fervent contempt. By contrast to these little-enticing role models, global girls like Nicole and Nena seem fluent in all kinds of languages, on top of things and ahead of their time: "I noticed [Nena] was wearing a very dark lipstick which matched her nail polish. Rouge Noir by Chanel. Oh no, these two had not been left behind one bit" (*RW* 77).

Bruce Robbins reminds us that "[c]*osmos* (world) in *cosmopolitan,* originally meant simply 'order' or 'adornment'—as in cosmetics—and was only later extended metaphorically to refer to 'the world.' Cosmetics preceded totality."[58] And indeed, these girls do not seek the totality of control or the totality of immersion, pragmatically "making up" their world as they go along, in accordance with a multiplicity of intricate dos and don'ts that constitute eventually not so much the "rules of the wild" but rather the "rules of civilization." Or the code of cosmopolitanism, if you will. According to this code you may have lunch—and do coke—in a Gujarati vegetarian restaurant, a place "on the wrong side of town" with "a decor straight out of a David Lynch set" and not frequented by white people (*RW* 8). "[T]o go native," however, is considered highly improper, and visitors who want to eat out in an African place are plain embarrassing: "It's like going to New York and begging people to take you to Harlem" (*RW* 211).

In this world stratified around the "Karen shopping centre," named after Karen Blixen, doing the right thing finally means nothing but going to cool places and buying the proper stuff. "[S]urvival consumerism," Esmé calls her practice of self-maintenance in the wilderness, a practice that radically does away with the white hunter credo of simplicity and discipline, embracing materialism and self-indulgence instead: "Material possessions haunt you. It could be a Wonderbra or a chunk of real Stilton cheese; the nature of the object is irrelevant. The object becomes the mantra on which to meditate whenever you feel your identity is starting to fade away" (*RW* 42).

Rules of the Wild has thoroughly imbibed the logic of cosmopolitanism: the identity markers of location, nationality, and cultural tradition have indeed lost much of their definitional power here, whereas the terminology of alienation, of homelessness and dislocation, acquires latently positive connotations. While birthplaces and hometowns, families and native communities no longer work as sites of identification, the "objects" and "things," whose power to constitute selfhood Robert Redford's Finch-Hatton once underestimated so blatantly, have unmistakably taken over. They form a reliable and unchanging system of orientation precisely because they are projection surfaces, empty slates to be inscribed with the consumers' varying desires and needs.

Esmé's "tribe of women" fully complies with Hunter Reed's requests for the African natives—of course, the global girl has no trouble operating a computer, and if she is not busy reading *Cosmopolitan* she might very well have a look at the *Economist*. The tribe of white women will survive long after the Samburu are extinct, as women like Esmé, Nena, and Nicole are exotic and versatile, foreign and familiar, their entire lifestyle incorporating Africanity in a way the locals never could: Nena's house, we learn, "has been featured in *World of Interiors,* giving the definite impression that you need only see that house in order to return home and say you have been treated to True African Ambience" (*RW* 62).

Yet there is a crucial difference between these women's Africanity and the African assimilation of white men I investigated earlier. From Christopher Lambert's Greystoke to Michael Douglas's Charles Remington, white men go native in contemporary popular fictions to discover or acknowledge a submerged part of their self, which is then projected upon the African situation, so that the white man becomes the representative African, up to the point of figuring as the exemplary victim of colonialism and exploitation. Contemporary narratives around white women in Africa, by contrast, seem to be much more skeptical about the prospect of identification and emulation, even if the imagery of masquerade and make-believe is just as prominent here as in white hunter narratives. Ever since Isak Dinesen took so much care to bracket the African farm of her life story off from the actual world, be it African or European, white women's ventures into the wilderness have been narrated time and again in terms of a careful negotiation of the foreign and familiar influences involved. The lives colonial ladies and global girls are seen carving out for themselves in Africa are strikingly artificial, exotic "African Ambiences," which signify Africanity while making totally clear that it is a construction. By this token, the colonial lady and the global girl become model cosmopolitans, so much better equipped to face the requirements of a new "global system of cultural exchanges"[59] than their male counterparts, but at the same time calling for a reassessment of this very system and the imageries around it. Thus Marciano's identification of white women with the globally "dispossessed" in *Rules of the Wild* obfuscates the fact that traveling (voluntarily and adventurously) is not the same as being on the move (by necessity or force) and that the "tribe of white women" is by no means the same as the hybrid community in the transit area evoked earlier on. While older categories of differentiation like national identity and descent are on the wane in certain contexts, they are speedily replaced by new concepts applying to a global scale, the effect of which is often enough no less hierarchical and segregative, if less obvious. Moreover, the very iconicity of the global girl, who seems to be beyond the confines of race and patriarchal culture, blots out the reality of the "local woman," who is, as critics from Saskia Sassen to Gayatri Spivak do not tire to point out, the first to suffer from the effects of global financialization.[60] Marciano's Nairobi may be amazingly close to Manhattan these days, but Harlem couldn't be farther away.

II ALTERNATIVE AFRICAS

FIVE

Free Trade? Postcolonial Empires, Global Corporations

Colonial nostalgia focuses on East Africa. Based largely upon agricultural exploitation, East African colonialism lent itself much more easily to romanticization than its western counterpart, although its effects were hardly less devastating for the local population. For West African colonies, where mining and trading prevailed, the mock bucolic imagery of *Out of Africa* or the pseudo–prairie fantasies of countless white hunter narratives seem inappropriate. It is the case of the Congo that brings this discrepancy most glaringly to the fore, as even around the turn of the century it was becoming obvious that the situation here called for other patterns of Africanist representation than the familiar ones of romance and adventure.[1]

This is not to say that classical colonial narratives and spectacular accounts of adventure and exploration did not play an important part in the creation of the West African empire. After all, the pioneers responsible for the violent takeover of the Congo tried to write their own history precisely along these lines. Thus Henry Morton Stanley, who acted as King Leopold II's agent, shamelessly made use of his international reputation as a true-blue adventurer which he had gained in the wake of his search for David Livingstone, using his positive acclaim in the worst possible way. Talking hundreds of Congo basin chiefs into treaties in which—mostly unknowingly—they signed their land over to Leopold, he set the basis for Leopold's international campaign, which led to diplomatic recognition for a system of colonial rule that would be characterized by previously unknown methods of exploitation and cruelty: the Congo Free State, under the administration of the International Association of the Congo.[2]

The international support for this scheme, articulated in the West Africa Conference in Berlin in 1884, derived from the widespread enthusiasm for the concept of free trade shared by all colonial powers, enmeshed with their reluctance to get too involved with the costly projects of imperial takeover and their "suspicion of each other's expansion."³ To turn the Congo into a neutral territory for the benefits of everybody involved sounded like a perfect solution for this predicament. And the International Association of the Congo seemed to grant the necessary neutrality, promising easy access to local resources and markets, flexible handling of frontiers and taxes, and the creation of new patterns of consumption to introduce Western civilization to the Africans.⁴ If this agenda had little to do with the system of *Raubwirtschaft* actually implemented by the Association—Leopold's cruel raid of the country—it seems to have found sympathetic if belated listeners in the cultural meddlers and global managers of our day.

It might thus not come as a surprise that Michael Crichton, whose *Congo* can be read as a blueprint for the logic of globalization, presents Henry Morton Stanley's Congo travelogue *In Darkest Africa* as a subtext for his own, pseudodocumentary, narrative. In contrast to the popular reading of Stanley as the individualist gentleman adventurer in the dark continent, Crichton reads Stanley as a "businessman-explorer" with a "grand commercial scheme." For that matter, it is Stanley's expedition to the Congo that interests Crichton much more than the anecdotally richer first trip in search of David Livingstone. The Congo expedition demarcates for Crichton a fundamental transformation that brings about the split of national and economic interests: "Stanley was financed by Leopold II of Belgium who intended to acquire *personally* a large piece of Africa" (C xii). Leopold, Crichton quotes a contemporary source, "possesses the Congo just as Rockefeller possesses Standard Oil" (C xii). Leopold's private involvement indicates a new economic order that will be dominated first by individual businessmen and then by multinational big businesses and corporations. In the course of this transformation the nationalist and missionary pathos of colonialism will be replaced by a functionalist rhetoric of common sense and compatibility, and the order of the nation-state will be subsumed under the rule of large-scale corporations and trusts.

While the story of Leopold and the Congo Free State often tended to be explained in terms of a retreat to barbarity, an individualistic monarchic power game, it should instead be read as indicating the upsurge of a new era, an era in which international associations and global corporations would rule the day, and takeovers would be enacted not by means of military intervention but by contracts and agreements—even if the contracts, like Stanley's treaties, might be enforced, the agreements forged, the mutual benefit made up. And the vehement debates around the regime attest to a pervasive transformation just as well, as Adam Hochschild pointed out: "It was the first major international atrocity scandal in the age of the telegraph and the camera. In its mixture of bloodshed on an industrial scale, royalty, sex, the power of celebrity, and rival lobbying and media campaigns raging in half a dozen countries on both sides of the Atlantic, it seemed strikingly close to our times."[5]

There are many ways of looking at the transition from colonialist rule to global organization, and I will present several readings in what follows. The most famous reading is, of course, Joseph Conrad's *Heart of Darkness* (1902), which provides a subtext for many of the later reflections around individual, national, and corporate power and its abuses in the twentieth century. However, while Conrad clearly intended his book to be a critique of the situation in the Congo, the larger thrust of his critique is less obvious. "*Heart of Darkness* is specifically about what Conrad saw in King Leopold's African empire in 1890; it is unclear how far this critique can be generalized to imperialism beyond the Congo," writes Patrick Brantlinger.[6] Much more, of course, is unclear about this story, and a lot of it due to the fact that Conrad refused to be clear and chose to remain ambivalent about the significance of the darkness he wrote about.

Conrad's approach is typical in that respect, as so many later narratives of African atrocities took similarly ambivalent stances, if often less intricately enacted. Hence, *Heart of Darkness* could also be said to have implemented the "realistic" Africanist imageries of our century—the perspective of "looking closely," to which we shall return a little later. Combined with the logic of "doing what has to be done," this perspective forms a powerful paradigm for a whole set of new aesthetic and sociocultural approaches to Africa, and I will try to get a grip on this paradigm by investigating the themes of commerce, trade, and economic interaction.

These issues are, after all, as central to the discussions on West African colonization as they are to Conrad's story and to many later narratives around Africa and the West. Investigating the representation of commercial and cultural exchange in a series of different texts, I mean to take up earlier reflections on the concepts of control, compatibility, and cosmopolitanism, concepts that seem to call for new representational models and different frameworks of evaluation. With this I enter the second stage of my project, as I will no longer be concerned with the impact of classical figures and genres of colonial representation but with marked deviations from the established course. If these new and alternative narratives need not necessarily mean a turn to the better, they certainly bring about a break with the established forms of talking about Africa, with consequences that I hope to bring into view.

5.1 Subtle Bonds and Unforeseen Partnerships: Joseph Conrad's *Heart of Darkness*

The Congo Free State was a business venture, not a colonialist project under the auspices of a European nation-state. Apart from Leopold's empty diatribes against African slavery it was his plea for free trade that would drastically further the cause of his International Association of the Congo. While the blunt rhetoric of exploitation was always somewhat unpopular in European political and public discussions around colonization, the rhetoric of commerce became increasingly important in the last years of the century. At the West Africa Conference in Berlin in 1884, Otto von Bismarck employed the familiar idealistic imagery of colonialism as a missionary and philanthropic project, but he cast this project in terms of commercial and administrative expansion. The "civilization of the African natives" was to be achieved "by opening the interior of the continent to commerce."[7] David Livingstone's famous "three *c*s"—Commerce, Christianity, and Civilization—demarcating the goals of "African liberation," had almost imperceptibly narrowed down to the first one: "during the 1890s," writes Edward Said, "the business of empire, once an adventurous and often individualistic enterprise, had become the empire of business."[8] This was the point of departure for Leopold's commercial scheme, a scheme that drew heavily on the popularity of free trade arrangements yet would prove only too tightly conjoined with a fourth, unacknowledged, *c*—conquest.

It is also the point of departure for Joseph Conrad's *Heart of Darkness*, this story around the rule of a Belgian "Company" modeled after the International Association of the Congo with its Brussels headquarters. Indeed, Conrad's novella documents the last stages of colonialism, mapping out a system of takeover completely devoid of the spirit of adventure or exploration. The blank spaces on the map have long "got filled . . . with rivers and lakes and names,"[9] and the intruders are no longer interested in the country but covet its resources alone, driven singlemindedly by the desire "[t]o make money" (*HD* 48). In Conrad's novella, the main incentive of the Belgian administrators in the Congo seems to consist in holding the country at bay and in paralyzing the people so that the project of drainage and pillaging can go on unobstructed. The system Conrad describes is a merciless and cold-blooded capitalist venture: "They were going to run an over-sea empire, and make no end of coin by trade" (*HD* 35).

But if imperialism turns into a commercial scheme in *Heart of Darkness*, it is not a very efficient one. The Company's local headquarter in the

Congo, the "Central Station," harbors a group of self-centered, pedantic bureaucrats, indicative of the entire system's deficiency: "There was an air of plotting about that station, but nothing came of it, of course. It was as surreal as everything else—as the philanthropic pretence of the whole concern, as their talk, as their government, as their show of work" (*HD* 54). The pompous figure of the station's manager puts into sharp relief the emptiness and futility of the huge machinery of commerce and administration at work between Brussels and the Congo:

> He had no genius for organizing, for initiative, or for order even. That was evident in such things as the deplorable state of the station. He had no learning and no intelligence. . . . He had originated nothing, he could keep the routine going—that's all. But he was great. He was great by this little thing that it was impossible to tell what could control such a man. He never gave that secret away. Perhaps there was nothing within him. Such a suspicion made one pause—for out there there were no external checks. Once when various tropical diseases had laid low almost every "agent" in the station, he was heard to say, "Men who come out here should have no entrails." (*HD* 51)

Hollowed out like the entire framework and rhetoric of a commercialized colonialism, the Company representatives stand in marked contrast to Marlow, whose account forms the core of the narrative. Marlow professes to follow a course of his own instead of mechanically pursuing the Company's aims, driven by an "impractical" desire for adventure and exploration, and intent from the very beginning to use the Company's resources for his own purpose.

The man he is sent to seek out, Kurtz, master of the "Inner Station," seems to have been fueled by the same ambition once, equally determined not to get drawn into the Company's scheme and to set his own rules instead. "The new gang—the gang of virtue" (*HD* 55)—Marlow and Kurtz are consequently called by a Company representative. Yet Marlow's attempts at steering an alternative course eventually reaffirm the overarching system, while Kurtz's project gives vent to its worst implication, so that in the end the Company's logic proves to be much more powerful and committing than its individual representatives seem to know. But then again, the Company itself will eventually appear confined in and protected by a larger, abstract order, an order that is not political or economic but metaphysical.

When Marlow sets out on his quest for Kurtz and the Inner Station, however, we still have reason to believe that he is leaving the Company's petty world and petty logic behind and is entering a new reality, a world in which things get done. Although he makes himself out as an observer, who takes account rather than taking part, Marlow eschews the notion of distantiation and reflection and draws instead heavily upon the imagery of action, prefiguring in that respect Ernest Hemingway's suspicion that to think too long might very well mean losing control.[10] Yet in Conrad's case action is neither grandiose nor daring. Marlow describes his advance into the wilderness in terms of doing what has to be done—work, rather than adventure:

I don't like work, —no man does—but I like what is in the work, —the chance to find yourself. Your own reality—for yourself, not for others—what no other man can ever know. They can only see the mere show, and never can tell what it really means. (HD 59–60)

In a certain sense, Marlow's work is not all that different from the Company agents' tautological activities, their "show." He seems to keep busy not so much to get a job done but to keep the noxious influences all around at bay. Consequently, civilization turns from a matter of "principles" or "fine sentiments"—idealism—into the result of hard work and discipline, figuring forth a network of superimposed constraints and regularized practices. Marlow did not go native, he explains, because he "had no time":

I had to mess about with white-lead and strips of woollen blankets helping to put bandages on those leaky steam-pipes, I tell you. I had to watch the steering and circumvent those snags, and get the tin-pot along by hook and by crook. There was surface-truth enough in these things to save a wiser man. And between whiles I had to look after the savage who was fireman. (HD 69–70)

Marlow's supervision of the "savage," seemingly an integral part of his regularized workday, is worth a closer look, as the very imagery of control and submission he endorses rests upon shaky ground. In fact, the captain and his fireman seem locked in a strange interdependence, a reciprocity grounded in the claim of their utter difference *and* their secret similarity. The fireman epitomizes the logic of work, which is so crucial to the advent of civilization, but also brings to the fore its inherent contradictions—the fact that it is on the basis of an alienating and self-serving activity that you stay what you are, or maintain what you have achieved:

He was there below me, and, upon my word, to look at him was as edifying as seeing a dog in a parody of breeches and a feather hat, walking on his hind-legs. . . . He ought to have been clapping his hands and stamping his feet on the bank, instead of which he was hard at work, a thrall to strange witchcraft, full of improving knowledge. He was useful because he had been instructed; and what he knew was this—that should the water inside that transparent thing disappear, the evil spirit inside the boiler would get angry through the greatness of his thirst, and take a terrible vengeance. So he sweated and fired up and watched the glass fearfully (with an impromptu charm, made of rags, tied to his arm, and a piece of polished bone, as big as a watch, stuck flatways through his lower lip). . . . But the snags were thick, the water was treacherous and shallow, the boiler seemed indeed to have a sulky devil in it, and thus neither that fireman nor I had any time to peer into our creepy thoughts. (*HD* 70)

While this African, like so many of his peers in imperial adventure fiction, has been tricked into compliance with the colonial scheme, his civilized appearance another ridiculous act, he is much closer to the white man who watches over him than any of his predecessors was. After all, Marlow seems as entrapped in, and safeguarded by, a superimposed routine as his fireman, and for both of them the regularity of their duties constitutes a precarious status quo, a means of momentarily fencing off the dangers all around. This is by no means to downplay the racist condescension of the above description. To the contrary, the assumption of a deepgoing difference (the fireman's primitive, animalesque, ridiculous status) confounds the imagery of sameness here, which is clearly not based upon equality and communication but on shared practices and conjoined action: the logic of compatibility. The "surface-truth" of modernity and capitalism is diametrically opposed to an older, more profound truth, a "truth stripped of its cloak of time" (*HD* 69).

It is on the basis of this "surface-truth" that the fireman and the captain can enter a relationship. Working alongside each other, they do not so much overcome their difference but functionalize it, interacting like individual components in a huge and complicated mechanism. This notion of everybody as a more or less functional part, a tool or instrument for unclear purposes, suffuses the entire first half of Conrad's narrative. Totalizing an imagery we have already encountered in the writing of Haggard and Burroughs, Conrad demarcates the entire framework of colonialism and commerce as trickery, yet here everybody seems to be in compliance and no one altogether in control:

"When you have to attend to things of that sort [the routine of work], to the mere incidents of the surface, the reality—the reality, I tell you—fades. The inner truth is hidden—luckily, luckily. But I felt it all the same; I felt often its mysterious stillness watching me at my monkey tricks, just as it watches you fellows performing on your respective tight-ropes for—what is it?—half-a-crown a tumble—"

"Try to be civil, Marlow," growled a voice and I knew there was at least one listener awake besides myself.

"I beg your pardon, I forgot the heartache which makes up the rest of the price. And indeed, what does the price matter, if the trick be well done? You do your tricks very well." (*HD* 67)

No wonder this is the first time Marlow is interrupted in his narrative. Whoever speaks up of the audience introduced in the frame story—the Director of Companies, the Lawyer, or the Accountant—has reason to feel concerned by the insinuation that his work is nothing but "monkey tricks," his position not much different from the natives' who mindlessly perform the tasks they have been assigned, resembling trained animals. To "be civil," it seems, is to maintain the belief that commerce and colonialism are meant to further civilization, as Otto von Bismarck put it in his endorsement of Leopold II, and to blot out the alternative possibility of civilization being just another cover-up for the schemes of exploitation and conquest, which have long gained a momentum of their own.

In Burroughs's *Tarzan of the Apes* civilization was cast as a tautological practice of differentiation on the grounds of difference. In Conrad's novella the same notion of civilization as ceaseless laboring for distinction shows up, but here the project has become all-inclusive, and only the more self-referential at that. There is no doubt that the advent and maintenance of civilization profits from and furthers the hierarchical and authoritative structures of colonialism, as Marlow's relationship to his African fireman indicates and as another link with an African worker makes altogether clear. Shortly before the climactic encounter with Kurtz, the expedition on the steamer is attacked by a native tribe, an incident launched by Kurtz, as Marlow will learn later. Marlow's African helmsman dies in this attack, and Marlow cannot stop thinking about him afterward, although during his lifetime the helmsman seemed even less efficient than the fireman, as he "had no restraint, no restraint" (*HD* 88):

I missed my late helmsman awfully,—I missed him even while his body was still lying in the pilot-house. Perhaps you will think it passing strange, this regret for a savage who was of no more account than a grain of sand in a black Sahara. Well, don't you see, he had done something, he had steered; for months I had him at my back—a help—an instrument. It was a kind of partnership. He steered for me—I had to look after him. I worried about his deficiencies, and thus a subtle bond had been created, of which I only became aware when it was suddenly broken. And the intimate profundity of that look he gave me when he received his hurt remains to this day in my memory—like a claim of distant kinship affirmed in a supreme moment. (*HD* 87–88)

The "subtle bond" between Marlow and the African, their "distant kinship," manifests itself in retrospect, after their actual cooperation, and thus comes across as utterly devoid of communication or exchange. Once more, the individual roles are clearly set off from each other: there is an agent and an instrument, a master and a servant, both of them confined in and sustained by the same conceptual framework. The stratified structures of colonialism are not suspended in this recollection but are seen to confound the link between the European and the African.

As Marlow shifts from the lived relationship with his fireman to the remembered relationship with the dead helmsman, the idealized "bond" becomes an exclusively one-sided affair—imagined, mapped out, and controlled by Marlow, while the African turns into a mere projection surface, a "silent partner," if you will. But then, this Euro-African "partnership" is not meant to last in the first place, as it is evoked in order to figure forth an altogether different and "unforeseen partnership"(*HD* 110) that will eventually blot out any other tie and responsibility on Marlow's part. The relationship with Kurtz, the "umbilical cord of culture"[11] connecting Marlow with this proto-European white man, to whose making "all Europe contributed" (*HD* 86), replaces his African bonding once and for all.

This replacement of Euro-African by intra-European bonding calls to mind the shift of emphasis in Isak Dinesen's *Out of Africa* from the Somali women on her farm to her Swedish friend Ingrid, another replacement of transcultural solidarity by white European bonding in Africa. And yet—the differences between Ingrid's and Karen's female relationship in Kenya on the one hand, and Marlow's and Kurtz's male relationship in the Congo on the other, are so much more striking than the similarities. *Out of Africa* focused on white solidarity in the wilderness to map out a realm of (white) female independence replacing older forms of female self-determination such as subversion and masquerade. The colonial space gained the status of a utopian enclave in turn. In *Heart of Darkness*, Marlow's relationship with his African workers is not replaced by a less complicated relationship but by a much more complicated one. White male bonding is enacted as a sinister plot or nightmarish obligation, forcing Marlow back into an order he has disavowed as unjust and cruel, as Benita Parry has shown.[12] In other words, the colonial space functions not as a utopian enclave in *Heart of Darkness* but as the epitome of an expanding order exemplifying a dominant logic rather than presenting a counterpoint or constituting a clear-cut alternative to the given system. Everything links up to everything else in this novella, which does end, after all, with the vision of a darkness encroaching not on Africa but on London.

By dint of this insight Kurtz, who seemed to demarcate the extreme alternative to the Company's empty and dispassionate maneuvers, turns out to be entangled in the very same framework, another "hollow" man (*HD* 97), whose only glaring difference from the machinations of the Company consists in greater radicality and persistence. Kurtz carries the logic of personal profit and control—the Company's logic—to its ghastly extreme, just as King Leopold's rule in the Congo culminated the politics of conquest and exploitation until the country itself collapsed like an empty shell. This is when the fourth *c*—conquest—enters the heart of Conrad's story and discloses itself as the flip side of colonial commerce.

The very notion of free trade in an enslaved country is unmasked as a farce—"To speak plainly," as Marlow sums up his understanding of Kurtz's activities, "he raided the country" (*HD* 94).

By extension, Kurtz does not so much disrupt the stratified Manichaean order laid out before but totalizes it. Marlow's bond to the Africans is effaced in a radical act of incorporation, as Kurtz embodies both master and servant, god and fetish, paradoxically collating the function of the agent and the function of the instrument, aspiring to the pleasure of control and of submission, and ultimately suffering nothing but the painful implications of both states, as his first appearance in the novella epitomizes:

> I saw the man on the stretcher sit up, lank and with an uplifted arm, above the shoulders of the bearers. . . . I could see the cage of his ribs all astir, the bones of his arms waving. It was as though an animated image of death carved out of old ivory had been shaking its hand with menaces at a motionless crowd of men made of dark and glittering bronze. I saw him open his mouth wide—it gave him a weirdly voracious aspect, as though he had wanted to swallow all the air, all the earth, all the men before him. (*HD* 99)

This image of white power-weakness seems to allegorize the conditions for imperial rule, with the white man in utter dependence acting unabashedly superior. And once more it is the trope of trick translation, this ultimate trope of colonial fetishism, that delineates the mechanisms at work. Not only does Kurtz pose as "white god" for his African audience; he falls for his own show eventually, turning from idealist into idol and thus undergoing the transformation Patrick Brantlinger located at the core of Conrad's story: "Conrad universalizes 'darkness' in part by universalizing fetishism."[13] Even more important, however, Conrad's narrative itself goes through the same suspension of disbelief and the same universalization—falling for its own tricks and becoming a fetish in its own right, as it were—as the entire fictional universe is pulled into the vortex of Kurtz's self-aggrandizement and totalizing desire.

With Kurtz's appearance the interdependence of idealism and idolatry, commerce and conquest, modernity and magic comes to the fore. The sickening and sick performance of the "white god" in front of his native audience confirms Marlow's earlier suspicion of civilization as universal trickery. And yet, this epiphany is not to lend final precision to the critique of colonialism laid out before but to terminate it. After all, Kurtz's appearance also demarcates the end of Marlow's travel narrative and the takeover of another, symbolicist, narrative that opts for abstraction rather than concreteness, and abandons the quest for the ideological underpinnings of colonialism, which motivated the first part of the novella.[14] Once it is translated into abstract terms, however, imperialism turns from a superimposed (European) scheme into an innate (African) practice, while the very grounds for political critique and protest are taken away.[15]

In a certain sense *Heart of Darkness* thus appears to be *about* the blank spot that Edward Said made out at the core of imperial narratives of the turn of the century, as Conrad's totalizing move seems to exemplarily express Said's insight that "[i]mperialism has monopolized the whole system of representation."[16] Affecting everything that comes into contact with it, imperialism is seen to elide analysis and control and to undermine the very categories of control or agency upon which it seems to be based. But then again, if *Heart of Darkness* tentatively approaches this radical insight, it is mitigated in the subsequent move in which the incomprehensibility of imperialism, its "blankness," is conceived of in metaphysical terms rather than epistemological ones, so that the political implications of the problem must necessarily drop out of sight. A slight shift of emphasis suffices to realign this narrative, turning a political argument into a generic philosophical reflection, so that the case study in colonial relations inadvertently flips over into a classical case of blaming the victim. Chinua Achebe called Conrad's technique of mythifying Africa "trickery." And indeed, the entire novella could be said to verge between the representation and the performance of trickery.[17] Once more, the structures of narration—the mix of conventions and genres, of established images and long-standing tropes, and the subtle transformations of this material by way of combination and contrasting—turn out to be of focal importance for the text's conceptual and ideological work, producing inconsistencies and ruptures that are as puzzling as they are irritating, and that will form the point of departure for countless later rewritings and revisions.

5.2 Uneven Exchanges: Nicolas Roeg's *Heart of Darkness*

Joseph Conrad's *Heart of Darkness* sets out to sketch the grand narrative of imperialism, only to lose sight of its ugly groundworks in turn, evoking a grandiose and tragic spectacle of power and submission, where the imagery of a dirty business venture would have been more appropriate—a corrupt scheme that does not become more honorable just because it is pursued systematically and on a large scale. If the "immanent contradictions" in Conrad's novella, which the text "intimates but does not confront,"[18] have given vent to many discussions in the meantime, this is not to say that the problem of colonial—and postcolonial—representation has been settled. In many respects matters seem to be as complicated as they were in 1902, but the parameters for approaching the messy layout of colonial interaction and its postcolonial extensions have changed: At the turn to the twenty-first century, Conrad's technique of "turning away" from concrete concerns to symbolic constellations has definitely fallen into disrepute. On the contrary, the maxim of our day for approaching Africa seriously could be called facing the facts. If only we could agree on what the facts are.

In Clint Eastwood's approach to the white man's quest in the wilderness, *White Hunter, Black Heart,* the differentiation of fact and fantasy runs along the lines of filmmaking and hunting, and it is filmmaking that comes to stand for the realistic project, standing off in its constructive and communicative potential against the destructive venture of the hunt. These days the most impressive trophies to be brought back from Africa are not ivory tusks but images, it seems. If for once this quest for images is associated with the project of shooting a film, however, Eastwood's film is also clearly concerned with another production site for images: the psyche. Like so many other recent white hunter narratives, *White Hunter, Black Heart* enacts the journey into the heart of darkness as a psychological trip of self-discovery, or rather, self-fashioning—and thus paradoxically locates the factual and true precisely where the fantastic and irreal used to dwell: in the imaginary. In contrast to Conrad's turn to symbolism, the psychological turn in contemporary white hunter narratives is not meant to abandon the cultural project of coming to terms with Africa, however, but to ground it. Time and again, the theme of psychological self-scrutiny is pitted against the negative concepts of self-absorption and totalitarian pathos in our day, and is thus enacted as a basis for processes of communication and contact.

Read against this background, I will argue, Nicolas Roeg's TV adaptation of *Heart of Darkness*[19] in 1994 must not necessarily seem as radically retrospective as it was made out to be. In contrast to its famous and spectacularly up-to-date predecessor—Francis Ford Coppola's *Apocalypse Now* (1979)[20]—which replaces the scenario of nineteenth-century colonialism with twentieth-century war, Roeg's *Heart of Darkness* sticks quite close to Conrad's novella, yet Roeg's obsessive enactment of the themes of mutuality, exchange, and psychological self-scrutiny resonates as much with contemporary concerns as it calls up bygone matters.

The most obvious evidence for a changed focus is Roeg's introduction of a third character into the formerly binary constellation of the white men in the wilderness: Mfumu (Isaach de Bankolé), who comes to act as Marlow's adviser, guide, and translator—a character vaguely based upon Conrad's main African characters, the fireman and the helmsman. And while Roeg arguably "was not attracted to the theme of doubleness,"[21] enacting Marlow (Tim Roth) and Kurtz (John Malkovich) in awkward distance, this is not to say that the film is not concerned with the imagery of male bonding—Mfumu dies calling Marlow "my friend," and Marlow, too, will come to remember him in terms of friendship rather than mere cooperation. Likewise, if Roeg adopts the Conradian theme of duty and work ethic, having Marlow (Tim Roth) spend "most of his time simply doing his job, from rebuilding the ship to cleaning up the mess at the inner station,"[22] the imagery around work and workers has undergone a significant shift from Conrad's day to ours. In Roeg's adaptation the binaries of agent and instrument, master and servant, which are so disturbingly mapped out in Conrad's novella, gain altogether different connotations.

Roeg may not have turned *Heart of Darkness* into a "bi-racial buddy movie," to use Ed Guerrero's term for a most popular filmic formula of the 1980s and '90s, but he was doubtlessly familiar with the pattern in which a white hero is equipped with a black sidekick, both to acknowledge black agency and simultaneously to "subtly reinscribe the cinematic racial hierachies of old."[23] "Buddy movies" from *Lethal Weapon* (1987) to *The Negotiator* (1998) time and again emphasize the theme of teamwork and partnership, a focal theme for the enactment of Western-African bonding in contemporary Hollywood films just as well—be it Eastwood's *White Hunter, Black Heart* or Pollack's *Out of Africa*. While the formula reaffirms long-standing racial hierarchies, it does not lend itself easily to an open enactment of white supervision and black subservience but discloses alternative, if by no means unproblematical, imageries of interaction and communication. If Conrad's phrasing in the description of Marlow and his helmsman—"he steered for me—I had to look after him"—figured forth a certain ambivalence, Roeg's film capitalizes on this indeterminacy, leaving no doubt that on foreign ground the one who steers might very well be in control, and that looking after somebody need not necessarily mean to have the upper hand. "Have you been assigned to me?" Marlow asks upon first meeting Mfumu. "Non, non," he replies, "c'est moi qui a demandé de le faire. I ask."

In Conrad's novella, to work was to fence off the wilderness, a huge and probably hopeless project as we saw in the end, with nothing much achieved and nothing whatsoever changed in the order of things—Kurtz may have been dead, but the darkness kept spreading. In Roeg's film, by contrast, work is enacted as a means of communication and bonding; we see Mfumu and Marlow gradually growing closer while they repair the steamer and finally forming a silent alliance against the Company representatives, when they hide on board to overhear a conversation about Kurtz. Their relationship delineates a model of interaction and understanding that Kurtz's later appearance can by no means efface—especially given John Malkovich's performance of the character as indifferent, detached, and morbid, very much along the lines he laid out in *The Sheltering Sky* for the decadent white man in Africa. This sick white god can hardly present a counterweight to Marlow's African friend, even if he manages to have him killed.

And while Kurtz is clearly Africanized here just as in Conrad's text, his affiliation with the dirty work of imperialism is less obvious: "Of the two issues that mainly drive the novella—the problematics of colonization, especially the ivory trade, and the temptations of regression to savagery—the first ceases to be problematic and the second is slighted," Seymour Chatman remarked about Roeg's film: "The requisite skulls are on view, but the worst that Kurtz does personally is to wring, absent-mindedly, the neck of his pet monkey."[24] This man might be disturbed, but he is not monstrous—a far cry from Conrad's "atrocious phantom" (*HD* 99) or Coppola's brutal Colonel Kurtz in *Apocalypse Now* at that.

In Roeg's film the white man's going native seems to have little to do with going wild. Rather, Kurtz comes across as altogether passive, devoid of willpower and energy. The ivory he gathered from his raids of the country just piles up in the Inner Station, useless and empty stuff. And while this may call to mind Conrad's totalizing move at the end of *Heart of Darkness,* the "hollowing out" of imperialism by way of its decontextualization, in Roeg's film the figure of Kurtz is not totalized but rather washed out by way of a panoply of different symbolic markers: at times he seems to be the ultimate anti-imperialist; at other times he figures forth the horrors of imperialism. "Zwei Seelen wohnen, ach, in meiner Brust," we hear him quote Goethe at the close of the film—and indeed, like so many other postcolonial colonial heroes, this white man has a split personality. Roeg's Kurtz does not grandiosely collate contradictory stances and conditions in his persona, as did his literary predecessor, but suffers from their incompatibility.

But then again, the centerpiece of Roeg's film is obviously Marlow, not Kurtz. And if the imperial venture has dropped out of view, the white man's precarious situation in the African jungle gains vital importance. Not that this Marlow would run a big risk of being corrupted. In fact, he seems miraculously unaffected by the darkness all around, his agenda of work and interaction standing in stark contrast not only to Kurtz's passivity but also to the Company's logic of commodification. Where Conrad's Marlow ended up entangled in the very logic he meant to contest, Roeg's hero manages to stay detached; another acultural expert and control-man who does what has to be done and does it in a team. In fact, depicting Marlow's relationship with Mfumu, Roeg both fosters the logic of communication and cooperation and manages to maintain the unambiguous focus on the white man—the silent African once more suggesting authentic communication without words, just like Eastwood's African guide Kivu or Pollack's Kanuthia.

Yet the desire for authenticity is acted out not only by way of the cultural contact scenario but even more fundamentally on the level of filmic representation itself. Conrad evoked the aura of a dream to characterize Marlow's experience of losing (narrative) control—"that commingling of absurdity, surprise, and bewilderment in a tremor of struggling revolt, that notion of being captured by the incredible which is of the very essence of dreams" (*HD* 57). Roeg, by contrast, enacts dream passages not to evoke the loss of control but its recuperation. While he, too, calls up a system of hidden links and analogies, references and cross-references, he makes it totally clear that he is not concerned with metaphysical questions but with a psychological predicament: the entire film stretches out along the lines of Marlow's unorderly recollections. Time and again, dreamlike flashbacks and flash-forwards, fantasy sequences, and hallucinatory intermissions disrupt the narrative flow, disorienting at first, yet oddly constructive eventually.[25] In a paradoxical move, familiar from the contemporary enactment of the white hunter, the highly subjective realm of personal recollection and fantasy gains the status of authenticity and truth as opposed to edited and objectified accounts of the past.

Like Conrad's narrative, Roeg's film sets out from a riverboat on the Thames, yet this time the boat does not belong to the Company but to Marlow, who is harassed by Company agents for information about Kurtz. If he eventually complies with their requests, it is to point out the futility of their endeavor, and to set his private recollections against their cynical quest for profitable information—no other personalized perspective complements or qualifies this stance. Marlow's account of Africa begins with one of Roeg's many flash-forwards, a brief crosscut from the boat to Kurtz's station with a dirty Marlow crouching in the flickering light of an open fire, and as the film proceeds more flash-forwards come up, which are then integrated step by step into the narrative—we shall eventually get to the scene at the station, and we shall eventually make sense of a setup that seemed utterly disconnected at first sight.

This alternation of disruption and narrative integration organizes the film on many levels: a central dream sequence figures forth future conflicts; shots of maps and photographs are intercut with glimpses of events to come or are briefly underlaid with an evocative sound score, hinting at (still) hidden dimensions of reality; and, finally, flash-forwards come to be replaced with flashbacks, as the narrative closes in on itself. Whereas in Coppola's version of Conrad's novella "the frame has been broken beyond repair,"[26] Roeg's narrative does acquire psychological closure at the very least, if via the detours of seemingly chaotic and disconnected scenarios. The entire film could thus be said to reiterate the motif of the journey, which is cast, however, not as a journey into darkness and uncertainty, as in Conrad's text, but as a journey to the "inner station" indeed—a psychojourney that may be painful, indirect, and full of losses but does reach its goal eventually, as Marlow survives the trip both physically and morally intact, refusing to take part in the Company's and in Kurtz's dirty business. After Kurtz's death, Marlow insists upon abandoning a loaded raft of ivory and thus terminates the "merry dance of trade and death" described by the director in the beginning. As the Company agents leave his boat empty-handed, the big history of imperial exploitation seems to have found its end, while small psychohistories around coping and communication take its place.

For once, Roeg's film thus personalizes and psychologizes colonial history in a manner reminiscent of white hunter narratives from Clint Eastwood to Irvine Welsh. But even if the film clearly lends focal weight to Marlow's project of meaning making, another plotline runs parallel to this narrative, which opens up an alternative perspective. From this different vantage point, the convoluted logic of exchange and exploitation appears much more committing and perverse than Marlow's psychojourney lets on.

The protagonists of this plotline remain obscure throughout the film. They are Africans, members of an unidentified tribe—the "jungle people"—and present themselves in stark opposition to Mfumu, who repairs and restores, and comes to a silent understanding with Marlow in the course of his labor. Instead of seeking understanding, the jungle people spread confusion, setting sabotage against cooperation, and rupturing exchange and communication instead of getting things done. This comes to the fore in the film's first contact scenario, if contact is the right word for the highly indirect encounter taking place. When the expedition on the lookout for Kurtz camps at the border of the jungle, some of their African carriers disappear overnight. They have been abducted, Marlow's companions say, by the jungle people. While these people are most certainly Kurtz's men or "emissaries," as a company agent suspects, their power is not his power: "This has nothing to do with Kurtz," Marlow recognizes—"this is much much older."

Mfumu seems to know more about "this" than Marlow, but he is clearly not altogether in on the jungle people's logic either. Before the carriers disappear, he sets out to cover them with leaves, concealing them from a danger he purports not to believe in: "First time they work for the Company. See: people think they good for trading. People think them to exchange for supplies. Mfumu laugh. Mfumu don't believe it." But Mfumu is wrong; the next morning the men are gone, and even a well-filled bundle for barter doesn't get all of them back—one is missing when they return to camp. Marlow is more furious about the natives' lack of business ethic than about the actual abduction: "Did they kill him? For God's sake, we gave them enough barter to get a bloody village for an entire year. You saying they didn't think it enough and they killed the boy just to make a point? Who are these people?" "Different people. . . . Hunters. They hunt," Mfumu replies cryptically.

Different people, indeed. The jungle people's difference seems to consist in their recalcitrance; they enter the game while breaking its rules and disregarding its conditions. If Conrad's Kurtz totalized the logic of commerce and thus exposed its hidden complicity with the logic of exploitation, Roeg's jungle people blow it up, refusing to stick to the set pattern of give-and-take, the logic of reciprocity and justice Marlow adheres to. In the course of this disruption, however, a much more pervasive incongruity comes to the fore: the fact that the underlying system itself is uneven and asymmetrical. The acts of sabotage thus lay bare the workings of a colonialist rhetoric that "translates the possessions and products of the Other (and the Others themselves) into alienable commodities which (who) were exchanged against European goods and entered a global market that was constituted by this very process," as Ulla Haselstein has pointed out.[27] By dint of this logic, men are turned into wares that must be hidden away at night, and can be weighed up against barter—if, that is, both sides agree on the exchange rate.

Echoing Conrad's Africanization of imperialism, Roeg will end up identifying the jungle people's tactics with the practices of colonialist commerce, thus blaming the victims after all and leaving only Marlow untainted by colonial corruption. But the final focalization on the white man's quest for understanding notwithstanding, the Africans' disruptive interference briefly discloses an altogether different option in the film, which it never manages to cancel out after that: understanding, the jungle people seem to argue, is *not* everything. With that they map out a line of action that is diametrically opposed to Marlow's project of communication and cooperation.

In a way, all of the narratives under investigation in this chapter will turn out to veer between the two poles marked out by Roeg's film: getting things done (Marlow's way) and messing things up (the jungle people's way). These options do not always appear in mutual exclusion; as a matter of fact we shall see that these days they may very well be thought of in terms of interdependence. With Marlow, a new kind of protagonist has entered the global scene who is neither hero nor agent in the classical sense but a pragmatic arranger and melancholic drifter, and in many contemporary fictions these attitudes go very well together with subversive projects of disruption and resistance, as we shall see.

Yet before we investigate this figure in more detail, let us cast a look at a trend in Africanist representation that could be said to epitomize the "global" perspective: Afropessimism and the logic of looking closely. Narratives that implement that logic often emphasize the aura of contingency, meaningless cruelty, and disruption that emanates from Roeg's jungle people. But we shall see that what is made out as utterly at odds with the familiar world often enough links up after all. The "heart of darkness" and the "horror" are still there, but a truly closer look will show that it is less clear than ever before where this darkness really stems from and where the horror is located.

5.3 Looking Closely: Afropessimism and Global Fictions

It is a disease, a mania with some people, that they never can relate the positive, literal, exact truth. Traveling in Africa is adventurous enough as it is, without any fiction.
—H. M. Stanley, *How I Found Livingstone* (1872)[28]

Conrad's Marlow averts his eyes from the concrete evidence of imperial injustice and abandons "looking too closely at the sordid realities of colonialism,"[29] turning to abstract reflections on good and evil instead. Roeg's Marlow, by contrast, never leaves the witness stand, representing the utterly foreign not in metaphysical terms but by way of close observations woven into a comprehensive, if seemingly unedited, "raw" report. With this, Roeg's film gives evidence of a shift of emphasis that characterizes many contemporary narratives of cultural difference: Since the early 1980s, journalists, travel writers, and popular authors concerned with "foreign affairs" have distanced themselves markedly from what they make out as the conventions of their fields, emphasizing their unbiased approach to their subject matter instead, unencumbered by the heavy weight of idealizing and exoticizing traditions and unfettered by political provisions and interests. Thus a rhetoric has evolved that could be called the rhetoric of looking closely.[30]

Mary Pratt has pinned down this development in the context of travel writing, where new "realistic" modes of representation have established themselves in marked contrast to the trite imageries of mass tourism: "In the 1960s and 1970s, exoticist visions of plenitude and paradise were appropriated and commodified on an unprecedented scale by the tourist industry. 'Real' writers took up the task of providing 'realist' (degraded, countercommodified) versions of postcolonial reality." The rhetoric of looking closely constitutes a "third worldism,"[31] Pratt argues, which not so much counters the long-standing imageries of imperial travel writing and modern mass tourism but rather supplements them. Now that exoticism is out, the detailed representation of corruption, hunger, poverty, and war is in: Afropessimism rules.

There is ample evidence that this trend has not abated since; in fact it seems more popular than ever in current writing on Africa, be it nonfictional or fictional. One example out of many may suffice to illustrate its ongoing effectivity. Keith Richburg, the Africa bureau chief for the *Washington Post* from 1991 to 1994, wrote an account of his experiences in Africa that was to become a best-seller in the United States and in Europe: *Out of America: A Black Man Confronts Africa* (1997). In order to come to terms with the traumatizing experiences of Somalian famine, Rwandan genocide, and South African postapartheid turmoils, Richburg turns against what he regards as the predominant modes of approaching Africa—Afrocentric romanticization and Western sentimentality—and opts for a close look instead. The result of this 1990s approach to the heart of darkness can be easily summed up in Kurtz's famous last words—the horror, indeed:

. . . while I know that "Afrocentrism" has become fashionable for many black Americans searching for identity, I know it cannot work for me. I have been here, I have lived here and seen Africa in all its horror. I know now that I am a stranger here, I am an American, a black American, and I feel no connection to this strange and violent place.[32]

For Richburg, looking closely is an honorable if dangerous endeavor—honorable in that it attacks the fallacies of the politically correct and ideologically misled, dangerous in that it is liable to bring about a proximity that is as revealing as it is infectious. You cannot look closely from a distance, after all, yet getting close might very well lead to losing the very objectivity and independence that should inspire journalism just like politics, according to Richburg.

The paradoxical twists of this logic come to the fore in a deeply disturbing account of global interaction: At one point, relatively early in the book, Richburg describes the United Nations' military action in Somalia in 1993, directed against General Mohamed Farah Aideed's Somali National Alliance. In the course of this action, a meeting place of Aideed's Alliance in Mogadishu was bombed and at least seventy people were killed, according to estimates of the International Red Cross. Richburg leaves no doubt that he vehemently objects to what he calls "the United Nations' first-ever officially authorized assassination," or, even more bluntly, "a slaughter" (*OoA* 79). In the riots after the event, four of Richburg's colleagues and friends were brutally killed by a Somali mob, one slaughter triggering another. The military intervention, he shows, clearly did not bring about a resolution but intensified an impending crisis. Given this account, Richburg's conclusion to the passage is all the more amazing:

> My own moral universe had just been turned completely upside down. We were the United States of America, and my country, I believed, did not go around assassinating people in houses and using the convenient cover of the UN flag to get away with it. We were supposed to be the good guys, the ones who always surrounded the house and told everybody inside to come out with their hands up. We read people their rights, gave them the chance to defend themselves in a court of law. But something had happened to the United States in this first postwar military expedition in Africa—we were behaving like they were. We had come into the jungle (or in this case, the desert) and adopted their survival-of-the-fittest rules. We had lost our moral high ground. (*OoA* 81)

For Richburg, Africa is doubtlessly a dangerous subject matter. Cultural contact and political interaction are problematical not because of longstanding projections, unacknowledged interests, and uneven positions, which complicate an allegedly symmetrical setup, but because they bring about the collapse of a hitherto absolutely unambiguous system of give-and-take, regularity and chaos, knowledge and ignorance. The United States as the "world police," adhering to a strict and inviolable code of law and order, represents the former aspects, while Third World countries around the globe stand for the latter. No wonder Richburg interprets the evidence of asymmetrical "exchange" exclusively in terms of African unreliability, a disorder emanating from one side only.[33] Once "infected" with the disease of African corruption, the stable and sound American system goes to pieces, giving way to primitivity unbound.[34]

This aside on *Out of America* may seem inappropriate given the overall focus of my study on fictional representations of Africa. But in view of the popular trend since the 1980s in film and literature of adopting techniques of cinema verité, docu-fiction, and the new journalism on a broad scale, both authenticating fiction and fictionalizing authenticity in turn, documentary accounts like Richburg's seem not that far away from psychohistories like Roeg's *Heart of Darkness,* not to mention the self-authenticating tone of contemporary white hunter narratives or a pseudodocumentary like Michael Crichton's *Congo.* Richburg's most striking counterpart, however, could arguably be Francesca Marciano's autobiographically infused novel *Rules of the Wild.* Indeed, Richburg, the real-life journalist based in Nairobi, by all likelihood would have gotten along splendidly with his fictional counterpart in Marciano's novel, Hunter Reed, another correspondent reporting out of Nairobi and propounding the unbiased view. Significantly enough, the Mogadishu bombing and the riots in its wake come up in *Rules of the Wild* as well—although drained of any political critique here—and again the events are made out as innately African, shocking and absolutely strange for the ones who dare to confront them:

So now you can see that things were beginning to take shape before my eyes; but the result was disheartening. The more I saw what living in Africa implied the less I understood where one was supposed to stand. Maybe my mistake was standing in the middle: I should commit to one side and stick to it. But would . . . it be the side of trendy European magazines, which chose Africa as the perfect backdrop for fashion shoots, or the side of those grieving young men, gathered to mourn the death of their friends stoned by an angry mob? That side, it seemed, revealed how hopelessly and mindlessly cruel Africa could be. (*RW* 111)

Of course, Esmé, being all the global girl, will never "commit to one side and stick to it." Her place is and will be "in the middle," and indeed, given the options between the true Africa, "hopelessly and mindlessly cruel," and the artificial "African Ambience" of Western commodities reassembled in a foreign space that she will come to cherish, who could blame her? Contemporary Africa comes across as so hopelessly beyond repair in both Richburg's journalistic account and Marciano's novel that the only options seem to be to stay away (Richburg's decision) or to make up your own alternative world (Marciano's choice). For your own good you had better come up with remedies against the infectious truth of Africa.

Unless, that is, you choose to adopt an altogether different approach. After all, these days the closest look is not necessarily achieved by way of direct confrontation and unmediated contact—as we learn at the beginning of Michael Crichton's *Congo,* when the American scientists invade the African jungle equipped with a multiplicity of mediating instruments: "We used goggles to see at night, and video to see during the day. We were using machines to see what we could not see otherwise, and we were totally dependent on them" (*C* 214). Transmitting their data back to the United States and receiving detailed evaluations in turn, the scientists first experience the jungle as an experimental scenario: complicated, but under control.

Bruce Sterling's novel *Islands in the Net* (1988) sets out with a similarly detached impression of Africa. Before the protagonist, Laura Webster, even thinks about experiencing Africa directly, she catches a glimpse of a computer simulation of the world, a "Worldrun game," in which Africa plays a characteristic part: "Long strips of the Earth's surface peeled by in a simulated satellite view. Cities glowed green with health or red with social disruption. Cryptic readouts raced across the bottom of the screen. Africa was a mess. 'It's always Africa, isn't it?' she said."[35] In a world depicted in terms of dazzling malleability and breathtaking change, the African chaos figures as a curious kind of stability. Throughout the novel, speaking about Africa means speaking in the negative but also with certainty—"[e]xcept for Africa" (*IN* 37), "[e]xcept in Africa" (*IN* 294), people keep qualifying whatever is said about the current state of affairs in the world. And when Laura returns to the United States at the end of the novel, after years of travel and trial, a brief glance at the screen is enough to get one thing settled at least: "A Worldrun game was on. Africa was a mess" (*IN* 374).

Just like Crichton, Sterling fashions his novel as a plausible account, an event that "could have been." Or rather, given the genre of cyber–science fiction, as an event likely to come about sometime soon. And just like Crichton, he eventually abandons the detached perspective and forces his characters to confront the facts on their own, without protective interfaces. Unmediated confrontation and the ensuing need for improvisation constitutes, after all, the most basic thrill of action adventure narratives. Therefore Laura will finally end up in Africa, physically experiencing a "mess" that easily tops the pessimistic horror visions of both Richburg and Marciano. A dumping ground for the rest of the world, Sterling's Africa hosts everything chaotic, grotesque, and negative still left in a world otherwise "netted together in a web . . . , a global system, an octopus of data" (*IN* 17). In Africa, remnants of older regimes still hold their power, and there is no end of terrorism, famines, corruption, pandemics, and environmental catastrophies: the horror, all over again. Yet in contrast to Richburg, Marciano, and many other propagandists of Afropessimism, Sterling locates the origin of the horror not in Africa but in the global network itself. Africa may be different from the rest of the world, but the difference is definitely not inherent.

Islands in the Net begins in the year 2022, at a time when almost all the world has been regularized underneath the order of the "Net," an order closely linked up with global corporations such as Laura's company—called, appropriately enough, Rizome. While these corporations seem so much more relevant than the old nation-states and a new world administration in Vienna, they do not stand unchallenged: "Data pirates," small semilegal operations all over the world, get to the new economic empires where it hurts most, acquiring and selling data trash, "scattered bits of information" collated, abstracted, and condensed to "a new and sinister whole" (*IN* 42). Laura Webster and her husband David, both Rizome employees, become caught up in a complicated plot as the conflicts between two such pirate operations, a Grenadan syndicate and the Singapore Islamic Bank, blow up, culminating in a guerrilla attack on Grenada.

With this thematic layout, the novel of 1988 set the tone for a new turn in cyberfiction, away from the playfully detached experiments of yore and toward much bleaker and less futuristic speculations around a global economy at large. In her reflection on the cyberfictional state of the art in 1999, Emily Apter casts light on a literary genre "rife with post-colonial scenarios that highlight the anachronicity of the future,"[36] and then continues to map out a catalogue of current fictional themes and concerns that are markedly at odds with a 1980s cyberaesthetics of black chrome, mirror shades, and leather: "multinational power brokering, world debt finance, transnational speculation."[37] Bruce Sterling, this founding father and spokesman of the cyberpunk movement, has always been drawn to such unglamorous ideological issues,[38] and *Islands in the Net* is certainly a case in point. This is why I choose to call his novel a "global" fiction rather than a cyberpunk novel—with its emphasis on transnational corporations and terrorist organizations, it certainly is as up-to-date as it was in 1988.

The world of corporations and multinationals in *Islands in the Net* only seems to have overcome the differentiations and conflicts of old. The Net is about to lose control, and greed, racism, nationalism, and other deepset desires and passions show their ugly faces again. An insight formulated toward the end of the novel could thus form its motto: ". . . the bright television world was brewing something dark and awful in its deepest voodoo corners" (*IN* 327).

At some point it will become apparent that a terrorist group consisting of outlaws from all over the world—"specialists, technicians [who] learned things, in Lebanon, Afghanistan, Namibia" (*IN* 326)—is behind the events that triggered the worldwide conflicts in the first place. This global group may be based in Africa, yet it is definitely not "African"—figuring forth the parody of a nation-state, as its leaders have taken over an entire country, Mali, turning its government into a puppet show and using the resources and people for the group's secret purposes. While clearly as opaque and destructive as Roeg's jungle people, this artificial African organization is much more efficient and much more up-to-date than its filmic counterparts. The terrorists from Mali are futuristic, not ancient—or rather futuristic atavists. While never ending meetings, investigations, and negotiations paralyze both the transnational corporations and the world government in Vienna, the terrorists have no qualms about taking action. Significantly enough, they call themselves FACT; an acronym that stands ironically for Free Army of Counter-Terrorism but of course primarily indicates the will to create facts, a will that is time and again associated with the semilegal, the outsiders, and the activists in this novel—with the "islands" in the "Net."

Laura, who tries to mediate between the various parties involved, finds out about FACT and is incarcerated in Mali to prevent her from going public. After almost two years of imprisonment she escapes, however, rescued by this book's white hunter update, called Jonathan Gresham. Gresham, an American journalist, directs the spearhead of local resistance against FACT, the so-called Inadin Cultural Revolution, an underground movement that insists on its African authenticity.

Of course, the Inadins' emphasis on their essential Africanness is considerably qualified by the very figure of their leader—Gresham, the American media person, activist, and "cultural meddler" (*IN* 364). Indeed, at second sight the Cultural Revolution has more in common with FACT than they let on. FACT makes itself out as an antiglobalization movement, yet the group's spokesmen and public statements seem facelessly and apolitically global themselves. The Inadins, too, seem determined to disrupt rather than take a stance. Their resistance is not to be grasped in political terms. Although their mastermind Gresham is once called a "right-wing intellectual"—and thus cast in political categories—he personally prefers to be seen as a "postindustrial tribal anarchist" (*IN* 388). Like the leaders of FACT, he defines his movement as a purely negative project, as negative as the artificial Africa that forms these groups' backdrop. The Inadins, Gresham proudly proclaims in an interview, do not really have a goal—except the project of remaining independent. Like all the other groupings in the novel, his organization has a telling name: "[I]t's not just another bullshit cover name, they *are* cultural, they're fighting for it, dying for it" (*IN* 343), he declares.

Sterling's "islands in the Net," his movements of global resistance and disruption, thus replicate a pervasive conceptual shift of the day, a shift that Fredric Jameson has defined in terms of abandoning the code and thematics furnished by the sixties—"that of the political"[39]—and in terms of embracing the so much more up-to-date code of "the cultural," a code that is deeply, if tacitly, enmeshed with the economic. In the postmodern era, Fredric Jameson argued, the formerly diversified levels of culture and economy merge with each other, "the cultural gradually becoming the economic, all the while the economic becomes the cultural."[40]

For Gresham's Cultural Revolution, culture means consumption, as we shall see. While Gresham vehemently argues for African difference and against its integration into the Net's dominant order, which would make it "[g]reen and pleasant and controlled and just like everywhere else" (*IN* 366), he steers a far from radically antimodern course. To fight the system, his logic runs, you have to know the system. But every so often, precisely this logic comes dangerously close to its paradoxical inversion: to fight the system, you have to join it. Gresham's description of a historical model figure is significant:

"Over a century ago, Lawrence . . . he was British, First World War . . . discovered how a tribal society could defend itself from industrial imperialism. . . . The Arab revolt stopped the Turkish cultural advance, literally in its tracks. They did this with guerilla assaults on the railroads and telegraphs, the Turkish industrial control system. For success, however, the Arabs were forced to use industrial artifacts—namely, guncotton, dynamite, and canned food. For us it is solar power, plastique, and single-cell protein." (*IN* 388)

By dint of this outline, Lawrence of Arabia turns out to be the first-ever cyberpunk, turning technology against its original use and fighting the enemy with its own weapons. But of course, once it is reintroduced into a context of international and intercultural relations, the image of the cyberpunk guerrilla fighter undergoes a curious twist. In William Gibson's *Neuromancer* (1984), the novel that launched the vogue of cyberpunk resistance, a group of social and racial outsiders comes against a faceless system of power and money. In Sterling's novel, by contrast, the outsider *is* the insider: Lawrence was British, Gresham is American—both of them have more in common with the enemy than with their self-chosen "people," and it is on these grounds that they promote the new use of industrial artifacts. Gresham steers resistance and monitors dissent, not unlike his filmic counterparts in action adventures of the period. And just as in these films, the native recipients of the gift of subversion seem largely unaware of its implications. At one point Gresham translates a local "folk" song for Laura:

> . . . we were the enemies of the grass,
> That is why we suffer.
> What our cows did not eat, the sheep ate.
> What the sheep refused, the goats consumed.
> What the goats left behind, the camels devoured.
> Now we must be the friends of the grass,
> We must apologize to it and treat it kindly.
> Its enemies are our enemies.
> We must kill the cow and the sheep,
> We must butcher the goat and behead the camel.
> For a thousand years we must praise the grass.
> We will eat the *tisma* food to live,
> We will buy Iron Camels from GoMotion
> Unlimited in Santa Clara California. (*IN* 363)

When Laura asks Gresham whether he has written the song, he denies: "'No,' he said proudly. 'It's an old song.' He paused. 'Retrofitted'" (*IN* 364).

Retrofitting culture means adapting the old to the conditions of the new, a strategic reinterpretation that seems to be lost on its recipients here. After all, the folk song cloaks the call for responsible consumption in the rhetoric of authenticity, intricately interlinking cultural and economic matters, while once more giving vent to the impression that the native mindframe allows for only so much innovation. In a curious repercussion of an earlier narrative of innovation by cultural manipulation, Haggard's *King Solomon's Mines*, Gresham's Cultural Revolution seems to aim at an ideal state of perfect isolation: "We will not be tamed or assimilated. By your very nature, by your very presence you would force assimilation on us. That will not be allowed" (*IN* 387). This sounds like a negative version of Haggard's Kukuanaland, sealed off from the rest of the world, this time not in timeless perfection but in eternal negativity.

And yet, at second glance Conrad's *Heart of Dearkness* figures more prominently as a subtext for Sterling's novel than Haggard's text. After all, just as in Conrad's novella, things turn out to be intricately and secretly connected in *Islands in the Net*. And it is Marlow, the pragmatic worker, who provides a more appropriate model for Gresham's "cultural meddling" than Haggard's Quatermain. The world of Sterling's novel is as "post-political" as it is "[p]ostindustrial" (*IN* 223), since other, seemingly more appropriate means of interaction and meaning making take the place of political interests and agendas. Enthusing about the working conditions in Grenada's science labs, Laura's geeky husband David states the obsoleteness of politics at the very outset of the novel: "The tech is more important than the politics" (*IN* 158), and his dismissal of a political line of thought in favor of technological "hard facts" seems to demarcate a general trend. In line with this logic, none of the many terrorist groups and pirate operations making an appearance raise political demands, as even the most radical of them are seen to be tied up in the forces of the market and in the logic of marketing. Nothing is behind the spectacular effects of disturbance and disruption all over the world: "this was not an act of politically motivated terrorism" (*IN* 66), runs the comment to the novel's first terrorist murder.

Of course, such tautological activism is not without its precedents in cyberfiction. William Gibson's media terrorists, the Panther-Moderns, come to mind, who contest the overall processes of co-optation and appropriation in the cybernetic world order of their day: "Terrorism as we ordinarily understand it is innately media-related. The Panther-Moderns differ from other terrorists precisely in their degree of self-consciousness, in their awareness of the extent to which media divorce the act of terrorism from the original socio-political intent."[41] If the media turn terrorism into a mere spectacle, dismissing its political interests and social critique as irrelevant, the Panther-Moderns turn spectacle into terrorism. "Chaos . . . is our mode and modus," explains their leader at one time, accentuating the circular quality of this resistance, which displays nothing but the potential to disrupt the ordered, to shatter conventions.

In *Neuromancer,* the anarchic project—as ironized as it is—figures as the only alternative to the co-optation of resistance movements by the market and the mainstream. Sterling's novel proves much more skeptical, as it does not really allow for such independence. For the Inadins and their leader the culturalization—and, by implication, the commercialization—of their project will ultimately turn out to be its most crucial shortfall. They will be reintegrated into the global Net on the grounds of their consumption patterns. Once she is back with Rizome, Laura Webster, who has learned from Gresham's retrofitted song about the Inadins' preference for "GoMotion Unlimited" motorbikes, knows precisely what has to be done in order to shatter the isolationist movement:

"Iron Camels, from GoMotion Unlimited in Santa Clara, California. We should make inquiries. . . . Don't you see it? Iron Camels—the Jonathan Gresham Look. Every would-be tough guy and rugged individualist and biker lunatic on this planet is gonna want one for himself. . . . And there's not a damn thing [Gresham] can do about *that.*" (*IN* 391)

If you cannot beat them, turn them into a fashion movement. Once more, the global girl's stance, the position in the midst of things yet on top of them, has proven superior to the classical white hunter's effort at individualist self-authentication, with Laura coolly negotiating African chaos and African difference because she is familiar with the rebels' consumption patterns.

5.4 It's Magic! Globalization Totalized

In Conrad's *Heart of Darkness,* the "monkey tricks" of imperialism gain a curious double function: For one, they are self-deceiving devices, deflecting from the dirty facts of racial inequality and colonial exploitation. But they are always also survival techniques. It is only because Marlow tends to his daily duties, working alongside his fireman, that he avoids being drawn into the dark vortex of the country, the "unspeakable rites" Kurtz falls for. The daily routine on the steamer, uniting Marlow and his crew in a strange choreography of interaction, resonates with the regularized machinations of capitalist enterprise, as set against Kurtz's private and unconstrained greed: "'My Intended, my ivory, my station, my river, my———' everything belonged to him" (*HD* 85). Kurtz's monomaniacal desire for private property is going to destroy him, just as Leopold's personal greed eventually brought the Congo Free State down. Marlow's "monkey tricks," by contrast, will win the day. As the logic of conquest gives way to the strategies of co-optation, new paradigms for cultural contact arise: the buzzwords of the age to come are interaction, compatibility, and communication.

Seen that way, Marlow's routine prefigures the survival schemes mapped out by Roeg and Sterling, as different as they are. Pragmatic coalitions and day-to-day negotiations take over and ultimately inflect not only the global lines of action but also local schemes of reaction and resistance, as Roeg's jungle people and Sterling's underground "islands" indicate. The noble project of individualist self-authentication dissolves into techniques of coping and make-do, while its counterforces undergo reconceptualizations just as well. In turn, guerrilla tactics replace heroic rebellion, and sheer disruption sets in where political dissent used to unfold.

The mastermind of this kind of shape-shifting in Sterling's *Islands in the Net* is not Jonathan Gresham, however, but the Grenadan Sticky Thompson, a man of many faces and even more devices, who dons cultural identities like other people put on their working clothes, appearing as Rastafarian hipster, terrorist hit man, and Tamil passerby in Singapore. In other words, Sticky, this incarnation of a Third World activist, is a cyborg: "Laura understood now why his skin color had varied. It wasn't makeup, but chameleon technical tricks, right down in the cells. Lots of changes—maybe too many" (*IN* 137). There might always be a rational explanation to Sticky's masquerades and maneuvers, but this is not the point: "With the tech they gave us, I can do things you can't tell from magic" (*IN* 223), he explains, before he helps to bring down the Singapore system by way of technomanipulations. If, that is, they really were technomanipulations and not magic in the first place. Time and again, the novel's narrative voice indicates that there is indeed a supernatural quality to the dark and awful events brewing in the world's "deepest voodoo corners" (*IN* 327).

Significantly enough, both Roeg and Sterling associate the most effective new modes of resistance to the powers of colonialism and globalization with magic and mysticism: the subversive schemes of Roeg's jungle people are presented as stemming from "another" logic, beyond and at odds with the logic of commerce and exchange, while Sterling confronts the bright new world of global capitalism with an alternative—dark and secretive—system of signification: voodoo. In contrast to Roeg's primitivist rebels, however, Sterling's outlaws are far from premodern. Obviously no strangers to the world of capitalist consumption and production, voodooists like Sticky Thompson continuously bridge the gap between trickery and magic, modernity and tradition, merging both spheres instead of casting them as mutually exclusive. But then this is nothing altogether new.

Voodoo, for one, this epitome of Africanity, has been enacted for quite some time now as a link between spheres that seem diametrically opposed. Thus Ishmael Reed's novel *Mumbo Jumbo,* published in 1972 and set in the 1920s, envisions a new kind of loa, a modernized voodoo spirit symbolically conjoining jazz age and postmodernity: "we have a Radio Loa who just came about during this war. It loves to hear the static concerning its victims' crimes before it 'eats' them. . . . This particular loa has a Yellow Back to symbolize its electric circuitry. We are always careful not to come too close to it. It's a very mean, high-powered loa."[42] If this modernization emphasizes voodoo's syncretic character, it also collates spiritual and social concerns, giving scope to a markedly new model of action and agency, as we shall see.

Reed insists upon voodoo's modernity, while simultaneously emphasizing its ancient power: voodoo messes things up, and it is dangerous to mess with, never altogether under individual control, with a momentum of its own that is as fascinating as it is frightening. This reenactment of voodoo can be linked back to an African diasporic tradition.[43] But *Mumbo Jumbo* has at least as much in common with "the whole tattered carnival of contemporary religion" in the West—"oily New Age gurus and Pentecostal crusaders, existential Buddhists and liberation theologians, psychedelic pagan ravers and grizzled deep ecologists."[44] That is, if it makes sense to draw a clear-cut line between certain spiritualist dimensions of the African diaspora and these Western trends in the first place. Both developments attest to a pervasive desire for a *"re-enchantment* of the world," after all, a desire that Zygmunt Baumann located at the core of postmodern culture.[45] In the course of this quest for sense and meaning, seemingly unrelated traditions and sources are resuscitated and reassembled: Western popular culture, African cults, Eastern rites, indigenous traditions, fairy tales and myths. John McClure has elaborated the idea of a "New Spiritual Awakening" since the 1960s, when he evoked a "post-colonial return of the repressed"[46] and pointed out the need to turn to "less academically accredited sources" to come to grips with this phenomenon.[47]

In the course of this development, the logic of getting things done supersedes the logic of things just happening. Or having things done to you. If this does not necessarily imply an overall view and total control, it does almost always evoke the imagery of coping and immediacy—drawing from whatever comes handy in a vast repertory of cultural references and religious traditions. Thus a mixed-up and asynchronic cultural scenario—a scenario usually associated with "exotic" cultures—comes to be located right at the core of "our world," as Bruno Latour has argued: "It is not only the Bedouins and the !Kung who mix up transistors and traditional behaviors, plastic buckets and animal-skin vessels. What country could not be called 'a land of contrasts'? We have all reached the point of mixing up times. We have all become premodern again."[48]

The question is, of course, whether our current condition is to be conceived of in terms of a "return" to premodern mindframes, or whether Baumann's notion of a re-enchantment makes more sense. After all, this is not about the surfacing of an old order but about the upsurge of a markedly new one: a hybrid concoction of different symbolic systems and schools of thought. "[T]echnology is becoming more and more like magic—with a class of people who know the incredibly complex spells and incantations needed to get the stuff to work," remarked the science fiction author Samuel Delany,[49] thus neatly inverting the modern (and colonialist) rhetoric about technology and magic we saw at work in H. Rider Haggard's novel.

Yet while the present situation clearly differs from Haggard's scenario, it is certainly no less ambivalent than the earlier constellation. The mixup of modernity and magic, technology and the spiritual, turns out to be as involved in the ideological act of distinction as were Haggard's juggling acts one hundred years ago. At a time when mainstream culture eagerly embraces marginality and difference, the demarcation of alternative stances becomes a crucial endeavor in its own right. By dint of this development, distinction turns from a means of fencing oneself off against the primitive (magical) other into the project of becoming this other.

From this vantage point, I would like to return briefly to Sterling's novel, this blueprint of so many other global fictions to come. It is interesting to note that Sterling's "modernization" of voodoo has far less fantastic implications than Reed's "voodoo virus" in *Mumbo Jumbo*. In *Islands in the Net,* the hint of magic in modernity does not really mean the existence of a radically different order of being at the heart of the familiar world. On the contrary, the voodooists in *Islands in the Net* are as grounded as their predecessors in William Gibson's *Count Zero*—where a group of cybervoodoo priests is once characterized as being "business men first."[50] In both cases, the difference between technological, commercial, and religious-spiritual concerns does not really matter any longer.

In line with this logic, Sterling's Caribbean magicians and wizards aim at the exact same things as the agents of global commerce. They want control—control of the images of reality, of information, and ultimately control of the world: "You see, we know everything about you. But you know *nothing at all* about us," a representative of the Grenadan syndicate tells Laura before confronting her with a dramatic display of voodoo

magic that might be "real" or just a "trick." But then—whether it is magical practices that control reality or electronic tricks is not all that important in the end: "Tricks you call it," another Grenadan ridicules Laura's
recourse to rationality, "[r]eality's nothing but levels and levels of tricks"
(*IN* 151). Sticky Thompson and his partners are successful not because
they move on truly different grounds than the corporate powers but because they manage to beat them at their own game—practicing a syncretic religion that is as down-to-earth functional as any of the novel's
business ventures. Seen that way, the claustrophobically closed world of
the newly strengthened globalists with which the novel ends—a world
that has nothing of the rhizome and everything of a net—is truly all-
confining. For Sterling, it seems, the corrupt control system of the global
world is so pervasive that to act means invariably to become part of it.
There is no outside any longer; even the "mess" of Africa figures as an integral part of the scenario at large.[51] Sticky Thompson, for one, seems to
have recognized this at the end of the novel. Back in the United States,
Laura reviews a tape of the Inadin Cultural Revolution and catches a
glimpse of somebody familiar in the background: "That walk, that sa-
lute. Under that veil, it's got to be him. Sticky—Nesta Stubbs. Of course,
where else would he go?" (*IN* 390).

Since Sterling's novel came out, a panoply of other global fictions has
appeared, and time and again Sterling's logic has been replicated—you
cannot escape, because the evil powers of greed and corruption have already enveloped the entire globe. These days even John Le Carré has
turned from Cold War scenarios of infiltration and espionage to the
theme of corporational corruption—played out along the lines of pharmaceutical business ventures and clinical trial series in Africa. A quick
glance at his *Constant Gardener* (2001) may suffice to demonstrate how
much of a routine both Afropessimism and the notion of a world "netted" irretrievably together has become. Le Carré evokes a convoluted
conspiracy on a global scale, calling to mind the immoral schemes in
Crichton's *Congo* and Sterling's *Islands in the Net,* and in his book too
the center of the corruption is hard to make out—it seems to have spread
to cover the planet. While there are many unsavory characters in Le
Carré's novel, no evil mastermind comes into view—nobody really seems
to be in charge and in control any longer. The evil is faceless and without
identity. The good guys, on the other hand, are mapped out in full and
positive detail. In fact, it seems as if the author took his heroes straight
out of a manual of cosmopolitan self-fashioning: Tessa Quayle, the
beautiful Anglo-Italian "Society Girl Turned Oxbridge Lawyer,"[52] her
companion Arnold Bluhm, "the Westerner's African, bearded Apollo of
the Nairobi cocktail round, charismatic, witty, beautiful" (*CG* 31), and

finally their Anglo-Indian friend Ghita Pearson, the "second most beautiful woman in Nairobi" (CG 256) after Tessa, who thinks of herself as of
an "unsavable hybrid" (CG 347).

The fact that the bulk of the action takes place after Tessa's and
Arnold's deaths, as Tessa's widowed husband, British diplomat Justin
Quayle, tries to uncover the circumstances of their murder, does not
really mitigate this emphasis: after all, the diplomat and agent might be
Le Carré's classical hero of choice, but here this figure in the service of the
queen clearly testifies to a bygone order—the days of the empire are over.
Traveling from Kenya to England, Italy, Germany, Canada, and South Africa, Justin has to learn the hard way what one of his opponents, the African gangster boss Kenny K, knew all along: "You're history," Kenny
once tells a colleague of Justin's. "You think *countries* run the fucking
world! Go back to fucking Sunday school. It's 'God save our multinational' they're singing these days" (CG 416). For Le Carré, just as for
Sterling over ten years before, politics are no longer an option. And just
like Sterling, Le Carré does not really present a way out. In the end, the
good guys are either dead or defeated. They might have won, but their
victory is far from spectacular or deepgoing.

But then, from the very beginning the novel is not really concerned
with a positive outcome or the concrete impact of resistance but rather
sets out to celebrate its sheer beauty. Justin's recollections of his love
story with Tessa are a case in point: "he had been drawn completely by
accident into a beautiful play, and was captivated by it. He was in a different element, acting a part, and the part was the one he had often
wanted to play in life, but never till now quite brought off" (CG 145).
Tessa, whose "theatrical" aura is mentioned time and again, transfers the
spirit of noble role-playing on everybody around. The "experience of
real tragedy," we learn at some point, did not dim her "theatrical impulses" (CG 111)—and indeed, why should it? To stay in character and
act one's part admirably is the only compensation these heroes will ever
get. Indeed, in the course of the novel, their performances of resistance,
while rather ineffective on the plot level, will easily blot out their
opponents' sorry displays of egotism and corruption by dint of their dramatic effect. Seen from this vantage point, the vantage point of effect, the
good guys win the game after all, precisely because they die for their
cause. The logic of pragmatic action gives way to the mode of high tragedy and virtually effaces the ambivalences and complications at the heart
of the crisis depicted. Here, the standard scenarios of Afropessimism—
suffering, corruption, environmental crisis—provide the stage set for a
highly individualized drama of classical scope.

But the totalizing turn to resignation or tragedy is not the only option.

For the rest of this chapter, I would thus like to turn to instances of "global" representation in a radically different mode—narratives that counter the logic of Afropessimism with the less grandiose tone of the tragicomic farce.

5.5 Swallow It All: Explorers and Cannibals

I saw him open his mouth wide—it gave him a weirdly voracious aspect, as though he had wanted to swallow all the air, all the earth, all the men before him.
—Joseph Conrad, *Heart of Darkness* (1902)

Twentieth-century culture has been rightfully called "cannibal culture,"[53] as processes of appropriation and incorporation, co-optation and takeover seem to constitute the very lifeline of contemporary cultural self-fashioning, in the West and almost everywhere else. Once one turns to the history of colonialism, however, the imagery of cultural "cannibalism" in its interrelation with the rhetoric of trade and exchange proves to have a much longer tradition, as we shall see. From the vantage point of colonialism, it has always been difficult to conceptualize trade as an ideal system of reciprocity and equality, a system aiming at mutual benefits yet sadly compromised the moment social hierarchies, personal convictions, and irrational impulses come in. Time and again, the inherent ambivalence of trade, its complicated interaction with the forces of power, ethics, and desire, have proved hard to ignore in this context.[54] This ambivalence becomes conspicuous in the debates around free trade at the outset of the Congo Free State—in response to the passionate (European) demands for equal opportunity, immediate access, and unobstructed interaction evolved one of the most unabashedly cruel systems of exploitation and subjugation in the colonial history of Africa.

If this is an extreme example of the clash between ideal and reality, the history of colonial relations gives ample evidence of similar if less spectacular cases. It also testifies, however, to an equally long-standing tradition of critique and contestation pitted against the practices of colonial commerce. The obviously unjust system of trade in the colonies caused unease on the European side from its outset and provoked a panoply of critical responses from conscientious observers and guilt-ridden participants of the colonial crusades and takeovers. As Stephen Greenblatt has shown in his analysis of such a line of criticism—Michel de Montaigne's "Of Cannibals"—the apprehensions about colonial trade and its conventions were triggered by the suspicion that the systematic implementation of deception, fraud, and force was bound to backfire at some point, affecting the perpetrators' culture and their self-perception just as it affected the world and worldview of the colonized.[55] Once more, Conrad's imagery of the "monkey tricks" performed knowingly or unknowingly on all sides comes to mind.

In Conrad's text, the critique of the colonial masquerade gives way to its aggrandizement, however, as the novella ultimately evokes an aura of tragedy and grandiose failure. Not accidentally, it is precisely this pathos that other approaches to the same theme set out to challenge: taking Kurtz and his moral dilemma seriously is seen to deflect from the actual focus of events—the "robbery with violence, aggravated murder on a grand scale" (*HD* 31) that Conrad deplored only to eventually lose sight of it.

Indeed, this much quoted indictment of imperialism in *Heart of Darkness* could be considered a motto for all kinds of revisionary projects concerned with colonialism. Time and again, such revisions aim at laying bare the links between commerce and cruelty that have been obfuscated for so long. One technique for emphasizing this connection is already given in Conrad's text when Kurtz's desire to "swallow . . . all the men before him" calls to mind earlier reflections around cannibalism, focusing on the African workers on the steamer: "Fine fellows—cannibals—in their place" (*HD* 75). Then, Marlow approached the subject in an altogether pragmatical tone, noting that the Africans' hunger for human flesh seemed quite justified, as they were paid with "three pieces of brass wire a week" but not fed: "So unless they swallowed the wire itself, or made loops of it to snare the fishes with, I don't see what good their extravagant salary could be to them" (*HD* 75). While the cannibals are forced to go civilized and starve in turn, the Western man aspires to go cannibal, taking part in "certain midnight dances ending with unspeakable rites" (*HD* 86). Both sides are linked via the rhetoric of economy and consumption: Kurtz's "hunger" for possession, the cannibals' inedible payment—the very concrete (cannibalism) and the very abstract (commerce) merging to form a curious and highly ambivalent alliance. "In cannibalism," wrote Michael Taussig about the Colombian colonial system around the turn of the century, "they [the colonists] and those who chose to represent them to the outside world found a 'way station,' so to speak, a point of strategic convergence in the rubber station where the assumed forms of life of the savage met the savagery assumed by the trade."[56]

Crystal Bartolovitch has analyzed this conceptual interlinkage and its implications recently with reference to early modern travel writing and Marx's later critique of capitalism. Anticannibalistic and anticapitalist rhetoric, she argues, come together not as equivalents but as supplements—cannibalism is envisioned in terms of "absolute consumption," whereas Marx characterizes capitalism as a technique of "disciplined" consumption or a consumption "under restraint": "the capitalist is a cannibal-manqué."[57] Even if Bartolovitch does not mention Conrad, her observations concur neatly with his differentiation of Kurtz's greed and the Company men's "restraint" (*HD* 77).

Cannibalism, commerce, and colonial rule turn out to be intricately connected phenomena in this light, and while Conrad both acknowledges and obfuscates the links, two other, more recent, takes on the scenarios of cultural takeover and economic exploitation draw upon the same imagery with much more disturbing concreteness. Both the play *Faustus in Africa!* (1995), performed by the South African Handspring Puppet Company and directed by William Kentridge, and T. Coraghessan Boyle's novel *Water Music* (1981) reenact colonialism in order to come to terms with constellations and contortions of the present time, and both present cannibalism and colonialism as interrelated practices that are far from extinct in our day, as their unacknowledged common ground—capitalism—is still very much alive. Hence both texts, I will argue, are as up-to-date as Crichton's, Sterling's, and Le Carré's much more openly "contemporary" fictionalizations of globalization and (post)modern cultural and commercial exchange, if not more so, since the detour to historical setups permits both the Handspring Company and Boyle to address the incongruities that are so central, and so obscure, in *Islands in the Net* and other global fictions. In the course of the Handspring Company's and Boyle's revision, the self-perpetuating practices of commerce, conquest, and communication at the heart of the colonial venture move into the foreground of representation, while the classical personae of colonial contact narratives—explorers, adventurers, and deep thinkers in the vein of Conrad's Kurtz—are flattened to the degree of caricature. Both texts, I argue, are not so much about people as about the conditions and circumstances that keep people going.

In *Faustus in Africa!*[58] it is Goethe's individualist hero, not Conrad's, who demarcates the center of revisionist attention, but the analogies between Kurtz and Faust are only too obvious—as Nicolas Roeg clearly saw when he had Kurtz quote Goethe's play to express his dread and despair. The play combines nearly life-size wooden puppets and live actors onstage, employs theatrical as well as filmic elements of representation (a large video screen with "background information" by way of maps, historical images, texts, etc., and animations of Kentridge's renowned charcoal drawings), and patches together passages of Goethe's *Faust* and *Faust, the Tragedy's Second Part* with impressions from Mikhail Bulgakov's *Master and Margarita* and texts of the South African poet Lesego Rampolokeng. Focusing on Faust's fate, the production thus approaches another canonical Western hero on the quest for knowledge, which every so often proved indistinguishable from the desire for conquest. But Kentridge and his company refuse to take Faustus's tragic predicament seriously. This Faustus is nothing but a puppet, moved by a master, the white puppeteer David Minaar, who is always in plain view. In fact, the only person on stage who does not handle a puppet is the black actor Leslie Fong, who plays Mephisto, and even he can be seen to be secretly controlled by a hidden puppet master: God (spoken by the actress Busi Zokufa).

Transferred to the colonial space of Africa, *the* Western drama of the estranged individual is fractured and rewritten to dismantle the very imagery of heroic individualism: Faustus's most dramatic and heartfelt gestures are nothing but acts, performed by a puppet, and the fact that one often tends to block out the puppeteer's presence only reinforces the overall effect of witnessing a masquerade on display for everyone but its participants. If this strategy of representation discourages any reception along the lines of cathartic self-scrutiny—and thus runs counter to the psychological turn that Nicolas Roeg's revisionary narrative underwent—it forces the audience into ever more complicated analytical maneuvers. A constant back-and-forth between explicit political critique and slapstick, spectacular effects and literary quotation, epitomizes the interconnectedness of the grand narratives of the past (the literary masterpieces just like the historiographical master narratives) with the fragmentary tales of the present and ultimately calls for a reading of colonialism under the insignia of postcolonial disintegration and reorientation. On the grounds of such techniques, the performance manages to avoid the pattern of the Afropessimistic "close look" without falling for the other extreme of a naively optimistic rhetoric of universal goodwill and understanding, steering a third course that gets a much better grip on the self-perpetuating structures at work.

Kentridge mixes up the second part of Goethe's tragedy, in which Faust goes capitalist, with the first part's seduction story—both plotlines coming across as stories of willful acquisition. Highly stylized, "naive" animations on the background screen call up and ironize the traditional imagery of conquest—be it maps documenting the thrust of Faustus's imperialist progression, or be it the comical depiction of a safari where almost every being or item coming into view is shot and thus "cleaned away." One of the most impressive scenes, "The Banquet," shows Faustus literally eating up the continent to the background sounds of loud masticating and swallowing. As he tears huge chunks out of an undefined entity on his plate, the screen behind his back shows a map of Africa being attacked with knife and fork—once more, as in Walter Abish's *Alphabetical Africa,* the effect of Africa's economic and political takeover by entrepreneurs and corporations is made out as its disappearance: here, Africa is the object, rather than origin, of cannibalism.

As tragedy is replaced by farce, depth by surface, cannibalism is not enacted as an early, "primitive" form of capitalism but as all there is to it; not a secret African practice but the spectacular expression of all-pervasive co-optation—after all, Faustus does not go native but performs his cannibalistic act under the refined circumstances of a banquet. By this token, however, cannibalism turns from an "unspeakable rite" into a quite mundane if not altogether palatable practice. Like so many other recent reenactments of the theme, *Faustus in Africa!* envisions the cannibal as the modern subject par excellence—civilization and refinement intricately linked up with the problems at hand, rather than holding them at bay. Reflecting upon a vogue of the cannibal theme in films from *Eat the Rich* (1987) to *The Cook, the Thief, His Wife, and Her Lover* (1989), *Delicatessen* (1991), and finally *The Silence of the Lambs* (1991), Maggie Kilgour noted a fundamental shift of focus:

I think that the function of cannibalism in culture and criticism today lies in its utility as a form of cultural criticism. Where in the past the figure of the cannibal has been used to construct differences that uphold racism, it now appears in projects to deconstruct them. . . . The man-eating myth is still with us, but now explicitly revealed to be a story about *ourselves*, not others, as the cannibal has moved from the fringes of our world to its very centre.[59]

This "centralization" of the cannibal is not only due to the theme's recently recognized critical potential, however, but also hinges on its iconicity, documented by countless cartoons, comic strips, and action adventures that set up the timelessly silly scenario we find neatly summarized in Lee Thompson's *King Solomon's Mines*: Sharon Stone and Richard Chamberlain in a huge cooking pot along with assorted vegetables, added—no doubt—for taste, while the African tribe who captured them war-dances around, working up an appetite for the feast to come. The two white heroes manage to escape, of course, but given the stupidity of the entire scenario, it is only too tempting to project the revisionary turn Kilgour detects in the late 1980s upon this film and to wish for the cannibals' success against the odds of genre convention and diegetic consecutiveness.

If this is not a likely turn for a 1980s action adventure to take, it suffuses a novel of 1981 that seems grounded in the technique of raising expectations only to shatter them in turn: T. Coraghessan Boyle's *Water Music*. Like "Big Game," the story written over ten years later and based upon Hemingway's "Macomber," *Water Music* draws upon other narratives—this time most notably Mungo Park's *Travels in the Interior*

Districts of Africa, describing the 1795 "discovery" of the course of the Niger. Again, to say that Boyle takes liberties with the literary and historical material at hand is to state the obvious. "Where historical fact proved a barrier to the exigencies of invention, I have, with full knowledge and clear conscience, reshaped it to fit my purposes," the author declares in a prologue.[60]

Water Music, like *Faustus in Africa!* exposes the rhetoric of disinterested exploration and benevolent colonization as the empty shell it is. In contrast to the South African Faust, however, who clearly has the upper hand until his final downfall, Boyle's individualist hero, Mungo Park, never stands a chance in Africa. He may survive his first trip out of sheer luck but fails dramatically at his second expedition, which brings about his death and the deaths of countless others, European and African, whom he dragged into his manic and vainglorious project to "know the unknowable, see the unseen, scale mountains and look behind the stars" (*WM* 90). When Mungo comes across Ali Ibn Fatoudi, the emir of Ludamar, during his first trip, the self-referentiality of this quest comes to the fore: "'I'm looking for the River Niger,'" Mungo proudly explains to the Emir. "Ali studied his great toe for a moment and then looked up. 'There are no rivers in your country?'" (*WM* 27). The great adventure of exploration—here, it turns into a farce of continuous misunderstandings and never ending miscommunication.

If the Africans Mungo encounters clearly do not see much sense in being discovered and explored, Mungo cannot imagine anything more important. This discrepancy calls up no end of conflicts and clashes, which Mungo is determined not to face. Time and again, he manages to "edit" his actual (grotesque, gruesome, absurd) experiences, so that they fit the expectations of his European readership. "[T]hey want a little glamour, a touch of the exotic and the out-of-the-way. . . . When they read about Africa they want adventure, they want amaze. They want stories like Bruce and Jobson gave them," he declares, after having turned a hilarious and utterly weird encounter with the potentate of Bambarra into a trite tale of benign cultural contact with a "rude but true prince of the jungle" (*WM* 120–122).

A detached and deeply ironic auctorial voice demarcates Mungo's entrapment in outmoded and distorting models of thought and thus undermines the eighteenth-century traveler's self-stylization as it goes along. But if Boyle dismantles the traditional discourses of representing difference—travel writing, anthropology, geography—it is not to replace them with more appropriate and more up-to-date approaches to alterity and difference. Mungo's approach to Africa may be criticized on the grounds of its naiveté, its blindness to the real world, but coming from T. C. Boyle, any critique of fantasy and any plea for realistic representation should be carefully examined. *Water Music* eventually deconstructs one set of stereotypes only to establish another one, no less pervasive, if harder to tackle than Mungo's obvious mistakes and misjudgments.

Boyle's novel discloses a world, writes Arndt Witte, in which "the relations of Africans and Europeans were not yet obfuscated by colonialism."[61] He is right, of course, with regard to the historical period depicted. But he could not be more wrong when it comes to the repertory of tropes and stereotypes at work in the novel. Boyle maps out the precolonial era in West Africa by means of images, styles, and tropes that are firmly grounded in what Edward Said called "the system of imperialist representation," as it was carried into the popular culture of our day. At one point, relatively early in the novel, Mungo's African companion and guide Katunga Oyo, or "jolly old Johnson," (*WM* 29), as Mungo chooses to call him, tries to make him face the facts for once. His intervention culminates in an invocation of African difference, based upon an imagery that is certainly original for 1795 but does seem somewhat worn-out from the perspective of today: "hey, this is *Africa,* man. The eye of the needle, mother of mystery, heart of darkness" (*WM* 92). The chapter in which this crucial, yet futile, call to reason is ventured forth bears the title "The Heart of Darkness." Against the old and obviously inadequate stereotypes of Africa to which Mungo adheres so religiously, Boyle sets a master trope of modernist literature that has long become a template term in its own right. Clichés, stereotypes, and trite images—this is all the "reality" we will ever get out of this disturbing novel.

And yet, *Water Music* differs significantly from this later story of Boyle's, "Big Game," in which cynical detachment rules supreme. In contrast to the short story, the novel time and again replenishes stereotypes with a sense of sudden depth or newness, as the language of detached observation switches inadvertently into an altogether different mode. A sense of tragedy arises precisely out of the farcical and produces scenarios that are always both funny and frightening, hilarious and touching.[62]

The character who comes to be associated most with this mode of oscillation and indeterminacy is Ned Rise, Mungo's second translator figure in Africa. Ned is a petty thief and fraud from lowest-class London, whose picaresque life story is related parallel to Mungo Park's, and who ends up, not altogether by his own choice, part of the second expedition to the Niger. His experiences of eighteenth-century London street life seem to prepare him far better for the dangerous and strenuous journey than any travel book or geographical account ever could, and in the face of Mungo's obvious incapability he quickly and expertly takes over the expedition's management.

Ned knows instinctively what Mungo will not accept: that there is no such thing as disinterested intervention and that the European intrusion into West Africa is bound to cause hostility and resistance, regardless of individual intentions or dreams. After all, the Niger expedition is to initiate an imperialist takeover like the one of North Africa, which by 1790 had been "staked out, mapped, labeled, dissected and distributed" (WM 4). The progress of Western civilization is incompatible with Mungo's vague ideals of peaceful and harmonious cultural contact, and the encounters of Western explorers and African natives are fraught with projections and misconceptions on both sides from the very beginning. Even Mungo, this naive dreamer, eventually has to acknowledge it: unnerved by the ongoing sabotage of his expedition by petty thieveries, he issues the order to shoot the African perpetrators on sight and is the first one forced to do so—killing an unarmed man who tried to steal his compass, of all things: "The explorer thinks of Sir Joseph Banks, of his book, of London and the whirl of celebrity, Ailie, the children, sun on the Yarrow. What am I doing? he thinks. What in God's name am I doing? Then he pulls the trigger" (WM 355).

If Mungo is entirely unprepared for the gruesome business of the colonial venture, Ned Rise is up to the task. His background is, after all, not that different from the African thief's, whose situation parodically mirrors Ned's earlier predicament before the gallows in London. It is due to this and similar experiences that Ned Rise, the London "Hottentot" (WM 84), learns to cope with the African situation, while Mungo never will.

And it is the imagery of cannibalism that brings the specific implications of Ned's "coping" to the fore. Like Roeg's protagonists, Ned makes a deal with this novel's "jungle people." Selling his old enemy Smirke, by then thoroughly established as one of the novel's least likable characters, to the Maniana, a tribe of cannibals, he goes native while staying on familiar grounds, conducting "a little business" (WM 359) in the full awareness of its grotesque implications. Where Roeg's scene of barter failed, however, Ned's deal works out neatly. In Water Music, pathos is suspended by parody:

Ned points down at the sleeping Smirke. "Trade?" he says in Mandingo. . . . Ned watches from the shadows as the five silently bind the slumbering Smirke with hemp cords, wrapping him like a mummy. . . . Electrified, Ned has drifted closer, fatally drawn like a moth to the taper, until he catches himself with a jolt—if he doesn't watch it he'll wind up in the pot alongside Smirke. Suddenly Cobra-head whirls round, one eye twitching, lips pulled back in a lewd unholy grin, the grin of one conspirator to another. Ned flinches as the savage holds out his hand. The smell of him, this close, is unbearable. Ned wants to tear his clothes off, run whooping through the trees, drink blood. There is something in the Maniana's hand, a black leather purse, small and smooth as a pear. Take it, he gestures, dipping his head and extending his arm. Ned reaches out for the soft black bag, wondering, and then realizes with a rush of giddy joy that this is his payment—Judas Iscariot—and he laughs deep in his head as he slips the bag into his pocket. He feels evil, powerful, exhilarated. A partner to demons and devils and things of the night. (*WM* 362)

Here too, the system of colonial commerce shines forth in its exaggerated repetition, especially as before we learned about the African belief that the "black man puts his slave to work, the white man eats him" (*WM* 182). Yet in contrast to Roeg's "jungle people," Boyle's Maniana are not heroic, wild, and aloof but grotesque and weird, comic-book cannibals confronted with comic-book explorers. There is nothing grandiose about this absurd instance of cultural contact and its description: "Then, suddenly, inexplicably, the wildman was grinning. A wild wet obscene grimace of a grin, big lips distended, teeth filed to points. And then he's gone. Poof. Like a degenerate elf" (*WM* 356).

Just as in the Hollywood action adventures of the 1980s, the foreign and the far-away is enacted as pure surface in Boyle's *Water Music,* too familiar to be horrifying and too absurd to be taken at face value. But where action adventures from the Indiana Jones trilogy to *King Solomon's Mines* focus on the spectacularity of special effects, suggesting that survival depends upon Western technology and its clever use, in *Water Music* Africa, or Africanity, sets the rules of the game. Trying to superimpose a European order and logic on the other continent, by contrast, means death and defeat, as Mungo will have to learn, when his expedition is eliminated eventually by a pan-African army in Boussa, welded together by the spirit of revenge:

The explorer can see them clearly now—the Tuareg army that had looked down on them from the bluff, the Hausa tribesmen in their *jubbahs* and turbans, a contingent of Maniana, ochre limbs and filed teeth. There—those are the Soorka, and there, the nameless savages from Gotoijege, hot to avenge their king. Every prerogative ignored, every snub, every wound given and drop of blood spilled has come back to haunt them. It is a day of ironies. (*WM* 424)

This huge confederation of dissociated tribes, formed on the grounds of their outrage against the intruders alone, is clearly one of Boyle's many "inventions," and an invention that manages to drive home the novel's function as a very peculiar alternative history—a history of precolonial contact that is inscribed with the knowledge of colonial and postcolonial conflicts and clashes, prefiguring the developments to come and the battles to be fought.

Mungo will go down in the imminent fight. Ned, however, will float on, although he will never return to England either and although

Mungo's English readership will never learn about this white man's heroic quest. While setting the individualist white man against the indigenous masses, a constellation only too familiar from countless white hunter narratives and action adventures to the present day, *Water Music* eventually turns against the logic of individualist self-reliance and the aesthetics of action. Ned, for one, survives not because he learns to gain control of Africa but because he knows how to cope with it, flexibly adjusting to whatever situation comes up—an expert in survival techniques.

This is not to say, however, that the novel ultimately abandons stereotypical setups and revalidates authentic experiences. After all, Boyle takes recourse to one of the oldest clichés in the colonial book—trick translation—to enact Ned's final delivery. Having escaped the massacre of Boussa, Ned is accosted by a group of natives led by an old magician, offering a strange gift:

Something glinting in the old man's hand: a knife? a gun? Was this it, was this what he'd been saved for? But then suddenly he knew what that refulgent, light-gathering object was, knew why they were offering it to him, knew what he would do and how he would survive. All at once he could see into the future. He was no outcast, no criminal, no orphan—he was a messiah. (*WM* 434–435)

The object in the old man's hand is Ned's clarinet, brought along from England, and by playing the instrument, Ned gets the natives to take him for a god. If this sounds like the epitome of a colonial adventure scenario, depicting the white man's taking control by manipulation, it can just as well be read along completely different lines—depicting Ned's final mastery of the African game of trickery and trading. By this token, going native here is not to maintain individual control and autonomy in the guise of the white hunter but to lose oneself.

Significantly enough, the moment of Ned's revelation also concludes the African adventure. Everything else is only rumor, myth, and hearsay: ". . . some trader would appear in Edinburgh with a story he had from a factor on the Gambia who had it from a native slaver who had it from a Mandingo priest: there was a white man in the Sahel, humble, saintly, living like a black" (*WM* 436). Ned Rise—a saint? To the end, irony rules.

Processes of cultural exchange and global interaction are not to be grasped in terms of individual agency alone, and both social theorists and artists emphasize the impact of collective practices, social structures, and cultural conditions—categories that mitigate and complicate the significance of personal intentions or isolated actions. In the exemplary practice of exchange—trade—this complication comes to the fore. While this is certainly a central insight of Conrad's *Heart of Darkness,* he nevertheless chose to enact the ensuing predicament in terms of personal tragedy and individual fate. The same turn can then be noted in Nicolas Roeg's 1994 revision of the theme, if translated into the more contemporary language of psychology: remembering, reflecting, self-scrutinizing. While the defiant jungle people figure forth a different mode of action—disruptive instead of restorative—their destructivity is carefully contained, as the film mythicizes the defiant jungle people into monolithic irrelevance.

Both the Handspring Company and T. C. Boyle set out to capitalize on the imagery of disruption, contained in Roeg's enactments. Moreover, the theatrical production and the postmodern novel challenge the confidence in the power of words and goodwill to dissolve long-standing scenarios of power, exploitation, and subjugation, highlighting the self-perpetuating mechanisms at work and dismantling the very notion of the individualist hero on foreign ground. If the Handspring Company turns the individualist into an empty mask, a grotesque if powerful puppet, Boyle eventually seems to abandon the very concept of individualist planned action, replacing it with a far less personalized pattern of agency and resistance—techniques of playing stereotypes to the full, rather than avoiding them. The "old" approach of the individualist explorer and travel writer is pitted against the "new" approach of the "London Hottentot" Ned Rise, a cultural meddler who opts for adaptation instead of control and decides to drift along instead of leading the pack. He is a trickster, just like Sterling's Sticky Thompson, and just like Thompson he manages to survive by (almost) dropping out of the picture, becoming the subject of hearsay, rumor—a shadow on a video screen.

Ned Rise and Sticky Thompson show little confidence in words; pragmatic action and sly manipulation are more to their taste. Seen that way, they collate the logic of getting things done with the logic of messing things up. The trickster's interference ruptures communication and unhinges reciprocity, creating disturbances that ultimately collapse the logic of commerce and trade as well: "Deftly done, a trickster's thieving calls into question the local property rights."[63]

By the same token, however, the trickster's survival means the end of representation, or at the very least its pervasive manipulation, reflecting a profound skepticism against the power of words, as Gilles Deleuze—echoing William Burroughs—put it in another context: "Maybe speech and communication have been corrupted. They're thoroughly permeated by money—and not by accident but by their very nature." Deleuze's premonitions, on the other hand, might also indicate a possible way out of the predicament we are faced with: "We've got to hijack speech. Creating has always been something different from communicating. The key thing may be to create vacuoles of noncommunication, circuit breakers, so we can elude control."[64] Let us have a closer look at some such efforts to break the circuit of communication and control, to contest the individualist grand narratives of guilt and agency.

SIX

In Between and Nowhere at All:
The Middle Passage Revisited

Due to new technologies and due to new economic and marketing strategies, our perception of the world has been fundamentally transformed within this century. Technologies of representation, travel, and communication have pulled the world tighter together, and simultaneously demarcated new trenchant lines of marginalization based on access and skill rather than location, race, or gender alone. Transnational enterprises and global corporations in the wake of colonialism, finally, have altered the way we conceive of distance and proximity, the familiar and the far-away, establishing a new grid of evaluation, appropriation, and dismissal that comes to the fore in narratives from Michael Crichton's *Congo* to Francesca Marciano's *Rules of the Wild* and Bruce Sterling's *Islands in the Net*—novels that map out the new conditions for corporate collaboration and cosmopolitan interaction in an age in which "communication is everything." Given the powerful, but often unacknowledged, impact of communication networks and their bulk of technological and economic support systems, a certain distrust seems appropriate—after all, the smoothly functioning lines of cooperation, exchange, and understanding celebrated time and again in contemporary mainstream culture might not be as innocent and disinterested as they are often made out to be.

There is abundant evidence of other narratives, however, that do not stress communication and cooperation at all, at least not in the sense of functioning and functional interaction. Instead, misunderstandings, deceptions, masquerades—"circuit breakers," as Gilles Deleuze called these phenomena—are enacted that reintroduce a trope we have encountered in colonial and postcolonial discourse before: trickery. This trope, I argued, for once serves as a means of stratifying contact zones and exchange lines, establishing more or less subtle techniques of manipulation and keeping communication under one-sided control. But that is not all there is to trickery, and in the following I will map out some lines of implementation, in which the trope of trickery and the tactics of deflection become techniques of resistance rather than domination, disturbance rather than (controlled) communication. Trickery has, after all, always been a means of subversion in minority cultures, and the case of African-American culture exemplifies this, as Lawrence Levine has pointed out with regard to the folk cultural figure of the slave trickster:

[This figure] epitomized the rewards, the limits, and the hazards of the trickster. He could improve his situation through careful deception, but at no time was he really in complete control; the rewards he could win were limited by the realities of the system within which he existed, and the dangers he faced were great. Time and again the more elaborate schemes of the slave trickster failed, and he saved himself only by last minute verbal facility and role playing—two qualities which these stories emphasized were crucial for all slaves to cultivate.[1]

If the trickster figure thus brings to the fore the limits of the system, it is confined by it just as well, the very trickery determined by the overall rules and superimposed conditions. Thus, to the present day, such minority narratives or alternative discourses should not be conceived in clear-cut opposition to the dominant models of social and cultural meaning making. The cultural spheres are too mixed-up for that, so that alternative visions and resisting imageries are most often infused with the same tropes we met before, yet invest them with new significance, turning them around rather than giving them up altogether. This is a tricky game, and it does not always work, as we shall see, but it seems to be the most promising strategy for addressing issues of power and control, and conceiving of exit lines and alternatives these days.

Once more, it is narratives of contact and exchange that foster such reflections, narratives that juggle the changing systems of signification and mix up the dichotomies of (Western) meaning making, forcing together the divergent repertoires of Africanity, primitivity, nature, adventure, and leisure, on the one hand, and the West, civilization, culture, business, and work, on the other. We witnessed the same approach to different symbolic systems before, in the setup of ape-man stories, but in the texts to be regarded in the following, this approach is not meant to suggest an underlying complicity or compatibility of cultural spheres but rather to expose their complicated and troublesome inflection with each other.

The setting of the following accounts itself invites this notion of a chaotic and catastrophic mixture: the Middle Passage, this Atlantic route from freedom to enslavement. The spatial dimension of this process, the fact that it came about during a trip, a journey, emphasizes the gradualness of the development in which human beings are transformed into commodities and independent agents into objects of use, and thus echoes uncannily these other trips and journeys—the explorers' and colonizers' trips over the sea to turn indigenous peoples into subjects of European crowns. At the same time, however, the Middle Passage is different from these other imperialist journeys in that it draws our attention to the sea, this paradigmatic open space of freedom that gained such radically different connotations in this context, as Hortense Spillers argued: "removed from the indigenous land and culture and not-yet 'American' either, these captive persons, without names that their captors would recognize, were in movement across the Atlantic, but they were also *nowhere* at all."[2]

I will take my departure in this chapter from another famous intermixture of historical fact and fiction: Herman Melville's novella *Benito Cereno* (1855), which is based, among other sources, upon the documentation of an upheaval and its ensuing legal history: the *Amistad* affair (1839). This affair comprised the events in the course of an uprisal on a Spanish-owned schooner, the *Amistad,* sailing between two ports in Cuba with a "cargo" of fifty-four African captives. The ship was taken over by its black captives, who meant to force their Spanish "owners" to sail back to Africa. But the two Spaniards tricked them by sailing northwest instead of east at night, so that they were finally intercepted by the American navy off the coast of New England. The Africans were incarcerated and put to trial for their revolt. Three spectacular trials ensued, the last one an appeal to the Supreme Court, which ended in the Africans' release. By that time the affair had gained huge public attention and turned into a model case for the abolitionist cause.

Of course, this affair has acquired even more fame through its recent filmic revision by none less than Steven Spielberg. In *Amistad* (1997) he enacts the historical case with significant changes that epitomize the changed conditions for conceptualizing cultural difference and transcultural communication then and now. While I pit these narratives, Melville's novella and Spielberg's film, against each other to bring to the fore dominant strains of representing the history of slavery, I will then turn to a series of different texts, equally more or less openly concerned with the Middle Passage, which invest the imageries of trickery, deceit, miscommunication, and resistance with new meanings.

When reenacted from the perspective of today, I argue, the Middle Passage acquires a whole set of new connotations, the theme of enforced displacement and violent abduction merging with other, more contemporary, scenarios of migration, dislocation, and contact. Paul Gilroy's study *The Black Atlantic* thus set out most impressively to trace the imageries of travel in the African diaspora, imageries that often enough managed to translate the starkly negative into accounts of liberation and self-fashioning, rewriting the past from the vantage point of the present. It is in the contemporary arts—literature, film, installation art, pop music—that such transformations become most obvious, and it is here that the passages between Africa and the Caribbean are most glaringly recast and transformed. In such revisions "the metaphor of travel is emptied of a purely retrospective thrust, in which the ship is envisioned as the vehicle of an original abduction or of the return to an original territory. Now the metaphor, especially in contemporary youth cultures of the African diasporas, is opened up to harbor all kinds of notions of development, mutation and crossover."[3] The vector connecting different cultural traditions and different geographical zones seems to have lost any unidirectional thrust, reaching back and forth instead, vacillating. And again it is an artificial Africa that figures as a means of orientation against all odds, providing the extreme ends of a line that stretches "between Africa as a lost continent in the past and between Africa as an alien future."[4]

6.1 "Spectacles of Disorder": Herman Melville's *Benito Cereno*

On his quest for Kurtz, the white man gone native in Joseph Conrad's *Heart of Darkness,* Marlow goes down the river Congo on a steamboat, experiencing a nightmarish sphere both in and outside of Africa, a sphere utterly unfamiliar and different from everything he "had known once—somewhere—far away—in another existence perhaps" (*HD* 66). Marlow's response to this frightening and disorienting experience of in-betweenness is to keep busy with the "monkey tricks" of labor, to erect a hybrid order in its own right, in which Africans and Europeans figure as mere tools, acting out a ritual of "busy-ness" to fence off the threatening reality all around. In the course of this ritualization of labor the category of race is by no means effaced, as we have seen: Marlow's fireman turns from savage to coworker not on the grounds of equality but on the grounds of difference. He has been trained to do his job like a "dog in a parody of breeches and a feather hat, walking on his hind-legs" (*HD* 70), and the fact that Marlow too likens himself to a trained animal at times does not mitigate the racism of this description one bit.

Captain Amasa Delano, through whose eyes we experience most of Herman Melville's novella *Benito Cereno* (1855), seems to be confronted with a very similar situation at the outset of his story—set in a location just as indeterminate and in-between as Conrad's Congo, it seems. The *San Dominick,* the "negro transportation-ship"[5] in distress that Captain Delano encounters and sets out to rescue, may be less well organized than Marlow's steamer, but the cooperation between its Spanish captain, Don

Benito Cereno, and his African slave Babo, seems to be just as smooth, and just as stratified, as Marlow's relations with his African fireman. And Babo's devotion conjures up the same imagery as in *Heart of Darkness*—Delano feels spontaneously reminded of a "shepherd's dog" (*BC* 167), an association that is further elaborated later on with reference to the American's "weakness for negroes":

At home, he had often taken rare satisfaction in sitting in his door, watching some free man of color at his work or play. If on a voyage he chanced to have a black sailor, invariably he was on chatty and half-gamesome terms with him. In fact, like most men of a good, blithe heart, Captain Delano took to negroes, not philanthropically, but genially, just as other men to Newfoundland dogs. (*BC* 213)

As we know, Melville's entire story revolves around the insight that Babo is anything but devoted and doglike, that together with the other "unsophisticated Africans" (*BC* 167) on his side he has taken over the *San Dominick* before Delano boarded it, and that the entire "spectacle of fidelity on the one hand and confidence on the other" (*BC* 176) is nothing but an intricate performance for the American, who seems only too willing to see just what he wants to see and to assume only what fits into his narrow frame of expectations. And the concept of a scheming African or a plotting black obviously does not.

This frame of expectations is, of course, in itself far from original or idiosyncratic, but is determined by a social and political situation that strategically conjoined blackness, stupidity, and servility: the system of slavery. Herman Melville's novella, written almost fifty years before Conrad's text, thus visualizes another scenario of systematic racial subjugation against a sociocultural backdrop of economic interests, political conflicts, and philanthropic concerns, a scenario that turns out as corrupting and explosive as the one of imperial takeover and commercial exploitation that I investigated in the previous chapter. In fact, no other institution mixed up commerce and conquest, trade and exploitation as blatantly as slavery, as here the goods to be exploited and appropriated were invariably and obviously human beings.

Where Conrad's story called up the messy history of the Congo under Leopold II, Melville related his narrative around African, American, and Spanish seamen with reference to a series of (then) equally well known historical events, most notably two spectacular cases of slave rebellion, the *Amistad* case and the mutiny on the Spanish slaver *Tryal*, recorded by captain Amasa Delano in his *Narrative of Voyages and Travels* (1807). By transposing his narrative to 1799, Melville moreover managed to give scope to the uprisings in Haiti of that same year, another dramatic—and traumatic—event for American race relations. Hence, *Benito Cereno* pulls into view "the convulsive history of the entire region and epoch—from the Columbian arrival in the Americas, through the democratic revolutions in the United States, Haiti, and Latin America, to the contemporary crisis over the expansion of the 'Slave Power' in the United States," as Eric Sundquist noted.[6] This multiplicity of historical cross-references is then further complicated when confronted with the multiplicity of projections and subsumptions raised in the story itself, which traces the interpolated force fields of perception and deception, self-fashioning and alienation.

Melville's story is, after all, a story about cultural contact and international relations. As was the *Amistad* affair, which called up heated debates on intersecting national and international claims and areas of jurisdiction in the 1840s. The Supreme Court decision of 1841, the last of a series of trials around the slave revolt, made this impact of international legislation—as opposed to an abstract concept of universal rights—perspicacious. The court ruled that the Africans' enslavement was illegal, due to the fact that they had arrived in Cuba after the abolition of the transatlantic slave trade by Spain in 1820. In the turn of these debates the standard conception of the high seas as indeterminate, open, and purely "natural" space was thoroughly challenged: "The courts . . . refused to define the high seas, where the mutiny had taken place, as an extraterritorial space only subject to the law of nature. That is to say, the judges denied the existence of any legal blank spaces on the map of the Atlantic world—any space that would be outside the jurisdiction of the various national governments," writes Gesa Mackenthun.[7]

According to Carolyn Karcher, who analyzed the analogies between the *Amistad* scenario and Melville's novella, it was precisely this lack of universality—the courts' refusal to turn the case into a general argument for or against the institution of slavery and their adherence to petty questions of national jurisdiction—that made Melville renarrate the episode, mixing it up with the earlier incident on board the *Tryal* and the Haiti revolts. By dint of this revision, Karcher argues, Melville managed to translate a narrow legal account into a challenge to "solve the life-and-death riddle of the nation's destiny,"[8] setting up a counterdocument to the fragmented and dry legal accounts in an attempt to "reconstruct the slaves' side of the story."[9]

But should he have tried to do so, then the story is clearly a failure. Up to the moment of Babo's "voiceless end" (*BC* 258) the slaves seem poised in silent defiance or deceptive cooperation, giving early expression to "the insight of postcolonial theorists that 'the subaltern cannot speak,'" as Mackenthun remarked.[10] Indeed, Babo, just like his fellow mutineers, remains a blank spot; they cannot come into view, because they are obscured by a highly flexible repertory of stereotypes—as the form of Delano's final "revelation" exemplifies: "When faced with the undeniable fact of the Africans' rebellion, he switches without apparent discomfort from assumptions of black submissiveness to black savageness."[11]

This is not to say that Delano's perspective will be absolutely committing—clearly, we learn quite soon that his account is unreliable, as his insights are often banal and his endless conjectures incongruent and contradictory. But even if Delano's account is not to be trusted, it is hard to abstract from it and to come to an independent conclusion about the events at hand. After all, the story's second part—the deposition cited at length at the end—does not provide an altogether satisfactory viewpoint either. While one account—Delano's story—unfolds never ending speculations about the motives and feelings of everybody involved, the other—the legal document—forgoes any such train of thought, focusing on the "bare facts," which fall just as short representing the complexity of what is going on. "Because Melville formulates no alternative himself," Brook Thomas comments upon this highly ambivalent structure of representation, "he allows readers either sharing Captain Delano's prejudices or believing in the objectivity of legal documents to accept the version of the story closest to their own perspective."[12]

Either way, we end up confronting a masquerade that seems so much more pervasive than the Africans' performance on the ship: the masquerade of race relations, set in the 1790s, resonating with the conflicts of the 1850s, and reaching well into our own times—as racist projections are to this day indissolubly entangled with the rhetoric of benevolence and open-mindedness. It would be wrong to conceive of this rhetoric exclusively in terms of strategic behavior—it works so well, after all, because people actually believe in it. "If white racism manifested itself exclusively through hostility and exclusion," observes George Lipsitz, "it would be easier to understand and to combat."[13] On the same grounds, Amasa Delano in Melville's story falls for his own rhetoric of goodwill, just as Melville's father-in-law, Justice Lemuel Shaw, seems to have done in reality.[14] In the world of and around *Benito Cereno* integrity and trickery, conviction and deception seem almost inseparable—forming a "knot" or "spectacle of disorder" (*BC* 194) that draws its effectivity from the fact that most often it does not even come into view.

Seen that way, the *San Dominick* does not figure forth a momentary suspension of the dominant order but its overblown and distorted mirror image. While for once the Africans seem to have turned the tables on their oppressors, with Babo reaching "true mastery" and establishing a "cunning authority,"[15] we should not forget that nothing whatsoever is achieved by this role reversal, as both parties involved remain "trapped in a mimicry of the old master-slave relationship."[16] Thus Babo's performance may illustrate the Hegelian paradox that "mastery (like slavery) both *is* and *is not*"[17] (both stances being dependent upon each other), but it certainly does not subscribe to a Hegelian notion of dialectic interaction and progress, in which master and servant positions are regularly exchanged. Rather, Melville approximated Frantz Fanon's later insight that once the category of "race" is introduced, the Hegelian dialectics of master and slave changes fundamentally: "For Hegel, there is reciprocity; here the master laughs at the consciousness of the slave. What he wants from the slave is not recognition but work."[18] Given the logic of the system he is caught up in, Babo may successfully undermine his master's power position, but he will never take over, as the only possibility for him to act publicly as a master is to play the slave, going as far as to cut his own face in a mock-serious simulation of punishment.

Of course, all of these tricks are said to be played with a specific goal in mind: Babo demands to be transported back to Senegal, we learn in the legal account, and it is to achieve this goal that he decides to let Delano board the ship—against the wish of his companion Atufal, who "was for sailing away" (*BC* 247). The question is, then, why Babo opts for confrontation and masquerade in the first place. Is it only to get the supplies needed for the journey back, as he purports, or is there more to it? Seen from a slightly different angle, the masquerade for Delano's eyes appears suspiciously tautological, enacted not as a means to return to Africa but as an end in itself, essentially confined and contained by the boundaries of the ship that forms its stage.

After all, what would Babo gain from a return to Africa? Atufal, who is so eager to get back, "was king in his own land" (*BC* 181), a truly "heroic slave" and "noble savage," in accordance with a standard imagery of blackness enacted time and again from Aphra Behn's *Oroonoko* to H. Rider Haggard's *King Solomon's Mines* and suffusing the public representation of Cinque, the leader in the *Amistad* affair, just as well.[19] Babo, however, does not look back on a history of autonomy and power: "poor Babo here, in his own land, was only a poor slave; a black man's slave was Babo, who now is the white's" (*BC* 183), he says of himself. Of course, half of this statement is clearly a lie, as Babo is not a white man's slave at the time of the utterance. But on another level, this brief glimpse at his past and future options—a black man's slave, a white man's slave— attests to the claustrophobic closure of this narrative universe: after all, neither Africa nor America offer a way out for this man, so that the *San Dominick* becomes the only space where he can momentarily act out his freedom—by impersonating a slave. Thus, the entire ship turns into a huge minstrel show, as Eric Lott noted:

The slaves-turned-mutineers disguised as slaves aboard the *San Dominick* are in virtual blackface, performing for the liberal northern visitor too blinkered to know better. . . . Melville's pessimism about the effects of white racial discourse is revealed in the way the rebelling slaves are, for most of the story, stuck in mid-drama, frozen in the midst of revolutionary activity. In Melville's view there is apparently no possible emergence from behind the minstrel mask even in the act of revolt, which is to say that the mask itself interrupts the attempt to throw it off.[20]

By dint of this insight, the ship may appear as an exemplary and exceptional place—fenced off from everyday reality like a stage—as it is indeed the only place where somebody like Babo can be in control. But at the same time the utopian dimension of this imagery is undermined even more unconditionally than in the Supreme Court's argumentation during the *Amistad* trial. As a matter of fact, the *San Dominick* proves to be utterly dependent on the dominant laws, regulations, and assumptions: Babo has to comply with the hegemonic rules even as he subverts them, his trickery and role-playing inadvertently repeating rather than disrupting the overall order. Seen that way, Melville does not abstract from the legal situation at hand but instead gives vent to the insight that there is no such thing as indeterminacy, openness, and freedom of imagination in an institutionalized order, that even the high seas have been charted and mapped, and that the only way out of a deceptive system at large is by adopting deception oneself. The moment the masquerade falls short, Babo is lost—his entire existence depending upon the convincing performance as a slave. That, however, sounds horribly like the predicament of his peers on the plantations in the United States, who are equally poised between the desire for freedom and the need to act as slaves.

6.2 True Translation: Steven Spielberg's *Amistad*

In Melville's *Benito Cereno* the rituals of cultural communication and social interaction are shown to be so strong and self-perpetuating that the very notion of free will seems to dwindle away next to them. In a rare moment of insight, Amasa Delano recognizes this powerful impact of the ritual and comes up with an imagery that shall resonate through the literature of cultural contact and colonial clashes:

To Captain Delano's imagination . . . there was something so hollow in the Spaniard's manner, with apparently some reciprocal hollowness in the servant's dusky comment of silence, that the idea flashed across him, that possibly master and man, for some unknown purpose, were acting out, both in word and deed, nay, to the very tremor of Don Benito's limbs, some juggling play before him. (*BC* 216)

Stronger even than their more famous successors—Conrad's imperialist "hollow men"—Melville's hollow men of slavery suggest that social (and racial) hierarchies are mere stage props, to be manipulated and inverted at will. Yet, if these institutions are indeed only illusions, they are also all there is, and their manipulation ends up not so much suspending power structures as "aping" them—performing another sort of "monkey tricks," a parody of the dominant system that evinces its arbitrary nature but can never establish an alternative order in its own right. Nevertheless, the Africans' survival on the ship depends upon this masquerade of communication, and once the network of tricks and deceit breaks down, its mastermind, Babo, resorts to another "comment of silence," his hostility and noncommunication suddenly out in the open: "Seeing all was over, he uttered no sound, and could not be forced to. His aspect seemed to say, since I cannot do deeds, I will not speak words" (BC 258).

Steven Spielberg's take on the history of slavery and revolution, his 1997 film Amistad,[21] revolves around similar issues as Melville's narrative, and again communication, misunderstanding, and silence turn out to be at the heart of the matter. The spectacular affair around the fifty-three Africans who survived the mutiny they staged against their Spanish abductors, only to be captured after all by the American navy, is enacted as a court drama, pulling into view the intersecting systems of international politics, cultures, and legislation. At the height of the film, Cinque (Djimon Hounsou), the leader of the revolt and hero of the film, withdraws into silence, just as Melville's Babo did over one hundred years before. Yet his refusal to communicate is not the film's last word. Nor does it bring about estrangement alone. After all, before we witness Cinque's lapse into silence, we get to know his point of view, in a scene that forms the film's cathartic turning point, a scene of confusion and conflict that will engender communication and understanding eventually.

The Africans have just won their case before the federal district court in Massachusetts, because their lawyer, Roger Baldwin (Matthew McConaughey), managed to prove that they came straight from Africa, speak Mende, and have no knowledge of the Spanish language. On this evidence, which proves that they must have been abducted after the abolition of the international slave trade by Spain, they should be allowed to go free. But things do not go as they should.

This is, after all, where the entire story starts all over again. President Van Buren (Nigel Hawthorne), anxious about his impending reelection and relations with the southern states and Spain, intervenes and compels an appeal to the Supreme Court. In Spielberg's film the action culminates as Baldwin bears the bad news of the appeal to his clients. By that time an interpreter for the Mende-speaking Africans has been found (Chjwetel Ejiofor), but explaining the complicated course of events is too much for him. A chaotic conversation ensues between Cinque, Baldwin, and the interpreter Covey, above the noise of the Africans' victory celebration going on around them. Cinque obviously is not up to the intricacies of the American legal system: "You said there would be a judgment. And if we won the judgment we would go free," he has Covey say. True enough, as Baldwin has to concede: "OK, I said it, I said it. But I shouldn't have. What I should have said—what I should have said. . . ." But here the interpreter, by now as excited as the two parties, interrupts: "I can't translate that. . . ." In Mende, it seems, there is no concept for error or misconception: "either you do something or you don't." What you say is what you mean. And laws are both absolute and binding. When Baldwin, increasingly desperate, goes on to explain— "Listen to me, understand what I am saying . . . What I said to you before the judgment . . . is almost how it works here. Almost. . . ." Cinque blows up. Withdrawing from his interlocutors, he steps in front of the big fire lighting the scenery and gives an angry speech, all the while undressing until he confronts his audience completely naked, discretely— and becomingly—backlighted by the fire. This time, as always in this film when cultural difference is to be emphasized, his words are not translated but subtitled: "What kind of a place is this? Where you almost mean what you say? Where laws almost work? How can you live like that?" It is after this outburst that Cinque withdraws into silence, obviously determined not to be part of a system in which people do not say what they mean. But unlike Babo, Cinque finds his voice again. Or rather, he finds *a* voice again.

As the actual *Amistad* case went before the Supreme Court in 1841, its abolitionist lobbyists were lucky to find a star lawyer supporting their cause: the former president and famous abolitionist John Quincy Adams took over and won the day. Thus it is only appropriate that in Spielberg's film a star actor should tackle the task of getting words and their meanings finally together again:[22] and Anthony Hopkins, famous for his impersonation of a cannibal who takes things literally in *The Silence of the Lambs,* fills the part brilliantly. In his thunderous plea before the Supreme Court he turns against the empty shell of legal discourse and opts for common sense: "Truth has been driven from this case," he sets out, to then enter an attack on the institution of slavery on the grounds of its incompatibility with natural law: "the natural state of mankind is . . . freedom." With this, Adams seems to subscribe to the Mende worldview that laws work unconditionally and words mean what they say. And indeed, when Cinque congratulates him for their success, asking "What words did you use to persuade them?" Adams answers: "Yours."

But of course, John Quincy Adams needed not go as far as Africa to find a point of reference for his plea, as the theme of uprisal against unjust rule clearly calls upon American historical traditions in the first place. Gesturing to the copy of the Declaration of Independence on the courtroom walls and dramatically addressing the marble busts of the founding fathers on display, Adams (both in the historical case and in its filmic revision) invoked *the* American template for the spirit of justified rebellion and universal freedom: the Revolution. Yet while in the historical case Adams's reference took up only a fraction of his extensive plea, and the actual decision remained firmly on the grounds of legal technicalities,[23] in Spielberg's film the revolutionary spirit takes over. When the filmic Adams calls upon the principles of the American Republic, it is not to inaugurate a liberal reading of the revolutionary past[24] but to implement a conservative reading of the history of slavery, which is thus presented as a momentary, and embarrassing, aberration from an otherwise unblemished tradition of liberty, honesty, and universal rights.[25]

Where the actual *Amistad* affair attested to a curious bifurcation of abolitionist rhetoric (taking recourse to the natural right of freedom) and a decision-making process completely independent of this rhetoric, Spielberg's film collapses the pleas for natural law and the legal debates, just as it collapses authentic Africanity (Cinque's outburst) and true Americanness (Adams's appeal). This move is firmly entrenched within the film's overall representation of cultural communication and conflict along the lines of goodwill and bad intentions—a logic of representation radically at odds with Melville's assessment of the self-perpetuating power of social rituals and institutions, as expressed in his use of the tropes of trickery and masquerade. In Spielberg's film, by contrast, trickery figures neither as an overall social condition nor as a strategy of resistance—let alone both of these—but is enacted exclusively as a mean-spirited plot to obscure the truth and to obstruct justice. Tricks are played by the slave "owners" José Ruiz and Pedro Montes, who submit tampered documents to court in order to prove their ownership, and by the Van Buren administration, which tries to manipulate the federal district court and the Supreme Court. All of these plots are characterized as selfish and isolated maneuvers, and all of them backfire eventually, as the film emphatically endorses (and Americanizes) Cinque's plea for sincerity and univocality—meaning what one says.

It might thus be argued that *Amistad* sets the utopia of true expression against the trope of trick translation, which proved to be so prominent in colonial discourse. But truth is a tricky business in itself, and in Spielberg's film its expression is too entangled with the practices of translation—be it the interpreter's obvious intervention or be it the less obvious intervention of subtitles—to allow for a clear-cut contrast. The issue, then, seems to be "true translation" rather than true expression—and with that an obvious question arises: when is a translation true? Or, in other words, who is to tell whether what is said is what was really meant?

Spielberg's film answers this question in a classical move of pragmatism: a translation is true when its recipients think so. According to this understanding, the audience in the courtroom and the audience watching the film decide upon Cinque's—and his translator's—credibility. Yet this decision is not based upon information and content alone—it is the form that counts most. Truth is what works: "Whoever tells the best story wins," Adams sums up his courtroom strategy at one point, and of course his maxim applies even more trenchantly to this other public spectacle intent on winning over an audience, the Hollywood blockbuster: "Thematizing history as his story—emphasis on the masculine pronoun—*Amistad* is shifting the locus of historical authority to Hollywood," writes Michael Rogin.[26] By dint of this strategy the Africans' experience needs to be translated not only into English but moreover into a story fit for the courtroom, and Covey turns out to be only one out of a panoply of translator figures. Culminating the earlier attempts of all kind of "translators," Adams, finally, totalizes translation and turns it into ventriloquism: casting an African concept in American terms, and pretending to give voice to an African's words. The film's most impressive act of translation, however, is not personalized, and even less obvious than Adams's operation: it is the camera's translation of words into images.

When Cinque finds a voice, because his advocates found a translator, his past experiences find expression. We hear him talking in Mende, his voice overlaid quickly by his translator's perfect, if accented, English. Then the mode of representation switches once more, and a flashback sequence provides the images to Cinque's recollections. When we return to the film's present time, the scenery has changed from the prison (where Cinque set out to speak to a small audience) to the courtroom (where he just finished speaking to a crowd), suggesting that the images we saw are one and the same as the information conveyed to court in the act of translation—a perfect story indeed. With this, Spielberg leaves no doubt that it is the institution of the slave trade itself that is put to trial—if the imagery of a trial or legal debate is still adequate here. After all, Cinque's story does not come across as a testimony to be contested, but as absolutely authentic—the truth in all its visibility, allowing for only one reaction: horrified indignation and commiseration.

Any attempt at legalistic intervention or debate must needs seem petty in the face of this evidence. Still this is what a trial calls for, and it is precisely what District Attorney Holabird (Pete Postlethwaite), Cinque's opponent in the federal court, tries to bring about. He expresses doubts about Cinque's account, questioning the episodes of extreme cruelty and violence he depicted on the grounds of sheer calculation: "After all, when you come down to it, it's all about money, isn't it? It's slaves—production—money." Why, he asks, would slave traders then have possibly wanted to "routinely slaughter their slaves" in the first place? In a seemingly most cynical response to Cinque's moving account he calls it an invention: "Like all good works of fiction it was entertaining. Nothing more."

Once more, the film confronts truth (Cinque's authentic account) with trickery (the attorney's allegations), clearly evaluating both stances in turn: Cinque is good, and the attorney is bad. And indeed, in view of the monumental visual evidence of Cinque's story, any doubt must seem insincere and petty. What should we make, then, of the fact that in the historical case itself the evidence was not as striking and monumental and the district attorney's intervention would have been very well justified? After all, in contrast to the actual case, Spielberg's film condenses the most horrifying incidents of the intercontinental slave trade within the last one hundred years in his peculiar "Middle Passage," distilling an image of the slave trade at its most horrific and gruesome, as Robert L. Paquette pointed out:

Had these and similar atrocities become the norm, the Atlantic slave trade might not have lasted a generation, much less four centuries. At the time of the Amistad, the average return on investment for individual traders involved in the contraband Cuban Trade had risen to almost 20 percent. Because of the risks associated with British suppression policies, however, many big traders were going bankrupt. In making economic sense of the Tecora atrocities, District Attorney Holabird (Pete Postlethwaite) was heading in the right direction.[27]

In contrast to Paquette, I have no problem with Spielberg's manipulation of historical facts as such—the film is, after all, clearly demarcated as a fictional presentation. But I do find it interesting to investigate the exact way in which Spielberg chose to deviate from his sources, that is, the documented history of the *Amistad* case and the current state of research on the Middle Passage. After all, Cinque's account as portrayed in the film not only envelops all kinds of other, earlier, and more dramatic accounts but also adopts the classical representational pattern of the abolitionist narrative: isolating specific episodes and turning them into exemplary experiences. The mother with child, going overboard to die rather than become a slave, the baby handed over in the ship's belly, and not least Cinque's own fate as the heroic slave—all of these episodes glaringly illustrate the injustices of slavery by both abstracting from and personalizing a vaster context.[28] Spielberg's very condensation of the horrors of slavery into one representative journey attests to what Peter Brooks called the "melodramatic imagination."

Melodrama, writes Brooks, "demonstrates over and over that the signs of ethical forces can be discovered and can be made legible,"[29] and by dint of this definition, Spielberg's *Amistad* is pure melodrama, while Melville's *Benito Cereno* might be called melodrama emptied out: the signs are there, yet they have lost their meaning. But of course, read along these lines it is not *Benito Cereno* that figures as *Amistad's* nineteenth-century counterpoint but another text, whose spectacular effect Spielberg clearly tried to emulate in the grandiose rhetoric around *Amistad's* release: *Uncle Tom's Cabin*. No other abolitionist text exemplified as glaringly as Harriet Beecher Stowe's novel the power of melodrama to make ethical dilemmas not only visible but "legible," and the countless stage productions of the novel finally brought to the fore the political effectivity of melodrama, forcing their audiences into identification and commitment.[30]

Over one hundred years later, the same technique of representation yields radically different effects. In Spielberg's film, District Attorney Holabird's derogatory comment about Cinque's "entertainment" value rings strangely true. By turning the Middle Passage into a spectacle of atrocities, Spielberg seals his strategy of representing slavery as a historical aberration in American history, completely unrelated to the current state of race relations and politics. The film enacts slavery along the lines of melodrama as a hidden evil, which, once made public, can be attacked and expurgated on the grounds of its amorality. The fact that slavery was an everyday affair, not the effect of vicious drives and bad intentions but part of a neat economic calculation—a drab routine effectively splitting up social reality into two intersecting but strangely unrelated worlds—drops out of view, although it briefly shines up in Holabird's objection: the peculiar institution was, after all, "all about money."

In Melville's novella, the institution of slavery is shown to be so powerful that it affects social relations on every level, forcing everybody into a minstrel show that is as tragic as it is grotesque. In Spielberg's film, on the other hand, the grotesque and all-comprising character of slavery cannot come into view, as race relations become a matter of goodwill—the conflict between Africans and Americans is resolved as soon as they get a chance to talk it over, and the courtroom provides the unbiased forum for this exchange.[31]

Yet there is a scene early in the film that—curiously out of place—briefly manages to visualize a gap between whites and blacks that seems so much more trenchant and so much more threatening than any later misunderstanding or silence. Having just taken over the *Amistad,* the

Africans detect another vessel, a European passenger ship, which comes dangerously close. To stay undetected, they put out all lights and keep absolutely silent. In an eerie and markedly fantastic scene, the *Amistad* is then seen drifting silently past the other ship, the African rebels within talking distance of the European travelers, watching utterly transfixed. Some of the Europeans stare back at them, taken aback by the Africans' appearance alongside them, while most are completely unaware of their presence as they chat, dine, and listen to a string quartet, which provides the scene's oddly inappropriate musical score. The camera includes Africans and Europeans in a series of tracking shots, emphasizing alternately the background and the foreground—the African mutineers or the European travelers—but there is absolutely no doubt that this oscillating link constitutes the only connection possible between these two types of travel and two types of travelers, who may take the same course but could not be farther apart.

In this momentary intake of glaring difference and enforced contact, the film for once captures the horrible logic of slave trade and slavery, the fact that thousands of people were dragged into a world that could not possibly make sense to them, and in which they had no social presence: no rights, no voice. That the scene in which this comes about adopts the tone and tinge of fantasy indicates already that it may very well take another sort of narrative and another structure of representation to capture this kind of estrangement and this kind of angst these days.

6.3 "Truth Is What *Works*": Charles Johnson's *Middle Passage*

The *Amistad* affair, giving vent to both Melville's and Spielberg's revisions of slavery, was a showcase for a new kind of political struggle. After all, the court debates around the Africans' legal or illegal status were only one facet of a much larger picture. Around these legal disputes revolved a huge machinery of public discourse: the case was investigated in journals, commemorated in poems, and enacted on stage well before Melville wrote his novella—and Spielberg produced his film. The Amistad Committee, an abolitionist organization formed around the publicist and activist Lewis Tappan, kept a pervasive and efficient public relations campaign going, cleverly steering public sentiments and thus transforming the case into the spectacular event it turned out to be.[32] In that respect the *Amistad* affair calls to mind the campaigns against the Belgian Congo in Europe and America some years later, this serious blow against colonialism, initiated by a group of efficient European activists who worked largely outside of official governmental and national institutions in what has been rightfully called "the first great international human rights movement of the twentieth century."[33] Clearly, the protest movement against King Leopold II profited directly from strategies conceived in abolitionist organizations such as the Amistad Committee.[34]

In Spielberg's film, however, the clever and intricate abolitionist public relations work drops completely out of view. The campaigners around Tappan come across as dull, inefficient, and prejudiced bigots, while Tappan (Stellan Skarsgard) himself is pictured as more interested in abstract moral questions than in the movement's effectivity, the entire portrayal of white abolitionism corresponding with "today's cynicism about broad social movements," as Eric Foner pointed out.[35] Abolitionism obviously figures as another abstract cause, standing off unfavorably against the categories of melodrama—exemplary experience and individual redemption.

This strategy of representation comes to the fore in the construction of Cinque as focalizer for the slave perspective, but even more than that it suffuses the African's black American counterpart—the fictional figure Theodore Joadson (Morgan Freeman), a former slave come to wealth who proves to be so much more committed to the abolitionist cause than Tappan's sorry crowd. The fantastic dimensions of Joadson's persona— an ex-slave who moves about in a slave state with the nonchalance of a twentieth-century businessman—remain unacknowledged as *Amistad* presents a black American protagonist in control—an agent, not a victim.

An honorable endeavor, no doubt, which bears only the slight flaw of historical inaccuracy. But then, to represent the dehumanizing institution of slavery along the conventional lines of (male) self-determination and agency has always been a problematical project, as we have known at least since the TV miniseries *Roots* (1977–1979) was broadcast all over the world. Melville's Babo faced the same predicament in an altogether different way, responding to a system that would not allow him the status of an agent by becoming an actor, transforming what was conceived to be his nature into a role, if a tragic one. And Charles Johnson, clearly drawing upon a multiplicity of earlier literary and pop cultural enactments of the black male, goes even further with his novel *Middle Passage* (1990). His protagonist and I-narrator Rutherford Calhoun reviews the history of African abduction from the perspective of an African-American ex-slave, poised between white Americans who reject him due to his color and black Africans who reject him due to his cultural background: "Rutherford Calhoun is confined, spatially and temporally, to a space 'in-between'—in-between the ship's crew and the [African] Allmuseri, in-between factions of the ship's crew, and in-between generations of African-Americans."[36] Rutherford is clearly not in control of his own life, much less the lives around himself.

Due to messy circumstances and a series of fantastic accidents, Rutherford lands a job as a cook's helper on the American slave ship *Republic*, on its way to Africa in 1830. After taking on a load of forty African slaves, all of them belonging to a fictional tribe, the Allmuseri, the ship sets out to return to the United States. Shortly, however, all kinds of conflicts flare up, and Rutherford becomes involved in plots and counterplots onboard, against his will and—once more—without any clear aim or intention on his side. The *Republic* is then taken over by the Allmuseri in a revolt that barely precedes the sailors' mutiny against their monomaniac captain. Eventually, almost all of them will perish in a huge storm—the *Republic* going down like Captain Ahab's *Pequod* in *Moby Dick,* and the African rebels ending up as unsuccessful as their predecessors in *Benito Cereno.*

In Spielberg's film, the African-American protagonist is time and again enacted as a fascinated disciple, taking in the Africans' protest against the white system on the basis of an understanding that seems to transcend all language barriers and eventually brings about his emancipation from the stifling "regime" of white abolitionism. By contrast, Johnson's narrative of contact is much more skeptical. Rutherford's encounter with the Allmuseri does not spawn self-cognizance and emancipation but fragmentation and loss, as he recognizes toward the end of his journey:

... in myself I found nothing I could rightly call Rutherford Calhoun, only pieces and fragments of all the people who had touched me, all the places I had seen, all the homes I had broken into. The "I" that I was, was a mosaic of many countries, a patchwork of others and objects stretching backward to perhaps the beginning of time.[37]

Yet Rutherford is not the only one to face the possibility that "the (black) self is the greatest of all fictions" (*MP* 171). The exposure of the Allmuseri to the "terrible forces and transformations" of the Middle Passage effects a similarly disturbing loss of identity, a "reshaping [of] their souls" that renders them "[n]o longer Africans, yet not Americans either" (*MP* 124–125).

Just like the colonial project, the Middle Passage, this "defining moment of the African-American experience,"[38] lays bare the dark underside of cultural contact, its potential to disrupt and to destroy. This potential evolves most disturbingly in seemingly harmless processes of exchange— most notably spoken communication. "I suspected . . . he did not recognize the quiet revisions in his voice after he learned English as it was spoken by the crew, or how the vision hidden in their speech was deflecting or redirecting his own way of seeing" (*MP* 124), Rutherford notes about one of the Allmuseri, just as he noticed before that his masters' accents "echo in the very English I spoke—as if I was no one—or nothing—in my own right . . ." (*MP* 47).

Personal identity, for Johnson the "deepest of mysteries,"[39] turns out to be a precarious category in this novel, as it easily succumbs to manipulation, shifting shape and changing scope almost imperceptibly according to highly unstable circumstances. The most subtle and most dangerous means of such manipulation is language, and thus to relate one's past and to communicate one's experiences, as Cinque did so impressively in Spielberg's film, becomes a risky business in Johnson's world.[40] Mixed up with the forces of desire, nostalgia, projection, and invention, narrations and revisions of the past turn out to shape and twist the very process of recollection, so that not only Rutherford's account seems somewhat unreliable but the Africans' past can be seen gradually slipping into artificiality, too. The problematic implications of this tendency come to the fore in the self-fashioning of an Allmuseri "leader," Diamelo, who "goes African" to cope with the situation onboard, finding a coherent sense of selfhood in a past he made up: "In three weeks the wastrel previously cool toward his tribe's culture became its champion, a change the older Allmuseri . . . found unconvincing, opportunistic at times, even false, though none could criticize him during their crisis below" (*MP* 154).

Where Spielberg's film seals the past off from the present, declaring slavery an unfortunate episode in American history that is once and for all over, Johnson interfuses past and present, taking the Middle Passage as a pretext for reflections on contemporary black culture—"transforming the middle passage into at once a microcosm of world history and an allegory of growing self-awareness," as Carl Pedersen wrote.[41] Diamelo's "identity politics" are a case in point for this technique of casting light on present constellations via the detour to the past, a technique we encountered before in T. C. Boyle's approach to precolonial African history in *Water Music*. Just like Boyle, Johnson mixes up historical and contemporary references to bring about a distantiation from the familiar perspective, complicating and contorting the grand narrative of the Middle Passage with a multiplicity of grotesque, funny, fantastical, and tragic tales veering between then and now.

One such fantastical detail lends an eerie closure to Rutherford's story and provides a backdrop against which the cultural and social differences on board the *Republic* fade away: in a conversation with the Captain, Ebenezer Falcon, Rutherford learns that the very man who controlled New Orleans both economically and politically and drove him out to sea in the first place is the owner of the ship he fled to. Papa Zeringue, the New Orleans gangster boss, seems to have his own ideas about identity politics and black solidarity:

Suddenly the ship felt insubstantial: a pawn in a larger game of property so vast it trivialized our struggle on board. My months on the *Republic* seemed to dissolve, delivering me back to Papa Zeringue's smoky restaurant, which I'd never left, and then it was he talking in front of me . . . , telling me there was no escape from the webs he had woven in New Orleans, across the sea, and even into the remotest villages of Africa. But how could he do this, I wondered? Buy and sell slaves when he himself was black? Was this not the greatest betrayal of all? (*MP* 150)

Middle Passage has the networks of the international slave trade fade into the postcolonial networks of global organizations, calling to mind Bruce Sterling's image of a world "netted together in a web . . . , a global system, an octopus of data" (*IN* 17). In this new world order, dated back to the nineteenth century, skin color is just one among many factors determining social and economical status, a marker of difference that can be of crucial importance in one context but need not mean anything in the next. If Papa Zeringue's omnipresence and omnipotence thus stands in glaring contrast to the powerlessness and dislocation of the ones "webbed in," his very persona also epitomizes the fact that this contrast can no longer be determined on the grounds of racial or cultural categorizing. The community of the underdogs, it seems, is hopelessly heterogeneous.

It is also huge. *Middle Passage* leaves no doubt about the system's pervasive reach, sketching a world in which almost nobody is in control, and almost everybody a victim. Thus the slaves and the sailors on Captain Falcon's ship are not as different as they would like to be, all of them in the thralls of a capitalist system that is as abstract as it is unassailable, the sailors working like slaves, "men and women who had no more stake in the fields they worked than these men in the profits of a ship owned by financiers as far away from the dangers at sea as masters from the rows of cotton their bondmen picked" (*MP* 87). This analogy can, of course, be further and further extended, so that eventually it even comprises the captain himself, who, Ahab-like, raves against the forces of the absolute, which quickly enough prove to be much more concrete than he lets on: ". . . was Ebenezer Falcon telling me that he, at bottom, was no freer than the Africans?" Rutherford muses after a conversation with the captain in which the economic foundations of the enterprise are laid bare. The very quest for imperialist power and possession, the desire to "Americanize the entire planet" (*MP* 30) for which the captain stands, gradually appears as a pretext, a means to think agency where pure alienation rules.

And yet, instead of acknowledging their common predicament, the captain and his men, and the sailors and the slaves, are pitted against each other, wasting all their energies in a fight that is purely destructive. Johnson does not allow for a utopia of solidarity, as did Barry Unsworth in *Sacred Hunger* (1992), where whites and blacks unite in a mutiny against their captain and actually manage to set up an alternative enclave of equality and freedom afterward, if only for a brief time. In *Middle Passage*, the men's anger and frustration rings hollow, everybody interlocked in a fight as futile as the one between "two men—one black, one the barbersurgeon" whom Rutherford watches during the mutiny: "working quietly, single-mindedly at the uphill chore of killing each other" (*MP* 129).

In view of the convoluted systems of domination and power, an alternative course of action, uniting the wronged ones and setting solidarity and bonding against subjugation and exploitation, seems hard to establish. After all, all lines of communication and exchange seem irretrievably obstructed, the words "despoiled"[42] and thought systems fraught with projections and ascriptions. On these grounds, a skepticism against organized political action shows up in Johnson's text that is no less pervasive than *Amistad*'s "cynicism against broad social movements"—if located on altogether different grounds. The new order of transnational capitalism, firmly based upon the dehumanizing mechanisms of the slave system, seems to be even more efficient than its secret predecessor at canceling out resistance and critique: it is just too huge to be affected, seemingly pulling any dissenting voice into its force field and turning it around to its own cause.

Before Charles Johnson interlinked the nineteenth-century system of slavery with the current rhetoric of globalization, Melville enacted a similar conceptual interlinkage between slavery and earlier projects of exploration and colonization. In *Benito Cereno,* the system's complicity is epitomized in the removal of the *San Dominick*'s "proper figure-head—the image of Cristobal Colon, the discoverer of the New World" (*BC* 245)— and its substution by the skeleton of the slaveholder Don Alexandro Aranda and the inscription "follow your leader" (*BC* 163). Aranda's body, stripped to its bare white bones, glaringly signifies the emptiness *and* importance of whiteness, which does, after all, constitute the most basic precondition for leadership, both in the context of colonization and in the context of slavery. In line with this move, Babo forces each Spaniard on the *San Dominick* to ponder the absurd question "whether, from [the skeleton's] whiteness, he should not think it a white's" (*BC* 245), once more turning the dead body into an icon of whiteness.

In *Middle Passage,* another white man's body is stripped to its bones. But where Melville kept the references to cannibalistic practices vague,[43] Johnson dwells upon them, mixing the grotesque and the grandiose, the tragic and the bizarre. While Rutherford succumbs to a grave illness, Peter Cringle, the ship's mate, loses his life. Yet this white man is not killed by the Africans in an act of horrible and primitivist revenge but by another white man, the ship's cook. Moreover, Cringle dies at his own wish, in order to pass a gruesome heritage on to the black and white rebels of the *Republic:* "I wish to leave you something for no man could ask for better shipmates than thee. You're brave lads. The lasses have given their full share as bluejackets too, and methinks 'tis scandalous how some writers such as Amasa Delano have slandered black rebels in their tales" (*MP* 173). The "something" Cringle leaves to his starving companions is his own body. As Rutherford has to learn after fully regaining his senses: "Yuh had Mr. Cringle fer supper, m'boy. We all did. . . . This was what he wanted" (*MP* 173).

Stylistically, the passage calls to mind T. C. Boyle's montage of the tropes of cannibalism and savagery in *Water Music* much more than Melville's gothic horror or—to call up another obvious literary model—Poe's *Narrative of Arthur Gordon Pym* (1838), but still Johnson's cannibalistic episode stays on the grounds Melville and Poe mapped out before. Where Melville collapsed the most savage (the skeletonized body) with the epitome of civilization (the discoverer's image), Johnson, too, forces together the imageries of savagery and civilization to render them finally indistinguishable. Yet here the rhetoric of race—Africanity and whiteness pitted against each other—which grotesquely bifurcated Melville's scenario, is drawn into the vortex of ambiguity. This is how Squibb, the cook, relates the event to his horrified friend:

> At first I couldn't do it. . . . I started to ask if it wouldn't be better fer us to die like men, but I checked meself before sayin' a thing so foolish, 'cause what could I mean? What was the limit of bein' human? How much could yuh take away and still *be* a man? In a kind of daze I done what he wanted, standin' back from meself, then unstringin' him, and it was in a daze that I lay back, short-winded and watchin' the Africans cut away Cringle's head, hands, feet, and bowels, and throw 'em overboard. Next they quartered him. They skinned him and quartered the meat into spareribs, fatback, bacon, and ham. (*MP* 174)

In this account, the outrageous act of cannibalism, this epitome of savagery, becomes a labor routine—a task that has to be done. Watching this grotesque procedure has an effect on Squibb similar to the effect the dehumanizing practices of enslavement had on the Africans before—he undergoes a "sea change" (*MP* 176), a profound transformation of identity. Clearly traumatizing and painful, Squibb's "sea change," just like the Africans' transformation, unhinges his cultural background, releasing "perfectly balanced crosscurrents of culture in him, each a pool of possibilities from which he was unconsciously drawing, moment by moment, to solve whatever problem was at hand" (*MP* 176).

Squibb's new mode of action, based upon this mixed-up cultural identity, sounds quite familiar: to solve the problems at hand means to turn away from overarching projects and grandiose schemes and to endorse a logic we encountered several times before—the logic of getting things done. This is, of course, precisely what motivated Cringle's sacrifice and the Africans' cool execution in the first place—all of these actions indicative of a changed system of values, arranged around "the only question of significance aboard ship, which was this: What must he do next?" (*MP* 175). And once more the new logic, the "sea change" coming over Squibb and Rutherford, unfolds within the framework of trickery and masquerade. Where Spielberg's *Amistad* locates truth in individual expression and emotion, Johnson puts more faith in appearances or—to invoke the writer's favored philosophical approach—phenomena.[44] At one point early in the novel, Rutherford tries to come to terms with the fact that the Allmuseri leader Ngonyama reminds him of "actors I've known in New Orleans (all unemployed)," as the strange African at times seems to resemble American pop culture caricatures of the noble savage: "'Universal Native,' I'd call it, the high-flown inscrutable way whites made the Cherokees talk in dime novels, or the Chinese in bad stage plays" (*MP* 83). He soon learns, however, that eventually it does not matter whether Ngonyama's act is true or tricked, whether he is a bad actor or a real sorcerer, whether his mode of action is a cultural cliché or an authentic expression. Where hidden motives and underlying principles are hard to determine, as they constantly shift, in line with the shifts and breaks of personal identity, the most important question turns out to be, not whether people mean what they say and intend what they do, but who performs with which effect for what kind of audience.

For Rutherford this logic, which sharply privileges the momentary and the performative over the absolute and heartfelt, is intricately linked up with the experience of the Middle Passage:

Looking back at the asceticism of the Middle Passage, I saw how the frame of mind I had adopted left me unattached, like the slaves, who, not knowing what awaited them in the New World, put a high premium on living from moment to moment, and this, I realized, is why they did not commit suicide. The voyage had irreversibly changed my seeing, made of me a cultural mongrel, and transformed the world into a fleeting shadow play I felt no more need to possess or dominate, only appreciate in the ever extended present. (*MP* 187)

Again, the concept's strength is also its weakness. Obviously, the notion of "living from moment to moment" merges almost imperceptibly with an aesthetics of inertia here. Getting things done and letting things go, taking effect and drifting along, discarding the grand view and losing orientation altogether—these stances, and their alternately negative and positive implications, come remarkably close in Johnson's novel. After all, the turn away from overarching moral and political questions to

immediate concerns and the problems at hand emulates the much ma-
ligned logic of commerce, based on the assumption that "truth is what
works, pragmatically" (*MP* 160). But be that as it may, Rutherford and
Squibb, like T. C. Boyle's trickster figure Ned Rise, manage to survive
precisely because they do not care about being co-opted and have abandoned their superior's will to possession and domination. They know
how to drift and float, which makes them the novel's true "specialist[s] in
survival" (*MP* 51), but also just that: specialists—or experts—who are
too much part of the dominant system to ever really challenge it.

6.4 Flying Africans: Rewriting the Middle Passage

"There was a whole lot of life before slavery. And we ought to know what it is. If we're
going to get rid of the slave mentality, that is."
"You're wrong, and if that's your field you're plowing wet. Slavery *is* our past. Nothing
can change that, certainly not Africa."
"We live in the world, Pat. The whole world. Separating us, isolating us—that's always
been their weapon. Isolation kills generations. It has no future."
                                                    —Toni Morrison, *Paradise* (1997)[45]

At one point in Spielberg's *Amistad,* Joadson, his fictional African-
American abolitionist, joins the lawyer Baldwin to search for evidence
supporting the Africans' case in the belly of the slave ship. By the dim
light of a lantern he looks over the traces of the Middle Passage—the
bloody scratch marks on wood, locks of hair, foot angles, and a crisscross
of chains. Panicking in the face of all these tools of terror, he drops the
lantern, trips over the chains, and falls. By the time Baldwin comes to his
rescue, relighting the lantern, we see Joadson utterly disoriented and horrified: the elegantly dressed black businessman all of a sudden thrown
back into the despondency and denigration of the slave system. In the
same scene, however, Joadson also finds Cinque's amulet, a lion's tooth,
which will convince Cinque of his integrity and will be awarded back to
the African-American at the film's end, demarcating the bond between
the black men, their common origin, and common project.

While the Middle Passage and its horrors thus figures as the negative
point of reference for the African-American's commitment, its imaginary and imaginative reenactment frightful, disorienting, and demean-
ing, a mythical African past (the lion's tooth and the story of male self-
empowerment around it) forms its positive counterpart, infusing the
diasporic African with the power to stand up for his own cause, as
Joadson does when he breaks with Tappan, the film's opportunistic
white abolitionist.

Both instances—the Middle Passage and the African past—are enacted as reference points for cultural commemoration, but their function differs radically. In *Amistad,* the recollection of an empowering African tradition compensates for the negative cultural memories of abduction, enslavement, and subjugation. The film carries this differentiation so far that eventually the entire history of slavery drops out of sight, an ugly episode to be blotted out by the grandiose and overpowering evidence of self-empowerment and personal struggle. With this, Spielberg neatly replicates a revisionist pattern by now firmly entrenched in American culture. From nineteenth-century slave narratives to late-twentieth-century pop culture, reenactments of the past tended to pit the negative history of slavery against a positive African tradition, as Paul Gilroy pointed out with respect to current black popular culture:

It seems as if the complexity of slavery and its location within modernity has to be actively forgotten if a clear orientation to tradition and thus to the present circumstances of blacks is to be acquired. Rebel MC's moving assertion in his track "Soul Rebel" that "there's more than just slavery to the history, we have dignity" typifies the best of these revisionist impulses. However, there is a danger that, apart from the archaeology of traditional survivals, slavery becomes a cluster of negative associations that are best left behind. The history of plantations and sugar mills supposedly offers little that is valuable when compared to the ornate conceptions of African antiquity against which they are unfavourably compared. Blacks are urged, if not to forget the slave experience which appears as an aberration from the story of greatness told in African history, then to replace it at the centre of our thinking with a mystical and ruthlessly positive notion of Africa that is indifferent to the intraracial variation and is frozen at the point where blacks boarded the ships that would carry them into the woes and horrors of the Middle Passage.[46]

Spielberg's film exemplarily figures forth the dangerous implications of such a strategic move of contrasting history and myth. Just as in parts of black popular culture, the history of slavery is made out as an "aberration" in Spielberg's film, but here Africa and the United States seem strangely interchangeable, the glorious African past echoing the no less glorious past of revolutionary America. Enacting a standard motif of black popular culture, *Amistad* inverts it radically, so that it no longer signifies resistance to the American mainstream, but turns the mainstream into the site of resistance, American history into African myth.

Given this blatant act of appropriation, it may not come as a surprise that the black pop cultural scene itself has for quite some time now shown signs of reorientation. For several years writers, directors, visual artists, and musicians have experimented with alternative approaches both to the African and to the African-American past. Increasingly, such accounts and reenactments of the past attempt to link back to the African traditions *by way of* a recollection of slavery. In the course of such revisions, the history of slavery is turned into a source of strength. Michael Jackson's remark that "[s]lavery was a terrible thing, but when black people in America finally got out from under that crushing system, they were stronger," enacts this counter-revisionist move almost paradigmatically.[47] Another instance of this reconceptualization of slavery, this transformation of a past of pain and suffering into a present of strength and self-determination, can be seen in the paraphernalia of hip-hop culture, the gold chains that signify upon the iron instruments of bondage by turning them into symbols of power and success.

Traces of such an alternative enactment of slavery—in collusion rather than contrast with African traditions—are given in Johnson's *Middle Passage,* but then Johnson's text tends to contest binary distinctions on a large scale, so that the merging of African myth and black American history only reiterates the much more pervasive merging of past and present, nineteenth-century configurations and twentieth-centuries concerns. In Haile Gerima's film *Sankofa* (1993),[48] by contrast, the historical and the mythical past might be similarly mixed up with a present perspective, but where Johnson suffuses the past with the present, Gerima undermines the present via the past, interspersing African myth and African-American history to challenge the current status quo. Hence, his revisionist return to the history of slavery not only questions the "interpretations . . . imposed by the dominant culture," as Gay Wilentz noted about Toni Morrison's *Song of Solomon,*[49] but transforms traditional African-American interpretations just as well in the very process of signifying upon them.

Haile Gerima, who grew up in Ethiopia and has lived in the United States since the 1960s, stages the history of slavery as part of the larger framework of black history originating in Africa.[50] The film enacts the fantastic and disturbing experiences of the African-American Mona (Oyafunmike Ogunlano), a fashion model on a shooting session in Elmina Castle on the Atlantic Coast of Ghana, experiences that bring about a fundamental rupture of her sense of identity, reality, and history. Lost in the cavern underneath the castle, Mona is forced into a nightmarish time travel back to the days of slavery. The setting, Elmina Castle, which used to be a central collecting camp for Africans to be shipped to the United States as slaves, suddenly comes to life again in all its former terror, confronting Mona with a reality to which she cannot relate in any way: "I am not an African!" she screams, as she is captured by white men in the cave, silently and mournfully watched by rows of chained black men and women. As she gathers what is going on, her screams change to "I am not a slave!" and of course both protestations highlight the perverse logic of slavery, which renders every black person an African and every African a slave. If Mona's objections are obviously true—she is neither an African nor a slave, after all—they are also absolutely futile, as "blackness," "Africanity," and slave status must not and cannot be differentiated, once the logic of slavery takes over.

The transformation of woman into slave takes place in a setup charged with sadomasochist sensationalism (invoked by the dungeon-cave, Mona's nakedness, and the "bondage" scenario) and the ambivalent dynamics of voyeurism (the silently watching Africans figuring forth the film's uneasy audience), a setup that has been rightfully said to be inflected with the logic of "porno-troping"—the spectacular enactment of black (female) suffering and pain for an audience both shocked and thrilled by it.[51] Thus, the film unfolds a weird Middle Passage in reverse, forcing the modern African-American to recognize and confront a past that seems to be the radical opposite of the present: leaving no grounds for agency, self-determination, and dignity.

Yet the disturbing scenes in the cave have to be seen in the context of what follows. After Mona's capture, the scene switches to a tracking shot of a flying buzzard, the Sankofa bird, which will come to stand for the fantastic travel to the days of slavery and back again. We then see southern cane fields fading with shots of shackled slaves, and then the buzzard again, landing. The sequence ends upon a close-up of Mona's face. Now her voice-over no longer denies but states: "I'm Shola. I'm a house slave on the Lafayette plantation. . . . You know, if you was born a slave like me, it was easier to accept things like they was." While visually the identity of Mona/Shola is unquestionably the same, this identity is never diegetically confirmed: it is only the body of the actress that collates the twentieth-century black model Mona and the nineteenth-century slave Shola. At any rate, the film's contemporary heroine seems to be as split up as Johnson's protagonist, her interaction with the past bringing forth the same fragmentation and dispersal that Rutherford described: "The 'I' that I was, was a mosaic of many countries, a patchwork of others and objects stretching backward to perhaps the beginning of time" (*MP* 163).

Strangely unrelated diegetically, yet clearly linked visually, Mona and Shola turn out to be complementary figures—interacting indirectly and along twisted lines, as comes to the fore most impressively in their respective encounters with Africanity. For Mona Africa presents an utterly disturbing, disempowering, primitive place, the origin of slavery, which deprives her of every positive self-definition, forcing her into negations—"I am not an African," "I am not a slave." Shola, conversely, will encounter African symbols as a means of personal empowerment, subversion, and resistance. If these ambivalent connotations imply the power of the Africanist image to cut both ways—it can be willfully super-imposed on a person to enslave her (as Mona experiences) yet also turned into an emblem of self-assertion against this imposition (as Shola learns)—they are resolved only at the end of the film on a markedly fantastic level: in a utopian reunion all characters eventually meet in Africa, sitting in the sun, listening to the African drummer Sankofa (Kofi Ghanaba), so that the temporal and spatial, just like the conceptual, dichotomies collapse.

The film does not marginalize the fact that slavery is represented from a contemporary perspective—after all, Mona's worldview "frames" the representation of the past. But in contrast to, say, Octavia Butler's revisionary turns to the past in *Kindred* (1979),[52] the present perspective is not enacted as a means of coming to terms with the past, as *Sankofa* merges past and present in a mythical continuity, suspending the very difference between then and now, history and myth, fact and fantasy. The film's narrative ends with Shola's fantastic escape from the plantation, parallel to Mona's escape from the cavern. In the course of a slave insurrection on the plantation, Shola runs away together with other slaves. At first, her voice-over relates their defeat, as one by one they are being overtaken by the dogs and the overseers on their horses. This is not what we see, however: the camera tracks smoothly backward through the same cane fields we saw before, as distant shouts and barks fade into music. In line with this strangely dreamlike transformation of the scenery, Shola's enthusiastic narrative changes from a description of running away to a fantastic tale of deliverance: "This buzzard was flying next to me and he spread his wings and he scooped me up and up and up. . . . Next thing I know is I'm in the air, going up and up and up and this miserable earth is getting smaller and smaller. . . . The buzzard brought me home." While she is speaking the cane fields turn to sea, the sea to land—the African coast. The historical narrative ends on this note of both defiance and visionary hope.

Thus Mona's enforced encounter with the past, her personal Middle Passage from present-day America to an Africa of suffering and bondage, is resolved by way of Shola's fantastical journey. As her flight back to Africa transcends spatial and temporal boundaries, it corresponds to the historical Middle Passage, which equally denoted a space in-between and nowhere at all. But simultaneously and more important, Shola's fantastical Middle Passage in reverse, ending in the utopian "reunion" in Africa, restores a sense of identity and belonging that seemed to have been irrevocably lost once the alienating and perverse machinery of the slave system took over.

The selfsame confrontation of force (the system of slavery) and imagination, corporeal confinement and fantastic flight, which lies at the heart of the film's imagery of escaping from the "prison of the flesh,"[53] runs through Toni Morrison's *Song of Solomon* (1977), where it motivates Solomon's fantastic "flight to Africa":

> That motherfucker could fly! Could fly! He didn't need no airplane. Didn't need no fuckin tee double you ay. He could fly his own self! . . . He just took off; got fed up. *All the way up!* No more cotton! No more bales! No more orders! No more shit! He flew, baby. Lifted his beautiful black ass up in the sky and flew on home. . . . my great-granddaddy could flyyyyyy and the whole damn town is named after him. . . . he went back to Africa. . . . He left everybody down on the ground and he sailed on off like a black eagle. "O-o-o-o-o-o Solomon done fly, Solomon done gone / Solomon cut across the sky, Solomon gone home!"[54]

Both Morrison and Gerima envision a new body too insubstantial to be kept in bondage, a body that can fly away or be swept away by a bird, take off and leave the confining and degrading systems of racist control and subjugation behind. And both correlate the fantasy of the flight with the perspective of grandchildren and descendants for whom the tale or vision of the mythical flight constitutes a cathartic point of departure and decision.

Both narratives—and Ishmael Reed's *Flight to Canada* (1976) would be another example—thus chose to break with the "realistic" setup of the trickster tale and its logic of getting things done within the confines of the system. Instead, *Sankofa* and *Song of Solomon* explode these confines by drawing upon another tradition of black culture: stories around "flying Africans."[55] Even more than Johnson or Boyle with their stories of trickery and sorcerers, the "flight narratives" of today embrace the fantastic and the grotesque to open up markedly different readings of a much represented past.[56] Such readings of the Middle Passage invert, distort, and reverse the historical facts, not even bothering to lay claim to historical accuracy, as they clearly approach the past with the present in mind.

Seen that way, it makes much more sense to read these stories as instances of cultural commemoration, which is invariably as concerned with the present as it is with the past, providing a repertory of practices and images that are to "stabilize and circulate a self-image, a collectively shared knowledge preferably (yet not exclusively) about the past from which a group derives its awareness of unity and specificity," as Jan Assmann held.[57] Translated into the realm of fiction, the memory of slavery is made to oscillate between the rhetoric of fact (the—at times "pornotropic"—display of the regime of slavery) and the rhetoric of fantasy (evoking time travels, African magic, flying slaves, and Middle Passages in all kinds of inversion), as the narratives of Johnson, Gerima, and Morrison exemplify.

Elizabeth Alexander has emphasized the strategic function of present-day slave narratives, their revision of a past of pain in terms of self-definition and agency. She thus places Gerima's film in a long tradition of African-American enactments of terror and suffering, a cultural history of witnessing pain, in which time and again the collective experience of watching violence is artistically remodeled to shape "our collective sense of who we are."[58] Alexander's correlation of slave narratives from Frederick Douglass to Harriet Jacobs with films and multimedia art and the public debates around the video of the beating of Rodney King elucidates the long-standing tradition in African-American thought of staging cultural memory as both a troublesome burden and an indispensable responsibility. From Douglass to Gerima she perceives the need to utilize the memory of witnessing violence for concrete social actions of resistance. Within the context of African-American thought, Alexander argues, cultural memory functions as a means of self-assertion, establishing links between "an African-American present, an African past, and the space of slavery between."[59]

Although I do agree that this revisionary appropriation of a black tradition, from Africa through the diasporic condition of enslavement and violation to the present day, is one of the most pertinent patterns of contemporary black thought, I would like to differentiate the contemporary turn to an African and Afro-diasporic past from a nineteenth-century thematization of black history and experience. While the associative pattern of thought conjoining the witnessing of violence with its recollection, its representation, and finally a passionate call for action was doubtlessly central to nineteenth-century black writing, the memories themselves were made out to be almost exclusively negative, so that the recollection of the past was staged primarily to prevent its repetition. One of the most impressive (and most famous) instances of this associative chain is given in Frederick Douglass's *Narrative* (1845), as he sets out evoking his feelings when witnessing his aunt Hester's whipping, feelings that he enacts as an irrepressible memory—"I remember the first time I ever witnessed this horrible exhibition. I was quite a child, but I well remember it. I never shall forget it whilst I remember anything"— and then stresses the impossibility of representing this experience (which of course only underlines the perversity of the event)—"I wish I could commit to paper the feelings with which I beheld it"—and finally reassesses the experience by dint of the later act of resistance to his master, which evokes self-control rather than passionate revenge and thus converts the former helplessness of the witnessing child into the well-conceived and careful action of the man.[60]

In a long reflection upon one of the first sentences in Douglass's *Narrative,* "I do not remember to have ever met a slave who could tell of his birthday,"[61] W. J. T. Mitchell comes to the conclusion that

Douglass plays here with two meanings of memory, the recollection of past experience by an individual, and the "passing on" ("telling") of memory from one person to another. . . . There is a simple reason Douglass and other slaves had no (collective) memory of their birthdays. They were separated from the one person who might pass on this memory, who might connect the personal and social, the directly experiential and the mediated forms of memory, namely, the mother who would likely be the only one with exact knowledge of the birthday based on personal experience.[62]

In this analysis the central feature of Douglass's enactment of memory comes to the fore: memory is something fundamentally foreign to the institution of slavery, which figures as a *"prevention* of memory," as Mitchell pointed out. Yet by the same token, remembering slavery becomes a highly ambivalent endeavor, as the commemoration of the pain and suffering can by no means provide a wholesome sense of identity and communal belonging—Douglass will never remember his birthday. It is only for later generations that the memory of slavery gains more than these utterly negative references.[63]

Houston Baker has shown in his reading of Frederick Douglass and Booker T. Washington how the rejection of slavery collated with a pervasive skepticism against the (African) past and brought about the adoption of an Euro-American symbolic system that lent itself only partially to the purposes of black Americans.[64] In the decades after the Civil War this tendency in black culture to fence Africa off would be reexamined and gradually replaced with more markedly diasporic modes of identity politics, so that step by step increasingly artificial Africas came to shape African-American self-fashioning.[65]

In contrast to the nineteenth-century stylization of memory as either a painful revelation of a lack never to be replenished, or as a focal means of fencing off the dreaded institution, the current enactment of slavery, stressing the aspects of trickery and magic, opens up an entirely different perspective.[66] In *Sankofa,* for one, both the recollection of Africa *and* the recollection of slavery, one a positive, one a deeply negative experience, are made out to provide hidden patterns of black communication. In view of the twentieth-century frame, the warning against slavery gives way to an excavation of its still valid underside, its recuperable codes of solidarity and resistance. Gerima's very emphasis on the diasporic condition—the interaction of African, African-American, and Caribbean slaves, and his virtual exclusion of white protagonists—points to a shift of interest, leading from social critique and political protest to a historical and anthropological probing into the possibility of diasporic self-fashioning against the diatribes of racism.

While this shift of interest is deeply entrenched within the structures of cultural commemoration as described by Jan Assmann, as it reflects the effort to reassess a past that cannot be accessed directly by way of personal experiences and recollections, there is more to it than that. In current diasporic reenactments of slavery and the Middle Passage, the lack of personal experience is turned into an asset. Time and again, the very act of creative transformation is emphasized, so that the return to the past is undertaken not in order to excavate a forgotten history but to reorganize a present scenario, if needs be against the historical evidence at hand. Bell hooks's reflection upon her own feelings about the African-American past is a case in point:

To remember is to empower. Even though these memories hurt, we dare to name our grief and pain and the sorrows of our ancestors. . . . I remember the drawings of sparsely clothed, shackled African slaves. I want to forget them even as they linger against my will in memory. . . . When I recall the shame I felt seeing those images . . . , I recognize that there is also rage there. I was not only angry at those images which did not feel right in my heart, I felt that being forced to look at them was like being forced to witness the symbolic enactment of a colonizing ritual, a drama of white supremacy. The shame was feeling powerless to protest or intervene.

We are not powerless today. . . . We remember our ancestors, people of color—Native American and African, as well as those individual Europeans who opposed genocide in word and deed. . . . We call on their knowledge and wisdom, present through generations, to provide us with the necessary insight so that we can create transformative visions of community and nation that can sustain and affirm the preciousness of all life.[67]

This move from the figure of the witness, "forced to look," to the figure of the powerful present subject who controls the communication with the past, does away radically with any conception of cultural commemoration as a passive reiteration of the past, a repetition or nostalgic return. Moreover, emphasizing the "transformative vision" and thus an act of creativity, bell hooks counterposes her imagery most clearly to Frederick Douglass's painful personal recollections of helplessness and subjugation. If Douglass too cast his story as a transformation from victim/witness into agent/subject, in his case the transformation is not presented as a revisionary move but as an emancipatory break with the past. It is thus precisely the aspect of re-creation that strikes me as most prominent in contemporary black cultural enactments of history. By dint of this turn, the interlinkage of the memory of slavery with the memory of Africa is significant, as it transforms both references and emphasizes this transformation at the same time. What Diedrich Diederichsen wrote about the structures of black music might thus pertain to a much wider development in black culture at the moment:

. . . Hip hop has always aimed at this original unity, which must have existed once before the process of diasporic fragmentation, restructuring this unity into a new virtual unity in the present time. Adopting all kinds of local forms of black music, the hip hop track refocuses the disparate strains from the past into a utopian reconstruction of the origin. . . . By this token the quotation functions no longer exclusively as a reference to the absent, but now must also reenact the absent—the lost unity, the origin—within the presence of the music. In other words: the loop functions paradoxically as a trace and a construction of a collective memory in the here and now.[68]

When the traces of the past—here the traditions of black music—are reassembled into a new unity, a timeless memory, "present" and "presence" indeed fall into one, as Diederichsen pointed out. This collapsing of the past into the present/presence could be seen as a dominant pattern in contemporary black culture, opposing itself to the nostalgic recuperations that have so long determined the mainstream's reaction to history, and opposing itself to the very pull of signification along the lines of conventional narratives. The history of slavery is too negative to lend itself to nostalgic reiteration, and the myth of Africanity is too vague to establish a pattern for cultural agency—interspersed, however, these two strains of remembering constitute a powerful symbolic system, which is capable of mapping out a point of departure rather than a point of origin.

6.5 Waterworlds and Alien African Futures: Pop Passages

There are no stories of the middle passage. One hundred million people were stolen and sold from their homes, shipped across the world, and not a single story of that journey survives.
—Carrie Mae Weems[69]

In Haile Gerima's *Sankofa* the process of enslavement unfolds as an experience of utter estrangement and humiliation. Mona, his African-American protagonist, is forced into a system in which she figures as nothing but a body, a material object of use. When the inner narrative around the American African Shola inverts this logic later on, it is not on the basis of intercultural communication as in Spielberg's *Amistad*—white Americans hardly enter the picture in Gerima's film—but on the

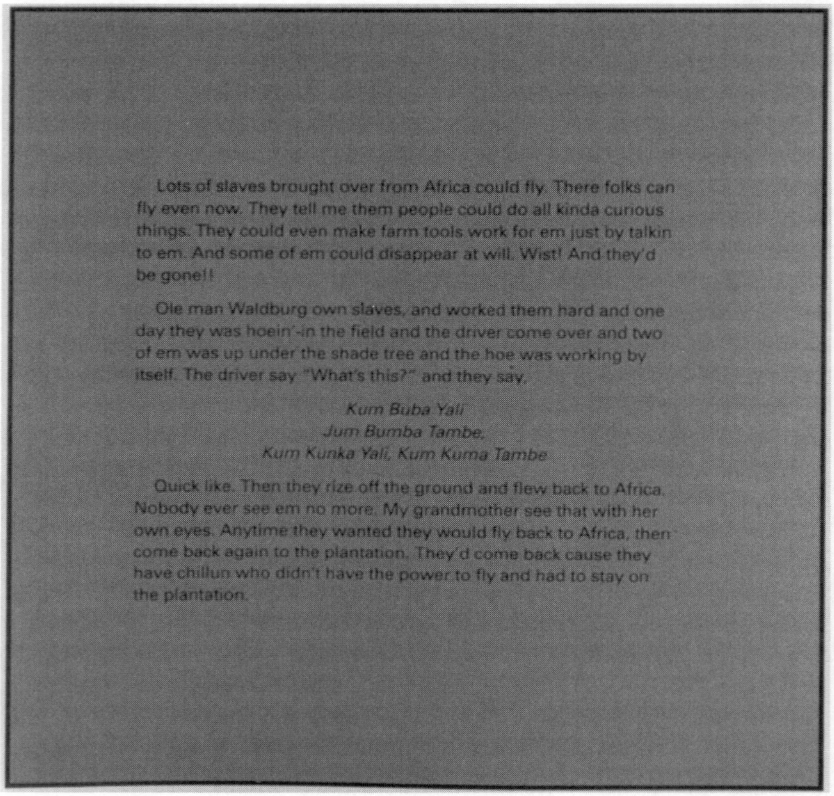

Lots of slaves brought over from Africa could fly. There folks can fly even now. They tell me them people could do all kinda curious things. They could even make farm tools work for em just by talkin to em. And some of em could disappear at will. Wist! And they'd be gone!!

Ole man Waldburg own slaves, and worked them hard and one day they was hoein'-in the field and the driver come over and two of em was up under the shade tree and the hoe was working by itself. The driver say "What's this?" and they say,

Kum Buba Yali
Jum Bumba Tambe,
Kum Kunka Yali, Kum Kuma Tambe

Quick like. Then they rize off the ground and flew back to Africa. Nobody ever see em no more. My grandmother see that with her own eyes. Anytime they wanted they would fly back to Africa, then come back again to the plantation. They'd come back cause they have chillun who didn't have the power to fly and had to stay on the plantation.

Fig. 6. Carrie Mae Weems, *Untitled* (Boone Plantation), detail (text panel).

basis of folk traditions and magic. Shola's escape from the system of slavery is enacted as the takeover of another—African—logic: the mythical story line of the Sankofa bird and the flying Africans replacing the historical story line of a subdued slave insurrection.

"Lots of slaves brought over from Africa could fly. There folks can fly even now. They tell me when people could do all kinda curious things. They could even make farm tools work for em just by talkin to em. And some of em could disappear at will. Wist! And they'd be gone!" This is how Carrie Mae Weems sets out to recount the tale of the flying Africans, then proceeding to relate specifically the fate of two men who "flew back to Africa" from a plantation on the Gullah Islands off the coast of Georgia and South Carolina.

Just like Gerima, the photographer and installation artist Weems jux-

Fig. 7. Carrie Mae Weems, *Untitled* (Boone Plantation), detail (photograph).

taposes folklore with visual evidence that neither contradicts nor corroborates the fantastic tale: a text panel relating the story (fig. 6) is conjoined
with a photograph of an island plantation (fig. 7) as a deserted and eerily
timeless setting. The piece *Untitled* (Boone Plantation) is part of an installation concluded in 1995, *Untitled* (Sea Island series), in which
Weems casts yet another glance at the entangled histories of Africa and
America. The bulk of the series consists of large-format landscape photographs combined with text. But Weems also resorts to a device familiar
from another series, titled, tellingly, *Commemorating* (1992), in which
she imprinted cheap ceramic dinner plates with the names of famous
Americans. In her Sea Island series she uses dinnerware to display general
reflections about the project under the joint heading "Went Looking for
Africa" (fig. 8). One such dinner plate inscription reads:

Went Looking for Africa

and found Africa here
in the proverbs
of McIntosh
In the voices
of Sapeto
In the songs
of St. Simons
Along the highways
of Jekyll
In the gardens
of Johns
In the grave-yards
of Hilton Head

By dint of this approach, Africa and America are no longer conceived as geographical entities, to be neatly separated, but as convoluted concepts, flight lines of beliefs, memories, and projections that are far too intersected to be told apart. Africa is ingrained in the very core of American culture, its language, its folklore, its soil. Characteristically, Weems expresses this insight both verbally and formally, the dinnerware figuring as an emblem of commemoration, invested with a significance that is visible only at second glance and to the initiate, as Houston Baker remarked: "The dishes are memory, and they are luxury. They pass through generations as family inheritance. Carrie Mae Weems reclaims such ceramics for the everyday uses of cultural conversation."[70]

In the Gullah Islands, once the last illegal refuge for slavery in the United States, a central predicament of contemporary African-American culture becomes visible: the fact that black history is both there and not there, evident in countless traces, scars, and memories yet largely submerged when it comes to written accounts and first-person documentations of the past from the viewpoint of the victims. To come to pass in its own right, the African presence in the United States has to be pried away from the mainstream culture of which it has become an integral part—not by choice but by necessity, as Samuel Delany pointed out:

. . . , until fairly recently, as a people we were systematically forbidden any images of our past. . . . [E]very effort conceivable was made to destroy all vestiges of what might endure as African social consciousness. When, indeed, we say that this country was founded on slavery, we must remember that we mean, specifically, that it was founded on the systematic, conscientious, and massive destruction of African cultural remnants. That some musical rhythms endured, that certain religious attitudes and structures seem to have persisted, is quite astonishing, when you study the efforts of the white, slave-importing machinery to wipe them out.[71]

WENT LOOKING FOR AFRICA

and found Africa here
in the proverbs
of McIntosh
in the voices
of Sapelo
in the songs
of St. Simons
Along the highways
of Jekyll
in the gardens
of Johns
In the grave-yards
of Hilton Head

Fig. 8. Carrie Mae Weems, *Untitled* (Went Looking for Africa).

Weems's series can be seen as an effort to remobilize these remnants and draw them to our attention, "reassembling traces of the past into new, if only temporary, unities,"[72] as Maren Stange put it. The same idea motivated a later project in which she documented the traces of New World slavery in West Africa—most notably around Elmina Castle, the very ground of departure for Haile Gerima's journey back. And just like Gerima's film, Weems's installions evince that in the field of the visual and narrative arts the project of excavating an African past will invariably deviate from its anthropological and historiographical premises and venture into the realm of fantasy and myth to compensate for the lack of concrete and indubitable material. This is what comes about in Weems's recounting of the folktale, which is related as fact, of a family past: "My grandmother see that with her own eyes." And this is what infuses the

Sea Island series in general, when time and again the rhetoric of historical fact is replaced with the vernacular of personal experience and sense impressions.

In *Untitled* (Ebo Landing), a triptych of two silver prints and a text panel, Weems displays two scenic views of the island St. Simons, framed in black and mounted one over the other. In between the photographs she inserted a panel set in circular print:

> Ebo Landing
>
> One midnight at high tide a
> ship bringing in a cargo of Ebo (Ibo)
> men landed at Dunbar Creek on the
> Island of St. Simons. But the men refus-
> ed to be sold into slavery; joining hands
> together they turned back toward the
> water, chanting, "the water brought us,
> the water will take us away." They all
> drowned, but to this day when the
> breeze sighs over the marshes and
> through the trees, you can hear the
> clank of chains and echo of
> their chant at Ebo Landing.

Here the African past becomes a ghostly present, and a collation of different time spheres sets in that is all the more disconcerting for the detached and depersonalized representation of the event. The Ibo men appear in strange isolation, because their enslavers do not come into view and because the Africans' desperate act is related as not so much a tragic group suicide but a weird and moving ritual. The photographs (fig. 9) emphasize this aura of timeless detachment or suspension of time and place: the marshland on view a curious mixture of water and earth, and the entire setup of irregular palm trees and lush vegetation looking as "African" as it is "American." The Ibos' act seems to have fundamentally affected the land, giving vent to a haunting that is intricately connected with the region's history—its function, along with the port of New Orleans, as "Ellis Island's antitheses for African-Americans: . . . the chief ports of call where ships from Africa unloaded their human cargo"[73]—even if, or precisely because, this history turns into fantasy and myth.

The same collation of history and myth, the repressed cruel past and a seemingly enlightened present, runs through *Benito Cereno*. After all, Melville's novella figures forth a "spectral marionette show,"[74] presenting the slave ship along the lines of gothic horror as a haunted place in the middle of nowhere:

Fig. 9. Carrie Mae Weems,
Untitled (Ebo Landing).

Always upon first boarding a large and populous ship at sea, especially a foreign one, with a nondescript crew such as Lascars or Manilla men, the impression varies in a peculiar way from that produced by first entering a strange house with strange inmates in a strange land. Both house and ship—the one by its walls and blinds, the other by its bulwarks like ramparts—board from view their interiors till the last moment: but in the case of the ship there is this addition; that the living spectacle it contains, upon its sudden and complete disclosure, has, in contrast with the blank ocean which zones it, something of the effect of enchantment. The ship seems unreal; these strange costumes, gestures, and faces, but a shadowy tableau just emerged from the deep, which directly must receive back what it give. (BC 166)

These observations foreshadow the story's later revelation of a pervasive masquerade enacted on the ship, a revelation that leaves no doubt that the phenomena that have "emerged from the deep" are not necessarily more truthful or significant than the "blank" surface they disrupt. To the contrary, their uncanny effect might reside exclusively in their meaninglessness, the "spectacle" or "shadowy tableau" only the more frightening because it has lost any melodramatic significance: it does not permit itself to be read.

In fact, it is only against the backdrop of the high seas, the "blank ocean," that the spectacle of social and cultural interaction (the "nondescript" foreign crew, presumably under Western leadership) fully reveals its cruel, uncanny, and absurd character. In *Benito Cereno* the sea figures not as the land's opposite but as its epitome: here the incongruities of the land—most notably the system of slavery—are too conspicuous to be entirely ignored. And this is where Melville's novella calls to mind Weems's installation, which likewise associates the sea with a repressed and gruesome past—the Ibos' death by drowning. But while for Melville the "blank sea," just like the "tableau" of the land, ultimately does not make sense, being an empty melodrama or tautological masquerade, Weems turns it into a meaningful entity. In her enactment the sea turns from blankness to myth—the history of slavery mixed up with the myths of Africa bringing about the dead men's return and their haunting takeover. Where Melville discloses a dead end, Weems's horror scenario figures as a point of departure for a new symbolic repertory.

With this, Weems posits herself firmly in a postcolonial scene that insists upon reading established dichotomies of meaning and insignificance, essence and blankness against the grain, siding with the "nondescript crew," or the drowned ones whose viewpoint is irretrievably lost, by implementing another concept of history and historiography. In Derek Walcott's poem "The Sea Is History," this new notion of history is associated with a new beginning out of the pain and horror of the Middle Passage, a new beginning stemming from the victims, the drowned slaves:

> Where are your monuments, your battles, martyrs?
> Where is your tribal memory? Sirs,
> in that grey vault. The sea. The sea
> has locked them up. The sea is history
>
> . . . .
>
> Sir it is locked in them sea-sands
> out there past the reef's moiling shelf,
> where the men-o'-war floated down;
>
> strop on these goggles, I'll guide you there myself.[75]

Insisting that the ocean's "blank pages" are not as empty as they seem, Walcott's poem fashions the very history it then sets out to pronounce in the last line: "in the salt chuckle of the rocks / with their sea pools, there was the sound / like a rumor without any echo / of History, really beginning."[76] Black diasporic history, it seems, is a thing of the future, not of the past, a subject of fantasies, dreams, and speculations—the currents and changes of the sea—which is created in the process of its recuperation.

Thus, Walcott refutes Melville's notion of the ocean as irretrievably "blank." But even more important, his turn to the sea as both a burial ground *and* the space of a new beginning, like Weems's enactment of memory as survival, indicates that the subject matter of black history requires a methodology of its own, new goggles, if you will, that make readable what seemed blank and reveal the ghosts of the past at loose in the present world. It is precisely the openness and indeterminacy of the sea, its "oceanic" quality of the "*nowhere* at all" as Hortense Spillers had it, that privileges this space for a pervasive revision from the vantage point of present needs and desires. This is why the underwater world, the submarine, gains so much attention in turn: in contrast to the charted and mapped high seas, this world below emerges as a realm beneath existing lines of power and signification, an ambivalent space, "neither European nor Caribbean, neither metropolitan nor colonial, neither within the 'West' nor without it," as Ian Baucom wrote[77]—a fantasy space that is always as much of the future as it is of the past.

Yet we must not forget that such futuristic fantasy spaces are always also spaces of retreat from very real pressures, testifying—if often only indirectly—to these pressures and their traumatic effects. "Black people live the estrangement that science fiction writers imagine,"[78] Greg Tate noted, and for that matter it is no accident that so much black art that currently deals with this "life feeling" is not only clearly futuristic but also and just as clearly highly morbid—telling ghost stories and tales of haunting. The

British director John Akomfrah thus cast this peculiar obsession with the past as an obsession with the dead: "I think necrophilia is at the heart of black filmmaking." To come up with a history of one's own against the pull of oblivion and decay—to enforce the return of the repressed—is to face some ugly truths:

The most powerful moment, for me, in my earlier film *Testament,* is the very end and the very beginning, which are both images of death, stultification, atrophy. When she goes to the graveyard and buries her father, or when the man walks into the river, which is a wish-fulfilment of death, a drowning wish going on there. There is a level of morbidity which I think people have to realise in the quest for identity. Identities are a morbid business.[79]

Of course, Akomfrah's emphasis on a morbid black imagination is to a certain extent polemic—pitted against only too familiar stylizations of blackness as mindlessly joyful, happy-go-lucky, and ahistorical. But there is more to the obsession with the alien and the uncanny in black culture than sheer provocation, as not only Weems's and Walcott's ghost stories exemplify but also Charles Johnson's enactment of cannibalism as a revelatory "sea change," and as comes even more trenchantly to the fore in contemporary pop cultural turns to the Middle Passage and its imagery of travel and displacement. It is in this context, the workings of pop culture, that the spirits and ghosts of yore turn into quite contemporary figures of horror and haunting: aliens, extraterrestrials, creatures from the deep.

Could it be possible for humans to breathe underwater? A fetus in its mother's womb is certainly alive in an aquatic environment.

During the greatest holocaust the world has ever known, pregnant America-bound African slaves were thrown overboard by the thousands during labor for being sick and disruptive cargo. Is it possible that they could have given birth at sea to babies that never needed air?

Recent experiments have shown mice able to breath liquid oxygen. Even more shocking and conclusive was a recent instance of a premature human infant saved from certain death by breathing liquid oxygen through its underdeveloped lungs.

These facts combined with reported sightings of gill men and swamp monsters in the coastal swamps of the Southeastern United States make the slave trade theory startlingly feasible.[80]

These are excerpts from the liner notes to the album *The Quest* by the Detroit electronic duo Drexciya, a project that has for many years fashioned itself around similar ruminations about "Drexciyans"—sea creatures of a superior submarine civilization invading the United States systematically.[81] Obviously, this narrative epitomizes the logic sketched above—from the move to the sea as an alternative history deeply infused with fantasy and myth, to the evocation of aliens arising out of alienation, up to the morbid imagery of creatures between death and life and beyond identification—which the entire album then sets out to consolidate.

The narrative of the liner notes is, after all, the only "information" we are given for the album. The music tells no story, apart from disjointed bits and pieces of lyrics that not so much add up to a narrative but disorient and confuse. Instead of learning more about the Drexciyans we are literally forced into an underwater world, a sound pattern meshing together the synthetic and the natural, bubble tones and electronic scales, which could be called breathtaking in more than one sense. An aesthetics of alienation takes hold, as Kodwo Eshun argued:

. . . there is no singer, no redemption, no human touch. Far from rehumanising electronics, Drexciyan fiction exacerbates this dehumanisation, populating the world with impalpable hallucinations that get on your nerves. . . . At Love Parade and Tribal Gathering you can still hear DJs saying electronic music is universal music. The frequencies can unite us all in a tonal consensus. After listening to Drexciya, it's audible that if electronics ever unites, then it does so through obfuscation. It communicates through mystification.[82]

By dint of this reading, electronic music could become *the* vehicle for dissent in a Deleuzean control society, an instrument to create precisely these "vacuoles of noncommunication, circuit breakers" that Deleuze deemed indispensable to "elude control."[83] For Eshun, Drexciya's aesthetics of alienation forms the blueprint for a new form of interaction and contact: "Each track title . . . functions as a component in an electronic mythology which the listener assembles. . . . A new geography of morals."[84]

Of course, such enthusiasm about the potential of music to bring forth a fundamental disruption, a new mythology, must always face up to the "fluidity" of musical expression—the fact that music, even when not purely instrumental, is so much more ambivalent than any other artistic medium, especially when it comes to ideological positions and projections. It is, after all, by way of lyrics, liner notes, performance, and artistic comments both on- and offstage that this ideological dimension enters the field of music. By consequence, the political and social effects of music, just as of fashion, turn out to be a matter of style—highly unstable, open to all kinds of adaptations, revisions, and appropriations.[85] While I hesitate thus to join into the enthusiastic chorus of critics like Eshun and celebrate electronic music as the manifestation of an altogether new "posthuman" form of expression, I do believe that Drexciya's style politics are indicative of an interesting turn, as they produce self-destroying narratives, fictions that strain against the conventional pull of identification and closure.

Seen that way, the effect of mystification evoked by Eshun is very well given in Drexciya, but located on an altogether different level, as it is inscribed in the very interaction of instrumental music and the narratives around it. While the narratives, presenting the Drexciyans as social outcasts and fighters from below, offer patterns of identification—if markedly fantastic ones—the music takes these patterns apart, moving between recognizable structures (the underwater sounds) and pure noise and thus discouraging any attempt at making sense eventually, erecting a code that cannot be deciphered.

Of course, Drexciya are not the first musical act to come up with this strategy. Indeed, their aesthetics can be traced back to the free jazz experiments of Sun Ra and his Arkestra, with regard not only to musical but also to conceptual developments. Time and again, the space narratives evoked in this context run analogous in their effect to the musical strategy of free jazz, to move from established harmonies to sudden transgressions and to confront closure with chaos. Just as the music veers between signification and rupture, so the space narratives establish recognizable structures only to disavow them in turn: "they have thrown their own identities into question, taking on a multitude of costumes and alter egos, each of them is a myth-making, alias-taking, self-styled postindustrial shaman," writes John Corbett on Sun Ra's and other musicians' "space madness."[86] By consequence, the aliens and extraterrestrials invoked by so many black musical projects of the 1950s and 1960s are not to be understood as neat inversions of the dominant value system but as more extensive tactics of confusion: instead of "only turning around the relation of 'us' against 'them,' and other binaries," Diedrich Diederichsen wrote, "most of these artists tend to mess up the entire matrix of binary distinctions."[87]

In the works of contemporary artists this technique of "messing up" has become a much more strategic—and theoretical—affair than in, say, Sun Ra's fantastical mythology. This comes to the fore not only in the musical projects of Drexciya, DJ Spooky, or 4hero but also in the films of John Akomfrah, the fiction of Darius James, or the art of Keith Piper. All of these artists, together with many more, have been subsumed under the heading "Afrofuturism,"[88] as all of them focus one way or another on the intersecting imageries of pastness and future in black culture, setting out not so much to rewrite the history of the African diaspora but to systematically deconstruct it, rendering Africa an "alien future," as Kodwo Eshun put it in John Akomfrah's film on the movement, The Last Angel of History (1995). The aliens and monsters haunting Afrofuturist narratives explode the confines of historiography and realism, collapsing established patterns of signification and identification, and time and again put forth undecipherable codes and fractured images.

One prominent means of generating the atmosphere of alienation so characteristic for many of these works is technology. In Drexciya's *Quest,* synthetic sounds imitate natural ones, sounding almost, but not altogether, the same, so that the underwater world disclosed seems strange in several respects—a sphere underneath the human world that is at the same time a realm outside of nature: artificial, alien, and uncanny. In the work of the British installation artist Keith Piper similar strategies of technological alienation are employed, and again the result is the collapse of long-standing symbolic systems, not in order to replace them, but to expose them in their artificiality and arbitrariness. And once more aquatic imagery, or what Kobena Mercer called the aesthetics of "oceanic feeling,"[89] is at the heart of these techniques of alienation and deconstruction: certainties are set afloat and stable identities go down the drain.

Piper's installation falls into three parts, all of them opening up different time frames to trace the interrelations between black British history and the African diaspora. One such part, "The Ghosts of Christendom," reflects the Middle Passage between Africa and the Caribbean, and leaves no doubt that Piper, too, conceives of black history as always also a horror story. The ship called Jesus is the *Jesus of Lubeck,* the first official British vessel to take part in the slave trade, sent off by Queen Elizabeth in 1564, and figuring forth the intricate convolution of religion and politics, spirituality and ideology, at the heart of colonial history and the history of slavery likewise, as we learn from an inscription on a tombstone displayed in the exhibition (fig. 11). And yet, religious history is not to be written along the lines of domination and subjugation alone, as Piper's project evinces: "[T]he slave ship called Jesus has experienced a mutiny of radical proportions. The same Africans for which the ship had been a mechanism of imprisonment had seized control of the helm and were steering the ship in a totally different direction."[90]

The exhibition, which comprises a variety of different representational techniques, unfolds around a series of huge computer-montaged transparencies mounted on light boxes to simulate stained glass church windows (fig. 10). Here, the obviously high-tech emulates the ancient, the up-to-date and the traditional enmeshed with each other, while African and Western symbols and emblems appear in intimate interlinkage. This effect is driven home most impressively in a cross-shaped montage showing the feet of a black crucified body, hanging over a water-filled basin with a broken mirror inside (fig. 11).

Ian Baucom has read this installation as a strategy of enforcing an impossible point of view, another means of pulling us under water:

Looking down into these waters, we see not simply a reflection of the agonized black body which hangs above, we see that bleeding figure as if from beneath,

Fig. 10. Keith Piper, *A Ship Called Jesus*, detail (transparency).

Fig. 11. Keith Piper, *A Ship Called Jesus,* detail (basin and crucifix).

from below the surface of the water. Manipulating a trick of light to reverse our optic of inspection and to reposition our space of observation, Piper's installation displaces the viewing subject, draws us beneath the water to gaze at the scene of violence played out above. The work forces us, if only for a moment, to occupy the submarine.[91]

If this relocation of the perspective is definitely one effect of the installation, there is more to it. The tormented black body on the cross, like the entire exhibition, points to a deep skepticism vis-à-vis the very symbolic systems at work here: the selfsame system—Christianity—that triggered the history of suffering figures now as a means of representing it. With this, Piper for once does invert a set of dominant signs and symbols, as his catalogue essay indicates. But he also goes beyond mere inversion, pinpointing the difficulty of representing positively what happened and what happens in the history of cultural contact and race relations. After all, the installation is not content with relating a clear-cut "other" story of salvation and redemption; it does not merely "blacken" the imagery of Christianity by depicting a black Christ. The doubly fractured reflection of the black body we see in the water instead brings about the shortcomings of such neat reversals, which merely turn around prefabricated values systems, ideologies, and props, and thus add speculations to speculations: fragments of meaning and knowledge that are as broken up and distorted as the body reflected in the water. Thus Piper's installation seems to comment on the other projects I presented here—all of them collapsing past, present, and future, and all of them interlinking historiographical and mythical rhetoric and imagery, not so much in order to reconstruct a lost history (as did Spielberg's *Amistad*), but to dismantle the established one and give scope to altogether different, highly fantastic scenarios instead, which are as much of the future as they are of the past. In any case we end up with strange sights—alien, aquatic, artificial— which force us to reconsider not only the past but most of all the present we like to take for granted.

Keith Piper, like Herman Melville, knows that institutions form reality, and that such mechanisms of reality formation are difficult to be sidetracked. Just as Babo, who sets out to invert slavery, ends up confirming and repeating this "peculiar institution," so the black figure on the cross in Piper's installation seems to both protest against a superimposed—imperial and Christian—system of signification and yet remain entangled in it. In contrast to Melville, however, Piper manages to unhinge the logic he is up against by refusing to stay within its confinement. Mixing his symbolic systems and fracturing his images to the point of absurdity, he explodes the very frame of reference he set himself, replacing history with something else: a fantastic, grotesque, weird conglomerate of images of pastness and futurism, of times that could have been and might once be.

Of course, this is a perspective that Melville could not possibly take, a perspective pertaining markedly to our time. With this, artists as different as Piper, Drexciya, Carrie Mae Weems, or Haile Gerima all manage to go beyond the logic of getting things done, which we encountered in the works of Gibson, Sterling, Boyle, and Johnson. Translating the trope of trickery into the realm of fantasy and myth, these artists both acknowledge its effectivity as a model for pragmatic cultural action *and* point out the need for more than just pragmatics—new concepts, different images. This is what the turn to the air and to the submarine epitomizes in its defiance of the laws of logic and linearity, and this is why formal and conceptual aspects play such an important role in all of these works and projects. Where *Amistad* pitted truth against trickery, and propounded translation—of Mende into English, words into images—as a means of bringing about clear and univocal communication, artists from Gerima to Piper insist upon the need to manipulate what is accepted as truth. Messing up the material they work with—the folk stories, the oral narratives, the historical documents—they introduce a different kind of trick translation. After all, this time trickery does not aim at writing history and safeguarding one-sided domination (as in the discourses of colonialism), but spreads confusion and undermines control. If this sounds like an altogether negative process, we shall see shortly how the utterly destructive (confusion, infection, morbidity, and disease) can inadvertently flip over to propel liberation and alternative action.

SEVEN

Don't Touch! Africa Is a Virus

Establishing contact is a vital project in the time of globalization. As people, funds, ideologies, and patterns of consumption travel around the world, areas that are still isolated and groups that are not yet in touch have to seem like a challenge to the smooth machinery of global translation and transformation. And yet, establishing contact is at the same time a dangerous undertaking, as the very imagery of contact reveals: coming close and getting in touch always also means exposure to foreign influences, unknown emanations of the other, so that the laudable project of initiating communication—or the less laudable scheme for implementing control—is ever liable to flip over into its opposite mode and open the door to infiltration, takeover, and contamination.

Etienne Balibar has consequently pointed out that the very concept of the border has to be reconsidered these days. Instead of celebrating cosmopolitan border crossing as a transgressive activity in its own right, Balibar points to the functional and formal transformations borders have undergone. Borders, he argues, "are no longer localizeable in an unequivocal fashion"—they "vacillate":

Vacillating borders . . . do not work in the same way for "things" and "people"—not to speak of what is neither thing nor person:—viruses, information, ideas—and thus repeatedly pose, sometimes in a violent way, the question of whether people transport, send, and receive things, or whether things transport, send, and receive people: what can in general be called the empirico-transcendental question of *luggage*.[1]

By dint of this conceptual turn, border crossing becomes a highly ambivalent activity, in the course of which basic notions of agency, autonomy, and responsibility are called into doubt. Once the focus changes from travelers with their intentions, aims, and incentives to traveling as a not necessarily personalized activity or, even more broadly put, from traveling to being on the move, an "alien" transgressivity comes into view that does not compute with the classical vocabulary of travel writing. And it is no accident that it is the virus that ranges first in Balibar's list of traveling forces (or the forces of traveling): the virus—which *is,* in a manner of speaking, pure information—is definitely not to be mapped along the lines of conscious, rational, self-asserting agency. Yet just as definitely this entity *does* act, and it *has* an impact, often a profound and devastating one.

It is on these grounds—its depersonalized, "alien" effectivity—that the figure of the virus, alongside the trope of the parasite, has come to haunt the popular imagination of our day. While it does take up other, older, imageries—vampirism, voodoo, and demon possession—to form the complex semantic field of infection and infiltration, contagion and contact, the virus imagery abandons the notion of an intentional or emotive thrust underneath. In turn, the virus may very well be demonized; it may be represented in anthropomorphized imageries. But its most fascinating feature is precisely *not* viciousness, but an utter lack of deliberation: viral infection is not to be grasped by means of moral or ideological evaluation alone, even if such value judgments invariably hover in the background of attempts at rationalization and explanation.

A "metaphoric field" has constituted itself within the last decades, "actualized with the advent of AIDS and organized around the figure of the virus or the parasite, which turned into a 'collective symbol' against the backdrop of aesthetic practices and theories of the so-called 'postmodern era,'" as Brigitte Weingart pointed out in her extensive account of the imagery and logic at work in virus narratives.[2] A popular theme comes to the fore, which runs through novels, films, comics, and pop songs these days, and is time and again enacted in tight conjunction with imageries of global interaction, communication, and contact.[3] Seen that way, the virus is a new trope, a trope of globalization if you will, even if or precisely because the trope refashions countless earlier fantasies around the issues of infection, contagion, and disease. And I decided to take the "newness" of this trope seriously, abandoning consequently in this last chapter the practice of setting out with a reading of a classical narrative. In the following I will trace the trope of viral infection and parasitical contact over a wide range of pop cultural material, setting out with a reading of a 1990s film—Wolfgang Petersen's *Outbreak*—that will figure as a counterpoint for the literary, graphic, and musical enactments of infection and contact investigated afterward.

The virus is an apt figure for concluding this study, not only because it lends scope to a broad variety of "global" topics in general, but also because it seems to have a special affinity to the imagery of Africanity. No other continent has ever gained as dangerous connotations as the

African, and the virus seems to slip easily into the place of older, colonial fears and projections, as Heather Schell has shown:

The virus emerges as a dangerous foreign being: a fecund, primitive yet evolving, hungry, needy, African predator unleashed by modern travel from the last recesses of the wild. . . . Virus discourse has become a covert means of negotiating identity and contact in the increasing multiculturalism of the global village. Western ideas of the non-self, the external threat, have not kept pace with the postmodern flexible self. The Other is still the same, tired old Other, that dark, unknowable native lurking in that dark, unknowable continent, waiting to erode our identity and leave us degenerated or reborn. Marlow or Tarzan, the Westerner who makes contact with the indefinable essence of Africa has always emerged a transformed soul. The only postmodern element of virus discourse is that now the African transformative being has become a global passenger with no need for a green card. Viral discourse is retelling old imperialist nightmares that, neutralized under cover of medical common sense, seem to justify exclusionary practices, surveillance and general prejudice that we would otherwise find inexcusable as well as politically untenable.[4]

While I clearly disagree with the notion that nothing much has changed in the implementation of the imagery of the "foreign" since the days of early imperialism, Schell's outline of the anxieties and fantasies involved in current enactments of viral infection indubitably traces the issues at stake: the obsession with travel, contact, and change, which entails as many paranoid ideas of losing control as it triggers fascinations about a pervasive reorganization and focalization on a global scale. By dint of this insight, the fusion of virus imagery and Africanity into the horror vision of a timelessly primitive aggressor turns out to demarcate only one trend in a wider semantic field. The Africanist virus, it seems, is not only savage and unchanging; it is also hypermodern and highly versatile.

Stereotyping is, after all, neither logical nor conclusive, and racial stereotypes need not "add up" to an overall picture in order to do their work. Indeed, the fact that contradictory ascriptions may exist harmoniously next to each other ensures the very functionality of stereotyping, providing a highly volatile and indeterminate backdrop for immediate evaluations and quick, quasi-instinctive judgments. Thus, the stereotypical setup of Africa as a wholesome, purifying space need not rule out the converse setup of Africa as a noxious influence, a dark, "viral" force at the borderlines of Western civilization; Africa as corruption and Africa as paradise seem to coexist happily next to each other in the Western imagination. And on the same grounds, the virus can be both an ancient evil force and an epitome of (post)modern versatility. The buzzword of our time, for one, crops up time and again in descriptions of viral and parasitical influence: flexibility.

And this is a curious development, given the term's overall positive connotations these days. After all, from economic theory to business politics and New Age philosophy, flexibility came to be celebrated as the quality of true up-to-dateness. The icons of our time—the expert, the cosmopolitan, the global girl—are time and again characterized on these grounds: it is because of their flexibility that they escape the confines of local culture and manage to live everywhere, or, for that matter, nowhere at all. Only in the field of immunology does the term gain a somewhat dubious connotation—after all, flexibility may refer to the adaptive capacity of the antibody, but the quality pertains first and foremost to the virus itself, signifying the unpredictable course of a viral infection.[5]

This ambivalence figures forth one of the most interesting aspects of popular approaches to the virus figure: the fact that this impersonal and relentlessly destructive force is envisioned in terms of definitional power. The virus lays down the rules of the game, or the conditions of battle, it seems: it can be conquered only once its operative principle, its "tactics," has been decoded. It is this quality that renders the virus a markedly modern force to be countered with modern means. Again, the implications of this turn become most obvious with regard to classical imageries of cultural contact: the individualist heroes of yore—the adventurer, the white hunter, the colonial lady—stand no chance against this predator figure, which may act ancient but is also as modern as it gets. As participant intermediaries or observers, such heroes are the first to be infected and the first to go.

The virus sets the tone for new modes of action and new kinds of agency, as we shall see. But more than that, it allows for strange alliances and interlinkages, eventually giving way to identification along crooked lines. If artists of the African diaspora have for quite some time now enacted their struggle in terms of an "alien" force, as we saw in the previous chapter, many such artists now set out to envision blackness as a virus—the epitome of an alien impact. And the implications of this alignment are certainly no less ambivalent than the developments traced before with regard to revisionist diasporic narratives.

As the binary constructions of Africa and the West, blackness and whiteness, the global and the local get entangled into an ever more complex web of signification, once more the power of trickery to manipulate meaning production comes to the fore. Earlier in this study I introduced Michel Serres's "parasitic turn" in cultural theory, the notion that the parasite, this sidekick of the virus, effects a communicative "relation without a reversal of direction." Now we shall see that there is more to the doings of viruses and parasites than the implementation of such a unidirectional thrust. We shall see that these figures culminate the work of human trickster figures delineated before, fundamentally redesigning cultural contact by messing up the poles of confrontation and forcing our attention toward the very channels in between these poles, a "mediate, a middle, an intermediary," as Michel Serres had it. The "essence of relation," the parasite, just like the virus, turns out to inscribe "a function of the relation . . . in a circular causality, a feedback loop."[6] Eventually, viruses will turn out to be the ultimate go-betweens of our day, intruding into and reshaping our concepts of communication and contact, and— even more than that—representations of such contact scenarios. The virus "infects" narrative, as it were, as a series of alternative narratives published from the 1970s to the 1990s conceive of viral outbreaks not so much as momentary deviations from a stable status quo but as its very essence,[7] offering new poles of identification and self-fashioning in turn. The virus becomes a role model. That may sound like a dangerous development, but then narratives are far from harmless in the first place, as we should know by now.

7.1 On the Air: *Outbreak*

Spotted fever, yaw, typhus and trypanosomiasis throve here. Hookworm, cholera and plague. There was bilharzia and guinea worm in the drinking water, hydrophobia in the sharp incisors of bats and wolves, filariasis in the saliva of mosquitoes and horseflies. Step outside, take a bath, drink the water or put a scrap of food in your mouth and you've got them all—bacilli, spirilla and cocci, viruses, fungi, nematodes, trematodes and amoeba—all eating away at your marrow and organs, blurring your vision, sapping your fiber, eradicating your memory as neatly as an eraser moving over the scribbled wisdom of a blackboard.
—T. C. Boyle, *Water Music* (1981)

Africa, this dangerous and chaotic ground, is better enjoyed from a distance. Once you get too close you might get attacked. Or sick. The distanced glance is a stock element of colonialist self-fashioning, as Mary Pratt pointed out with reference to travel writing and what she called the trope of the "monarch of all I survey," in which an elevated vantage point allows for an overall view without immediate contact.[8] Conveying unquestionable superiority and unquestioning submission, the entire setup on the hill, in the treetops, or in the sky moreover effectively rules out communication. In Edgar Rice Burroughs's *Tarzan of the Apes* we once witness his protagonist's surveyal of a native village in precisely these terms, the very wording of the passage suggesting one-sided control, disciplined distance, and the safety associated with such precaution:

At length he came to a great tree, heavy laden with thick foliage and loaded with pendant loops of giant creepers. From this almost unpenetrable bower above the village he crouched, looking down upon the scene below him, wondering over every feature of this new, strange life. (*TA* 96)

The trope of the "monarch of all I survey" is far from defunct, although the means of distantiation may have changed. In Michael Crichton's novel *Congo* it is technology that first provides the distancing and safeguarding screen for perusal without involvement. Once the technological interfaces come down, a less alienated communication sets in, but not between Americans and Africans, as could be expected, but between Americans and apes. The incongruity of this development is pinned down at the end of the novel, when the Americans barely escape from an attack of a cannibal tribe, the Kigani, by mounting a gas balloon. From this vantage point they look back on their aggressors: "Pale white arrows sliced up in the fading light, but they fell short, arcing back down to the ground again. The balloon rose steadily into the sky" (*C* 310). No communication will ever be established with the Kigani, not only because they speak another language but, more important, because their symbolic system has proven incompatible; it is not to be integrated. An earlier remark in the novel comes to mind: "The Kigani haven't seen that times have changed and their beliefs don't work. And they're going to be extinct" (*C* 150). The glance back at them from the safe distance of the balloon demarcates the nostalgic contemplation of a world in decline, a "culture" at its vanishing point.

In a way, *Outbreak*, Wolfgang Petersen's film produced fifteen years after the publication of *Congo*,[9] seems to operate on the principle of discouraging precisely this feeling of security in distance. In this film, to be airborne and leave the dangerous ground behind does not necessarily mean to escape. Or to enjoy nostalgia at that. What Heather Schell called the "image of Africa's *getting out*"[10] prevents such easy relief time and again. At an early point in the film we see an American plane take off from African ground, leaving a scenario of disease and death behind. As the plane approaches the foreground, the camera refocuses, drawing our attention to a horde of monkeys on a tree branch. The monkeys carry the very disease that wiped out the African village. And one of them will make it to the United States, infecting a small American town in turn. The parallels between the events in the African village and in the American small town are trenchant and impossible to ignore, especially as we get to know the village in the Motaba River Valley and the California town Cedar Creek from strikingly similar perspectives: bird's-eye views.

This is, after all, the film's most favored perspective. Thus it opens with a long shot very similar to the one ending the film *Congo*[11]: looking down on Africa. Dwelling upon an endless, majestic sight of treetops at first, the camera then moves down to the shrubbery in a crane shot. The moment the ground level is reached, a wheezing sound sets in, and the peaceful forest scenery explodes. A series of jump cuts to the close-up of a screaming monkey, soldiers firing machine guns, and back to the animal underscores the disruptive effect of this intro—a technique that will then organize the entire film. In line with action adventure conventions and the disaster movie formula, *Outbreak* runs upon surprise effects and disillusionment: scenarios and settings are almost never what they seem to be at first glance. Over and over again, the beautiful turns into the dangerous, the pretty into the horrible—as when the cute little monkeys disclose their sharp teeth and screech their shrill screams.

To the displeasure of many critics Petersen mixed two genres: disaster movie and conspiracy film.[12] Thus the outbreak of a devastating epidemic of Motaba fever, caused by an Ebola-like virus that proceeds even faster, is for one shown to be triggered by "negligence, disobedience and intentional irresponsibility"[13] but then escalates due to the secretive strategies of two military physicians, Major General McClintock (Donald Sutherland) and General Ford (Morgan Freeman). The two of them were involved in the disease's first upsurge in the Motaba River Valley in 1967, with which the film begins. Determined to use the virus in biological warfare, they had the infected mercenary camp in Zaire firebombed instead of inoculating the soldiers with the vaccine they developed. When the virus hits again in "present time," they hold back with the antiserum until it is too late, as the virus mutates to become even more dangerous—going airborne.

Of course, eventually an antibody serum is found, thanks to nonconformist virologist Sam Daniels (Dustin Hoffman), who stubbornly follows his own course and conscience to save the country, and who comes up with the idea that the original carrier of the virus, a monkey on the loose in the United States, must also carry the antibodies required. Hundreds of liters of antiserum are miraculously distilled out of a tiny ape body, and the small town where the virus principally hit is restored to health and order, and the villains are exposed. The monkey, of course, will by then be dead.

If Tarzan seemed obsessed with distance and discipline, this film comes across as plain paranoid. The very imagery of contact gains a tinge of the perverse when the Westerners in Africa don astronaut-like outfits guarding them securely from the dreaded contaminating touch. In the course of the film, especially as the disease becomes airborne, this gear is associated with survival: step outside, touch, breathe, contact—and you're dead.

While the protective suit provides a spectacular means of visualizing the virus's versatility and omnipresence,[14] it also underscores the awkward insight that the consequences of contact—infection—are outside of personal control and independent of willpower, yet located and manifest in the body. Hence the intricate body wraps not only prevent contamination by exterior influences but eventually seem to provide a means of keeping the body intact and together: ensuring, in other words, containment.

Both functions, preventing contamination and granting containment, could be said to be the key concerns of contemporary virus narratives. Maintaining and reestablishing boundaries is envisioned as the foremost goal in fighting the virus, as Heather Schell points out: "Recent writing about viruses carefully and repeatedly details the relationship between individual human bodies and the seemingly boundless geography of emerging viruses. Like a cell ready to burst from the crowded virus copies within, Africa appears to be seething with infection that resists confinement."[15] While this certainly applies to the causal logic of *Outbreak*, matters are more complicated when it comes to the projected resolution. After all, containment procedures require not only quarantine here but eventually the much more drastic turn of wiping out an infected idyllic town. When urging White House officials to support this course, General McClintock shows them a video map of the United States on which the devastating spread of the disease is simulated. His final plea, however, seems to envision a much wider scope: "Containment procedures must be viewed globally. Be compassionate, but be compassionate globally." Coming from a person by then firmly established as the film's villain, this plea for global compassion has to be received with a certain skepticism. And indeed, in an earlier conversation with his much more sympathetic, conscience-ridden accomplice General Ford, McClintock's true incentives came to the fore. When arguing against the release of the vaccine, he laced the rhetoric of containment with the spirit of secrecy: "We have to proceed with conventional containment. And you have to maintain an absolute media blackout. Control your subordinates." From the outset, the conspirators are seen to lag behind the developments due to their determination to keep the situation "contained" and secret, incapable of coming up with a viable means of crisis management. The logic of "get in, get out"—General Ford's order to Sam Daniels before sending him off to Africa—does no longer apply, as "Africa" is everywhere, always one step ahead of the efforts to get it back where it belongs.

If the crisis is resolved eventually, it is precisely because Ford's subordinates do run out of control. Sam Daniels and his ardent *adlatus,* Major Salt (Cuba Gooding, Jr.), break through the cold war logic of containment and secrecy, introducing a much more contemporary model of action, which simulates the very patterns of viral transmission they mean to confine: as the virus goes airborne, so do they.

Initiating the final showdown, Sam Daniels and Major Salt hijack an army helicopter, going up while Salt shouts triumphantly—"We're airborne"—echoing Sam's earlier, horrified recognition of the viral mutation: "It's airborne." Apart from this literal turn to the air, however, Sam makes use of a panoply of other instruments for going on the air, forcing his entrance to a TV station to broadcast his search for the host monkey to the nation, and making his plea to the bomber pilots via radio in a climactic confrontation of helicopter versus plane. Emulating the virus's versatility, Sam endorses guerrilla techniques of subversion and appropriation, techniques that in the 1990s are no longer characteristic of the underdog but demarcate successful business strategies instead. As the film defies the logic of containment and secrecy, it touts the spectacular and the visible, along the lines laid out by Guy Debord: "The spectacle manifests itself as an enormous positivity out of reach and beyond dispute. All it says is: 'Everything that appears is good; whatever is good will appear.'"[16] Sam's relentless crusade for disclosure, openness, and truth testifies to this spectacular order, suggesting the immediate comprehensibility of a world laid bare.

Yet this turn to the spectacular also means the ultimate break with the idea of communication as an exchange, the spectacle demarcating, in Debord's words, the "opposite of dialogue."[17] Dustin Hoffman's totalized trick translation in Ishtar comes to mind, where communication became a performance, a show. If Outbreak downplays the performative aspect of communication and its subversive implication of a drainage of meaning, the film ends upon an imagery of spectacular action no less onesided than in Ishtar. The disciplinarian society of the cold-war conspirators in the film can be seen giving way to a more up-to-date system, fashioned along the lines of technocommunication and control, as Sam contacts the bomber pilots via radio, urging them not to destroy Cedar Creek. He talks to them without seeing them, and without verbal response from their side ("they've been trained not to," Major Salt explains)—but finally they will do precisely what he tells them.

As Africans vanish, as apes turn into carriers of disease and African viruses represent the ultimate other, the unidirectional and acultural logic of expertise takes over, a logic that comes so much closer to manipulation than to mediation—beating the virus on its own turf indeed. From this vantage point, the spectacle functions no longer as a technique of exposure, or distraction at that, but becomes all there is. Expert figures gain focal importance in global fictions, not because they lay bare hidden causes and unknown reasons, but because they add to the aura of spectacular action: even if we do not get it, the buzz of scientific probing and last-moment intervention looks good.

But projecting the force of this turn on the expert figure in the film, Sam Daniels, would be to miss the point. The actual trajectory for the logic of spectacular expertise is not personalized in *Outbreak:* when switching from the opening scenes in Africa to the first US location, the US Army Medical Research Institute of Infectuous Diseases in Maryland, the film introduces the true point of origin for the spectacular: the camera eye. In a much praised sequence, Michael Ballhaus's camera tracks along the four different safety levels of the biolab, with a smooth, persistent thrust that never lets off, even as the conditions for access, indicated by changing dress codes, intricate decontamination devices, and identifying mechanisms become more and more complicated. Overcoming all obstacles and gaining easy access to the most dangerous and secret parts of the laboratory, the camera designates a mode of action that Sam Daniels acquires only at the film's very end: flexible, spectacular, and relentlessly probing. This is where the logic of expertise goes viral.

7.2 Infectious Whiteness: Vampirism and the Demise of the Superhero

Outbreak is obsessed with the issue of globalization, with themes of traveling, traffic, and transnational exchange, themes that come to be interlaced with the imagery of the virus in the course of the film. The only way of coping with the problems in the wake of an inevitable and irreversible process of global interaction, it seems, consists in going viral yourself. Being even more flexible, compatible, and volatile than the virus. "Get me on a plane" is the order bellowed out by Sam Daniels for the first half of the film, until he finally proceeds to use less conventional means of (air) transportation.

By implicitly determining the film's status quo, the virus acquires curious connotations, figuring eventually not only as the epitome of abhorrence but providing also, if much less obviously, a perverse kind of template for efficient action. The very correlation of spectacular expertise in terms of control rather than discipline, moreover, evokes new modes of global interaction and superimposition.

As fear and fascination are closely conjoined, the fear of extermination by a virus may inadvertently merge with the desire for emulation and imitation. Seen that way, it is not such a long way from Sam Daniels's reluctant acknowledgment of the virus's definitional power to a more recent virologist character, Barbara Kingsolver's protagonist Adah Price in the novel *The Poisonwood Bible* (1998), whose turn to the virus is clearly tinged with admiration. But then, the American Adah comes of age in Africa, and it is against this background that she is seen to develop the notion of a "partnership," rather than a battle, between viruses and humans: "I must sometimes appear at public functions where I am lauded as a savior of the public health. This startles me. I am nothing of the kind. Certainly I'm no mad exterminator bent on killing devil microbes; on the contrary, I admire them. That is the secret of my success."[18]

Adah's success, however, is just as clearly based upon a clear-cut distinction between virologist and virus, "predator and prey."[19] Just as in *Outbreak*, the expert position—outside and above—is never jeopardized. Neither Sam Daniels nor Adah Price goes as far as some recent white hunters, whom we have seen only too ready to collapse the dividing line between predator and prey and to identify with the object of their quest. Thus, Irvine Welsh's *Marabou Stork Nightmares* mercilessly did away with any notion of superiority or difference on the side of the human hunter. In this novel, the hunted turns out to be the hunter himself, predator and prey becoming one and the same, while the very notion of individualist heroism or distanced expertise is thoroughly dismantled. As the novel's gory ending exemplifies, this is a dangerous road to take. To give up (the illusion of) control and to let oneself go by identifying with the prey may bring about redemption, but just as clearly it brings about death: the demise of the white hunter in the guise of his castration and violent dismemberment.

In his seminal essay "White," Richard Dyer has traced this logic, pointing out that the conceptualization of whiteness in terms of self-control, containment, and constraint always runs the risk of keeling over into its opposite—bringing about disintegration, loss of control. In his reading of George Romero's "living dead" films, most notably *Night of the Living Dead* (1969), Dyer shows how whiteness comes to signify zombielike indifference, rigidity and lifelessness, set against black "vitality."[20] In the course of this polarization, the imagery of control and containment, or "boundedness" as Dyer has it, is inadvertently seen to come apart:

The hysterical boundedness of the white body is grotesquely transgressed as whites/zombies gouge out living white arms, pull out organs, munch at orifices. The spectre of white loss of control is evoked by the way zombies stumble and dribble in their inexorable quest for blood, often with intestines spilling out or severed limbs dangling. . . . "The fear of one's own body, and how one controls it and relates to it" (Brophy) and the fear of not being able to control other bodies, those bodies whose exploitation is so fundamental to capitalist economy, are both at heart of whiteness. Never has this horror been more deliriously evoked than in these films of the *Dead*.[21]

Where white rigidity undergoes disintegration, black flexibility takes over. In Romero's film, whiteness and blackness are shown to be interdependent categories, with blackness gaining the upper hand. These days, however, the color line has become so much more permeable—at least with regard to ascriptions and projections—so that today a confrontation very similar to the one mapped out by Romero in 1969 has to take a glaringly different form.

In *Bite of the Scarab* (1994), the third issue of the American superhero comic *Captain Africa* drawn and written by Dwayne Ferguson,[22] the themes of blackness and whiteness, containment and contamination, flexibility and individuality are tackled once more and spun around considerably. The chaotic plot of this comic, which is no less trashy than the 1960s B movie and doubtlessly inspired by Romero's work, involves corrupt Western megacorporations and ancient African spirits, vampirism and global economics, contaminated pharmaceutical supplies shipped all over Africa, and a superhero almost corrupted by the prospect of absolute power.

The comic is set in a fantastic scenery—part Pan-African utopia, part high-tech futurism. In line with pop culture trends of the 1980s and 1990s, from cyberpunk to the *X-Files,* trends that we already saw at work in the writings of Bruce Sterling, mythical and technological imageries converge, so that modernity and magic turn out to be far from mutually exclusive concepts. In addition, complying with the conventions of the superhero genre,[23] Captain Africa has an everyday identity as a cover for his superhero self, but his daytime appearance is far from mundane here: his real name is Prince Najee M'witu, and he is made out as "[h]eir to the throne of Juba Castle in the Kingdom in M'lele, which is twenty-five miles from Mt. Kilimanjaro, and ten miles from the high-tech metropolis called Egyptica" (*CA* 3). Finally, the issue's central conflict equally enacts a mélange of apparently weirdly disconnected themes. It sets in with Captain Africa captive in a vampire dungeon, complete with the tragic vampire beauty Hannah, who asks him to relieve her from her sinister fate, yet not until he has shown her "the . . . love of a man, his touch" (*CA* 12). This is followed by a dramatic kiss and kill sequence. In between we learn about the "real-world" background for this scenario: Captain Africa is up against a Western megacorporation called LifeScope, an exploitative pharmaceutical enterprise "shipping low-quality vitamins and pharmaceutical supplies across the globe to poor nations" (*CA* 8), headed by a CEO, Johan Southerland, who is involved in all kinds of dirty mafia-like schemes. Of course, pharmaceutical exploitation and vampirish blood-sucking prove to be one and the same eventually, so that a series of cover organizations come to the fore: the respectable organization LifeScope turns out "a cover-up to millions of dollars worth of illegal activities" (*CA* 8), while these illegal activities in turn are nothing but covers for a vampirish cult intent on draining Africa and the rest of the world of blood, willpower, and life.

While no virus narrative in the immediate sense, *Bite of the Scarab* spawns a panoply of viral and parasitical tropes. First and foremost, to enact a vampirish cult in an artificial Africa these days means to face up to the metaphoricity of HIV/AIDS, with its manifold Africanist implications.[24] Moreover, even before the advent of AIDS in the early 1980s, the vampire theme called up fears of contact and contagion, as Paul Barber has shown in his analysis of folk beliefs around it[25] and as Patrick Brantlinger claimed with regard to *the* literary vampire tale, Bram Stoker's *Dracula:* "*Dracula* itself is an individual invasion or demonic possession fantasy with political implications."[26] In *Bite of the Scarab,* this fear of contact undergoes a curious revision. After all, in order to fight the vampirish conspiracy, Captain Africa does not confront it on the grounds of his purity and difference but on the grounds of his sameness. He becomes part of the cult, joining their ancient blood bond to strike from within, as Hannah, his vampire ally, tells him to do: "Drink this . . . Southerland's blood which runs through all his clan. It will heal you and with your warrior skills, it will make you almost his equal." The rhetoric of "equality" is disconcerting here, and will come to dominate the comic both on a narrative and on a visual level. When Captain Africa is first transformed into a vampire, his amplified face with bared fangs seems both in setup and perspective a blown-up repetition of an earlier panel, revealing Southerland's vampire identity (figs. 12 and 13).

On a generic level, this notion of "equality" points to the fact that the vampires' self-healing invulnerability, their agelessness, and their double identities render them inverted versions of the very concept of the superhero. On a more immediately plot-relevant level, finally, Captain Africa's becoming "equal" points to the tendency in contemporary narratives to merge hero and villain, predator and prey, and calls up the insights of *Outbreak* or Kingsolver's *Poisonwood Bible* that to defeat the noxious influence you have to emulate its workings.

But Ferguson's comic goes further than emulation. The story culminates in the showdown between Captain Africa and Southerland, an African prince and a villain whose very name calls to mind South African and US histories of racist subjugation.[27] Little surprisingly, Captain Africa wins the fight, the last panel showing him towering over the prostrate figure of his opponent, peace and order apparently restored. And yet, the formulaic superhero narrative undergoes a significant shift here, as the hero is not as individualist, independent and self-reliant as he might seem at first glance.

The parallels between Captain Africa and Southerland, black superhero and white villain, pervade the entire text, yet culminate in the final panel, which shows Captain Africa wiping his mouth with a bloody

Fig. 12. *Bite of the Scarab* (Captain Africa's transformation).

Fig. 13. *Bite of the Scarab* (Southerland's transformation).

gloved hand (fig. 13). The figure seems to have stepped outside of the panel, whose borders only partially confine it. Rectangular squares, descending from left to right, convey the character's reflection on the events, not so much commenting upon the image but rather framing it, completing it with a narrative of "before" and "after":

I end our relationship by locking my jaws against his jugular vein.

With Southerland's destruction, the blood tie shared by his clan and myself is violently shattered. It feels like my lungs have been ripped out.

The pain is indescribable.

The salty taste of his blood fades into nothingness as Southerland's body turns into dust. The pure power of his ancient blood floods my mind. I never want this power to go away.

But I know it must.

Call me crazy, but I think I enjoyed ripping into his neck. Or maybe I'm just acting out what Hannah would have wanted his death to be like. I pray the real answer is the second choice. (*CA* 21)

While drinking somebody's blood is a curious way of "ending a relationship" in the first place, the strangely meandering reflections testify to a similarly indecisive back-and-forth between vampirism and superhero detachment, between power and righteousness, clan and individual independence. And the fact that the last image sets forth Captain Africa displaying his vampire teeth and wiping his mouth rather than visualizing the restoration of order (which is related in a written afterword without image) does not seem to tip the scales in favor of "the second choice." In fact, the vampire cult in its ancient rootedness seems so much more powerful than the superhero's lonesome quest.

Fig. 14. *Bite of the Scarab* (Captain Africa's victory).

The next issue of *Captain Africa* sets in with the hero back in balance, but the indication of moral and bodily corruption at the end of this issue is hard to miss. Where the early version of the superman on African ground, Tarzan, fenced himself efficiently off from all the contaminating influences around him, Captain Africa has to undergo contamination to stand a chance in a different kind of contest. The very polarization between contact and corruption, contamination and containment, which Dyer found at the heart of *Night of the Living Dead,* seems no longer to make sense here, as whiteness and blackness, the global corporation, and Africanist resistance come to be mapped out along much more convoluted lines: Captain Africa, for one, is deeply involved from the outset, and the spheres the comic depicts are integrated from the beginning—technology, economy, and mythologies forming a complicated network that does not allow for withdrawal or isolation. In line with this logic, the vampire myth itself, this ur-myth of contamination by too close contact, is inverted: now fear of contamination is inflected with the desire to contaminate in turn, to appropriate a foreign system for one's own ends—playing the games of globalization.

The vampire—epitome of a noxious influence—gains an aura of power in *Bite of the Scarab* that seems hard to overcome and hard to subdue at the narrative's close. If that might call to mind the dark romantic appeal of Bram Stoker's Dracula, Ferguson's vampire shows none of his predecessor's tragic individuality; on the contrary, his power seems to consist in his clan membership, or corporate identity. This evil is not ancient but hypermodern—which makes it so hard to contest with conventional means.

The very confrontation between isolated individual and conspirational complex thus also points to the final takeover of tactical flexibility on all grounds, emanating most strongly from the machinations of the global corporation. At least in this enactment, vampirism comes across not so much as white rigidity and stasis but as an all-enveloping force of action and agency, transcending personal weaknesses and individualist schemes. No wonder Captain Africa is severely tempted in the end. Playing around with corporate vampirism is not likely to leave you unaffected—or uninfected at that.

7.3 The Voodoo-Virus: Ishmael Reed's *Mumbo Jumbo*

Captain Africa is an "African" superhero, but it is the powerful and multilayered white corporation LifeScope, or rather its inscrutable, "dark" underground side, that is inscribed with the traditional repertory of Africanity here: no wonder Johan Southerland's face is tinged black for most of the final struggle, while Captain Africa looks white. In turn, blackness and whiteness, Africanity and Westernness, are no longer to be clearly differentiated, as the latter term has already swallowed the symbolic markers of the former, establishing a "dark" realm of whiteness gone global, cleverly interlacing the mythical and the economical, smoothly integrating the utterly foreign—be it African magic or Haitian voodoo or vampirism—into its overarching system. Given this imagery of a vast, ramified, intricate organization of evil, the final confrontation in the guise of the showdown seems inappropriate—the individualist old-school superhero strangely out-of-date. The very themes of contamination and infection call for less personalized accounts of contact and conflict, and less individualized concepts of resistance: Captain Africa, after all, kills the carrier of the disease in the end only to fall under suspicion of becoming a carrier himself.

If Captain Africa seems corrupted at the end of *Bite of the Scarab,* he is superhero enough to pull out for the time being. In a world without superheroes, however, such distantiation and containment seems much harder to maintain. As traditional boundaries collapse and long-standing dichotomies of good and bad get lost, a new world order discloses itself in which it is no longer important to do the right thing but rather to go with the flow in order to survive. This is the conclusion of narratives from the Handspring Company's *Faustus in Africa!* to T. C. Boyle's *Water Music* to Charles Johnson's *Middle Passage,* texts that set out to undermine the concept of heroic individualism and go back to the past in order to reflect upon present constellations. John Edgar Wideman's short story "Fever" (1989) is another case in point, even if this author is doubtlessly much more skeptical about the constructive cultural work of pragmatic action. But then, in Wideman's work the dominant system comes across as so much more powerful and all-comprising than in Johnson's or Boyle's writing.

In "Fever" the insight that *Bite of the Scarab* manages to hold at bay—that in a world gone corrupt, corruption might be the only way to survive—takes center stage. Like Johnson, Wideman locates the beginning of the global age in the history of the slave trade, evoking a neverending history of suffering and pain, based—then as now—on the biases of race and class. Set in Philadelphia during the yellow fever epidemics of the late eighteenth century, at a time when the viral character of the disease was still far from known, "Fever" traces the "black" history of the epidemics, the fact that African slaves were blamed both as being the carriers of the "noxious influence" and as being immune to it, although they died in even greater numbers than the more affluent white population. The story depicts a world in disarray, in which the standard measures of distinction and containment have lost grip: "What should be separated was running together. Threatened to burst. Nothing contained the way it was supposed to be. No clear lines of demarcation. A mongrel city. Traffic where there shouldn't be traffic. An awful void opening around him, preparing itself to hold explosions of bile, vomit, gushing bowels, ooze, sludge, seepage."[28]

If this perverse release of debris and excretions has subversive implications, they seem to exhaust themselves in pure destructivity. As the city's long-standing system collapses and its boundaries cave in, a fever takes over, which seems to have been there all along—an explosive force buried in everyday life that bursts forth the moment things run out of control. Yet at the end things are back in control, the epidemics have subsided, and order has been reestablished. And from this vantage point, the fever's disruptive energy seems purely negative, causing a momentary breakdown without any liberating consequences, as the system at the story's conclusion seems to be identical with the old one before its outset:

The city was recovering. Commerce thriving. Philadelphia must be revictualed, refueled, rebuilt, reconnected to the countryside, to markets foreign and domestic, to products, pleasures and appetites denied during the quarantine months of the fever. A new century would soon be dawning. We must forget the horrors. The Mayor proclaims a new day. Says let's put the past behind us. Of the eleven who died in the fire he said extreme measures were necessary as we cleansed ourselves of disruptive influences. ("F" 161)

The system is strong enough to make us forget the past, Wideman suggests, as he analogizes "extreme measures" against the viral disease with the "extreme measures" taken by the city of Philadelphia against the African-American project MOVE, whose quarters in Philadelphia were bombed in 1985, leaving eleven people dead. The viral disease, this "disruptive influence" of the 1890s, inadvertently erupts again in the guise of a radical black political organization. Yet if the virus turns political here, this is not to ascribe any concrete effectivity to it; it remains futile, as the dominant system with its many links and interrelations, its effectivity and flexibility, seems always to gain the upper hand eventually.

The name of the virus's mosquito carriers—*Aedes aegypti*—brings the story's pessimism to the fore: "New Latin *Aëdes*, from Greek *aedes,* unpleasant: a –, not + edos, pleasant . . ." ("F" 131). Unpleasant, nonpleasant—in Wideman's bitter revision, acts of disruption present themselves as exclusively reactive, momentary inversions of the dominant logic, which might momentarily unmask the ruling injustices only to meet with more effective strategies of silencing and subjugation eventually. Nothing ever changes in this fictional universe, which ultimately projects a vague hope for change and resistance not so much through the trope of viral infection but by the sheer act of narration—laying bare connections that are suppressed and a history that has been blotted out.

And this is precisely where another, earlier narrative steers a different course, as it interlinks viral activity and the act of narration on a much more fundamental level than Wideman, thus enacting the virus as a transformative force in its own right. The virus, this other text argues, brings about a radically different symbolic order, an order that may look suspiciously like chaos to the proponents of the status quo but presents an interesting alternative precisely for that reason.

With the astonishing rapidity of Booker T. Washington's Grapevine Telegraph Jes Grew spreads through America following a strange course. Pine Bluff and Magnolia Arkansas are hit; Natchez, Meridian and Greenwood, Mississippi report cases. Sporadic outbreaks occur in Nashville and Knoxville, Tennessee as well as St. Louis where the bumping and grinding caused the Gov to call up the Guard. A mighty influence, Jes Grew infects all that it touches. (*MJ* 13)

This is one of the several beginnings of Ishmael Reed's novel *Mumbo Jumbo,* published as early as 1972, a narrative that curiously anticipated the symbolic system of later virus narratives, most notably narratives around HIV/AIDS. And the passage already reveals a lot about the specific enactment of imageries around infection and contamination in the entire novel. The steady spread of the disease, delineated by means of its geographical course, calls to mind the dramatic device of the video map in *Outbreak,* which illustrated a national worst-case scenario in order to radically reformulate the concept of global interlinkage, "global compassion." But then, the very mention of the notorious "Grapevine Telegraph," this means of alternative communication during the days of slavery, indicates that the phenomenon of rapid infiltration and secret progression might not be as negative here as in other virus narratives. In addition, the strange musical and sensual subtext called up by the town names and by way of the "bumping and grinding" reference curiously refashions the imagery of contamination. This virus, we are soon to learn, triggers a "dance epidemic" and thus does not bring about pain and destruction, but pleasure and empowerment. Virus and antibody seem to have become exchangeable terms here. In a system as "sick" as US race relations, the novel argues, a viral disruption has to come across as healing rather than destructive: "Actually Jes Grew was an anti-plague. Some plagues caused the body to waste away; Jes Grew enlivened the host" (*MJ* 6).

In line with the subtext of race and race relations, it is not a sudden and unknown disease that erupts in *Mumbo Jumbo* but a viral infection with a long history of outbreaks, spreads, and containments, indicative of a primeval force and transhistorical power at its core:

You see it is not 1 of those germs that break bleed suck gnaw or devour. It's nothing we can bring into focus or categorize, once we call it 1 thing it forms into something else. No man. This is a psychic epidemic, not a lesser germ like typhoid yellow fever or syphilis. We can handle those. This belongs under some ancient Demonic Theory of Disease. (*MJ* 5–6)

Mumbo Jumbo is set in the 1920s, the jazz age in its febrile sensuality and excitement forming an apt context for the dance disease. But the narrative is not confined to this period, moving back and forth between historical and geographical settings, between modernity and myth, rationality and rituals, presenting another exemplary case of the strategy to dismantle (rather than rewrite) historiography, a strategy we saw at work before in so many recent turns to the Middle Passage. Like Haile Gerima, Carrie Mae Weems, or Keith Piper, Reed takes recourse to familiar images and "types" of the past (the Harlem Renaissance, the jazz age, etc.), only to tinge them in markedly fantastic and grotesque colors. Yet this time, the deviation from and disruption of the well-known and familiar is enacted along the lines of viral infection, which seems to affect the novel's very mode of representation, bringing forth a text that time and again "slops out over its own boundaries [and] spills into alternative genres."[29]

Moreover, with *Mumbo Jumbo* once more an epidemic undergoes Africanization, but this time the connotations of Africanity differ radically from the enactments investigated before. Jes Grew is made out as an African disease and its upsurges in the United States attest to the interfusion of African and American history since that early forceful imposition of cultural contact zones by way of slavery: "Jes Grew carriers came to America because of cotton" (*MJ* 16). Not unlike the ongoing repercussions of this history, the virus affects everybody coming into contact with it, regardless of race, sex, or social status, acting like a concrete manifestation of African diasporic culture and figuring forth the "diaspora as pandemic," as Barbara Browning put it.[30]

Its celebration of chaos and disruption notwithstanding, the novel is a conspiracy novel, obsessed with plotting, paranoia, and pervasive patterns of power and resistance throughout history. Two secret organizations try desperately to get a grip on the developments at hand. A secret community of HooDooists[31] is determined to prevent Jes Grew's renewed retreat and to render it pandemic instead, while their opponents, organized in the white supremacist Wallflower Order, are equally intent on effacing the disease once and for all.[32] Not an easy task, as Hinckle Von Vampton, the order's "undercover agent" in Harlem, makes clear when reviewing the situation at hand:

Individuality. It couldn't be herded, rounded up, it was like crystals of winter each different from one another but in a storm going down together. What would happen if they dispersed, showing up when you least expected them; what would happen if you couldn't predict their minds? The Holy War in Haiti was going badly. . . . And what made it so confusing was that the new humfo only resembled the preceding 1 in essential ways so that not detecting a pattern they could not have a plan to attack. Everyone . . . had become an expert on Haiti. (MJ 140)

While the very polarization of individuality versus control, dispersal versus containment, calls to mind the binaries at work in *Outbreak* and in *Bite of the Scarab*, the constellations are far less clear-cut here. As traditional categories of individuality such as autonomy, free will, self-consciousness, or intentionality move into the background, apersonal concepts of dispersal, chaos, confusion, and decentralized action gain central importance for defining the subversive power of the individual. Just as in *Outbreak*, this logic equates individuality with going viral—behaving capriciously, versatile and unpredictable—and turns the viral into the ultimate form of expertise. But in contrast to *Outbreak*, the fact that everyone becomes an expert also means that the extraordinary quality of this status is abandoned. The above passage continues:

The men dressed in white linnen suits; the women wearing the most outlandish geegaws and long colorful skirts. The colors blended Hinckle. He preferred grey and black colors. They would have to outlaw color this time around. Better make a note of this. (MJ 140)

These experts enact their expertise in a purely performative mode here, setting flashy styles and erratic patterns against Hinckle's ideal of order and predictability. In the course of such transformations, any attempt at control on a personal, conscious, or strategic level must needs fail.

But then, regardless of its many background sketches, digressions, and subplots, *Mumbo Jumbo* in general shows a remarkable lack of depth. Its depiction of resistance stays on the level of ritualistic gestures or styles, spectacular actions, and flamboyant confrontations. Reed enacts a complex scenario of withdrawal, in which flexibility turns from an individualist strategy into minority tactics, along the lines laid out by Michel de Certeau: spontaneous, often unconscious moves, tricks and decoys, maneuvers "within enemy territory"[33,] or—viral behavior. Such tactics are highly effective because they leave the traditional grounds of action and agency behind, discarding the notion of self-authentication and self-possession, and embracing instead the notion of possession as an alien force. In *Mumbo Jumbo* the most personal merges with the utterly foreign, in a manner reminiscent of John Edgar Wideman's imagery of manipulative spirituality in *The Cattle Killing*. But in striking contrast to Wideman, Reed maps out such a takeover of the innermost as a far from altogether negative process.

Mumbo Jumbo is obsessed with tropes of impersonation and masquerade, travesty and transformation: While Jes Grew carriers lose control over their body movements and speak in tongues, we see HooDoo spirits, loa, take possession of their followers' bodies in takeovers that are sometimes alienating and dangerous, yet not necessarily destructive. After all, the foreign impulse, be it African virus or Haitian god, raises distinctly positive associations in this novel.

For that matter, Reed presents neither viral infection nor spiritual possession exclusively in terms of losing control. As Sämi Ludwig pointed out, "possession goes both ways" in *Mumbo Jumbo,* the humans can "own" and "ride" the loas just as they are "owned," "ridden," possessed by them—if such a clear-cut differentiation of two poles still makes sense here.[34] Possession and empowerment are intricately linked, both Jes Grew and HooDoo holding the precarious poise between deindividuation and pragmatic self-fashioning, cast in a markedly fantastic vein.

This two-sided imagery then reverberates with the novel's second trope of impersonation: masquerade. After all, while the HooDooists speak in tongues and move in the thrall of the virus, the followers of the Wallflower Order seem hardly more self-possessed. Their representative's very name—Von Vampton—once more calls to mind the semantics of vampirism, this other symbolic system around possession and the loss of self-control. If this system was racialized in *Bite of the Scarab,* Reed goes much further, evoking an intricate interrelation between white vampirism and mainstream practices of co-opting black culture in the 1920s, an interrelation that comes to the fore in the other connotation of Von Vampton's name—Van Vechten. The incentives of vampirish bloodsucking and cultural co-optation merge indissolubly in Von Vampton's project of setting up a "Talking Android," "a new kind of robot" (*MJ* 80) to destroy the HooDooist movement by way of infiltration and appropriation—"White talking out of Black" (*MJ* 80).

The scheme is bound to fail. As much as the systems of whiteness try to pass themselves off as setting the tone, being in control, they invariably turn out to be enmeshed and entangled in a larger logic whose complexity they do not even begin to grasp. The HooDoo priest PaPa LaBas easily exposes the Talking Android as the fraud he is: "grazing a quick finger over his face, leaving a white streak, he then displays the black paint on his finger to the audience" (*MJ* 160). This should not be read as a plea for depth and sincerity against the logic of make-believe and masquerade, however. HooDoo's complex system of impersonation and possession shows that the Wallflower people fail not because they go too far but because they go not far enough. In order to gain "the Know" (*MJ* 194) you have to embrace a new mode of knowledge and cognition, another, "stylistic" type of expertise, abandon the effort of staying in control of your performances.

While in narratives from *Congo* to *Islands in the Net* and *Outbreak* technocommunication and expertise were envisioned as strategies for maintaining control against all odds, *Mumbo Jumbo* sets out to manipulate the very notion of communication and expertise, figuring forth transformations instead of exchanges, and substituting for the logic of analytic evaluation (the outside stance) the logic of impersonation (the inside perspective). By consequence, the very idea of stable selfhood, or self-conscious action, loses ground. But then, in a social system based upon appearances—black/white distinctions—that have inscribed themselves indelibly into the public consciousness, practices of ritualistic impersonation and performances of communication and expertise might present the only conceivable way out. By dint of this turn, the alien and alienating viral impact and possession by foreign powers present themselves as viable if paradoxical means of genuine self-expression: "He started to speak in tongues. There are no isolated cases in this thing. It knows no class no race no consciousness" (*MJ* 5).

7.4 Elvis Zombies and Hip-Hop Hoodoo: Darius James's *Negrophobia*

The age of superheroes is over. The virologist's spectacular expertise in films like *Outbreak* is but a weak replication of the impersonal pattern of action prefigured by the virus, while the superhero Captain Africa defeats his vampirish opponent only on the grounds of adopting his "corporate" techniques of infiltration and takeover. The same turn takes center stage in Ishmael Reed's *Mumbo Jumbo,* where the very notion of expertise is redefined to signify the demise of conscious action and the conceptual relocation of resistance onto the level of style, camouflage, and tactics— viral behavior patterns.

This imagery relies not only on the symbolic system of voodoo and spirit possession, however, but also on the trope of trickery, which turned out so central to narratives of cultural contact before. The virus could be said to be the ultimate trickster figure. But then, this is not a highly original insight on my part—in fact, the parallels between viruses, parasites, and tricksters seem to be so self-evident that even a study on trickster figures that never questions the individualist character and individualizing function of trickery, Lewis Hyde's *Trickster Makes This World,* analogizes the trickster and the parasite at one point. This is when the individualist notion of trickery as willful and willed action briefly gives way to another pattern of thought in this book:

Seizing and blocking opportunity, confusing polarity, disguising tracks—these are some of the marks of trickster's intelligence. The last of them leads to the final item on this initial list: if trickster can disguise his tracks, surely he can disguise himself. He can encrypt his own image, distort it, cover it up. . . . Because the mythology suggests it, I have been deriving each of trickster's tricks from predator-prey relationships; to illustrate skin-changing, let's take a case in which the prey is humankind and the predator is a microbe, *Trypanosoma brucei,* the protozoan that causes African sleeping sickness. This worm-like creature kills thousands of people each year in Africa. It enters the bloodstream through the bite of the tsetse fly and then begins to multiply. Once the invader is detected, the victim's immune system fights back with the single weapon at its command: it produces antibodies specific to the shape of the intruder's skin, or outer protein coat. But this trypanosome can change its skin in as many as a thousand shapes, and the immune system never catches up. Each time it produces an antibody specific to any one skin, *brucei* drops that skin and produces another from its enormous wardrobe. *Brucei* is like a con man at a masquerade; it is not attached to any particular mask or face or persona, but fluidly alters each as the situation demands.[35]

In this passage, all of the characteristics of virus imagery we came across up to now crop up: Africanity, the predator-prey imagery, the notion of style, politics, and masquerade, and the idea of flexibility and shape-shifting. And while Hyde ultimately returns to his concept of the trickster as a "male" individualist figure, for me the aspect of deindividualization that comes up here seems to be of interest in its own right, as it figures forth processes no longer controlled by force of willpower and thus at a remove from the schedule of good and bad intentions that so often rules the enactment of trickery and, on another level, cultural contact in general. By contrast to the animal heroes of, say, the classical African-American trickster tale, predator figures in the shape of viruses and parasites hardly lend themselves to identification—a "worm-like creature [that] kills thousands of people each year in Africa" is just difficult to sympathize with. It is precisely on these grounds, however, that such a shift of perspective gives scope to new concepts of cultural agency. While such concepts are on the way in Reed's highly ambivalent enactment of spirit possession, another text, clearly very much influenced by *Mumbo Jumbo,* focuses on them, if focusing is an appropriate term for this narrative's frantic manipulation of perceptions and perspectives.

Negrophobia (1992), Darius James's weird concoction of a novel (posing as a film script) promotes the same agenda of flexibility and masquerade as Reed in a style clearly signifying upon *Mumbo Jumbo,* yet complicates matters further. The text seems to lack a cause or fixed project, precisely because it lacks a hero—it is, in fact, quite impossible to sympathize with any of the exaggeratedly flat characters, let alone identify with their plights or manic worldviews. The novel is about a disease, negrophobia, which seems to have infested the very narrative perspective—no way of gaining a clear picture, an unmarred view.

Drawing upon the huge reservoir of racist fears and prejudices in the United States, James enacts an explosive mixture of bawdy details and obscene scenarios, a mélange of pop culture quotes and voodoo allusions, in the course of which black culture is seen to merge with its phobically distorted representations, and voodoo, this epitome of black subversion and power, comes paradoxically to collapse with its opposite, negrophobia, this epitome of white strategies of demonization. The novel sets out with a juxtaposition, in Hanjo Berressem's words, of "images of material abjection (connected to images of negritude) and images of phantasmatic identification and objectification (connected to images of whiteness)."[36] But eventually these different images fall into one. Possession and infection become almost synomymous terms.

Casting negrophobia as a disease, strategically planted to disrupt the Western world so much more efficiently than the Ebola virus ever could, James, like Wideman or Reed, projects the entire scenario of US race relations upon the screen of virus discourse—unconscious infiltration, flexible action, guerrilla maneuvers. And of course, in line with all kinds of virus narratives, the noxious influence is crafted as African—voodoo figuring forth *"magick's African face in the West"* and Africa constituting *"the repository of all that is vile and taboo in the dark subconscious,"*[37] as we learn on the very first page. Magic, masquerades, and manipulations abound in the entire text—the scenario of trickery all over again, if under changed insignia.

The novel relates the hallucinatory travels of a white teenage girl, Bubbles, through the nightmarish world of negrophobia. Bubbles came to be infected with the disease, or possessed with the spirit of negrophobia, because her black maid put a spell on her, punishing her for tackling her mojoes, her sacred books. If this seems to indicate a purist conception of magic and spirituality—voodoo for the initiate only—the description of one of the maid's possessions strikes a different chord:

A hard wave of convulsions thunders through the Maid as she falls to the floor. Her teeth gnash. Her limbs thrash. The boom blaster's computerized Petrorhythms pound concurrently with her disjointed movements.

Her head, arms, hands, legs, and feet move with an independence of their own. They begin to talk, change shape, and emit sounds: Music. Radio white noise. Reptile skin. A bird's head. A cat with a coat of flames. TV commercials. Radio white noise. The BERNHARD GOETZ confession mixed to hip-hop rap rhythms. Pentecostal tent-house shouts. Police sirens. MALCOLM X speeches. Harlem bar talk. The bark of heroin pitchmen. The assassination of JOHN F.

KENNEDY cross-edited with the *Amos and Andy* radio show. And the recurrent image of a YOUNG BLACK BOY repeating the phrase, "*Yo, man! You got five dollars? Yo, man! You got five dollars?*" answered with gunfire. (N 52)

James's version of voodoo is definitely no less syncretic than Reed's, whose modernized "radio loa" he seems to revive, and calls to mind the high-tech vampirism in *Captain Africa,* a narrative equally unconcerned with the borderlines between the new and the ancient. Yet where Reed and Ferguson focus on the correlation of seemingly incongruent stances— the mythical and the modern, magic and technology—James highlights the symbolic framework that enables such convergences in the first place: pop culture. Infused with the logic of the mix, the logic of inversions and repetitions, interpolations and refashionings, pop culture sets forth the ground on which the most contradictory and converse stances can meet and merge. Often enough, though, this means smoothening the edges, making invisibile the seams and transitions between disparate matters. Darius James's novel rips the tight textures of pop culture apart again, exposing the incongruity between TV, musical, and streetwise representations of race, giving the lie to the neat media and mainstream images of integration and showing their dark subtext and gruesome flip side.

This is not to say, however, that James gives up on pop culture as a subversive instrument, a means of resistance, altogether. Pop is depicted as deeply ambivalent, open to manipulations and maneuvers of all sorts. Thus it does provide a recalcitrant code based upon voodoo practices:

. . . present-day urban America has spawned a new generation of loa out of concrete and steel, out of radio and TV, out of comics and film. The new loa are invoked by beat-box rhythm, Burroughsian cutup, industrial music, and the extreme edges of performance art. (N 2)

But then, there is a reactionary force to pop culture just as well. The maid, for one, underestimates its propensity to cut both ways, just as she misjudges the powers of whiteness to vampirishly appropriate cultural material at hand—the "pure power of blood" invoked in *Bite of the Scarab,* if you will. Having "messed" with the white girl's menstrual blood, the maid smokes a reefer and puts on a record, Marlene Dietrich singing "Hot Voodoo": "Dis dat blond Venus Nazi ho bitch singing that phony hoodoo song she sang in a gorilla suit 'mongst all them big-lipped jungle Niggas" (N 54). This turns out to be a fatal combination of influences:

On the floor below, the maid had gone mad—her blubbersome black bulk flopping and flailing about the floor, bellowing for a pink-skinned god who would never come. . . . If only she had taken the precaution of wearing a pair of rubber gloves. Or had simply wiped the unguent from her hands. She hadn't. Instead she chose to underestimate the power of the Blond Venus. (N 55)

Here bodily fluids, as the epitome of dangerous contact matter, and pop culture, as the epitome of appropriation and inversion, are made out as one and the same. Just like Wideman before him, James insists on the immediate and gruesomely physical impact of processes of contact and exchange (race relations in Wideman, pop cultural appropriation in James), montaging increasingly grotesque "images of bodyfragmentation invariably related to sex, violence, dread and abjection," as Berressem showed.[38] Pop culture's volatility comes across as viral, impossible to pin down and control once and for all, because always enmeshed in a complex scheme of quotation and takeover, a scheme that repeats and slyly discloses the logics of race relations: "love and theft" as Eric Lott called this pattern. This resonates with the depiction of vampirism and zombification as voodoo's other face. Just like *Bite of the Scarab*, *Negrophobia* casts whiteness as a powerful movement that has gained a dangerous momentum of its own, precisely because it managed to incorporate techniques and tactics first conceived in black culture. A later product of Bubbles's hallucinations, The Elvis Zombie, pins this logic down:

With a complicated series of karate kicks and jabs, the Elvis Zombie moves like he's just returned to the Vegas stage. Unfortunately, as a result of advanced decomposition, his body parts fly straight into the lens of the camera. (*N* 112)

If this performance of white pop culture definitely testifies to Dyer's equation of whiteness and death, the gory evidence of zombification reaches out well beyond the realm of whiteness. Just like Ferguson's comic book, *Negrophobia* enacts whiteness and blackness, and the cultural spheres associated with these categories, as deeply enmeshed with each other: after all, the novel equally presents an abundance of black zombies and undead, coming complete with a gruesome black "Zombie Master" (*N* 104), so that in a further turn of the screw black culture seems now to have emulated white culture, appropriating its own distorted images for quite converse purposes.

This process of reappropriation, or rather, reorientation within a profoundly transformed territory, entails a shift of perspective. Eventually, *Negrophobia* stages a new kind of colonial contact narrative, retelling the old story of the cultural encounter from a "cosmic" vantage point, "universalizing" the logic of contact, while giving the lie to the very idea of an all-embracing code or universal understanding. *Negrophobia*, too, goes Afrofuturist. Bubbles comes across an extraterrestrial power, the Talking Dreads, who turns out to have for a long time tried to make "contact with your world," in order to establish "intelligent communication" (*N* 124). But soon the Talking Dreads, this icon of black power, comes to recognize that "[i]ntelligent communication is not a quality your world is known for in this or any other galaxy" (*N* 131). As communication fails, he decides to resort to other means, concentrating on the very manifestation of difference now—skin color. Going utterly superficial, he decides to attack whiteness, turn white skin into black skin. Communication gives way to manipulation, and the quest for exchange turns into a cosmic game of trickery.

In another absurd twist of the plotline, a midwestern small town, called significantly enough "Garvey's Corner," is staged as a guerrilla camp of whiteface minstrels steered behind the scenes by the Talking Dreads, preparing for the takeover of the entire country. The epitome of Americanness, the small town or suburb, which we saw to figure as a blueprint setting for the enactment of homogeneous harmony in Disney's version of the *Tarzan* story, turns into a host of dangerous forces here:

Located at the heart of America's most dangerous slum, Garvey's Corner is a mock town where blacks are trained to *look, act,* and *think* like ordinary law-abiding white citizens in order to undermine all the rights and freedoms America has to offer the white race without the slightest detection!

These agents of subversion are so expert in the chameleon's art of camouflage they can even mimic the actual smell of whites by bathing in tubs of *rancid milk*! (*N* 139)

Here as in *Outbreak* the infection of the small town figures forth the decline of the national order under the impact of moral corruption and viral intrusion. Yet echoing *Mumbo Jumbo,* James mixes masquerade, mimicry, and expertise in order to collapse the very distinction between experts and viruses, agents of supervision and "agents of subversion": his "expert[s] in the chameleon's art of camouflage" are clearly no longer above things. Almost the same, but not quite, they resemble Hyde's infamous trickster parasite, which "can change its skin in as many as a thousand shapes," as we learned before. And in a further analogy to Hyde's parasite, James's con men in whiteface pursue a purely destructive project—spreading disruption and disaster, as the novel relates in a (mock-)horrified tone.

Once again James enacts his imagery of infection and intrusion via the discourses of pop culture, calling upon and inverting the traditions of minstrelsy and blackface to stage a new kind of "Talking Android"—black talking out of white—and thus to finally blow up the explosive mixture of racist phobias:

It could happen. Anywhere. At any time. . . . The fallout from the exploding Negro's darkening melanin agents could infect millions of innocent Caucasian men, women, and children close to the point of ground zero, reducing this country to a nation of lumbering Al Jolsons in mammy-whining blackface. (*N* 145)

Race pride and racial phobias, secret rites of blackness and sinister cults of whiteness come across as different aspects of the same phenomenon in this novel, suggesting surface variations at best. And yet these chimeras clearly testify to profound and deeply consequential apprehensions, fears, convictions, and conflicts ingrained in American culture. As the conceptual complex of race and Africanity itself is made out to be superficial, extraneous, spectacular, so are all of its countermeasures. While James, just like Reed, inverts the concepts of disease and health, siding with the virus rather than the virologist, if you will, he stops short right there: the sick and the infectious do retain their negative connotations in his novel, as James refuses to replace negative stereotypes with positive counterimages. In this negativitiy, *Negrophobia* resembles Wideman's "Fever," but with the notable difference that there is no trace of Wideman's tragic in James's novel. Moreover, while the Talking Dreads's intervention might very well call to mind the spirit intervention of the Xhosa girl's mind Wideman staged in *The Cattle Killing*, as both texts suggest a pervasive loss of individual control and a totalization of trickery, which is seen to infect the innermost realms of the psyche now, the differences between the two enactments could not be more blatant: James gleefully changes sides, evoking in Afrofuturist fashion a new—cosmic—level of action and trickery, and thus reveling in a (fantastic) scenario of disjunction rather than mourning the loss of agency, as Wideman does.

Perhaps *Negrophobia* makes most sense when placed into an altogether different context. Instead of reading it alongside Wideman's tragic writing, it should be placed against the backdrop of pop musical developments of its time. Gangsta rap did, after all, equally experience its heyday in the early 1990s and equally thrived on imageries of violence and hatred, disdaining the explicit statements of 1980s polit rappers and cherishing the spectacular effects of pure negativity. While this is admittedly not a constructive stance to take, it proved a highly effective way of visualizing the problems at hand, a point of departure for a pervasive reorientation in black popular culture.

7.5 The Massive Global Telecommunication: Hip-Hop Virology

Long before the days of HIV the experiences of sensuous or erotic pleasure were often cast as dangerous states of vulnerability and alienation, strongly connoted with the loss of self-control and ultimately the corruption or fundamental transformation of selfhood.[39] While complicated by a more recent history of "sexual liberation" and sensual self-exploration, this associative pattern is far from extinct today, as manifested by the conceptual interlinkage of sexuality, infection, and music, an interlinkage especially pertinent for black music, as Barbara Browning has shown:

[W]hile a drumbeat is not *simply* the "black heart beating back to Africa on a steady pulse of dub," [Dick Hebdige] the resonance of this image still matters.

Hip-hop is one moment in the dispersion and popularization of black musical idioms, a process of cultural exchange which was concomitant with the first processes of global economic exploitation—that is colonization. Reggae presents another such moment. Funk. Soul. Mambo. All "infectious" rhythms—all spread quickly, transnationally, accompanied by equally "contagious" dances, often characterized as dangerously, usually as overly sexually explicit, by white critics.[40]

Revised and fractured, such associations take center stage in virus narratives from *Mumbo Jumbo* to *Negrophobia,* motivating the inversion of established narrative patterns of identification and distantiation. From Reed's dance epidemic to James's "Hip-Hop hoodoo" (*N* 121) the notion of subversive viral impact resonates with the idea of black music as an alternative powerful mode of communication—a "Grapevine telegraph" if you will.

Yet both narratives also acknowledge in numerous instances of ironic detachment and disclaiming that such a correlation of (black) music and the unconscious, the sensual, the other, is a by no means unproblematical turn. Of course, the popular conjunction of the (black) body and rhythm, as the operative principle of black music, always hovers on the verge of "benign racism" and by no means accounts for the complex processes at work in either the production or the reception of music, as Simon Frith has pointed out. He contested the widespread notion of pop as a prediscursive, purely instinctive, sensual experience and argued for its conceptualization as a specific cultural code that involves, among other things, sensuality and feeling:

> . . . the pleasures of rock music continue to be explained by intellectuals in terms of *jouissance,* the escape from structure, reason, form, and so forth. As should by now be obvious, what's involved in such assertions is not a musical (or empirical) judgment at all, but an ideological gesture, a deviant expression of respectable taste. So-called "hot" rhythms, that is to say, don't actually mean bodily abandon but signify it, signify it in a particular ideological context.[41]

While concerned with rock and pop, Frith's intervention seems equally appropriate in view of the debates around hip-hop. The stylistics of pure sensuality and authentic abandonment attached to hip-hop were, after all, not the inventions of "white critics" alone but actively endorsed by numerous hip-hop artists just as well, who enthusiastically promoted the imagery of "truthful," "real," "immediate" expression and thus contributed to the implementation of a powerful symbolic system of "inauthentic authenticity."[42] While the evidence of signification was backgrounded, however, hip-hop foregrounded an alternative pattern of articulation that calls to mind the practices of "signifyin'," this black cultural code of representation based upon parody, quotation, and inversion, or in hip-hop's lingo: toasting, sampling, versioning.[43] And not accidentally, the representational practices in hip-hop, just as elsewhere, were associated with a diasporic recuperation, an excavation and reinterpretation of the themes and (musical) structures of Africanity, as hip-hop acts from A Tribe Called Quest to Jungle Brothers exemplified time and again.

As hip-hop moved away from the radical, explicit, and outspoken political presentations of the 1980s, these representational strategies of indirection gained more and more significance. The very evidence of hip-hop's mainstream co-optation led to new experimental formations and acts conjoining hip-hop techniques with other musical styles, less obsessed with authenticity and street-cred—calling to mind Darius James's techniques of alienation and provocation. This is where the late-1990s act Spearhead comes in, who employ the imagery of infection and indirection, flexibility and ambivalence, the global and the local, once more to give scope to a complex project of expression and resistance, if with much more constructive effects than in Darius James's narrative.

Spearhead, headed by Michael Franti, a central figure in the 1980s and '90s independent pop scene, presents a striking example for a new aesthetics "post-hip-hop," an aesthetics that registers the current state of the art in many respects.[44] They are clearly entrenched with hip-hop postures and themes, yet doubtlessly also at an ironic distance, in playful detachment. This comes to the fore on all kinds of levels: in their style mixes (rap, reggae), in a complex system of allusions to both British and American pop history, and in the interpolation of black musical traditions from blues to the most recent hard-core rap, let alone the peculiar montage of classical hip-hop techniques from scratching to sampling in terms of smooth integration rather than irritation or rupture.

In "Comin' to Gitcha," one of the songs on Spearhead's album *chocolate supa highway*,[45] irony and radical political critique, fantasy and commitment are conjoined in a way typical for the entire album. On first hearing, "Comin' to Gitcha" seems to be a weird love song, enacted with all kinds of allusions to and quotations of black cultural history. It sets in with a spoken intro drawing on the gospel theme of the enslaved Israelites, then moves into the chorus "I'm coming to gitcha," a multilayered sequence dominated by Michael Franti's low, obsessive, stuttering voice, before it turns to the strange love theme, which interlinks love and disease, virus and sex: "you're like Ebola in my system / I'm sick with you but you're the serum." This sequence, which strangely reiterates the conventional collation of blackness, sexuality, infection, and music, is later taken up by background vocalist Trinna Simmons, who tears the already fragmented text completely apart with her sexualized moaning and mumbling. Finally, the song undergoes another curious shift—the sex and virus theme takes a political turn:

> Baby making music for the massive
> global telecommunication
> aboriginal Black Militia Broadcastin' system
> the chocolate melter, the helter skelter
> the skull rattler, the bush doctor
> the part the Red Sea boom shocka
> Una Bomber supa jamma
> Jungle business melt in the mic in your hand
> jah! master mind the master plan

Michael Franti's voice does not change in the course of this semantic transformation; his staggering, driven, obsessive performance saturates the song, so that the vocals, the regular beats, and the languorous drift of the entire song deflect from the semantic level, instilling a vague impression of infiltration and takeover, which could be sexual, viral, ritual, political, or terrorist (signifying on lovesickness, Ebola, voodoo, black power, and the Unabomber). A break beat on "jah!" and before "master mind the master plan" finally demarcates the common ground for all of these themes, suggesting both a divine master plan and a global underground organization, a "telecommunication" network or the "Black Militia Broadcastin' system." While the trajectory of this system—alternative or destructive—remains unclear and its stylistics undergo complex shifts, the impetus of secrecy, confusion, and—at least at the second hearing—of a vague threat pervades the entire album's semantic and musical structure.

"Comin' to Gitcha" suffuses the harmless pop themes of love and desire with the rhetoric of the virus, the love song mutating and traveling all the way through the African diaspora back to a mystical African jungle, modern technologies merging with "primitive" practices and magic. In the course of this fusion of incongruent systems of signification, the metaphor of the "noxious influence in the system" gains more and more scope—it could be anything from Ebola to a computer virus or voodoo charm disrupting established means of communication and representation. Just as in Reed, the relentless spread of this influence signifies the disruption of established power structures and the insurrection of a new underground system of global interaction. And just as for Reed, who eventually seemed to associate the text *Mumbo Jumbo* itself with the virus Jes Grew, for Spearhead the song itself seems to figure as the viral carrier, the means of transportation.

Even if the old polit rap idea of hip-hop as an alternative CNN clearly shines up in Spearhead's Black Militia Studio, the disjunctive themes and incongruent levels of signification do not allow for a linear reading. Instead of a message, the song communicates a powerful emotional stance, and instead of suggesting alternative institutions or a concrete political project, the song stops short at the vague idea of a powerful underground network or a secret alternative order—an idea conveyed both explicitly on the semantic level and in a striking move by the very convolutions of musical and semantic elements, which turn a love song into a tale of subversion and threat.

Yet by contrast to James—and by stark contrast to gangsta rap—the declaration of defiance and denial is not acted out openly, spectacularly, and provocatively, but takes the form of an oscillation between explicit yet fragmentary semantic references and an almost countereffective score of smooth rhythms. This is a pattern into which most songs on the album fall, easy listening and mellow sounds interfusing with dark themes and piercing critique. In that respect, Spearhead's project resembles another major act of the nineties, the Fugees, who similarly de-emphasize toughness and radicality without giving up on agitation. Is this an indication of withdrawal? Or, as Andrew Ross argued in view of the seemingly entirely apolitical styles of New Harmony and swingbeat, an indication of just another shift in black music to resist appropriation and claim an independent ground?[46]

Either way, Spearhead's smooth and easy aesthetics of confusion are not that far away from the much more openly alienating aesthetics of electronic music, which often enough equally evokes a narrative only to deflect from it again, mixing up the effects of mystification and estrangement to bring about disorientation *and* pleasure—or the pleasure of disorientation, as we saw with respect to Drexciya's *Quest*. And in their complicated dependence on the imagery of "space madness,"[47] both trends call to mind another contemporary "school" in black pop music:

While explicitly political hip-hop bands like Public Enemy fall into eloquent silence, other acts safeguard their "clandestine" communication within the community by way of public displays of "craziness." A Tribe Called Quest member Q-Tip calls himself "ill figure" on the Beastie Boys album *Ill Communication,* and the Wu-Tang Clan affiliate Ol' Dirty Bastard just like Ex-Leader of the New School rapper Busta Rhymes perpetuate with their stammering sounds a kind of new "Black Dada Nihilismus" (Amiri Baraka).[48]

Deflection, secrecy, and confusion seem to be the most promising options of the day, momentary self-stylizations and diversionary strategies that ultimately testify not to a pervasive "cultural nihilism," as deplored by Cornel West,[49] but to a "Dada Nihilismus" indeed, which allows the conceiving of both cultural identity and cultural contact in terms of construction, provisionality, and change.

"If the parasite is a man," writes Michel Serres, "he is an actor. He goes on stage, sets up the scenery, invents theater, and imposes theater. He is all the faces on the screen."[50] If he is a man, that is. If the parasite is neither man nor woman, it still makes use of play-acting and masquerade, as we have seen, but the notion of an "imposition," a willed and conscious agency, necessarily recedes. The parasite, this epitome of infiltration, and the virus, this epitome of shape-shifting, come across not so much as agents and actors than as manipulative forces—confusing, multifaceted, looped. They are "all the faces on the screen," because they have no face of their own, no individuality or personhood—there is nothing behind their masks. By dint of the conceptual shift from classical trickster figures—be they human or animal—to these impersonal unfeeling entities, trickery reconfigures itself as an automatically unfolding process, a pervasive structure instead of an isolated, willed or willful, strategy.

Shape-shifting and highly flexible, the virus embodies the key qualities of the global age, yet under markedly negative insignia. It discloses the flip side of global contact scenarios, giving vent to the fearful insight that the bright new world of compatibility, cosmopolitanism, and communication is only to be realized at the cost of systemic instability and vulnerability. *Outbreak* illustrates succinctly the phobic dimension of this "global" reading of the virus figure, a dimension that seems to pertain to virus narratives in general, even if they set forth resistance and endorse disruption. Time and again, we saw alternative virus narratives reiterating the phobias and fears at large, inverting and blowing up the dominant imageries of contact and contagion rather than trying to avoid them altogether.

The reluctance to envision a radically different or utopian outlook and the tendency to set forth repetitions with a difference instead also manifest themselves in the historical loops and geographical conjunctions performed by these narratives, the mix-ups of past and present, colonialism and globalization, Africa and America that give scope to an even more pervasive crisis of differentiation and distinction than the one evoked by Etienne Balibar with his notion of "vacillating borders." Obviously, such conceptual developments foster paranoia. From Ferguson's vampirish corporation to Reed's global underground organizations and James's cosmic superpower up to Spearhead's master plan, systems of power and flight lines of resistance are mapped out in terms of hidden patterns and invisible interlinkages, echoing insofar the conspiracy logic of a film like *Outbreak*. But then, in contrast to *Outbreak* and in pointed analogy to contemporary revisions of the Middle Passage, none of the alternative virus narratives enacts its paranoid pattern of power in terms of the rhetoric of the "could have been" or "about to happen." While adhering to the material of the real—history, politics, culture—all of them montage this material into markedly irreal accounts, coming up with patterns of explanation that are tentative, optional, bracketed, often contradictory or absurd.

As genres, conventions, and traditions converge and collapse, and as thematic and structural borderlines vacillate, momentarily, the tricks of ideology come into view, which otherwise every so often take the guise of dazzling disappearance acts. This is not to say, however, that these texts would present case studies in postmodern metatextuality, parody, or self-reflexivity,[51] as all of them invariably mitigate the effect of critical distantiation at one point or level: think of Spearhead's montage of confusing lyrics and harmonic song lines, or of James's mixture of sardonic critique and Afrofuturist fantasies. The Handspring Company's enactment of *Faustus in Africa!* comes to mind, where the puppet players are always in full view and still tend to drop out of sight, alienation and illusion, distantiation and mystification working hand in hand. Such enactments, be they theatrical, literary, filmic, or musical, are always unsettling in their confusing mixture of effects and techniques. None of them provide satisfactory explanations or viable solutions. But in times when understanding and harmony are increasingly cast as the prerequisites of cultural communication rather than its possible outcome, the disturbing insistence on—and enactment of—uneven, chaotic, and malfunctioning contact scenarios is so much more constructive than it seems: setting the mode for cultural encounters and political negotiations that take difference and disagreement into account.

Roots and Role-Play: A Conclusion

This study set out with reflections on the "Old World" of European power politics, investigating the representation of colonial contact scenarios in the nineteenth century and in the present time. It ended upon a reading of some provocative enactments of race relations in the United States, this self-acclaimed center of a "New World" order. The field that thus came into view turned out amazingly homogeneous, at least with respect to its symbolic repertory—the tropes and stock figures of Africanity. In present-day actualizations, we have seen this repertory being psychologized (as in Hudson's *Greystoke*, in Eastwood's *White Hunter, Black Heart*, or in Roeg's *Heart of Darkness*), ironized (as in countless filmic action adventures of the 1980s), being blown up into melodrama (as in Pollack's *Out of Africa*, in Bertolucci's *The Sheltering Sky*, or Spielberg's *Amistad*), or boiled down to the rhetoric of looking closely (as in Marciano's *Rules of the Wild* or in Sterling's *Islands in the Net*). We have, in fact, seen artists, authors, and filmmakers employ a variety of such techniques in one and the same enactment. And while a certain skepticism is evident in most rewritings and reiterations of the established material, it is also quite evident that the imagery of Africanity is tougher and more resistant than one might think, liable to withstand explicit critique and ironic detachment likewise, and to reappear just slightly transformed, on a different level of representation, after it has been dismantled.

Given this tenacity, and flexibility, of the Africanist repertory, other modes of contestation seem called for, and it is in narratives that not so much rewrite the past but rather infiltrate and explode it that I find evidence for such an alternative project in our time. The fantastic fictions of African and Afrodiasporic history investigated in the last two chapters rarely confront Africanist stereotypes head-on, by dint of explicit critique of the established images. Nor do they resort to irony or parody alone. Combining ironic detachment with revisionary appropriation, the structure of identification with the effects of alienation, these texts tackle

Africanity at its core, probing viruslike into its operative system, and manipulating it by way of that intrusion.

This is why a text like Darius James's *Negrophobia* could be said to demarcate the extreme other end of narratives of adventurous contact like Haggard's *King Solomon's Mines* or Burroughs's *Tarzan of the Apes,* precisely because James is obsessed with the very workings of the symbolic system of contact and communication, translation and trickery, a system that we have already seen to inform colonial and early imperialist writing. Where a novel like *Tarzan of the Apes* enacted Africa as a hidden comment on the situation in the United States, the fictional jungle laid out along the lines of identification and segregation established in an America thoroughly stratified by the markers of class, race, and gender, James's novel signifies precisely on that unacknowledged mirror function. The jungle he presents in an imaginary book within his book, titled "Lil' Black Zambo," is nothing but a neat replication of American stereotypes around blackness and poverty—a tabloid ghetto with palm trees:

Zambo's pappy, Tambo, who liked to drink cheap coconut wine, ran off long before Zambo was born, so Zambo and his mammy were very, very poor. They didn't give out welfare checks in the Jungle. The Jungle was uncivilized. Or at least that's what Zambo's mammy, Mambo, said. "When we gwine git civilized so I can git on d'welfare?" (*N* 125)

It is when the Talking Dreads, James's cosmic contact figure, comes across this skewered narrative that he finally gives up any "attempt at intelligent communication" (*N* 124) with the human race and takes recourse to other means of contact—manipulation and mimicry. Classical narrative, it seems, does not lend itself easily to projects of contestation or radical critique, as it is always already infused with the very categories to be questioned.

If James has his "cultural meddler," the Talking Dreads, eventually turn away from talk and writing, as he is seen to endorse simulation and deceit, this turn once more forms a counterpoint to rather than an echo of colonial and imperial structures of representation. After all, the Talking Dreads's maneuvers of deception differ dramatically from Tarzan's trickery—or, for that matter, Greystoke's mimicry—as *Negrophobia* clearly does not propound one-sided control and individualist self-fashioning. Where both Burroughs and Hudson endorse trickery and mimicry as a means of gaining control (over others, as in Burroughs's case, or over one's self-image, as in Hudson's), James gleefully focuses upon the chaotic dimension inherent in these techniques, epitomizing trickery's liability to run out of control and mimicry's propensity to bring about disruption: his trickster figures, the exploding negroes in whiteface, call the very notion of individual agency into doubt. Turning from trick translation to special effects means also abandoning a clear focus of heroic action in this narrative.

While *Negrophobia* and other recent takes on the repertory of Africanity grapple with the awareness that the modes and mechanisms of agency and resistance have changed considerably within the last thirty years, all of these texts also revolve around the insight that racism, too, is no longer to be located on the level of conscious and willful action alone: clearly, expressed racist aggression is widely considered déclassé and anachronistic in wide parts of the contemporary United States—most notably its mainstream media. But just as clearly, race has far from disappeared as a category of differentiation and marginalization, even if it comes to bear on social reality in a way that is not always easy to grasp. This is what Patricia Williams described in her analogy comparing the logic of racism to a familiar room emptied of its furniture:

The power of that room, I have thought since, is very like the power of racism as status quo: it is . . . strong enough to make everyone who enters the room walk around the bed that isn't there, avoiding the phantom as they did the substance, for fear of bodily harm. They do not even know they are avoiding, they defer to the unseen shape of things with subtle responsiveness, guided by an impulsive awareness of nothingness, and the deep knowledge and denial of witchcraft at work.[1]

The image of the empty room calls to mind Renée Green's installation *Vistavision,* set forth in the same year as Williams's book. Where Green exhibited the stage props of Africanity, Williams—clearing the room—takes even these props away and still insists on the power of the setup: racism becomes a body memory. And by the same right Africanity could be made out as a set of cultural techniques of differentiation and ideological truisms that need not be consciously called up or actively embraced to be effective.

This is not to say, however, that racism and Africanity are quasi-pathological influences, hovering somewhere in the human unconscious since the beginning of time. Racist and racializing patterns of meaning making should rather be understood as a changing "historically concrete articulation of an abstract 'apparatus,'" an apparatus that is never independent of its context of social practice, as Mark Terkessidis has argued,[2] and thus always also subject to revision, reconsideration, and change. This is precisely the basis for the continual reenactments I have traced in this study, all of them illustrating that the very same image can mean markedly different things and can be put to glaringly different uses.

There is no atavistic power at the roots of race relations and cultural contact, but for that matter the claims to newness at the heart of so many

contact scenarios should not be taken at face value either: even first encounters always actualize older patterns of thought and structures of signification, patterns and structures that are, of course, far from objective
and distinterested in their own right, as we have seen. The "documents
and stories of 'discovery,'" Myra Jehlen pointed out, should thus not be
read "as records of fulfillment, but as components of a historical process.
These documents and stories themselves participated in an 'encounter'
whose unfolding was so far from being a natural process that at times it
unfolded first in the telling."[3] The scenarios of cultural contact might time
and again be cast in terms of the utterly new and the never before seen,
but this rhetoric itself soon becomes a commonplace, laden with preconceived ideas and preformulated incentives.

"People are trapped in history and history is trapped in them,"[4] James
Baldwin once wrote, indicating a reciprocity that is frightening, but by no
means as deterministic as it sounds. Baldwin came up with his insight in
the context of a very special and highly interesting cultural contact narrative of his own. And this narrative, which was first published in 1953
under the title "Stranger in the Village," will serve as the first of three con-
trapuntal examples here to conclude some of my earlier reflections on
cultural contact, masquerade, and the constructive function of stereotyping, sharpening these reflections with regard to notions of diasporic identity as pitted between (nationalist) roots and (hybrid) role-play.

Baldwin's little essay, I argue, demarcates the transition from a colonial world order to a global system, although he does not use the latter
term. The text relates several visits to a Swiss mountain village in the
early 1950s. The first of these journeys brings about a strange revelation
for the African-American intellectual, who reaches Switzerland via Paris:
he finds himself in a first contact situation "reversed"—the first black
man to discover this "white wilderness" ("SV" 160). The account he
gives of this experience signifies on the pattern of colonial narratives of
cultural contact and on the tales of Western adventurers and anthropolo-
gists traveling in Africa:

If I sat in the sun for more than five minutes some daring creature was certain to
come along and gingerly put his fingers on my hair, as though he were afraid of an
electric shock, or put his hand on my hand astonished that the color did not rub
off. In all of this, in which it must be conceded there was the charm of genuine
wonder and in which there was certainly no element of intentional unkindness,
there was yet no suggestion that I was human: I was simply a living wonder.
("SV" 162)

Baldwin, the cosmopolite and intellectual, clearly casts himself as the
superior party in this encounter—more cultured, sophisticated, civilized
than these mountain folks whose worldview seems to him as limited as

the notions of African villagers appeared to travelers from Mungo Park to Henry Morton Stanley: "It did not occur to me—possibly because I am an American—that there could be people anywhere who had never seen a negro" ("SV" 159).

But that is not to say that Baldwin would (or could) neatly invert the colonial contact scenario. And irony, too, carries him only so far in his reflections. The situations are after all similar, but very definitely not the same: "People are trapped in history and history is trapped in them." Being an African-American in the twentieth century in Europe, Baldwin cannot possibly come up with an attitude corresponding to either Haggard's chuckling condescension or even Burroughs's disgusted distantiation vis-à-vis the natives he encounters. This contact scenario is inscribed with markedly different evaluations and sensations:

> I thought of white men arriving for the first time in an African village, strangers there, as I am a stranger here, and tried to imagine the astounded populace touching their hair and marveling at the color of their skin. But there is a great difference between being the first white man to be seen by Africans and being the first black man to be seen by whites. The white man takes the astonishment as tribute, for he arrives to conquer and to convert the natives, whose inferiority in relation to himself is not even to be questioned, whereas I, without a thought of conquest, find myself among a people whose culture controls me, has even in a sense created me, people who have cost me more in anguish and rage than they will ever know, who yet do not even know of my existence. ("SV" 163–164)

Commenting upon this passage, bell hooks pointed to the inherent unevenness that characterizes this account of reciprocal projections, the fact that "whiteness exists without knowledge of blackness even as it collectively asserts control."[5] Yet while the categories of whiteness and blackness, and the corresponding system of evaluations and ascriptions, doubtlessly inform this scenario and its logic profoundly, Baldwin does not stop short there. He continues to reflect upon the very representativity of such binaries—black-white and African-European—to come up with a third term that for him ends up throwing the entire symbolic system into disarray: American.

The United States of America demarcates a space where contact has irretrievably happened, where the encounter that the Swiss people are just living through took place long ago and on a scale impossible to dismiss. This is why Baldwin makes out a deep rift, an "abyss," separating not only him, the black man, and the white villagers, but the situations in America and Europe at large. This "dreadful abyss" opens up between the Swiss children shouting "Neger" and the American mob of his youth shouting "Nigger," "between the streets of this village and the streets of the city in which I was born." For Baldwin the abyss is "the American experience" per se: "I am a stranger here. But I am not a stranger in America and the same syllable riding on the American air expresses the war my presence has occasioned in the American soul" ("SV" 168).

There is a fundamental difference between America and Europe, Baldwin holds, and that difference is based upon the history of cultural contact and race relations. It is on these grounds that being black in the United States differs from being black in Europe, and that whiteness does not mean the same everywhere either:

> Europe's black possessions remained—and do remain—in Europe's colonies, at which remove they represented no threat whatsoever to European identity. If they posed any problem at all for the European conscience, it was a problem which remained comfortingly abstract: in effect, the black man, *as a man*, did not exist in Europe. But in America, even as a slave, he was an inescapable part of the general social fabric and no American could escape having an attitude toward him. ("SV" 170)

While this differentiation does capture the different stances of, say, the British colonialist author H. Rider Haggard and the American imperialist writer Edgar Rice Burroughs—their delineations of contact to be sought and abandoned at will (Haggard), and of contact already irrevocably established (Burroughs)—and while it manages to get a grip on the situation in the 1950s, today matters have clearly changed. Europe, too, has opened up—and not even Swiss mountain villages may rest in oblivion of racial and ethnic differences anymore. The world, as Baldwin predicts when ending his reflections, "is white no longer and it will never be white again" ("SV" 175). And all of the contemporary narratives around Africanity and the Western world investigated in my study try to come to terms in one way or another with this insight that the cultural spheres are irretrievably mixed up these days and that cultural contact has lost its spectacular exceptionality almost everywhere, as it comes to demarcate the logic of everyday interaction on both a private and a public scale.

Seen that way, Baldwin's very presence in the Swiss mountains already indicates the demise of the world order he describes. But the fact that contact has in the meantime set in on an unprecedented scale does not mean that understanding and interaction have correspondingly increased, as another instance of cultural contact described by Baldwin exemplifies. Writing about his encounter with North African students in Paris, he comes to quite bleak conclusions with regard to the prospect of a Pan-African political mobilization: "They face each other, the Negro and the African, over a gulf of three hundred years—an alienation too vast to be conquered in an evening's good-will, too heavy and too double-edged ever to be trapped in speech. This alienation causes the Negro to recognize that he is a hybrid."[6] This other contact situation in a European setting seems so much more up-to-date, pointing not at a world in decline but at a global order to come, which is "white no longer" but not necessarily any less hierarchical or alienated for that.

For Baldwin, the identity of the "Negro," the diasporic African, configures itself in stark contrast to a "European" and an "African" sense of selfhood. It is predicated on the experience of alienation, hybridity—rootlessness. But of course, at exactly the same time that Baldwin formulated these thoughts, Frantz Fanon approached the issue from another angle in *Black Skin, White Masks* (1952), demarcating the situation of postcolonial Africans as no less "hybrid" and artificial than the one of African-Americans, if definitely laid out along different lines. And these days, finally, hybridity seems to have lost its negative connotations altogether, as it has become a fashionable marker signifying independence, flexibility, and cosmopolitan cool. Not accidentally Francesca Marciano's Esmé, this epitome of the global girl, sums up her situation in the same words that Baldwin used—"I was a stranger and would always be" (*RW* 94)—while John Le Carré, not exactly a radical minority writer, comes to celebrate a protagonist as an "unsavable hybrid" (*CG* 347). Today, to be a stranger, a hybrid, an outsider (regardless of whether you are in New York, Naples, or Nairobi) is not necessarily a deficit. If you have the right cultural background, the right education, the right profession, and enough money, that is. North African students still tend to be cast in terms of unfashionable roots, rather than chic hybridity.

In line with such differentiations, hybridity and nationalism are time and again made out as oppositional terms, while the quest for national identity and specificity comes to be characterized as another atavistic impulse outside the confines of modernity. But to assume such an atavistic force is to ignore the flexibility and historicity of nationalism, as Gayatri Spivak, among many others, pointed out:

Nationalism, like culture, is a moving base—a *socle mouvant* (to quote Foucault . . .)—of differences, as dangerous as it is powerful, always ahead or deferred by definitions, pro or contra, upon which it relies. Against this, globality—or postnationalist talk—is a representation—both as *Darstellung* or theatre and as *Vertretung* or delegation as functionary—of the financialization of the globe, or globalization. . . . Fundamentalist nationalism arises in the loosened hyphen between nation and state as the latter is mortgaged further and further by the forces of financialization, although the determinations are never clear. The first items in the following couples are fuzzy, the second abstract: nation-state, subject-agency (institutionally validated action), identity-citizenship. Much manipulation, maneuvering, and mobilization can take place in the interest of the latter in the name of the fuzzy partner.[7]

Seen that way, economic globalization becomes a highly ambivalent process. While it weakens national institutions and "financializes" politics, it does not necessarily weaken the desire for "nation," "subjecthood," "identity"—terms that are "fuzzy" indeed. But fuzziness has never stood in the way of political motivation, let alone national commitment, even if it allows for the profound reconfiguration of such stances—national commitment, for one, seems to have become largely independent of categories such as the local or the territorial: "the nationalist genie, never perfectly contained in the bottle of the territorial state, is now itself a diasporic," writes Arjun Appadurai. "Where soil and place were once the key to the linkage of territorial affiliation with state monopoly of the means of violence, key identities and identifications now only partially revolve around the realities and images of place."[8]

While clearly the dissociation of territory and notions of national identity has gained an unprecedented momentum within the last decades, in the United States this is far from a new phenomenon. By this token, black identity politics throughout the twentieth century set the tone for the new "diasporic nationalities," whose invocations of "home" have come to be tinged with the same artificiality that has characterized the African "motherland" of Pan-Africanism and black nationalism for a long time. This is Africanity's "other" face—the continent's function not within mainstream discourses of exoticization or demonization, but within minority politics and diasporic self-stylizations. And even if numerous artists have recently come to cast Africa as an "alien future" rather than as "a lost continent in the past," to use Kodwo Eshun's term once more, nationalist patterns of thought are far from defunct in contemporary black culture.

But even where the concept of African roots is taken literally, the "motherland" often enough gains surprisingly hybrid connotations in the Afrocentrist narratives of today. An anecdote told by the black nationalist scholar Leonard Jeffries is a case in point. The little story revolves around Jeffries's involvement with Alex Haley's *Roots* (1976), this epitome of an Africanist narrative of self-empowerment and authentication, which came to shape what countless Americans think about when they think about African identity. Before Haley's novel appeared, its manuscript disappeared, as Jeffries relates: the author called him in panic from Philadelphia, to tell him that he had lost the novel's only copy somewhere in the airport. Jeffries joined in the search, "ran around the airport of Philadelphia and found *Roots*." He then continues to tell how he came to work as an adviser for the producers of the miniseries *Roots* (1977–1979), growing more and more disillusioned with the project and finally withdrawing altogether after having learned that the term "Mother Africa" was to be cut from a scene in which two abducted Africans on a slave ship give voice to their spirit of heroic resistance.

It is difficult to read this anecdote in terms of a struggle of authenticity versus fabrication, even if it is clearly laid out along these lines. Unfolding on quite mundane grounds—an airport and a movie set—the struggle to recover and safeguard a glorious African past appears fundamentally tinged with artificiality and hybridity, suggesting a quest for symbolic and political empowerment rather than historical truth. If the story seems laden with surplus meaning in its own right, its context and the way in which it came into circulation convey even more layers of signification: the anecdote is part of the performance *Fires in the Mirror,* staged by Anna Deavere Smith in 1992, a performance that revolves around the Crown Heights riots in Brooklyn the previous year. This performance, and specifically Smith's enactment of Jeffries's anecdote in the course of it, will serve as my second counterpoint here, a means of recapitulating my earlier argumentation around the functions of masquerade and mimicry in contemporary culture.

The riots in Brooklyn erupted after a seven-year-old Guyanese-American boy had been killed in a car accident caused by a driver who belonged to a local sect of Hasidic Jews, the Lubavitcher, and after a Hasidic Jew visiting from Australia had been killed in a revenge act. Smith's performance captures the explosive mixture of cultural ascription, projections, and aggressions set free in Crown Heights, a community largely constituted by two diasporic groups, which came to perceive each other as uncooperative, hostile, overpowering—and altogether different.[9] And obviously Jeffries, the professor teaching at City University of New York who gained notoriety by his public postulations of an antiblack Jewish conspiracy in the United States, plays a role in this kind of confrontation.[10]

Smith's technique of representing cultural conflict is based upon mimicry—she acts out interviews conducted with public personae, local representatives, and anonymous witnesses, putting forth impersonations that have been praised for their lifelikeness and similitude—almost like the original. Almost, but not quite: to describe Smith's act in terms of illusion or special effects, as holding "the mirror up to America"[11] or accomplishing "a morph without aid of digitization,"[12] is to grasp only part of her technique, which does, after all, rely as much on effects of alienation as it does on identification. This is not docudrama, and much less cinema translocated onto a stage, but performance theater—and markedly so. And precisely because Smith's endorsement of masquerade and mimicry achieves an effect glaringly at odds with the "special effects" of so many current mainstream representations of cultural contact, it provides an excellent counterpoint to these enactments.

Smith may not take an explicit stance vis-à-vis the statements she performs, and she certainly refrains from parody or ironic detachment. But this is not to say that she would disappear behind her work—or other people's words. Her impersonation of Leonard Jeffries is a case in point—since his tenet of a "rooted" patriarchal black community threatened by Jewish conspiracies all around is considerably qualified not only by the thrust of the material Smith chose to enact but by the very fact that Jeffries comes to be impersonated by a light-skinned black woman who will at the very next moment take off the African hat that serves as a prop here and don glasses to figure forth the liberal Jewish author Letty Cottin Pogrebin.

Explicating her method, Anna Deavere Smith evoked a breakdown of boundaries between self and other, "learning about the other by being the other," as she put it in her introduction to the book version of *Fires in the Mirror* (*FM* xxvii). Yet watching her act, I rather felt that the boundary between self and other becomes the very site of representation here, with Smith herself, the actress, moving in and out of focus, just as the puppet players do in *Faustus in Africa!*—the Handspring Company's take on the ideological force of make-believe and identification. "Mimicry," writes Smith, "is *not* character. Character lives in the obvious gap between the real person and my *attempt* to seem like them. I try to close the gap between us, but I applaud the gap between us. I am willing to display my own *unlikeness*" (*FM* xxxiii).

On the basis of this mix-up of "acts" with "agency" and role-play with roots, Smith eventually throws into doubt the power of spoken language itself. To "talk it over" is clearly not an option in the kind of conflicts she investigates: "I am interested in the lack of words and mistrustful of the ease with which some people seem to pick up new words and mix them with the old" (*FM* xii), she insists. It is consequently the "gaps" of self-fashioning that she focuses on—the syntactical breaks, the pauses, the fillers, the slips of the tongue, and the logical inconsistencies in oral expression: not the "smooth-sounding words" but "the very moment that the smooth-sounding words fail us" (*FM* xii). Concentrating on the point when language disintegrates and communication breaks down, Smith refrains from closure and contiguity, leaving us instead with disjointed bits and pieces, a patchwork of perspectives and opinions that is only the more disturbing and disorienting because some patterns are clearly given—and the quest for roots in an "uprooted" world is certainly one such pattern, surging up not only in Jeffries's statement but in many other accounts too.

In Crown Heights, rootlessness could be said to form the status quo. Yet this is not the chic hybridity of the global girl but has an effect like the gulf James Baldwin made out between diasporic Africans in Paris—a negative commonality, which does not bring about solidarity or even functional interaction in the long run. Smith's performance epitomizes this lack of alliance, although the very fact that it presents a reenactment, a second take, does also point at an effort to provide an alternative "common ground" in order to come to terms with the situation at hand, as Tania Modleski argued:

> ... the very premise of Smith's performance is diasporic consciousness. Further, *Fires in the Mirror* suggests that what blacks and Jews have in common is the condition of diaspora; their common ground is their 'groundlessness.' Ironically, this condition has been the source of intense mimetic rivalry between the two groups, particularly over the question of whose experience in the diaspora has been worse. . . . Yet insofar as it disputes the validity of claims to original rights and original wrongs, diasporic consciousness marks a shift from mimetic rivalry to solidarity—a shift, again, that is inherent in the very concept of Smith's work, one of the most intriguing aspects of which is its undermining of certainty about origins. Giving priority, as it were, to the copy over the original, Smith radically and viscerally contests ideals of authenticity, in effect "deterritorializing" her characters and getting them to act on new common ground—the stage.[13]

Smith's mimicry highlights the fact that rootlessness is a condition that cannot be suspended, that the point of departure, the motherland, will always be a phantasmic entity, and that roots may be recuperated, but most likely in the guise of fictions that can get lost again in airports and train stations all over the world. The master narrative, for one, will never be found, even if what Gayatri Spivak called the "representation of globality" tries to provide just that—an all-comprising frame for the diversity at large. Figuring forth the masquerade of smoothly functioning global interaction and suppressing the evidence of conflict and contingency, globalization constitutes a "theater" in its own right that stands in stark opposition to Smith's performance.

And this contrast—between the masquerades of globalism and the performance of "diasporic consciousness," if you will—also demarcates the extreme ends of contemporary endorsements of masquerade and mimicry. Vis-à-vis the pragmatic credo of global action—and acting—Smith epitomizes the mixture of rage and resignation arising "backstage," the suspicion that "they runnin' the whole show" (*FM* 138), as Carmel Cato, the dead little boy's father, put it: "they"—the Lubavitcher, the Jews. Where pragmatism no longer works, paranoia sets in all too easily—providing the ultimate master narrative.

The quest for the master narrative, whether it takes the extreme form of outspoken paranoia or whether it limits itself to the global rhetoric of contiguity, time and again welds stereotypical imageries and heartfelt expression together. Significantly enough, Smith claims to have come up with her technique of impersonation by watching talk shows, celebrity interviews, and real-life drama on TV, modes of representation and narration that "exploded in popular culture" (*FM* xxix) in the early 1980s, propelling an intricate machinery of "talk" and "understanding" infused with the logic of stereotyping. Yet where the mainstream media obfuscate the stereotypical form that their "true events" invariably take on, Smith's performances render it pivotal, showing time and again that stereotypes do not envelop meaning—they *make* it.

In this effect, *Fires in the Mirror* calls to mind the work of artists like Walter Abish, Renée Green, or Keith Piper, who presented the paraphernalia of colonial and imperial meaning making as so much more central than might seem at first glance, displaying the alphabet of adventure, the glass cases of science, and the symbols of religion not as some kind of arbitrary props to the theater of imperialism but as all there is to it—its essence, or rather its internalized operating system. The selfsame logic of internalization and unconscious infiltration has been captured by James Baldwin in his evocation of people "trapped in history," and by Patricia Williams in her comparison of racism with a body memory. But if Smith's performance exemplarily discloses the hidden power of stereotypical forms of expression and representation over people, it also insists that people have power over these seemingly abstract forces, precisely because they are made up of words and images—signs that are subject to change and may undergo manipulation. The very reenactment of "ideological work" onstage brings about a change of focus, envisioning a quite radical infiltration and manipulation of stereotypical form, another viral act that explodes stereotypes into absurdity: roots in an airport.

Stereotypes are always constructive; they make meaning, if highly unstable meaning, and their very volatility and arbitrariness may well be used against the tempting pull of ideological simplification and closure. Let me conclude these reflections with a glance at a third counterpoint, an artistic project that accomplishes the effect of exploding stereotypes exemplarily and breathtakingly, once more drawing on the aesthetics of the masquerade, yet this time in close interlinkage with the Africanist implications of this aesthetics—the imagery of primitivist masking.

The concept artist David Hammons claims to have always been fascinated by stereotypes. In an interview, he elaborated on this fascination, explaining why he came to work with one particular stereotype of blackness—the spade—in an installation series:

I was trying to figure out why black people were called spades, as opposed to clubs. Because I remember being called a spade once and I didn't know what it meant; nigger I knew but spade I still don't. So I just took the shape, and started painting it. I started dealing with the spade the way Jim Dine was using the heart. . . . Then I started getting shovels (spades); I got all of these shovels and made masks out of them. It was just like a chain reaction. . . . I was running my car over these spades and then photographing them. I was hanging them from trees. Some were made out of leather (they were skins).[14]

Like Baldwin, Hammons finds himself confronted with the objectifying gaze and language of racism. His reaction is to refer the symbolic insult back to a material level, objectifying the objectification—"I . . . took the shape"—and thus to drain it of its meaning. Turning the spade into a mask, however, Hammons also moves beyond a mere culmination of trite images in the style of Jim Dine, as the racist insult is called up and transformed in the very course of allusion. By rendering the "alphabetical" "spade" a literal spade, the literal spade a mask, and finally associating this mask with "skin," Hammons explodes the confines of stereotypical discourse and of Africanity.

One of these "spade" assemblages is called "Laughing Magic": a "primitive" spade/mask adorned with colorful rags and ties from which a chain dangles, forming a laughing mouth. The best way of ending these reflections might be precisely this image: the grotesque laughter of the mask at and by way of the chain.

Notes

INTRODUCTION, PP. 1–21

1. Walter Abish, *Alphabetical Africa* (New York: New Directions, 1974) 133.
2. I will use the term "postcolonial" in a strictly historical sense here, denoting the period after colonial rule. With this I draw upon Stuart Hall's argumentation in "When Was 'the Postcolonial'? Thinking at the Limit," in *The Postcolonial Question: Common Skies, Divided Horizons*, ed. Iain Chambers and Lidia Curti (London: Routledge, 1996) 242–260. For a wider debate about the terminology of postcolonialism that has influenced this work cf. Benita Parry, "Problems in Current Theories of Colonial Discourse," in *The Post-Colonial Studies Reader*, ed. Bill Ashcroft, Gareth Griffiths, and Helen Tiffin (London: Routledge, 1995) 36–44; Laura Chrisman, "The Imperial Unconscious? Representations of Imperial Discourse," *Critical Quarterly* 32:3 (Autumn 1990) 38–80; and Robert Young, *Colonial Desire: Hybridity in Theory, Culture, and Race* (London: Routledge, 1995).
3. Strictly speaking, the term "globalization" could be employed synonymously with the term "modernity," so that Columbus would figure as an early representative of the "global logic." Nevertheless, I chose to use the term in a much narrower—and more conventional—sense in the following, to demarcate what Gayatri Chakravorty Spivak called a "financialization of the globe," an economic development in tight conjunction with political and social transformations (Gayatri Chakravorty Spivak, *A Critique of Postcolonial Reason: Toward a History of the Vanishing Present* [Cambridge, Mass.: Harvard U Press, 1999] 364). The beginnings of this period of globalization coincide and overlap with the end of colonial rule and are certainly deeply entrenched with neocolonial tendencies, as will become clear. About the concept and its cultural implications see, among others, Immanuel Wallerstein, *The Politics of World-Economy: The States, the Movements, and the Civilization. Essays* (Cambridge: Cambridge U Press, 1984); *Challenging Boundaries: Global Flows, Territorial Identities*, ed. Michael J. Shapiro and Hayward R. Alker (Minneapolis: U of Minnesota Press, 1996); *Globalkolorit: Multikulturalismus und Populärkultur*, ed. Ruth Mayer and Mark Terkessidis (St. Andrä-Wördern: Hannibal, 1998); *The Cultures of Globalization*, ed. Fredric Jameson and Masao Miyoshi (Durham: Duke U Press, 1998); Saskia Sassen, *Globalization and Its Discontents* (New York: New Press, 1998); and *Cosmopolitics: Thinking and Feeling beyond the Nation*, ed. Pheng Cheah and Bruce Robbins (Minneapolis: U of Minnesota Press, 1998).

4. Of course, similar tendencies at stereotypical streamlining can be noted with respect to every other continent. But no other continent has been subjected to projections as pervasive as the ones of African primitivity, savagery, and time-lessness. Cf. on that development and its aesthetic and cultural implications, among others, V. Y. Mudimbe, *The Invention of Africa: Gnosis, Philosophy, and the Order of Knowledge* (Bloomington: Indiana U Press, 1988); Kwame Anthony Appiah, *In My Father's House: Africa in the Philosophy of Culture* (New York: Oxford U Press, 1992); *Africa's Media Image*, ed. Beverly G. Hawk (New York: Praeger, 1992); Annie E. Coombes, *Reinventing Africa: Museums, Material Culture, and Popular Imagination in Late Victorian and Edwardian England* (New Haven: Yale U Press, 1994); *Africanisms in American Culture*, ed. Joseph E. Holloway (Bloomington: Indiana U Press, 1990); and Kadiatu Kanneh, *African Identities: Race, Nation, and Culture in Ethnography, Pan-Africanism, and Black Literature* (London: Routledge, 1998).

5. Edward Said, *Culture and Imperialism*, 1993 (New York: Vintage, 1994) 22.

6. Coombes, 3.

7. Terence Ranger, "Invention of Tradition in Colonial Africa," in *The Invention of Tradition*, ed. Eric Hobsbawm and T. Ranger (Cambridge: Cambridge U Press, 1983) 211–262, 212. See also Mudimbe; and Appiah, "The Invention of Africa," in *In My Father's House* 3–27.

8. Kwame Anthony Appiah, "Out of Africa: Topologies of Nativism," in *The Bounds of Race: Perspectives on Hegemony and Resistance*, ed. Dominick LaCapra (Ithaca: Cornell U Press, 1991) 134–163, 143–144.

9. On the beginnings of "imperial filmmaking" see Ella Shohat and Robert Stam, *Unthinking Eurocentrism: Multiculturalism and the Media* (London: Routledge, 1994) 100–110.

10. *Khartoum*, dir. Basil Dearden and Eliot Elisofon, with Charlton Heston, Laurence Olivier, and William Blackstone. Cinerama, 1966.

11. Shohat and Stam, 113.

12. Anne McClintock, *Imperial Leather: Race, Gender, and Sexuality in the Colonial Contest* (New York: Routledge, 1995) 13.

13. Amy Kaplan, "'Left Alone with America': The Absence of Empire in the Study of American Culture," in *Cultures of United States Imperialism*, ed. Amy Kaplan and Donald Pease (Durham: Duke U Press, 1993) 3–21, 12.

14. Cf., for instance, Eric Cheyfitz, *The Poetics of Imperialism: Translation and Colonization from* The Tempest *to* Tarzan (New York: Oxford U Press, 1991); John McClure, *Late Imperial Romance* (London: Verso, 1994); Eric Sundquist, *To Wake the Nations: Race in the Making of American Literature* (Cambridge, Mass.: Harvard U Press, 1993); and the contributions in the excellent volume *Cultures of United States Imperialism*. For a theoretical discussion of these issues, most notably an international turn in American Studies, cf. Amy Kaplan, "'Left Alone with America'"; Gesa Mackenthun, "State of the Art: Adding Empire to the Study of American Culture," *Journal of American Studies* 30:2 (1996) 263–269; Paul Giles, "Virtual Americas: The Internationalization of American Studies and the Ideology of Exchange," *American Quarterly* 50:3 (Sept. 1998) 523–547; and Janice Radway, "What's in a Name? Presidential Address to the American Studies Association, 20 November 1998," *American Quarterly* 51:1 (1999) 1–32.

15. Toni Morrison, "black matters," in *Playing in the Dark: Whiteness and the Literary Imagination* (Cambridge, Mass.: Harvard U Press, 1992) 3–28, 5, 8.

16. Roland Barthes, *Mythologies*, 1957, tr. Annette Lavers (London: Jonathan Cape, 1972) 118. For a reading of Barthes's early work alongside Frantz Fanon's writing as an effort "to develop an analytical apparatus for theorizing white consciousness in a postempire world," cf. Chéla Sandoval, "Theorizing White Consciousness for a Post-empire World: Barthes, Fanon, and the Rhetoric of Love," in *Displacing Whiteness: Essays in Social and Cultural Criticism*, ed. Ruth Frankenberg (Durham: Duke U Press, 1997) 86–106, 88.

17. Amiri Baraka, "Ka 'Ba,'" in *The Heath Anthology of American Literature*, vol. 2, ed. Paul Lauter et al. (Lexington: D. C. Heath and Co., 1994) 2702–2703.

18. Paul Gilroy, *The Black Atlantic: Modernity and Double Consciousness* (London: Verso, 1993) 96.

19. Homi K. Bhabha, "The Other Question: Stereotype, Discrimination, and the Discourse of Colonialism," in *The Location of Culture* (London: Routledge, 1994) 66–84, 67.

20. Michael Taussig, *Mimesis and Alterity: A Particular History of the Senses* (New York: Routledge, 1993) 16.

21. Taussig, *Mimesis*, 186.

22. Taussig, *Mimesis*, 191.

23. Taussig, *Mimesis*, 189.

24. Homi K. Bhabha, "Of Mimicry and Man: The Ambivalence of Colonial Discourse," in *The Location of Culture* 85–92, 89. Of course, such reflections about the productivity of stereotypical discourse in the realm of cultural contact, minority discourses, and diasporic identity formation have been formulated not only by Bhabha or Taussig but also by Henry Louis Gates, Jr., with respect to African-American cultural self-fashioning, James Clifford with respect to ethnological contact situations, or Stuart Hall with respect to diasporic cultures—"new ethnicities"—in Great Britain. Cf. Henry Louis Gates, Jr., *The Signifying Monkey: A Theory of African-American Literary Criticism* (New York: Oxford U Press, 1988); James Clifford, *The Predicament of Culture: Twentieth-Century Ethnography, Literature, and Art* (Cambridge, Mass.: Harvard U Press,; 1988); and Stuart Hall, "New Ethnicities," in *Stuart Hall: Critical Dialogues in Cultural Studies*, ed. David Morley and Kuan Hsing Chen (London: Routledge, 1996) 441–459.

25. For a detailed critique of such trends see Ruth Mayer and Mark Terkessidis, "Retuschierte Bilder: Multikulturalismus, Populärkultur und *Cultural Studies* in Deutschland," in *Globalkolorit* 7–23; and my "Vielbevölkerte Zone: Kulturwissenschaften zwischen Gutmenschentum und dem Glamour der Rebellion," in *Die kleinen Unterschiede: Reader Cultural Studies*, ed. Jan Engelmann (Frankfurt/Main: Campus, 1999) 231–243.

26. Thomas Frank, *The Conquest of Cool: Business Culture, Counterculture, and the Rise of Hip Consumerism* (Chicago: U of Chicago Press, 1997) 19, 26.

27. I rely heavily on the theories of British cultural studies following Raymond Williams, most notably Stuart Hall's reflections on popular culture, although I will argue for a reexamination of his stances with regard to a changed cultural context of the 1990s and 2000s. Cf. the contributions in *Stuart Hall*, most notably "On Postmodernism and Articulation: An Interview with Stuart Hall," *Stuart Hall* 131–150.

28. Walter Benjamin, "Die Aufgabe des Übersetzers" (1923), in *Illuminationen: Ausgewählte Schriften 1* (Frankfurt/Main: Suhrkamp, 1977) 50–62, 55—my translation.

29. Benjamin, 53.

30. Cf. Kadiatu Kanneh's reflections on the paradigmatic project of cultural translation, ethnography: Kanneh, 2–21. On the issue of cultural translation see also Talal Asad, "The Concept of Cultural Translation in British Social Anthropology," in *Writing Culture: The Poetics and Politics of Ethnography*, ed. James Clifford and George E. Marcus (Berkeley: U of California Press, 1986) 141–164.

31. Fredric Jameson, "Foreword," in Jean-François Lyotard, *The Postmodern Condition: A Report on Knowledge* (Minneapolis: U of Minnesota Press, 1984) vii–xxv, xi.

32. Winfried Fluck, *Das kulturelle Imaginäre: Eine Funktionsgeschichte des amerikanischen Romans, 1790–1900* (Frankfurt/Main: Suhrkamp, 1997) 21— my translation. For a sociological definition of the term "imaginary" see Cornelius Castoriadis's *The Imaginary Institution of Society* (1975), tr. Kathleen Blamey (Cambridge: Cambridge U Press, 1987).

33. Wolfgang Iser, *Das Fiktive und das Imaginäre: Perspektiven literarischer Anthropologie* (Frankfurt/Main: Suhrkamp, 1993) 490.

34. Hayden White, "The Value of Narrativity in the Representation of Reality," in *On Narrative*, ed. W. J. T. Mitchell (Chicago: U of Chicago Press, 1981) 1–23, 11.

35. W. J. T. Mitchell, "Foreword," in *On Narrative* vii–x, viii.

36. Michel de Certeau, *The Practice of Everyday Life*, tr. Steven Rendall, 1984 (Berkeley: U of California Press, 1988) 23.

37. De Certeau, 37.

38. Taussig, *Mimesis*, 16.

39. Michael Taussig, *Shamanism, Colonialism, and the Wild Man: A Study in Terror and Healing* (Chicago: U of Chicago Press, 1987) 10–11.

40. Fredric Jameson, *The Political Unconscious: Narrative as a Socially Symbolic Act*, 1981 (Ithaca: Cornell U Press, 1982) 49.

41. See my *Selbsterkenntnis, Körperfühlen* (München: Fink, 1997), for an extensive debate on the benefits and perils of new historical approaches, and a model of accounting for discursive and cultural difference within the field of textual analysis. For a wide-ranging analysis of the new historicizing approaches and their role within American Studies, which has very much influenced my work, cf. Donald Pease, "New Americanists: Revisionist Interventions into the Canon," 1990, in *The New Historicism Reader*, ed. H. Aram Veeser (New York: Routledge, 1994) 141–160.

42. Sara Mills, *Discourses of Difference: An Analysis of Women's Travel Writing and Colonialism* (London: Routledge, 1991) 52, 55. For a similar critique of postcolonial theories that conflate different imperial regimes, different historical periods, and different sociocultural contexts into one big spectacle of "imperiality," see Benita Parry, "Narrating Imperialism: *Nostromo*'s Dystopia," in *Cultural Readings of Imperialism: Edward Said and the Gravity of History*, ed. Keith Ansell Pearson, Benita Parry, and Judith Squires (New York: St. Martin's Press, 1997) 227–246.

43. For a general debate on this development within popular culture see Lawrence Grossberg, *"We gotta get out of this place": Popular Conservatism and Postmodern Culture* (New York: Routledge, 1992); and Tom Holert and Mark Terkessidis, "Einführung in den Mainstream der Minderheiten," in *Mainstream der Minderheiten: Pop in der Kontrollgesellschaft*, ed. Tom Holert and Mark Terkessidis (Berlin: ID-Archiv, 1996) 5–19.

44. Christian Metz, "The Fiction Film and Its Spectator," 1973, tr. Alfred Guzzetti, in *The Imaginary Signifier: Psychoanalysis and the Cinema* (Blooming-ton: Indiana U Press, 1982) 109–147, 110.

45. Fluck, 20—my translation.

46. Pierre Bourdieu, *Distinction: A Social Critique of the Judgement of Taste* (1979), tr. Richard Nice (London: Routledge, 1984).

47. Holert and Terkessidis, 6.

48. Stephen Heath, "*Jaws*, Ideology, and Film Theory," 1976, in *Movies and Methods*, vol. 2, ed. Bill Nichols (Berkeley: U of California Press, 1985) 509–514, 514.

49. Heath, "*Jaws*," 514.

50. Christian Metz, "Story/Discourse (a Note on Two Kinds of Voyeurism)," 1975, tr. Celia Britton and Annwyl Williams, in *The Imaginary Signifier*, 89–98, 91–92. Formulated in the 1970s, Metz's critique naturally does not take into account the current turn in Hollywood cinema to ironic rupture—what could be called the "pulp-fictionalization of Hollywood." But even if these days irony rules, its modes of rupture do not per se counteract the pull of totalization, as diegetic, visual, and aural effects (such as the thrill of the plotline, the intricate machinery of special effects, or a riveting musical score) interact smoothly to create a new kind of totality that is certainly no less efficient than the older one of classical Hollywood film.

51. Craig Owens, "Earthwords," *October* 10 (Fall 1979) 121–130, 127.

52. John McClure, *Late Imperial Romance*, 4.

53. Isak Dinesen, *Out of Africa*, 1938 (New York: Vintage Books, 1989) 365.

54. Joseph Conrad, *Heart of Darkness*, 1902 (Harmondsworth: Penguin, 1973) 33.

I. SPECIAL EFFECTS: ENCOUNTERS IN AFRICA, PP. 25–47

1. John G. Cawelti, *Adventure, Mystery, and Romance: Formula Stories as Art and Popular Culture* (Chicago: U of Chicago Press, 1976) 35, 18. See also Martin Green, *Dreams of Adventure, Deeds of Empire* (New York: Basic, 1979); and Brian Taves, *The Romance of Adventure: The Genre of Historical Adventure Movies* (Jackson: U of Mississippi Press, 1991).

2. Said, *Culture and Imperialism*, 188–192. See also Abena P. A. Busia, "Manipulating Africa: The Buccaneer as 'Liberator' in Contemporary Fiction," in *The Black Presence in English Literature*, ed. David Dabydeen (Manchester: Manchester U Press, 1985) 168–185; Gina Marchetti, "Action-Adventure as Ideology," in *Cultural Politics in Contemporary Africa*, ed. Jan Angus and Sut Jhally (New York: Routledge, 1989) 182–197; Andrea White, *Joseph Conrad and the Adventure Tradition: Constructing and Deconstructing the Imperial Subject* (Cambridge: Cambridge U Press, 1993); McClure, *Late Imperial Romance*; and Shohat and Stam, *Unthinking Eurocentrism*.

3. Richard Phillips, *Mapping Men and Empire: A Geography of Adventure* (London: Routledge, 1997) 165–166.

4. Metz, 91.

5. Quoted in Stephen Greenblatt, "Invisible Bullets," in *Shakespearean Negotiations: The Circulation of Social Energy in Renaissance England* (Oxford: Clarendon Press, 1988) 21–65, 27.

6. Mary Louise Pratt, *Imperial Eyes: Travel Writing and Transculturation* (London: Routledge, 1992) 7.

7. "Fourth Voyage of Columbus," in *The Four Voyages of Columbus,* tr. and ed. Cecil Jane (New York, Dover, 1988) 134.

8. Of course, colonial narratives of trick translation not only stressed English technological and scientific advances but insisted on the colonizers' mental superiority as well. This is what another famous line of trick translation narratives brings to the fore. Time and again, such narratives dwell upon the exchange of "worthless trinkets" against valuable goods, thus attesting to an English cleverness, as Jeffrey Knapp pointed out, which "never seems so clever as when it is contrasted with the credulity of strangers." Jeffrey Knapp, *An Empire Nowhere: England, America, and Literature from* Utopia *to* The Tempest (Berkeley: U of California Press, 1992) 124; see also Mary Fuller, *Voyages in Print: English Travel to America, 1576-1624* (Cambridge: Cambridge U Press, 1995) 85–140.

9. Peter Hulme, *Colonial Encounters: Europe and the Native Caribbean, 1492-1797* (London: Methuen, 1986) 128.

10. Cheyfitz, 78, 79.

11. For early American contact scenarios, such a representation of the "other side" is, of course, almost impossible to bring about in the first place, as no written accounts of the natives' perspectives exist. Cf. Myra Jehlen's reflections on early American culture for a more pervasive analysis of this lack: "The Literature of Colonization," in *The Cambridge History of American Literature,* vol. 1, gen. ed. Sacvan Bercovitch (Cambridge: Cambridge U Press, 1994) 11–168, 37–58. For ethnological debates around these issues cf. Asad; Renato Rosaldo, *Culture and Truth: The Remaking of Social Analysis,* 1989 (Boston: Beacon Press, 1993); and Taussig, *Mimesis;* for the conditions of colonial contact in Africa, discussed from an ethnological perspective, cf. Jean Comaroff and John Comaroff, "Through the Looking Glass: Heroic Journeys, First Encounters," in *Of Revelation and Revolution: Christianity, Colonialism, and Consciousness in South Africa,* vol. 1 (Chicago: U of Chicago Press, 1991) 188–197.

12. Ulla Haselstein, "Stephen Greenblatt's Concept of a Symbolic Economy," *Real: Yearbook of Research in English and American Literature* 11 (1995) 347–370, 363.

13. Cf. Greenblatt, "Invisible Bullets."

14. Gesa Mackenthun has put Greenblatt's remarks on the "subversive" dimensions of Harriot's account into perspective, pointing out that "Harriot's quibbles with church authority, which were very common at the time, [can hardly] be called subversive, as the undermining of theological doctrine in the *Report,* again, was prerequisite for the extending of colonial power to America." This critique notwithstanding, Mackenthun too points out the two-sidedness of this and other colonial texts, which give scope to a "'magic technology' of English scientific inventions" that "operates less on the minds of the Algonkians at Roanoke in an actual colonial setting than as a trope within colonial discourse by which the colonial power demonstrates its cultural superiority to itself." Gesa Mackenthun, *Metaphors of Dispossession: American Beginnings and the Translation of Empire, 1492-1637* (Norman: U of Oklahoma Press, 1997) 150–151.

15. Chrisman, 47.

16. Quoted in Dennis Butts's introduction to H. Rider Haggard, *King Solomon's Mines* (1885), ed. Dennis Butts (Oxford: Oxford U Press, 1989) vii. Hereafter cited in the text as *KSM.*

17. Butts, *KSM* xviii.

18. The implications of this interlinkage of Sir Henry and Ignosi are significant, as Ignosi is "Anglicized" in its course, while the 'Africanization' of Sir Henry is less emphasized. Eventually both are decontextualized by way of exotic associations, as the very first description of Sir Henry exemplifies: "I never saw a finer-looking man, and somehow he reminded me of an ancient Dane. Not that I know much of ancient Danes, though I remember once seeing a picture of some of those gentry, who, I take it, were a kind of white Zulus" (*KSM* 11). Later on, Ignosi's light skin and European ("Grecian") features are emphasized as testifying to the same noble tradition, the "white Zuluism."

19. These objects may be trite, but they are still clearly different from the trinkets of yore, which had no use value whatsoever to the colonizers. It is precisely the long-established ordinariness of civilization, and its intricate interior distinctions, that gains focal importance here.

20. Taussig, *Mimesis,* 198.

21. Pierre Bourdieu, "Outline of a Sociological Theory of Art Perception" (1968), in *The Field of Cultural Production: Essays on Art and Literature,* ed. Randal Johnson (New York: Columbia U Press, 1993) 217–237, 234.

22. Laura Chrisman has noted that Gagool occupies "the sites both of perverter and preserver of African custom, as epitome and aberration." Due to the splitting of Africanist images in this novel it is never clear what precisely is made out as "genuinely" African—Ignosi's noble savagery or Gagool's perverted rites: "Gagool's knowledge is essential but of necessity evil; it matches imperialism's own, in this text exposing imperialism as the conscious process it claims not to be. . . . Gagool may . . . be seen as a product of imperial discourse's own bad faith. She is its bad mirror, engendered by the conflicting desires, fears and self-knowledges that imperialism cannot acknowledge to itself." Chrisman, 53.

23. Although explicitly denounced as "evil" and perverted, African magic does very well have fascinating connotations in this novel. As Patrick Brantlinger has shown with respect to Haggard and other imperialist writers, magical and fantastic plotlines were often enacted in close analogy and open reference to traditions of the gothic, so that horror was intricately tied up with pleasure. Patrick Brantlinger, *Rule of Darkness: British Literature and Imperialism, 1830–1914* (Ithaca: Cornell U Press, 1988) 227–253.

24. Indeed, the isolation of the African country seems to comply with native needs and customs, most notably the practice of commemorating in silence: "your names . . . shall be as the names of dead kings, and he who speaks them shall die. So shall your memory be preserved in the land for ever" (*KSM* 307), declares Ignosi upon his visitors' leave-taking. By dint of this insight, the decision to cut the Kukuana off from contact, change, and transformation seems not only justified from a European point of view but moreover in accordance with an African tradition of thought that fosters seclusion, cherishes isolation, and totalizes silence.

25. Kenneth Cameron has delineated the changing themes and plotlines of the Hollywood adventures drawing on Haggard. Cf. *Africa on Film: Beyond Black and White* (New York: Continuum, 1994) 17–32, 167–169.

26. *King Solomon's Mines,* dir. J. Lee Thompson, with Richard Chamberlain, Sharon Stone, and Ken Gampu, Golan-Globus Production, 1985.

27. Cf. Gina Marchetti's delineation of the action adventure hero in terms of a mediator between "the domain of the villain and the everyday world of the

ordinary person." Marchetti, 194. On this logic see also Yvonne Tasker, *Spectacular Bodies: Gender, Genre, and the Action Cinema* (London: Routledge, 1993).

28. In a curious inversion Haggard of course took back this declaration the moment he wrote it down, continuing the quoted passage: "—except Foulata. Stop, though! there is Gagaoola, if she was a woman and not a fiend" (*KSM* 9). Sandra M. Gilbert and Susan Gubar have commented upon the interlinkage of the "female" and the "native" in Haggard's novels by dint of which "any of the 'dark' colonized places on the globe, inhered in what seemed to be a subliminal conspiracy between 'strange' races and the (eternal) feminine." *No Man's Land: The Place of the Woman Writer in the Twentieth Century*, vol. 2 (New Haven: Yale U Press, 1989) 39–40. As the passage quoted above shows, however, this binary distinction of the feminine/native and masculine/European does not invariably run along the same lines, as the ideological ascriptions and affiliations constantly change. Cf. Laura Chrisman's critique of Gilbert/Gubar and Gayatri Spivak: Chrisman, 41–49.

29. For a survey of the filmic action adventure genre and its themes cf. Taves; and Georg Seeßlen, *Abenteuer: Geschichte und Mythologie des Abenteuerfilms* (Marburg: Schüren, 1996).

30. Michael Rogin, "'Make My Day!' Spectacle as Amnesia in Imperial Politics," in *Cultures of United States Imperialism* 499–534, 521.

31. *Allan Quatermain and the Lost City of Gold*, dir. Gary Nelson, with Richard Chamberlain, Sharon Stone, and James Earl Jones, Golan-Globus Production, 1986.

32. *Live and Let Die*, dir. Guy Hamilton, with Roger Moore, Jane Seymour, and Yaphet Kotto, Eon Productions, 1973.

33. Stephen Heath, "The Cinematic Apparatus: Technology as Historical and Cultural Form," in *The Cinematic Apparatus*, ed. Teresa de Lauretis and Stephen Heath (Houndsmills: Macmillan Press, 1980) 1–13, 6.

34. Edward Buscombe, "Sound and Color" (1977) in *Movies and Methods* 83–92, 91.

35. Thomas Elsaesser and Michael Wedel, "The Hollow Heart of Hollywood: *Apocalypse Now* and the New Sound Space," in *Conrad on Film*, ed. Gene M. Moore (Cambridge: Cambridge U Press, 1997) 151–175, 154.

36. *The Jewel of the Nile*, dir. Lewis Teague, with Michael Douglas and Kathleen Turner, Twentieth Century Fox, 1985.

37. *Ishtar*, dir. Elaine May, with Dustin Hoffman, Warren Beatty, and Isabelle Adjani, Columbia, 1987.

38. Anthony Schirato, "Comic Politics and Politics of the Comic: Walter Abish's *Alphabetical Africa*," *Critique* 33:2 (Winter 1992) 133–144, 134. On Abish's text and its enactment of cultural contact see also Klaus J. Milich, "Lektüre der fremden Zeichen: Walter Abishs Literarisierung der Wahrnehmung," *Amerikastudien* 38:2 (1993) 181–202.

39. Walter Abish, *Alphabetical Africa*, 2. Hereafter cited in the text as *AA*.

40. John Edgar Wideman, *The Cattle Killing* (Boston: Houghton Mifflin, 1996) 146. Hereafter cited in the text as *CK*.

2. MONKEY BUSINESS: OF APE-MEN AND MAN-APES, PP. 48–75

1. Bhabha, 6.

2. My reading of *Tarzan of the Apes* thus clearly differs from Marianna

Torgovnick's, who understood these textual disruptions as ideologically subversive. Yet, as Gail Bederman's contextualizing analysis of Burroughs's novel shows, what has subversive implications in the 1980s need not necessarily cause subversion in the 1910s. Cf. Marianna Torgovnick, *Gone Primitive: Savage Intellects, Modern Lives* (Chicago: U of Chicago Press, 1990) 42–72; and Gail Bederman, *Manliness and Civilization: A Cultural History of Gender and Race in the United States, 1881-1917* (Chicago: U of Chicago Press, 1995) 217–239.

3. Of course, the English system of colonialism relied no less upon imperialist practices than American politics around the turn of the century. Differentiating between "colonialist" and "American imperialist" ideologies in the following, I endorse Edward Said's definition of the term "colonialism" as a specific version of imperialist rule. Modern American imperialism, by contrast, demarcates another instance of the project of international expansion, unfolding along different ideological lines. Cf. Said, *Culture and Imperialism;* Parry, "Narrating Imperialism"; and for a discussion of American imperialism, among others, David F. Healy, *US Expansionism: The Imperialist Urge in the 1890s* (Madison: U of Wisconsin Press, 1970); Hans-Ulrich Wehler, *Der Aufstieg des amerikanischen Imperialismus zur Entwicklung des Imperium Americanum, 1865-1900* (Göttingen: Vandenhoeck & Ruprecht, 1974); George Liska, *Career of Empire: America and Imperial Expansion over Land and Sea* (Baltimore: Johns Hopkins U Press, 1978); Richard Drinnon, *Facing West: The Metaphysics of Indian-Hating and Empire-Building, 1980* (Norman: University of Oklahoma Press, 1997); and the contributions in *Cultures of United States Imperialism.*

4. For the shifts and reconceptualizations of cultural contact both in- and outside the United States in the early twentieth century, see among many others T. J. Jackson Lears, *No Place of Grace: Antimodernism and the Transformation of American Culture, 1880-1920* (New York: Pantheon, 1981); John Higham, *Send These to Me: Immigrants in Urban America* (Baltimore: Johns Hopkins U Press, 1984); Werner Sollors, *Beyond Ethnicity: Consent and Descent in American Culture* (New York: Oxford U Press, 1986); Paul Boyer, *Urban Masses and Moral Order in America, 1820-1920* (Cambridge, Mass.: Harvard U Press, 1987); and *Ethnic Cultures in the 1920s in North America*, ed. Wolfgang Binder (Frankfurt/Main: Peter Lang, 1993). On the interrelation of imperialist and anti–imperialist rhetorics in terms of conceptualizing the other see Drinnon, 307–351.

5. Cf. Paulo Medeiros, "Simian Narratives at the Intersection of Science and Literature," *Modern Language Studies* 23:2 (1993) 59–73.

6. Donna Haraway, *Primate Visions: Gender, Race, and Nature in the World of Modern Science* (New York: Routledge, 1989) 11.

7. Edgar Rice Burroughs, *Tarzan of the Apes* (1914), ed. G. Vidal (New York: Signet, 1990) 49. Hereafter cited in the text as *TA*.

8. For a discussion of *Tarzan of the Apes* within the context of twentieth-century American imperialist politics see Cheyfitz, 3–21. Catherine Yurca has criticized Cheyfitz's reading of *Tarzan* along the lines of a project of imperial expansion, pulling into view instead the context of early-twentieth-century debates around immigration and migration in the big cities: "Tarzan is more interested in keeping his black neighbors at bay than in mastering them, and thus he is hardly driven here by the imperialist fantasy of controlling Africa. Uncompromising in its support for the geographic separation of the races, and viewing their integration as a particular threat to the sanctity of the Anglo-Saxon home, *Tarzan of the Apes* begins to look like a novel of white flight rather than white rule." "Tarzan,

Lord of the Suburbs," *Modern Language Quarterly* 57:3 (Sept. 1996) 479–504. While I find Yurca's reading of the novel brilliant, I do think that she overlooks the fact that twentieth-century imperialism often enough combined the idea of "necessary" intervention with the paranoiac imagery of too close contact. In *Tarzan of the Apes* both contradictory impulses find expression.

9. On the concept of civilization in the late nineteenth and early twentieth centuries, and its implementation in *Tarzan of the Apes*, see Bederman.

10. Bederman sees these figures as the epitome of Victorian "civilized manliness," a concept that *Tarzan* sets out to overcome in line with changed cultural conceptions of gender and race. The intellectuals' "manliness," Bederman argues, is consequently confronted with Tarzan's "perfect masculinity"—a much less refined (or "civilized") notion of manhood. Bederman, 226.

11. Letter of January 28, 1919, to Piny P. Craft of Monopol Pictures, N.Y., quoted in Irwin Porges, *Edgar Rice Burroughs: The Man Who Created Tarzan* (Provo: Brigham & Young U Press, 1975) 315–316.

12. Richard Dyer, "The White Man's Muscles," in *White* (London: Routledge, 1997) 145–183, 164. On this pattern of thought see also Antony Easthope, *What a Man's Gotta Do: The Masculine Myth in Popular Culture,* 1986 (Boston: Unwyn Hyman, 1990) 35–58; Bill Brown, "Science Fiction, the World's Fair, and the Prosthetics of Empire," in *Cultures of United States Imperialism* 129–163, 139; and Michael S. Kimmel, "Consuming Manhood: The Feminization of American Culture and the Recreation of the Male Body, 1832–1920," in *The Male Body: Features, Destinies, Exposures,* ed. Laurence Goldstein (Ann Arbor: U of Michigan Press, 1994) 12–42.

13. Lears, 110.

14. Walt Morton, "Tracking the Sign of Tarzan: Trans-Media Representations of a Pop-Cultural Icon," in *You Tarzan: Masculinity, Movies, and Men,* ed. Pat Kirkham and Janet Thumim (London: Lawrence & Wishart, 1993) 106–125, 113.

15. Cf. Yurca. For a more extensive discussion of the interrelation of the terminology of heredity and training with regard to a reconceptualization of race in the nineteenth century see my "'Ther's somethin' in blood after all': Late Nineteenth-Century Fiction and the Rhetoric of Race," *Real: Yearbook of Research in English and American Literature* 11 (1995) 119–138.

16. Cheyfitz, 13.

17. Walter Benn Michaels, *Our America* (Durham: Duke U Press, 1995) 13.

18. Michaels delineated this logic in view of the construct of "Navajo" identity, which actually lends itself much more easily to this logic of "acting out" than the categories of whiteness and masculinity, their similar artificiality notwithstanding. Cf. Michaels, 125. *Tarzan,* just like other imperial adventure fiction of the day, could consequently be seen as the attempt to define white male identity along the lines of ethnicity—in terms of practice, training, and blood.

19. *Greystoke: The Legend of Tarzan, Lord of the Apes,* dir. Hugh Hudson, with Christopher Lambert, Ian Holm, and Andie McDowell, Warner Bros., 1984.

20. Torgovnick, *Gone Primitive,* 71.

21. Quoted in John Tibbetts, "A New Screen Tarzan," *Films in Review* 35:6 (June/July 1984) 360–364, 360.

22. Ed Guerrero has phrased the term "buddy formula" to pinpoint a classical constellation of white hero and black supportive sidekick in Hollywood movies of the 1980s and 90s. I will discuss this formula and its significance for other

than action adventure films at a later point in this book; for the moment suffice it
to say that the black partner of the buddy constellation traditionally figures as the
"physical" component in the partnership, while his white companion represents
the "brain"—a differentiation that inadvertently shines up when Greystoke takes
care of D'Arnot to profit from his superior knowledge in turn. Cf. Ed Guerrero,
Framing Blackness: The African American Image in Film (Philadelphia: Temple U
Press, 1993).

23. Of course, as Catherine Yurca pointed out, Burroughs's Tarzan, too, is a
victim figure—"Tarzan's enabling myth of settlement posits the white European
as the persecuted victim of imperial aggression, a fantasy of reverse colonization
that operates within a distinctively twentieth-century American context." Yurca,
480. But just as clearly, Burroughs's critique of imperialism is exclusively directed
at the Africans, simultaneously exculpating the European and the American enterprise of expansion. Hudson's film, by contrast, victimizes Tarzan by Africaniz-
ing him on the sly.

24. For broader reflections on the classical museum of natural history and its
techniques of representing Africa see Donna Haraway's reflections on the African
Hall in the American Museum of Natural History and its designer Carl Akeley in
her *Primate Visions,* Annie E. Coombes's *Reinventing Africa,* and Alison Griffiths, "'Journeys for Those Who Can Not Travel': Promenade Cinema and the
Museum Life Group," *Wide Angle* 18:3 (1996) 53–84.

25. For an extensive reflection on the differentiation between Africa and Europe in *Greystoke* see Griselda Pollock, "Empire, Identity, and Place: Masculinities in *Greystoke: The Legend of Tarzan,*" in *Me Jane: Masculinity, Movies, and
Women.* ed. Pat Kirkham and Janet Thumin (New York: St. Martin's Press, 1995)
128–147.

26. Bhabha, 86, 92.

27. Maurice Berger, Brian Wallis, and Simon Watson, "Introduction," in *Constructing Masculinity,* ed. M. B., B. W., and S. W. (New York: Routledge, 1995) 2.

28. Fredric Jameson, "The Cultural Logic of Late Capitalism," in *Postmodernism* 20–21.

29. *Tarzan,* dir. Kevin Lima and Chris Buck, art dir. Daniel St. Pierre, ed.
Gregory Perler, Tarzan character animator Glen Keane, with the voices of Tony
Goldwyn, Minnie Driver, and Glenn Close, Walt Disney Pictures, 1999.

30. Marie Woolf, "Me Tarzan, You Jane, We PC: Disney Sanitizes Lord of the
Jungle's Dark Continent Adventures," *The Guardian* (Nov. 12, 1995) 4.

31. Janet Maslin, "'Tarzan': Monkey Business—Rewriting the Jungle Book,"
New York Times (June 18, 1999).

32. Critics cited in "Tarzan without Africans," *St. Louis Post* (June 28, 1999)
D16, one of the few reviews to point out the exclusionary practices at work in the
film.

33. Edward Rothstein, "From Darwinian to Disneyesque. In Tarzan's Evolution, a New Theory: The Survival of Nearly Everything." *New York Times* (July
15, 1999) E1, E8, E8.

34. Jon Wiener, "Tall Tales and True," *The Nation* (Jan. 31, 1994) 134.

35. If this implementation of American identity in the African jungle is more
subtle than similar moves in earlier Disney projects, it still calls to mind the use
of language in a film like *Aladdin,* where the bad guys have an Arab accent
while Aladdin speaks perfect American English. "Racism in Disney's animated
films does not simply appear in negative imagery," Henry A. Giroux pointed out

consequently: "it is also reproduced through racially coded language and accents." *Fugitive Cultures: Race, Violence, and Youth* (New York: Routledge, 1996) 106.

36. Andrew Ross, "The Great White Dude," in *Constructing Masculinity* 167–175, 170.

37. Episode 14, "Tarzan and the Unwelcome Guest," 1991.

38. Gilles Deleuze, "Control and Becoming" (conversation with Toni Negri, 1990), in *Negotiations, 1972-1990,* tr. Martin Joughin (New York: Columbia U Press, 1995) 169–176, 175.

39. Holert and Terkessidis, 15—my translation.

40. De Certeau, 7.

41. *Congo,* dir. Frank Marshall, with Laura Linney, Dylan Walsh, and Ernie Hudson, Paramount, 1995.

42. Haraway, *Primate Visions,* 140.

43. Jonathan Crary, "Eclipse of the Spectacle," in *Art After Modernism: Rethinking Representation,* ed. Brian Wallis (Boston: The New Museum of Contemporary Art, 1984) 283–294, 293.

44. Michel Serres, *The Parasite,* tr. Lawrence R. Schehr (Baltimore: Johns Hopkins U Press, 1982) 5.

45. Haraway, *Primate Visions,* 135.

46. Deleuze, "Control and Becoming," 174.

3. BEING GAME: THE WHITE HUNTER AND THE CRISIS OF
    MASCULINITY, PP. 76–120

1. Bederman, 176. About this logic of being "like the Indians" and yet "superior to them" see also Richard Slotkin's seminal *Regeneration through Violence. The Mythology of the American Frontier, 1600-1860,* 1973 (New York: HarperPerennial, 1996).

2. Paul Smith, "Introduction," in *New Essays on Hemingway's Short Fiction,* ed. Paul Smith (Cambridge: Cambridge U Press, 1998) 1–18, 11.

3. Morrison, *Playing in the Dark,* 88–89.

4. Cawelti, 19.

5. Catherine McGehee Kenney, *Thurber's Anatomy of Confusion* (Hamden: Archon Books, 1984) 49. Cf. James Thurber, "The Secret Life of Walter Mitty" (1939), in *The Thurber Carnival* (New York: Harper & Brothers, 1945) 47–51.

6. Berger, Wallis, and Watson, 3.

7. Ross, "The Great White Dude," 172.

8. Haraway, *Primate Visions,* 53.

9. Peter Messent, "Geographies, Fictional and Non-fictional: America, Spain, Africa," in *Ernest Hemingway* (New York: St. Martin's, 1992) 124–163, 148.

10. Ernest Hemingway, "The Short Happy Life of Francis Macomber" (1936), in *The Short Stories* (New York: Simon & Shuster, 1995) 3–37, 4. Hereafter cited in the text as "M."

11. Hugh Kenner, *A Homemade World: The American Modernist Writers* (New York: Alfred A. Knopf, 1975) 136.

12. Ernest Hemingway, *Green Hills of Africa,* 1935 (New York: Simon & Schuster, 1996) 116.

13. Kenner, 138. Hence I disagree with Nina Baym's reading of the story in

terms of a critique of brutality and violence. Macomber's development, for one, is clearly shown to depend on the very cruelty and corporeality of hunting so that these qualities seem indispensable, vital to the entire project of "coming of age." Cf. Nina Baym, "'Actually, I Felt Sorry for the Lion,'" in *New Critical Approaches to the Short Stories of Ernest Hemingway,* ed. Jackson J. Benson (Durham: Duke U Press, 1990) 112–120.

14. Michaels, 74.

15. Hubert Zapf has pointed out the daydreamlike quality not only of this passage but of Macomber's entire development from coward to "man." However, he reads Macomber's death not as the culmination of this process but at its violent disruption. Cf. Hubert Zapf, "Reflection vs. Daydream: Two Types of the Implied Reader in Hemingway's Fiction," in *New Critical Approaches to the Short Stories of Ernest Hemingway,* 96–111.

16. Hemingway, *Green Hills,* 16.

17. On Hemingway's representation of Africans see also Debra A. Moddelmog, "Re-Placing Africa in 'The Snows of Kilimanjaro': The Intersecting Economies of Capitalist-Imperialism and Hemingway's Biography," in *New Essays on Hemingway's Short Fiction* 111–136.

18. *White Hunter, Black Heart,* dir. Clint Eastwood, with Clint Eastwood, Jeff Fahey, and George Dzundza, Warner Bros., 1990.

19. About analogies and allusions to Huston's films see Robert Benayoun, "Clint et John: une saison infernale (*Chasseur blanc, coeur noir*)," *Positif* 351 (Mar. 1990) 2–4.

20. Laurence F. Knapp, *Directed by Clint Eastwood* (Jefferson: McFarland, 1996) 152.

21. Verena Lueken, "Weißer Jäger, schwarzes Herz," *epd Film* 7:6 (June 1990) 32.

22. Susan Jeffords, *Hard Bodies: Hollywood Masculinity in the Reagan Era* (New Brunswick: Rutgers U Press, 1994) 186.

23. Richard Combs, "Do the Wrong Thing: *White Hunter, Black Heart,*" *Sight & Sound* 59:4 (Autumn 1990) 278–279.

24. Paul Smith has described a similar logic in Clint Eastwood's later films, which, much more than his early work, emphasize a body "hysterically acting out": so that role playing becomes increasingly significant "for the way in which the male body appears . . . as excessive—or, another way of reading it, as defective in relation to the image to which is aspires at the narrative's end." Paul Smith, "Eastwood Bound," in *Constructing Masculinity* 77–97, 94.

25. Knapp, 152, 154.

26. Metz, *The Imaginary Signifier,* 135–137.

27. Eric Lott, "White Like Me: Racial Cross-Dressing and the Construction of American Whiteness," in *Cultures of United States Imperialism* 474–495, 491.

28. Judith Butler, *Gender Trouble: Feminism and the Subversion of Identity* (New York: Routledge, 1990) 139.

29. Abigail Solomon-Godeau, "Photography after Art-Photography," in *Art after Modernism* 75–85, 76.

30. Roland Barthes, *Camera Lucida: Reflections on Photography* (1980), tr. Richard Howard (New York: Hill and Wang, 1997) 80, 76.

31. Cf. Leni Riefenstahl, *The Last of the Nuba* (New York: Harper & Row, 1974).

32. Guy Trebay, "*Tribe,*" *Village Voice Literary Supplement* (July/Aug. 1998) 7.

33. Barthes, *Camera Lucida,* 9.
34. Owen Edwards, "The Toast of Society Photographs the Death of a World: Peter Beard, Photographer," *Village Voice* (Dec. 29, 1975) 18–19.
35. Peter Beard, "Introduction," in *The End of the Game: The Last Word from Paradise* (New York: Doubleday, 1977) 19–21, 20–21.
36. Beard, *The End of the Game,* 21.
37. Barthes, *Camera Lucida,* 78–79.
38. Barthes, *Camera Lucida,* 82.
39. Introduction to "Oltre la fine del mondo," Italian exhibition in 1997.
40. Cf. David Harvey, "What's Green and Makes the Environment Go Round?" in *The Cultures of Globalization* 327–356, 341.
41. Press release, "Vistavision: Landscape of Desire," Pat Hearn Gallery, 1991.
42. Renée Green, "Various Identities" (interview), in *World Tour* (exhibition catalogue), ed. Russell Ferguson (Los Angeles: Museum of Contemporary Art, 1994) 52–61, 55.
43. Rogin, "'Make My Day!'" 521.
44. *The Young Indiana Jones Chronicles,* dir. Dick Maas, with Corey Carrier, Sean Patrick Flanery, and George Hall, Lucasfilms, 30 episodes, 1992.
45. While the series carries the mindframe of the present into a past that is pure pastiche, it purports, conversely, to enlighten the present via the past: each episode has a frame, set in the present, where the aged Indiana (George Hall) confronts a case of cultural or ideological misunderstanding and then relates his experiences of the past in order to settle the problem, thus exemplarily performing time and again the postmodern suspension of historical depth and geographical distance, collapsing present and past, the familiar and the far-away.
46. T. Coraghessan Boyle, "Big Game," in *Without a Hero* (Harmondsworth: Penguin, 1994) 10. Hereafter cited in the text as "BG."
47. Michael Walker, "Boyle's 'Greasy Lake' and the Moral Failure of Postmodernism," *Studies in Short Fiction* 31 (1994) 247–255, 52–53.
48. In fact, the tendency of cynical distantiation becomes even more obvious in Boyle's recent work (most notably *The Tortilla Curtain*), as he comes to adopt increasingly more traditional narrative techniques, moving away from the more experimental "postmodern" style of his early writing, as evinced in *Water Music* (1981) and *World's End* (1987). Yet even this early work stood in stark contrast to the work of postmodern writers like Thomas Pynchon or Don DeLillo, which—while admittedly lacking an overarching moral horizon—was and is deeply inflected with ethical questions and concerns. For a reading of postmodern literature in terms of moral commitment and therapeutic engagement see Martin Klepper, *Pynchon, Auster, DeLillo: Die amerikanische Postmoderne zwischen Spiel und Dekonstruktion* (Frankfurt/Main: Campus, 1996).
49. Thus Boyle seems to come closer to the second type of Hemingway's writing, characterized by Hubert Zapf as not so much emphatic but rather reflective. But even in *The Sun Also Rises,* where "an almost pathological distance from, and indifference of the narrator toward, the narrated world" is to be noted, "the focus of the reader is all the more turned away ('re-flected') from the reported facts toward an inner, subjective world beneath the external surface world of appearances." Cf. Zapf, 100. As we have seen, there is nothing underneath "the external surface world of appearances" in Boyle's writing.
50. Theo D'haen, "The Return of History and the Minorization of New

York: T. Coraghessan Boyle and Richard Russo," *Revue française d'études américaines* 17:62 (Nov. 1994) 393–403, 397.

51. Steve Engelhart (text), Neil Yokes and Jay Geldhof (graphics), et al., *Ape Fear, Congorilla* 4 (New York: DC Comics, 1992). Hereafter cited in the text as *AF*. Pagination assigned.

52. Jeffords, 191.

53. *The Ghost and the Darkness,* dir. Stephen Hopkins, with Michael Douglas, Val Kilmer, and John Kani, Paramount, 1996.

54. Lee Clark Mitchell, *Westerns: Making the Man in Fiction and Film* (Chicago: U of Chicago Press, 1996) 57–93, 121–149.

55. Metz, 134.

56. Irvine Welsh, *Marabou Stork Nightmares* (London: Jonathan Cape, 1995) 4, hereafter cited in the text as *MSN*.

57. Rowena Chapman and Jonathan Rutherford, "The Forward March of Man Halted," quoted in Fred Pfeil, *White Guys: Studies in Postmodern Domination and Difference* (London: Verso, 1995) ix.

4. COLONIAL LADIES, GLOBAL GIRLS, PP. 121–159

1. Not only does Mrs. Macomber make bad use of the gun; by shooting from the car she violates one of the basic honor codes of the hunt—"You don't shoot them from cars" ("M" 14), Wilson had admonished Macomber earlier on.

2. *Out of Africa,* dir. Sydney Pollack, with Meryl Streep and Robert Redford, Universal Pictures, 1985.

3. Isak Dinesen, *Out of Africa,* 1938 (New York: Vintage Books, 1989) 224, hereafter cited in the text as *OA*.

4. Sidonie Smith, "The Other Woman and the Racial Politics of Gender: Isak Dinesen and Beryl Markham in Kenya," in *De/colonizing the Subject: The Politics of Gender in Women's Autobiography,* ed. S. S. and Julia Watson (Minneapolis: U of Minnesota Press, 1992) 410–435, 425.

5. Significantly enough, Dinesen's letters relate the episode in a dramatically different version, as Judith Lee has pointed out. For a closer reflection on Dinesen's logic of evasion or "masking," her ongoing reenactment of her own life, see Judith Lee, "The Mask of Form in *Out of Africa*" (1985), in *Isak Dinesen: Critical Views,* ed. Olga Anastasia Pelensky (Athens: Ohio U Press, 1993) 266–282, 276.

6. Mills, 63.

7. For a more detailed reflection on the ideological function of style cf. Dick Hebdige, *Subculture: The Meaning of Style* (London: Methuen, 1979); Kaja Silverman, "Fragments of a Fashionable Discourse," in *Studies in Entertainment,* ed. Tania Modleski (Bloomington: Indiana U Press, 1986) 139–152; McKenzie Wark, "Fashion as a Culture Industry," in *No Sweat: Fashion, Free Trade, and the Rights of Garment Workers,* ed. Andrew Ross (New York: Verso, 1997) 227–248; and Andrew Ross, "Tribalism in Effect," *On Fashion,* ed. Shari Benstock and Susanne Ferriss (New Brunswick: Rutgers U Press, 1994) 284–300.

8. I will differentiate in the following between "Isak Dinesen" as the author of *Out of Africa* and Karen Blixen as its protagonist.

9. McClintock, *Imperial Leather.*

10. Abdul R. JanMohamed, "Isak Dinesen: The Generation of Mythic Consciousness," in *Manichean Aesthetics: The Politics of Literature in Colonial Africa* (Amherst: U of Massachusetts Press, 1983) 49–77, 51.

11. JanMohamed, 57.

12. Lucien Dällenbach has reflected extensively on the logic of the *mise en abyme*. For my purposes, it is most significant that Dällenbach defines the *mise en abyme* not only as a "modalité de la *réflexion*" but also as modality of "distraction"—pointing to its capacity to *invert* the logic of the dominant order it figures forth: "De manière très générale, on peut donc conclure que toute mise en abyme inverse le fonctionnement qui l'utilise: réagissant aux dispositions prises par le contexte, elle assure au récit une espèce d'auto-réglage." Lucien Dällenbach, *Le récit spéculaire: Essai sur la mise en abyme* (Paris: Édition du Seuil, 1977) 16, 94.

13. Judith Lee has traced the complicated subtext of this passage, Dinesen's effort to come to positive terms with a setup inherently foreign to her: "I am instinctively against it all to such an extent that I have to give up any idea of getting much out of it from the outset," she writes in a letter. Of course, her account in *Out of Africa* is just that—the effort to "get something out of it." Cf. Lee, 274–275.

14. Lee, 270, 275–276.

15. Paul de Man, "Autobiography as De-facement," *Modern Language Notes* 94:5 (Dec. 1979) 919–930, 922.

16. Renato Rosaldo, "Imperialist Nostalgia," *Culture and Truth: The Remaking of Social Analysis*, 1989 (Boston: Beacon Press, 1993) 68–87,68.

17. Jameson, *Postmodernism*, 19.

18. Laura Kipnis, "'The Phantom Twitchings of an Amputated Limb': Sexual Spectacle in the Post-colonial Epic." *Wide Angle* 11:4 (Oct. 1989) 42–51, 43.

19. Tasker, *Spectacular Bodies*, 18–19.

20. Shohat and Stam, 166. Cf. also Laura Kipnis, who comes to a similar conclusion when she claims that the film's "liberal sentiments are completely dependent on [its] misogyny," "that the woman is constantly undercut, ridiculed, instructed and put in her place by a white male anachronistic fount of postcolonial enlightenment." Kipnis, 45.

21. Cf. Laura Mulvey, *Visual Order and Other Pleasures* (London: Macmillan, 1989).

22. Yvonne Tasker, *Working Girls: Gender and Sexuality in Popular Cinema* (London: Routledge, 1998) 144. See also Mary Anne Doane, *Femmes Fatales: Feminism, Film Theory, Psychoanalysis* (London: Routledge, 1991).

23. Judith Williamson, "Woman Is an Island: Femininity and Colonization," *Studies in Entertainment: Critical Approaches to Mass Culture*, ed. Tania Modleski (Bloomington: Indiana U Press, 1986) 99–115, 115.

24. *The English Patient*, dir. Anthony Minghella, with Kristin Scott-Thomas, Ralph Fiennes, Juliette Binoche, and Willem Dafoe, Tiger Moth Productions, 1996.

25. Scott-Thomas curiously and certainly unintentionally pinned down this function of fashion when she stressed in an interview on the costumes in the film, headlined "Fashion is ridiculous and beneath my dignity," that she thinks herself "much more exciting in my dirty desert gear in *The English Patient* than in the white seduction dress" ("Mode ist lächerlich und unter meiner Würde," *SZ Magazin* 12 (Mar. 21, 1997) 90–91—my translation). The point is not, however, that the one is fashion and the other is not. The point is that the one (the white dress)

demarcates the norm, and the other (the dirty desert gear) its exotic transgression in the wilderness. Of course, the latter is more exciting in a film that yokes together exoticism and eroticism, declaring the white lady in the dark continent the bearer of both.

26. Ioan Davies, "Negotiating African Culture: Toward a Decolonization of the Fetish," in *The Cultures of Globalization* 125–145, 141.

27. Report of the Royal Commission on Agriculture, 1867. Quoted in McClintock, *Imperial Leather*, 117–118.

28. Seeßlen, 190—my translation.

29. *White Mischief,* dir. Michael Radford, with Greta Scacchi and Charles Dance, White Umbrella Film, 1987.

30. Mills, 22.

31. Marjorie Garber, "The Chic of Araby," in *Vested Interests: Cross-Dressing & Cultural Anxiety,* 1992 (New York: Routledge, 1997) 304–352, 309, 311.

32. Miriam Hansen, "The Return of Babylon: Valentino and Female Spectatorship," in *Babel and Babylon: Spectatorship in American Silent Film* (Cambridge, Mass.: Harvard U Press, 1991) 243–294, 254, 262.

33. *The Sheltering Sky,* dir. Bernardo Bertolucci, with John Malkovich, Debra Winger, Campbell Scott, and Eric Vu-An, Warner Bros., 1990.

34. Vincent Canby, "Toward the Heart of the Sahara: Chic but Lost in Its Vastness," *New York Times* (Dec. 12, 1990) C15.

35. Garber, 11, 13.

36. Garber, 335.

37. Lidia Curti has outlined an alternative set of texts, confronting themselves to Bertolucci's and Bowles's *Sheltering Sky* and these artists' pessimistic reading of female self-fashioning in the wilderness. In the works of Jane Bowles, who figured as a model for Kit in Paul Bowles's book, Curti traces the same notion of self-loss, yet with significantly different implications, as she points out with regard to the novel *Two Serious Ladies:* "Paradoxically [the protagonist] discovers that salvation, her only interest in life, means going to pieces and leads to the undoing and loss of the self. It seems to be at one with its opposite, perdition." Lidia Curti, "Alterity and the Female Traveller: Jane Bowles," in *Female Stories, Female Bodies: Narrative, Identity, and Representation* (New York: New York U Press, 1998) 133–154, 152.

38. Rogin, "'Make My Day!'" 499.

39. Amy M. Spindler, "Taking Stereotyping to a New Level in Fashion," *New York Times* (June 3, 1997) A:21.

40. Cf. Spindler. For a more extensive reflection on this logic of the mix see Tom Holert, "Mischkalkulationen und Gesichter der Zukunft: Noah Gabriel Becker, Tiger Woods, ein 'bi-rassischer' Androgyn und das 'vibe thing,'" in *Globalkolorit* 25–39.

41. Robin Givhan, "The Problem with Ugly Chic," in *No Sweat* 263–274, 273.

42. Lisa Feldmann, "Editorial," *Cosmopolitan* 6 (June 1996) 10—my translation. Like most European versions of established fashion magazines, the German edition of *Cosmopolitan* takes a much more radical stance, both in view of defining its cultural function and in view of introducing new representational techniques, contexts, and provocative links, than its American equivalent. About the difference between the European and the American fashion market cf. Amy M. Spindler, "The Splash Heard round the World," *New York Times* (Sept. 13, 1998) sec. 9, 1, and about the decline of feminist and political rhetoric in American

fashion magazines Alex Kuczynski, "Enough about Feminism: Should I Wear Lipstick?" *New York Times* (Mar. 28, 1999) sec. WK, 4.

43. For a closer reflection upon this section and its enactment of feminism and globalization see my "Cosmo-Politisch: Feminismus, Globalisierung, und Modemagazine in den Neunzigern," in *Globalkolorit* 163–179.

44 "Cosmos Orient—Reise ins Morgenland," *Cosmopolitan* 5 (May 1997) 120–148.

45. Of course, when it comes to North Africa, the repertory of Orientalism, as described by Edward Said, plays a central role for Africanist representation just as well, as we saw with respect to *Ishtar, The Sheltering Sky,* and the *Condé Nast* advertisement. The photography series' technique of interlacing Orientalist images and quotations out of *The English Patient,* a novel set in Africa, further epitomizes the interdependence between exoticist imageries of Africa and the Middle East.

46. *Gorillas in the Mist,* dir. Michael Apted, with Sigourney Weaver, John Omirah Miluwi, and Bryan Brown, Universal City Studios/Warner Bros., 1988.

47. Tania Modleski, "Cinema and the Dark Continent: Race and Gender in Popular Film," in *Feminism without Women. Culture and Criticism in a 'Postfeminist' Age* (New York: Routledge, 1991) 115–134, 123.

48. For an analysis of the figure of the "ape-lady" along the lines of long-standing tropes of colonial adventure fiction and exploration literature, cf. James Krasner, "'Ape Ladies' and Cultural Politics: Dian Fossey and Biruté Galdikas," in *Natural Eloquence: Women Reinscribe Science,* ed. Barbara T. Gates and Ann D. Shteir (Madison: U of Wisconsin Press, 1997) 237–251.

49. Modleski, "Cinema and the Dark Continent," 122.

50. Haraway, *Primate Visions,* 135, 154.

51. Haraway, *Primate Visions,* 182.

52. "Fashionable plot: When Italian socialite Kuki Gallmann (Basinger) heads to Africa to help save endangered species in the true-life tale, she leaves behind her Valentino gowns—they just don't work when there's elephant poop around. The budding preservationist nevertheless avoids becoming a blight in the landscape by wearing 'safari' fare from the Gap, Calvin Klein, DKNY, and Jigsaw (England's answer to Banana Republic)." "10 very fashionable films: A look at the upcoming movies that give fashion designers—from Banana Republic to Dolce & Gabbana—starring roles," *Movieline* (Sept. 1999) 84–86, 85.

53. Marianna Torgovnick, *Primitive Passions: Men, Women, and the Quest for Ecstasy* (New York: Knopf, 1996) 81.

54. Francesca Marciano, *Rules of the Wild* (New York: Pantheon, 1998) 115–116. Hereafter cited in the text as *RW*.

55. Kwame Anthony Appiah, "Cosmopolitan Patriots," in *Cosmopolitics* 91–114, 92.

56. Appiah, "Cosmopolitan Patriots," 91–92.

57. Amanda Anderson, "Cosmopolitanism, Universalism, and the Divided Legacy of Modernity," in *Cosmopoliticis* 265–289, 275.

58. Bruce Robbins, "Comparative Cosmopolitanisms," in *Cosmopolitics* 246–264, 253.

59. Appiah, "Cosmopolitan Patriots," 92.

60. Cf. Saskia Sassen, *The Global City: New York, London, Tokyo* (Princeton: Princeton U Press, 1991); Spivak, 312–421.

5. FREE TRADE? POSTCOLONIAL EMPIRES, GLOBAL
   CORPORATIONS, PP. 163–206

1. Adam Hochschild has pointed out the analogies between the Congo situation and regimes of power in other West African colonies and discussed the reasons for the international focus on the Belgian Congo rather than, say, the French Congo or Nigeria: Adam Hochschild, *King Leopold's Ghost* (Boston: Houghton Mifflin, 1998) 275–283.

2. See, apart from Hochschild's study, Neal Ascherson, *The King Incorporated: Leopold II in the Age of Trusts* (New York: Doubleday, 1964); and Georges-Henri Dumont, *Léopold II* (Paris: Fayard, 1990) 178–196.

3. Ascherson, 126.

4. Cf. Ascherson, 128–135; Dumont, 178–196.

5. Hochschild, 4.

6. Brantlinger, 256.

7. Quoted in Thomas Pakenham, *The Scramble for Africa: White Man's Conquest of the Dark Continent from 1876 to 1912* (New York: Avon Books, 1991) 241. See also Ascherson; Dumont, 178.

8. Said, *Culture and Imperialism,* 25.

9. Joseph Conrad, *Heart of Darkness,* 1902 (Harmondsworth: Penguin, 1973) 33. Hereafter cited in the text as *HD*.

10. Seen that way, Conrad's narrative attests once more to the popularity of adventure fiction. For a closer inspection of the genre conventions involved and rewritten cf. Andrea White, *Joseph Conrad and the Adventure Tradition: Constructing and Deconstructing the Imperial Subject* (Cambridge: Cambridge U Press, 1993); and Brantlinger, 255–274.

11. Benita Parry, "*Heart of Darkness,*" in *Conrad and Imperialism: Ideological Boundaries and Visionary Frontiers* (London: Macmillan, 1983) 20–39, 35. On the substitution of bonding see also Chris Bongie, "Exotic Nostalgia: Conrad and the New Imperialism," in *Macropolitics of Nineteenth-Century Literature: Nationalism, Exoticism, Imperialism,* ed. J. Arac and H. Ritvo (Durham: Duke U Press, 1991) 268–285; and Sarah Cole, "Conradian Alienation and Imperial Intimacy," *Modern Fiction Studies* 44:2 (Summer 1998) 251–281.

12. Parry, "*Heart of Darkness,*" 35.

13. Brantlinger, 262.

14. On this change of narrative formulas see Michael Levenson, "The Value of Facts in the *Heart of Darkness,*" *Nineteenth-Century Fiction* 40:3 (1985) 261–285; and Allon White, "Joseph Conrad and the Rhetoric of Enigma," in *The Uses of Obscurity: The Fiction of Early Modernism* (London: Routledge & Kegan Paul, 1981) 108–129.

15. Brantlinger, 262. On the representation of Africa and Africans, and the fact that anti–imperialism need not go together with antiracism, cf. Chinua Achebe, "An Image of Africa: Racism in Conrad's *Heart of Darkness,*" *The Massachusetts Review* 18 (1977) 782–794.

16. Said, *Culture and Imperialism,* 27.

17. Achebe, 784.

18. Parry, "*Heart of Darkness,*" 39, 38.

19. *Heart of Darkness,* dir. Nicolas Roeg, with Tim Roth, John Malkovich, and Isaach de Bankolé, Turner Network Television, 1994.

20. As I confine myself to Africanist fictions here, I will not go into an analysis of Coppola's film. For a close reading in view of Conrad's text and a postmodern context of spectacular action see Simon During, "Postmodernism or Postcolonialism Today," in *Postmodernism: A Reader,* ed. Thomas Docherty (New York: Columbia U Press, 1993) 448–462; E. N. Dorall, "Conrad and Coppola: Different Centers of Darkness," in *Joseph Conrad: Heart of Darkness,* ed. R. Kimbrough (New York: Norton, 1988) 303–311; Thomas Elsaesser and Michael Wedel, "The Hollow Heart of Hollywood: *Apocalypse Now* and the New Sound Space," and Seymour Chatman, "2½ Film Versions of *Heart of Darkness,*" both in *Conrad on Film* 151–175, 207–223.

21. Chatman, 219.

22. Chatman, 221.

23. Guerrero, 128.

24. Chatman, 218.

25. Christoph Decker has investigated at greater length various techniques of inscribing mnemomic practice into contemporary film, which "has been influenced by models of animated remembrance or the psychoanalytic notion of reinscribing a past that is in a state of constant change and subjected to interpretations." Christoph Decker, "Interrogations of Cinematic Norms: Avant-Garde Film, History, and Mnemonic Practices," *Amerikastudien* 43:1 (1998) 109–130, 119–120.

26. Chatman, 222.

27. Haselstein, "Stephen Greenblatt's Concept of a Symbolic Economy," 358.

28. Henry Morton Stanley, *How I Found Livingstone: Travels, Adventures, and Discoveries in Central Africa* (London: Low, 1872) 583.

29. Russell West, *Conrad and Gide: Translation, Transference, and Intertextuality* (Amsterdam: Rodopi, 1996) 145.

30. As indicated before with reference to Hemingway's aesthetics of action, the logic of looking closely does have a prehistory: of course, even before the 1980s, travel writers, journalists, ethnologists, and many artists have emphasized their unbiased perspective on the foreign context. But within the last twenty years, the claims to "tell nothing but the truth, as ugly as it may be," have gained unprecedented popularity in their explicit or tacit resistance to political correctness and exoticization likewise.

31. Pratt, 221, 220.

32. Keith B. Richburg, *Out of America: A Black Man Confronts Africa* (1997), with a new afterword (San Diego: Harcourt Brace, 1998) 227. Hereafter cited in the text as *OoA.*

33. For a "prehistory" to Richburg's distantiation from Africa and an account of African and African-American interrelations, focusing on African-American travel writing in the 1950s to 1970s, see John C. Gruesser, "Afro-American Travel Literature and Africanist Discourse," *Black American Literature Forum* 24 (Spring 1995) 5–20. For a differentiated account on the repercussions of African, American, and African-American identity constructions, see Manthia Diawara, *In Search of Africa* (Cambridge: Harvard U Press, 1998).

34. I will come back to the implications of such an imagery of infection with regard to Africa in my last chapter. For the logic of Afropessimism see also Patricia Williams's reflections on seemingly unbiased media representations of Africa,

which time and again suggest a pervasive analogy between African and American conditions, so that the depiction of African corruption and chaos implies a secret commentary on the situation in African-American communities and "Africans" become a foil for "African-Americans": *The Rooster's Egg: On the Persistence of Prejudice* (Cambridge, Mass.: Harvard U Press, 1995) 182–212.

35. Bruce Sterling, *Islands in the Net,* 1988 (New York: ACE, 1989) 5. Hereafter cited in the text as *IN.*

36. Emily Apter, *Continental Drift: From National Characters to Virtual Subjects* (Chicago: U of Chicago Press, 1999) 213–223, 215.

37. Apter, 215.

38. See Andrew Ross, "Cyberpunk in Boystown," in *Strange Weather: Culture, Science, and Technology in the Age of Limits* (London: Verso, 1991) 137–167, 146; see also Istvan Csicsery-Ronay, "Cyberpunk and Neuromanticism." *Mississipi Review* 16:2/3 (1988) 266–278. For a reflection on Sterling's role within the early cyberpunk movement cf. Pavel Frelik, "Return from the Implants: Cyberpunk's Schizophrenic Futures," in *Simulacrum America: The USA and the Popular Media,* ed. Carolin Auer and Elisabeth Kraus (Rochester: Camden House, 2000) 87–94, 91. On cyberpunk in general see Scott Bukatman's seminal study *Terminal Identity* (Durham: Duke U Press, 1993). See also my "Cyberpunk: Eine Begriffsbestimmung," in *Hyperkultur: Zur Fiktion des Computerzeitalters,* ed. Martin Klepper, Ruth Mayer, and Ernst-Peter Schneck (Berlin: Walter De Gruyter, 1996) 221–233.

39. Fredric Jameson, "Class and Allegory in Contemporary Mass Culture: *Dog Day Afternoon* as a Political Film" (1977), in *Movies and Methods,* vol. 2, 715–733, 720.

40. Fredric Jameson, "Notes on Globalization as a Philosophical Issue," in *The Cultures of Globalization* 54–77, 70.

41. William Gibson, *Neuromancer,* 1984 (London: HarperCollins, 1993) 75.

42. Ishmael Reed, *Mumbo Jumbo,* 1972 (New York: Atheneum, 1988) 204. Hereafter cited in the text as *MJ.* On the "New Age" dimensions in Reed's novel see also my "Magical Mystery Tours: Ben Okri, Ishmael Reed, and the New Age of Africa," *Zeitschrift für Anglistik und Amerikanistik* 45:3 (1997) 226–235.

43. Cf. Barbara Browning's reading of *Mumbo Jumbo,* William Gibson's *Count Zero,* and Neal Stephenson's *Snow Crash* (1992) in *Infectious Rhythm: Metaphors of Contagion and the Spread of African Culture* (New York: Routledge, 1998) 18–30, 121–140.

44. Eric Davis, *TechGnosis: Myth, Magic, and Mysticism in the Age of Information* (New York: Harmony, 1998) 7.

45. Zygmunt Baumann, *Intimations of Postmodernity* (London: Routledge, 1992) x.

46. John A. McClure, "Postmodern/Post-secular: Contemporary Fiction and Spirituality," *Modern Fiction Studies* 41:1 (1995) 141–163, 147. See also Robert S. Ellwood, Jr., *The Sixties Spiritual Awakening* (New Brunswick: Rutgers U Press, 1994).

47. McClure, "Postmodern/Post-secular," 156–157. For the historical and conceptual backgrounds of this trend cf. Andrew Ross, "New Age—a Kinder, Gentler Science?" in *Strange Weather* 15–74.

48. Bruno Latour, *We Have Never Been Modern,* tr. Carolyn Porter (Cambridge, Mass.: Harvard U Press, 1993) 7. Cf. also Eric Davis.

49. In Mark Dery, "Black to the Future: Interviews with Samuel R. Delany,

Greg Tate, and Tricia Rose," *The South Atlantic Quarterly* 92:4 (Fall 1992) 735–778, 748.

50. William Gibson, *Count Zero,* 1987 (London: HarperCollins, 1993) 234. By contrast to Gibson's much praised concept of a pragmatist *"street religion,"* which professes to "get the thing *done"* (112), Sterling's enactment of voodooism focuses on the emptiness and banality of this creed—in his Caribbean voodoo rituals the spirit of business, with all its negative implications, is not to be ignored.

51. Cf. also Andrew Ross's critique of Bruce Sterling's resigned stance in *Strange Weather,* 156–158.

52. John Le Carré, *The Constant Gardener* (London: Hodder & Sloughton, 2001) 62. Hereafter cited in the text as *CG.*

53. Cf. Deborah Root, *Cannibal Culture: Art, Appropriation, & the Commodification of Difference* (Boulder, Colo.: Westview Press, 1996).

54. For an extensive analysis on the logic of exchange and its anthropological and sociological implications see Pierre Bourdieu, *The Logic of Practice* (1980), tr. Richard Nice (Stanford: Stanford U Press, 1990). On the theoretical and cultural debates around these issues see Ulla Haselstein, *Die Gabe der Zivilisation: Kultureller Austausch und literarische Textpraxis in Amerika, 1682–1861* (München: Wilhelm Fink, 2000).

55. Cf. Stephen Greenblatt, *Marvelous Possessions: The Wonder of the New World* (Oxford: Clarendon Press, 1991) 146–150.

56. Taussig, *Shamanism,* 109.

57. Crystal Bartolovitch, "Consumerism, or the Cultural Logic of Late Cannibalism," in *Cannibalism and the Colonial World,* ed. Francis Barker, Peter Hulme, and Margaret Iversen (Cambridge: Cambridge U Press; 1998) 204–237, 213.

58. *Faustus in Africa!* dir. William Kentridge, with Busi Zokufa, David Minaar, and Leslie Fong, Handspring Puppet Company, 1995.

59. Maggie Kilgour, "The Function of Cannibalism at the Present Time," in *Cannibalism and the Colonial World* 238–259, 242, 247.

60. T. Coraghessan Boyle, *Water Music,* 1981 (Harmondsworth: Penguin, 1983) unpaginated prologue. Hereafter cited in the text as *WM.*

61. Arndt Witte, "Fremd- und Eigenerfahrung in Westafrika: Am Beispiel von Gertraud Heises *Reise in die schwarze Haut* und T. Coraghessan Boyles *Water Music,"* in *Reisen im Diskurs: Modelle der literarischen Fremderfahrung von den Pilgerberichten bis zur Postmoderne,* ed. Anne Fuchs and Theo Harden (Heidelberg: Winter, 1995) 374–390, 382—my translation.

62. One of many examples for this oscillation is the chapter "The Beginning of Sorrow (Plish, Plash)," the very heading of which already delineates the movement I pointed out. In this chapter, the situation after a monstrous thunderstorm that brought along an epidemic killing many of Mungo's men is related as a farcical confusion, grotesque and ridiculous rather than tragic. However, the chapter ends on the description of a crying eighteen-year-old in the midst of the apocalyptic chaos: "The sound of it is nearly lost in the cacophony of flapping canvas, thunderous rainfall and bowel-wrenching grunts and groans, but it is there all the same, a whimper in the interstices, a full-throated sob, the sound of hopelessness, the sound of failure, self-pity and annihilation" (*WM* 347). Time and again, Boyle enacts similarly grotesque scenarios, and time and again he contrasts the highly ironic detached narrative perspective with a personal perspective of pain, failure, and loss, which due to the strategies of exaggeration and irony is indeed "nearly lost" but "there all the same."

63. Lewis Hyde, *Trickster Makes This World: Mischief, Myth, and Art* (New York: North Point Press, 1998) 210.
64. Deleuze, "Control and Becoming," in *Negotiations* 175.

6. IN BETWEEN AND NOWHERE AT ALL: THE MIDDLE PASSAGE
REVISITED, PP. 207–255

1. Lawrence Levine, *Black Culture and Black Consciousness: Afro-American Folk Thought from Slavery to Freedom* (Oxford: Oxford U Press, 1977) 127–128. Henry Louis Gates, Jr., has elaborated the conceptual implications of this trope of tricking in his *Signifying Monkey*.
2. Hortense Spillers, "Mama's Baby, Papa's Maybe: An American Grammar Book," in *Within the Circle: An Anthology of African American Literary Criticism from the Harlem Renaissance to the Present*, ed. Angelyn Mitchell (Durham: Duke U Press, 1994) 454–481, 466. On the Middle Passage in African-American literature see also Wolfgang Binder, "Uses of Memory: The Middle Passage in African-American Literature," *Slavery in the Americas*, ed. W. B. (Würzburg: Könighausen & Neumann, 1993) 539–564; and Carl Pedersen, "Middle Passages: Representation of the Slave Trade in Caribbean and African-American Literature," *Massachusetts Review* 34:2 (1993) 225–239.
3. Diedrich Diederichsen, "Verloren unter Sternen: UFOs, Aliens und das Mothership," in *Globalkolorit* 237–252, 239–240—my translation.
4. Kodwo Eshun in an interview in *Last Angel of History*, dir. John Akomfrah, with Edward George, researchers Kodwo Eshun and Floyd Webb, Death Audio Film Production, 1995.
5. Herman Melville, *Benito Cereno* (1855), in *Billy Budd and Other Stories* (Harmondsworth: Penguin, 1986) 165. Hereafter cited in the text as *BC*.
6. Sundquist, 28.
7. Gesa Mackenthun, "Spectacle as Amnesia: The *Amistad* Case and the Sacrifice of Historical Truth," paper presented at the EAAS Conference in Lisbon, 1998. On the conceptualization of the high seas in terms of "natural law" and legal space see also Robert Cover, *Justice Accused: Antislavery and the Judicial Process* (New Haven: Yale U Press, 1975) 108–109.
8. Carolyn L. Karcher, "The Riddle of the Sphinx: Melville's 'Benito Cereno' and the *Amistad* Case," in *Critical Essays on Herman Melville's "Benito Cereno*," ed. Robert E. Burkholder (New York: G. K. Hall, 1992) 196–229, 221.
9. Karcher, 211.
10. Gesa Mackenthun, "Postcolonial Masquerade: Antebellum Sea Fiction and the Transatlantic Slave Trade," in *Early America Re-explored: New Readings in Colonial, Early National, and Antebellum Culture*, ed. Fritz Fleischmann and Klaus H. Schmidt (Frankfurt/Main: Peter Lang, 2000) 537–567, 542.
11. Maggie Montesinos Sale, *The Slumbering Volcano: American Slave Ship Revolts and the Production of Rebellious Masculinity* (Durham: Duke U Press, 1997) 160.
12. Brook Thomas, "The Legal Fictions of Herman Melville and Lemuel Shaw," in *Critical Essays on Herman Melville's "Benito Cereno"* 116–126, 123.
13. George Lipsitz, *The Possessive Investment in Whiteness: How White People Profit from Identity Politics* (Philadelphia: Temple U Press, 1998) 118.

14. On the entanglement of personal, public, and literary history around Melville's novella see Thomas.

15. Sundquist, 156, 162.

16. Michael P. Rogin, *Subversive Genealogy: The Politics and Art of Herman Melville* (Berkeley: U of California Press, 1983) 209.

17. Sundquist, 156. On the analogies between Hegel's system of thought and Melville's writing see my *Selbsterkenntnis, Körperfühlen,* 91–140.

18. Frantz Fanon, *Black Skin, White Masks* (1952), tr. Charles Lam Markmann (New York: Grove, 1967) 220.

19. On the representation of Cinque in the media of the day cf. Sale, 66–84.

20. Eric Lott, *Love & Theft: Blackface Minstrelsy and the American Working Class* (New York: Oxford U Press, 1993) 234–235.

21. *Amistad,* dir. Steven Spielberg, with Djimon Houson, Matthew McConaughey, Anthony Hopkins, and Morgan Freeman, Dreamworks, 1997.

22. I will not go at large into the manifold deviations of Spielberg's film from the historical case history—for one, because I do believe that a fiction film may very well personalize and edit history, even if it is interesting to see what is altered and to which effect. Secondly, however, I need not concentrate on this aspect, as it has already been investigated. Cf. Gary Rosen, "'Amistad' and the Abuse of History," *Commentary* 105 (Feb. 1998) 46–51; Robert L. Paquette, "From History to Hollywood: The Voyage of 'La Amistad,'" *The New Criterion* 16 (Mar. 1998) 74–78; see also Gesa Mackenthun's "Spectacle as Amnesia" and Michael Rogin's "Spielberg's List," *New Left Review* 230 (1998) 153–160.

23. Cover, 109–116; Paquette, 76; Karcher, 206.

24. As Maggie Montesinos Sale has shown with reference to Sacvan Bercovitch's concept of the "American Jeremiad," referencing the American Revolution in the eighteenth and nineteenth centuries did very well go together with a conservative stance vis-à-vis slavery—so that abolitionist invocations of this tradition have to be seen as markedly oppositional stances: Sale, 10–11.

25. "In celebrating the exception as a court room spectacle, the movie makes us disremember the Fugitive Slave Law, Dred Scott, the Jim Crow Laws, and the Ku Klux Klan; it mythologizes the history of African America as a story of intercultural understanding with a happy ending," writes Gesa Mackenthun in her analysis of the film and its historical points of reference. Cf. "Spectacle as Amnesia."

26. Rogin, "Spielberg's List," 156.

27. Paquette, 77. On the exigencies and customs of the US slave trade in the 1800s see also James A. Rawley, *The Transatlantic Slave Trade: A History* (New York: W. W. Norton, 1981) especially 432–433.

28. On this narrative strategy and its use in nineteenth-century abolitionist fiction see Philip Fisher, "Making a Thing into a Man: The Sentimental Novel and Slavery," in *Hard Facts: Setting and Form in the American Novel* (New York: Oxford U Press, 1985) 87–127; Susan Gilman, "The Mulatto, Tragic or Triumphant? The Nineteenth-Century Race Melodrama," in *The Culture of Sentiment: Race, Gender, and Sentimentality in Nineteenth-Century America,* ed. S. Samuels (New York: Oxford U Press, 1992) 221–243.

29. Peter Brooks, *The Melodramatic Imagination: Balzac, Henry James, Melodrama, and the Mode of Excess,* 1976 (New Haven: Yale U Press, 1995) 20.

30. On this connection see Lott, *Love & Theft,* 211–233.

31. After all, the same Africans who cannot relate to the concept of error, as their language does not allow for it, have no trouble at all making sense out of the

complicated courtroom scenario, as their subtitled conversations show, so that the American legal system, with its highly complicated concept of representation, comes across as an immediately accessible, "natural" order.

32. On the debates and public spectacles around the case see Karcher; and Sale.

33. Hochschild, 2.

34. On the interactions between American abolitionists and Congo activists see Hochschild, 211.

35. Eric Foner, "Hollywood Invades the Classroom," *New York Times* (Dec. 20, 1997) A:13.

36. Brian Fagel, "Passages from the Middle: Coloniality and Postcoloniality in Charles Johnson's *Middle Passage*," *African American Review* 30:4 (1996) 625–634, 625.

37. Charles Johnson, *Middle Passage*, 1990 (New York: Plume, 1991) 162–163. Hereafter cited in the text as *MP*.

38. Pedersen, 225.

39. Michael Boccia, "An Interview with Charles Johnson," *African American Review* 30:3 (1996) 611–618, 615.

40. In his *Being and Race* Johnson called this predicament "Caliban's dilemma," demarcating the precarious "compromise between the one and the many, African and European, the present and the past." Cf. *Being and Race: Black Writing since 1970* (Bloomington: Indiana U Press, 1990) 40. See also Ashraf H. A. Rushdie, "The Phenomenology of the Allmuseri: Charles Johnson and the Subject of the Narrative of Slavery." *African American Review* 26:3 (1992) 373–394.

41. Pedersen, 236.

42. Johnson, *Being and Race*, 39.

43. For a reflection on such references and their montage in Melville's text see Sterling Stuckey, "'Follow Your Leader': The Theme of Cannibalism in Melville's *Benito Cereno*," in *Critical Essays on Herman Melville's "Benito Cereno"* 182–195.

44. On Johnson's dependence on phenomenological models of thought see Rushdie; Boccia; and Johnson's *Being and Race*.

45. Toni Morrison, *Paradise*, 1997 (New York: Plume, 1999) 210.

46. Gilroy, 189.

47. Gilroy quotes Jackson's statement yet does not go into the implications of such a revisionist turn to the history of slavery as an empowering past analogous rather than opposed to an ancient African tradition. Pointing out the analogies between the histories of Jews and blacks, Gilroy argues convincingly for an interlinkage of approaches to the Holocaust and slavery without collapsing these histories into one. Nevertheless, the specific and actual turns to the history of slavery in black (popular) culture differ significantly from Jewish rituals of recollection, and it is the differences and specifities that interest me here.

48. *Sankofa*, dir. Haile Gerima, with Oyafunmike Ogunlano, Kofi Ghanaba, Alexandra Duah, and Mutabaruka, DiProCi/Ghana National Commission on Culture/Negod-Gwad/NDR, 1993.

49. Gay Wilentz, "Civilizations Underneath: African Heritage as Cultural Discourse in Toni Morrison's *Song of Solomon*," *African American Review* 26:1 (1992) 61–76. On recent narrative returns to the issue of slavery see also Klaus Ensslen, "The Renaissance of the Slave Narrative in Recent Critical and Fictional Discourse," in *Slavery in the Americas* 601–626.

50. On Gerima and the conceptual framework of the Los Angeles school of black independent filmmakers from which he derives, see Ntongela Masilela, "The Los Angeles School of Black Filmmakers," in *Black American Cinema*, ed. Manthia Diawara (New York: Routledge, 1993) 107–117; and Chris Norton, "Black Independent Cinema and the Influence of Neo-Realism" <http:\\images-journal.com/issue05/features/black.htm>.

51. The term "porno-troping" is Hortense Spillers's, and it was Sabine Bröck who applied it to *Sankofa* in a discussion around the film at the Annual Conference of the German Association of American Studies in Würzburg in 1996. Cf. Spillers, 67.

52. It would be interesting to compare this film in detail with Octavia Butler's novel, which equally envisions the time travel of an African-American woman back to the days of slavery. Butler's novel, however, is organized around the univocal identity of the protagonist, as it enacts the translocation of a twentieth-century black feminist into a nineteenth-century setting. *Sankofa* certainly stages the same kind of frightening idea of a sudden confrontation with a communal past, yet by "splitting" the female protagonist's identity her body gains a sometimes almost eerie significance as the bearer of a continuity that otherwise can be repressed and forgotten. As this continuity is emphasized almost exclusively on an extradiegetic level, Gerima dwells less on the aspect of psychological anguish (unlike Butler who closely relates the feelings and fears of her protagonist) but rather focuses on the gap between then and now, which the spectator has to bridge for herself by taking in the undeniable visual evidence given.

53. This transition from a realistic to a fantastic setting echoes an earlier scene when Nunu (Alexandra Duah), Shola's motherly friend, curses her body, her "flesh," which keeps her within the confines of slavery: "They can never do nothing to my soul. . . . Only to this flesh. This flesh, that's all. This is the only chain they have on us. Not because of this flesh, this meat, we'll be flying in the air, we'll go swim the river, walk under the sea, and soon we'll be home, we'll be home, we'll be home." And then too, a bird's-eye view of the sea and the African coast expresses freedom and release.

The very interlinkage of symbolic and concrete enactments of escape and dissolution, which culminates in the contrast of fantastic flight and realistic threat, is reflected in the image of the buzzard in this film, which always functions on two levels: the concrete (the Sankofa bird that Shola wears as a necklace) and the symbolic (the buzzard in the narratives).

54. Toni Morrison, *Song of Solomon*, 1977 (London: Picador, 1989) 328–329.

55. On this tradition see Levine, 87.

56. This current turn to myth and magic is interesting, as it runs counter to nineteenth-century modes of folk narration, to which both flight story and trickster tale can be traced back. As Lawrence Levine writes, it "is significant that, with the exception of the stories of flying Africans, mythic strategies . . . played almost no role in the lore of nineteenth-century slaves; not until well after emancipation do tales of exaggeration, with their magnification of the individual, begin to assume importance in the folklore of Afro-Americans." Levine, 104.

57. Jan Assmann, "Kollektives Gedächtnis und kulturelle Identität," in *Kultur und Gedächtnis*, ed. J. A. and Tonio Hölscher (Frankfurt/Main: Suhrkamp, 1988) 9–19, 15—my translation. For a concretization of such thoughts with regard to ethnicity see Michael Fischer, "Ethnicity and the Post-modern Arts of Memory," in *Writing Culture* 194–233; and my reflections on cultural memory and ethnic-

ity in the American 1920s in "'Taste It!' American Advertising, Ethnicity, and the Rhetoric of Nationhood in the 1920s," *Amerikastudien* 43:1 (1998) 131–141.

58. Elizabeth Alexander, "'Can you be BLACK and look at this?': Reading the Rodney King Video(s)," in *Black Male: Representations of Masculinity in Contemporary American Art,* ed. Thelma Golden (New York: Whitney Museum of American Art, 1994) 91–110, 110, 101.

59. Alexander, 101.

60. Frederick Douglass, *Narrative of the Life of Frederick Douglass* (1845), in *The Classic Slave Narratives,* ed. Henry Louis Gates, Jr. (New York: Penguin, 1987) 258.

61. Douglass, 255.

62. W. J. T. Mitchell, "Narrative, Memory, and Slavery," in *Picture Theory: Essays on Verbal and Visual Representation* (Chicago: U of Chicago Press, 1994) 183–207, 188. On this passage in Douglass's narrative see also Henry Louis Gates, Jr. *Figures in Black: Words, Signs, and the 'Racial' Self* (New York: Oxford U Press, 1989) 88–97. For an extensive reflection on the interaction of commemoration and witnessing cf. Shoshana Felman and Dori Laub, *Testimony: Crises of Witnessing in Literature, Psychoanalysis, and History* (New York: Routledge, 1992).

63. Mitchell goes on brilliantly to interlink his reading of Douglass with a reading of Toni Morrison's *Beloved.* Just like Elizabeth Alexander, he assumes that the recollection of slavery responds to similar "obligations" or follows the same function in both texts. While Morrison draws heavily on Douglass and other slave narratives, however, her historical novel opens up a different perspective on the system of slavery and the "obligation" to remember.

64. Houston A. Baker, Jr., "Autobiographical Acts and the Voice of the Southern Slave," in *The Slave's Narrative,* ed. C. T. Davis and H. L. Gates, Jr. (Oxford: Oxford U Press, 1985) 242–261, 249.

65. On this gradual reorientation see Sundquist; Wilson J. Moses, *The Golden Age of Black Nationalism, 1850–1925* (New York: Oxford U Press, 1978); Kwame Anthony Appiah, "The Uncompleted Argument: Du Bois and the Illusion of Race," in *'Race,' Writing and Difference,* ed. Henry Louis Gates, Jr. (Chicago: U of Chicago Press, 1985) 21–37; and Kenneth Warren, "Appeals for (Mis)recognition: Theorizing the Diaspora," in *Cultures of United States Imperialism* 392–406.

66. This is not to deny that there are definitely trickster elements in Douglass's self-fashioning. But by contrast to contemporary writers and artists, Douglass's trickery does not purport the suspension of his historical narrative but rather a momentary manipulation of its conditions, which are thus accentuated rather than collapsed. On Douglass as a trickster see Hyde, 203–280.

67. bell hooks, "Columbus: Gone but Not Forgotten," in *Outlaw Culture: Resisting Representations* (New York: Routledge, 1994) 197–206, 204–206.

68. Diedrich Diederichsen, "Hören, Wiederhören, Zitieren," *Spex* 1 (Jan. 1997) 43–46, 45—my translation.

69. Quoted in Maren Stange, "Memory and Form in Recent African American Photography: From *12 Million Black Voices* to Carrie Mae Weems," paper presented at the EAAS Conference in Lisbon, 1998, 10–11.

70. Houston A. Baker, Jr., "Islands of Identity: Inside the Pictures of Carrie Mae Weems," in *Carrie Mae Weems: In These Islands, South-Carolina–Georgia* (exhibition catalogue) (University of Alabama, Sarah Moody Gallery of Art, 1995) 12–19, 16.

71. In Dery, 747.

72. Stange, 12.

73. Patricia J. Williams, "'In the Times of the Drums'" (book review), *New York Times Book Review* (Aug. 15, 1999) 24.

74. Rogin, *Subversive Genealogy*, 209.

75. Derek Walcott, "The Sea Is History," in *Poems 1965-1980* (London: Jonathan Cape, 1980) 237-240, 237, 238.

76. Walcott, 238, 240.

77. Ian Baucom, "Charting the 'Black Atlantic,'" *Postmodern Culture* 8:1 (1997) <http://muse.jhu.edu/journals/postmodern_culture/v008/8.1baucom.html>.

78. In Dery, 767-768.

79. Kass Banning, "Feeding off the Dead: Necrophilia and the Black Imaginary. An Interview with John Akomfrah," *Borderlines* 29-30 (Winter 1993) 33.

80. Drexciya, *The Quest* (Detroit: Submerge, 1997), liner notes.

81. For an analysis of the act and its aesthetics see Kodwo Eshun, "Fear of a Wet Planet," *The Wire* 167 (Jan. 1998) 19-20. I came across Eshun's piece by way of Diedrich Diederichsen's edited volume *Loving the Alien: Science Fiction, Diaspora, Multikultur* (Berlin: ID Verlag, 1998), in which a German version of this text appeared.

82. Eshun, "Fear of a Wet Planet," 20.

83. Deleuze, "Control and Becoming," 175.

84. Eshun, "Fear of a Wet Planet," 20. For a more detailed discussion of electronic music and its cultural potential see Eshun's *More Brilliant Than the Sun: Adventures in Sonic Fiction* (London: Quartet Books, 1997).

85. On this issue, especially with regard to so-called protest music, see Simon Frith, *Performing Rites: On the Value of Popular Music* (Oxford: Oxford U Press, 1996); and my "Pop as a Difference Engine: Music, Markets, and Marginality," in *Simulacrum America* 149-160.

86. John Corbett, "Brothers from Another Planet: The Space Madness of Lee 'Scratch' Perry, Sun Ra, and George Clinton," in *Extended Play: Sounding off from John Cage to Dr. Funkenstein* (Durham: Duke U Press, 1994) 7-24, 7.

87. Diederichsen, "Verloren unter Sternen," 242—my translation. On this aesthetics and its implications see, apart from Corbett and Diederichsen, the contributions to Diederichsen's edited volume *Loving the Alien*, especially Tobias Nagl's "'I wonder if heaven's got a ghetto': Aliens, Ethnizität und der SF-Film"; and Renée Green's "Leidige Liebe: My Alien/My Self—Readings at Work," 68-87 and 134-151, respectively.

88. For a definition of the—awkward—term "Afrofuturism" and an introduction to the development at its outset see Dery, 735-743.

89. Kobena Mercer, "Witness at the Crossroads: An Artist's Journey in Postcolonial Space," in *Keith Piper: Relocating the Remains* (exhibition catalogue) (London: Institute of International Visual Arts, 1997) 13-85, 79.

90. Cf. Keith Piper, *A Ship Called Jesus* (exhibition catalogue) (Birmingham: Ikon Gallery, 1991) unpaginated.

91. Baucom, unpaginated.

7. DON'T TOUCH! AFRICA IS A VIRUS. PP. 256-291

1. Etienne Balibar, "The Borders of Europe," tr. J. Swenson, in *Cosmopolitics* 216-229, 219.

2. Brigitte Weingart, "Parasitäre Praktiken: Zur Topik des Viralen," in *Über Grenzen: Limitation und Transgression in Literatur und Ästhetik,* ed. Claudia Benthien and Irmela M. Krüger-Fürhoff (Stuttgart: Metzler, 1999) 207–230, 209—my translation.

3. For a detailed account of the social and scientific dimensions of this development see Lisa Lynch, "The Neo/bio/colonial Hot Zone: African Viruses, American Fairytales," *The International Journal of Cultural Studies* 1:2 (1998) 233–252; Heather Schell, "Outburst! A Chilling True Story about Emerging-Virus Narratives and Pandemic Social Change," *Configurations* 5:1 (1997) 93–133; and Iliana Alexandra Semmler, "Ebola Goes Pop: The Filovirus from Literature into Film," *Literature and Medicine* 17:1 (1998) 149–174. For the African and African-diasporic reverberations of this theme see Browning.

4. Schell, 96–97. On the media exploitation of such fears and the increasingly intricate interlinkage of Africa and AIDS/HIV especially see Paula Treichler, "AIDS and HIV Infection in the Third World: A First World Chronicle," in *Remaking History,* ed. Barbara Kruger and Phil Mariani (Seattle: Bay Press, 1989) 31–86; Simon Watney's "Missionary Positions: AIDS, 'Africa,' and Race," in *Out There: Marginalization and Contemporary Cultures,* ed. Russell Ferguson et al. (Cambridge, Mass.: MIT Press, 1990) 89–103; and Cindy Patton, *Inventing AIDS* (New York: Routledge, 1990).

5. Emily Martin, *Flexible Bodies: The Role of Immunity in American Culture from the Days of Polio to the Age of AIDS* (Boston, Mass.: Beacon Press, 1994). On the rhetoric and ideology of viral infection and immunity see also Brigitte Weingart, *Ansteckende Wörter: Repräsentationen von AIDS* (Frankfurt/Main: Suhrkamp, forthcoming 2002); and Donna Haraway, "The Biopolitics of Postmodern Bodies: Constitutions of Self in Immune System Discourse," in *Simians, Cyborgs, and Women: The Reinvention of Nature* (New York: Routledge, 1991) 203–230.

6. Serres, 63, 79.

7. Apart from the texts I will be concerned with here, there is, of course, another postmodern "tradition" of textual and strategic identification with the virus, leading from poststructuralism and William S. Burroughs through Jean Baudrillard to cyberpunk and its "computerization" of the virus, as Brigitte Weingart shows in her brilliant reading of this field of signification. Cf. Weingart, "Parasitäre Praktiken."

8. Pratt, 201–208.

9. *Outbreak,* dir. Wolfgang Petersen, with Dustin Hoffmann, Rene Russo, Morgan Freeman, Donald Sutherland, and Cuba Gooding, Jr., Warner Bros., 1995.

10. Schell, 106.

11. While Frank Marshall's film actually ends upon the balloon perspective— having left out the African attack before—Crichton's novel adds a last passage wrapping up the protagonists' future developments, in line with the novel's journalistic tone.

12. Cf. Semmler, 162.

13. Schell, 107.

14. Cf. Schell, 114.

15. Schell, 112.

16. Guy Debord, *The Society of the Spectacle* (1967), tr. Donald Nicholson-Smith (New York: Zone Books, 1995) 15.

17. Debord, 17.

18. Barbara Kingsolver, *The Poisonwood Bible* (New York: HarperFlamingo, 1998) 530.

19. Kingsolver, 529.

20. Richard Dyer, "White," in *The Matter of Images: Essays on Representations* (London: Routledge, 1993) 141–163, 157.

21. Dyer, "White," 160.

22. Dwayne Ferguson, *Bite of the Scarab, Captain Africa* 3 (Glen Ridge, N.J.: Diehard Studio, 1994). Hereafter cited in the text as *CA,* pagination assigned. The American comic is not to be mixed up with the Nigerian comic by the same title.

23. For the formulaic background of the genre see Reinhold Reitberger and Wolfgang Fuchs, "Super-heroes," in *Comics: Anatomy of a Mass-Medium,* 1971 (London: Studio Vista Publishings, 1972) 100–129. For the complex refashionings of the imagery in the 1980s see Scott Bukatman, "X-Bodies (the torment of the mutant superhero)," *Uncontrollable Bodies: Testimonies of Identity and Culture,* ed. Rodney Sappington and Tyler Stallings (Seattle: Bay Press, 1994) 93–129; and Martin Schüwer, "Superhelden in der Krise: Revision eines Pop-Mythos in Alan Moores und Dave Gibbons's *Watchmen,*" Master's thesis, U of Cologne, 1998.

24. A short story attached to the comic strip, written by Mark-Wayne Harris, illuminates this obvious associative interlinkage further, as here Captain Africa comes to be infected with a disease clearly laid out along the lines of AIDS.

25. Paul Barber, *Vampires, Burial, and Death: Folklore and Reality* (New Haven: Yale U Press, 1988).

26. Brantlinger, 233. For the fictional ramifications of this imagery see Nina Auerbach, *Our Vampires, Ourselves* (Chicago: U of Chicago Press, 1995); and Elisabeth Bronfen, *Over Her Dead Body: Death, Femininity, and the Aesthetic* (New York: Routledge, 1992) 295–322.

27. Apart from such indications and allusions it is sometimes hard to make out racial figurations in this comic. While it does not indicate race other than by facial features (all faces are white), it does very well invoke black and white contrasts: the hooded vampires' faces are black, and Southerland's face too is blackened by shadows for the most part of the fight.

28. John Edgar Wideman, "Fever," in *Fever* (New York: Henry Holt, 1989) 127–161, 135. Hereafter quoted in the text as "F."

29. Browning, 20. For reflections on the novel's narrative techniques, its intermixture of comic book aesthetics, metafictional reflections, visual material, postmodern experimentation, and African-American traditions see Henry Louis Gates's highly influential reading in *Figures in Black,* 235–276. See also Günter Lenz,"'Making Our Own Future Text': Neo-HooDooism, Postmodernism, and the Novels of Ishmael Reed," in *Theorie und Praxis im Erzählen des 19. und 20. Jahrhunderts,* ed. W. Herget, K. P. Jochum, and I. Weber (Tübingen: Gunter Narr, 1986) 323–344; and Reginald Martin, *Ishmael Reed and the New Black Aesthetic Critics* (New York: St. Martin's Press, 1988).

30. Browning, 17.

31. For the HooDoo/voodoo imagery in the novel and its relevance in a wider system of viral and diasporic meaning making see Browning; Lenz; and Robert Elliot Fox, "Blacking the Zero: Toward a Semiotics of Neo-Hoodoo," *Black American Literature Forum* 18 (1984) 95–99.

32. Much has been written about the interesting fact that all of these efforts revolve around a lost "Text" that is supposed to lend stability and finality to Jes Grew, doing away with its "ineloquence" (*MJ* 34) and providing it with the longed-for "1ˢᵗ anthology written by the 1ˢᵗ choreographer" (*MJ* 164), a set of stable meanings, a referential system. See especially Günter Lenz's reflections on the "multi-dimensional" quality of Reed's text, which time and again presents itself as provisional and prerequisite—and still the "best thing yet."

33. De Certeau, 37.

34. Sämi Ludwig, "Dialogic Possession in Reed's *Mumbo Jumbo*," in *The Black Columbiad: Defining Moments in African-American Literature and Culture*, ed. Werner Sollors and Maria Diedrich (Cambridge, Mass.: Harvard U Press, 1994) 325–336, 333.

35. Hyde, 51.

36. Hanjo Berressem, "'Negrophobia!?' Abjection in Darius James' *Negrophobia*," in *Cultural Encounters: American Studies in the Age of Multiculturalism*, ed. Mario Klarer and Sonja Bahn (Tübingen: Stauffenberg Verlag, 2000) 51–65, 53.

37. Darius James, *Negrophobia*, 1992 (New York: St. Martin's Press, 1993) 2. Hereafter cited in the text as *N*.

38. Berressem, 55.

39. See my *Selbsterkenntnis, Körperfühlen*, for a reflection on imageries of bodily contact, sensuality, touch, and infection in the nineteenth century.

40. Browning, 5–6.

41. Frith, 144.

42. Lawrence Grossberg introduces the term "authentic inauthenticity" in his reflections on a postmodern rock scene and defines the attitude as "assuming a distance from the other which allows it to refuse any claim or demand which might be made on it." While this attitude becomes a central trajectory of "the postmodern sensibility" for Grossberg, I would like to draw attention to its flip side, "inauthentic authenticity"—self-conscious gestures of emotionality, traditionality, and belonging in the face of their groundlessness and volatility. Cf. Grossberg, *"We gotta get out of this place,"* 224–225. For a more detailed reflection of these developments see my "Schmutzige Fakten: Wie sich Differenz verkauft," in *Mainstream der Minderheiten* 153–168.

43. For a closer reflection on signifyin' and hip-hop see Tricia Rose, *Black Noise: Rap Music and Black Culture in Contemporary America* (Hanover: Wesleyan U Press, 1994); and Diedrich Diederichsen, "Schwarze Musik und weiße Hörer," in *Freiheit macht arm* (Köln: Kiepenheuer & Witsch, 1993) 53–96.

44. It is significant that Michael Franti, whose former projects (Beatnigs, Disposable Heroes of Hiphoprisy) clearly drew upon European experimental pop mixed up with rap, foregrounds black musical traditions (rap and reggae) with Spearhead—testifying to a new understanding of these traditions, which even more than before are cast as disposable material rather than fixed points of reference and identification. See also my "Pop as a Difference Engine."

45. Spearhead, *chocolate supa highway,* Capitol Records, 1997.

46. Andrew Ross, "Pop-Politik: Schwarze Musik und weiße Identität," tr. Esther Fritsch, in *Globalkolorit, 59–64.

47. Where Sun Ra comes to mind with regard to Drexciya, another self-acclaimed "alien" and "crazy man" looms large in the background of Spearhead's project—Lee "Scratch" Perry. On the aesthetics of madness in

black music see Corbett, 7–24; and Akomfrah's documentary film *Last Angel of History*.

48. Holert and Terkessidis, 9–10—my translation.

49. Cf. Cornel West, "Nihilism in Black America," in *Race Matters* (New York: Vintage, 1993) 15–31.

50. Serres, 64.

51. I hesitate to enter the vehement, and somewhat contentious, debates around the differences between postmodern and postcolonial representation here, as I prefer to use both terms in a historically descriptive sense (after modernity/after colonialism) anyway, as should have become clear by now. If I distinguish minority narratives like the above from postmodern narration, this is consequently to be read as a pragmatic approximation to a complex and thoroughly entangled field, reaching from John Edgar Wideman's "postcolonial" commitment to Thomas Pynchon's conjunction of myth and history to Ishmael Reed's and Darius James's practices of parodic alienation to a postmodern writer like Robert Coover, who pursues a political project exclusively on the basis of alienation, pastiche, and irony. For a much more pervasive and detailed discussion of the positions at stake see, apart from Martin Klepper's aforementioned study on the "therapeutic" dimensions of postmodern literature, During; Linda Hutcheon, "'Circling the Downspout of Empire': Postcolonialism and Postmodernism," *Ariel: A Review of International English Literature* 20 (1989) 149–175; and Kwame Anthony Appiah, "Is the Post- in Postmodernism the Post- in Postcolonial?" *Critical Inquiry* 17 (Winter 1991) 336–355.

ROOTS AND ROLE-PLAY: A CONCLUSION, PP. 292–304

1. Patricia J. Williams, *The Alchemy of Race and Rights* (Cambridge, Mass.: Harvard U Press, 1991) 49.

2. Mark Terkessidis, *Psychologie des Rassismus* (Opladen: Westdeutscher Verlag, 1998) 255–256. Cf. also Barbara Fields, "Ideology and Race in American History," in *Region, Race, and Reconstruction: Essays in Honor of C. Vann Woodward*, ed. J. Morgan Kousser and James M. McPherson (New York: Oxford U Press, 1982) 142–177.

3. Jehlen, 24.

4. James Baldwin, "Stranger in the Village" (1953), in *Notes of a Native Son*, 1955 (Boston: Beacon Press, 1984) 159–175, 163. Hereafter cited in the text as "SV."

5. bell hooks, "Representing Whiteness in the Black Imagination," in *Displacing Whiteness* 165–179, 167.

6. James Baldwin, "Encounter on the Seine: Black Meets Brown" (1950), in *Notes of a Native Son* 117–123, 122.

7. Spivak, 364. For reflections on the logic of nationalism in the times of modernity, see also Benedict Anderson, *Imagined Communities: Reflections on the Origin and Spread of Nationalism*, 1983 (London: Verso, 1991); *Race, Nation, Class: Ambiguous Identities*, ed. Etienne Balibar and Immanuel Wallerstein (London: Verso, 1991); and Arjun Appadurai, "The Heart of Whiteness," *Callaloo* 16: 4 (1993) 796–807.

8. Appadurai, 798.

9. Anna Deavere Smith, *Fires in the Mirror: Crown Heights, Brooklyn, and*

Other Identities, dir. Christopher Ashley, Joseph Papp Public Theater, 1992. *Fires in the Mirror* has in the meantime come out in a television version, produced by PBS American Playhouse in 1993 and directed by George C. Wolfe, although this version does not comprise all of Smith's stage enactments (Jeffries's interview, for one, is missing).

10. My quote of Jeffries's interview is based on the printed collection of the interviews: Anna Deavere Smith, *Fires in the Mirror: Crown Heights, Brooklyn, and Other Identities* (New York: Anchor Books, 1993) 40–49, 41, 45, 44. Hereafter cited in the text as *FM.*

11. Barbara Johnson, "No Short Cuts to Democracy," in *Fires in the Mirror: Essays and Teaching Strategies,* ed. Pamela Benson (Boston: WGBH Educational Print and Outreach, 1993) 9–11, 10.

12. Carol Martin, "Bearing Witness: Anna Deavere Smith from Community to Theatre to Mass Media," in *A Sourcebook of Feminist Theatre and Performance: On and Beyond the Stage,* ed. Carol Martin (London: Routledge, 1996) 81–93, 83. For an analysis of the performance's techniques of representation and a reflection on the differences in the representation on stage and on video see also Janelle Reinelt, "Performing Race: Anna Deavere Smith's *Fire in the Mirror,*" *Modern Drama* 39 (1996) 609–617; and Tania Modleski, "Doing Justice to the Subjects. Mimetic Art in a Multicultural Society: The Work of Anna Deavere Smith," in *Female Subjects in Black and White: Race, Psychoanalysis, Feminism,* ed. Elizabeth Abel, Barbara Christian, and Helene Moglen (Berkeley: U of California Press, 1997) 57–76.

13. Modleski, "Doing Justice to the Subjects," 68–69.

14. David Hammons interviewed by Kellie Jones (1986), quoted in *David Hammons: Rousing the Rubble* (exhibition catalogue), ed. Tom Finkelpearl et al. (New York: The Institute for Contemporary Art, P.S. 1 Museum, 1991) 24.

Bibliography

Abish, Walter. *Alphabetical Africa*. New York: New Directions, 1974.

Achebe, Chinua. "An Image of Africa: Racism in Conrad's *Heart of Darkness*." *The Massachusetts Review* 18 (1977) 782–794.

Africanisms in American Culture. Ed. Joseph E. Holloway. Bloomington: Indiana U Press, 1990.

Africa's Media Image. Ed. Beverly G. Hawk. New York: Praeger, 1992.

Ahmad, Aijaz. *In Theory: Classes, Nations, Literatures*. London: Verso, 1992.

Alexander, Elizabeth. "'Can you be BLACK and look at this?': Reading the Rodney King Video(s)." In *Black Male* 91–110.

Anatomy of Racism. Ed. David Theo Goldberg. Minneapolis: U of Minnesota Press, 1990.

Anderson, Amanda. "Cosmopolitanism, Universalism, and the Divided Legacy of Modernity." In *Cosmopolitics* 265–289.

Anderson, Benedict. *Imagined Communities: Reflections on the Origin and Spread of Nationalism* (1983). London: Verso, 1991.

Appadurai, Arjun. "The Heart of Whiteness." *Callaloo* 16:4 (1993) 796–807.

Appiah, Kwame Anthony. "Cosmopolitan Patriots." In *Cosmopolitics*, 91–114.

———. *In My Father's House: Africa in the Philosophy of Culture*. New York: Oxford U Press, 1992.

———. "Is the Post- in Postmodernism the Post- in Postcolonial?" *Critical Inquiry* 17 (Winter 1991) 336–355.

———. "The Uncompleted Argument: Du Bois and the Illusion of Race." In *'Race,' Writing, and Difference* 21–37.

———.Apter, Emily. *Continental Drift: From National Characters to Virtual Subjects*. Chicago: U of Chicago Press, 1999.

Art after Modernism: Rethinking Representation. Ed. Brian Wallis. Boston: The New Museum of Contemporary Art, 1984.

Asad, Talal. "The Concept of Cultural Translation in British Social Anthropology." In *Writing Culture* 141–164.

Ascherson, Neal. *The King Incorporated: Leopold II in the Age of Trusts*. New York: Doubleday, 1964.

Assmann, Jan. "Kollektives Gedächtnis und kulturelle Identität." In *Kultur und Gedächtnis* 9–19.

Auerbach, Nina. *Our Vampires, Ourselves*. Chicago: U of Chicago Press, 1995.

Baker, Houston A., Jr. "Autobiographical Acts and the Voice of the Southern Slave." In *The Slave's Narrative* 242–261.

———. "Islands of Identity: Inside the Pictures of Carrie Mae Weems." In *Carrie Mae Weems: In These Islands* 12–19.

Baldwin, James. *Notes of a Native Son* (1955). Boston: Beacon Press, 1984.

Balibar, Etienne. "The Borders of Europe." Tr. J. Swenson. In *Cosmopolitics* 216–229.

Banning, Kass. "Feeding off the Dead: Necrophilia and the Black Imaginary. An Interview with John Akomfrah." *Borderlines* 29–30 (Winter 1993) 33.

Barthes, Roland. *Camera Lucida: Reflections on Photography* (1980). Tr. Richard Howard. New York: Hill and Wang, 1997.

———. *Mythologies* (1957). Tr. Annette Lavers. London: Jonathan Cape, 1972.

Bartolovitch, Crystal. "Consumerism, or the Cultural Logic of Late Cannibalism." In *Cannibalism and the Colonial World* 204–237.

Baucom, Ian. "Charting the 'Black Atlantic.'" *Postmodern Culture* 8:1 (1997) <http://muse.jhu.edu/journals/postmodern_culture/v008/8.1baucom.html>.

Baym, Nina. "'Actually, I Felt Sorry for the Lion.'" In *New Critical Approaches to the Short Stories of Ernest Hemingway* 112–120.

Beard, Peter. *The End of the Game: The Last Word from Paradise*. New York: Doubleday, 1977.

Bederman, Gail. *Manliness and Civilization: A Cultural History of Gender and Race in the United States, 1881–1917*. Chicago: U of Chicago Press, 1995.

Benayoun, Robert. "Clint et John: une saison infernale (*Chasseur blanc, coeur noir*)." *Positif* 351 (Mar. 1990) 2–4.

Benjamin, Walter. *Illuminationen: Ausgewählte Schriften 1*. Frankfurt/Main: Suhrkamp, 1977.

Berressem, Hanjo. "'Negrophobia!?' Abjection in Darius James' *Negrophobia*." In *Cultural Encounters* 51–65.

Bhabha, Homi K. *The Location of Culture*. London: Routledge, 1994.

Binder, Wolfgang. "Uses of Memory: The Middle Passage in African-American Literature." In *Slavery in the Americas* 539–564.

Black American Cinema. Ed. Manthia Diawara. New York: Routledge, 1993.

The Black Columbiad: Defining Moments in African-American Literature and Culture. Ed. Werner Sollors and Maria Diedrich. Cambridge, Mass.: Harvard U Press, 1994.

Black Male: Representations of Masculinity in Contemporary American Art. Ed Thelma Golden. New York: Whitney Museum of American Art, 1994.

Black Popular Culture: A Project by Michele Wallace. Ed. Gina Dent. Seattle: Bay Press, 1992.

The Black Presence in English Literature. Ed. David Dabydeen. Manchester: Manchester U Press, 1985.

Boccia, Michael. "An Interview with Charles Johnson." *African American Review* 30:3 (1996) 611–618.

Bongie, Chris. "Exotic Nostalgia: Conrad and the New Imperialism." In *Macropolitics of Nineteenth-Century Literature* 268–285.

Bourdieu, Pierre. *Distinction. A Social Critique of the Judgement of Taste* (1979). Tr. Richard Nice. London: Routledge, 1984.

———. *The Field of Cultural Production: Essays on Art and Literature*. Ed. Randal Johnson. New York: Columbia U Press, 1993.

———. *The Logic of Practice* (1980). Tr. Richard Nice. Stanford: Stanford U Press, 1990.

Boyer, Paul. *Urban Masses and Moral Order in America, 1820-1920.* Cambridge, Mass.: Harvard U Press, 1987.

Boyle, T. Coraghessan. *Water Music* (1981). Harmondsworth: Penguin, 1983.

———. *Without a Hero.* Harmondsworth: Penguin, 1994.

Brantlinger, Patrick. *Rule of Darkness: British Literature and Imperialism, 1830-1914.* Ithaca: Cornell U Press, 1988.

Bronfen, Elisabeth. *Over Her Dead Body: Death, Femininity, and the Aesthetic.* New York: Routledge, 1992.

Brooks, Peter. *The Melodramatic Imagination: Balzac, Henry James, Melodrama, and the Mode of Excess* (1976). New Haven: Yale U Press, 1995.

Brown, Bill. "Science Fiction, the World's Fair, and the Prosthetics of Empire." In *Cultures of United States Imperialism* 129-163.

Browning, Barbara. *Infectious Rhythm: Metaphors of Contagion and the Spread of African Culture.* New York: Routledge, 1998.

Bukatman, Scott. *Terminal Identity.* Durham: Duke U Press, 1993.

———. "X-Bodies (the torment of the mutant superhero)." In *Uncontrollable Bodies* 93-129.

Burgoyne, Robert, Sandy Flitterman-Lewis, and Robert Stam. *New Vocabularies in Film Semiotics: Structuralism, Poststructuralism, and Beyond.* London: Routledge, 1992.

Burroughs, Edgar Rice. *Tarzan of the Apes* (1914). Ed. G. Vidal. New York: Signet, 1990.

Buscombe, Edward. "Sound and Color" (1977) In *Movies and Methods* 83-92.

Busia, Abena P. A. "Manipulating Africa: The Buccaneer as 'Liberator' in Contemporary Fiction." In *The Black Presence in English Literature* 168-185.

Butler, Judith. *Gender Trouble: Feminism and the Subversion of Identity.* New York: Routledge, 1990.

Butts, Dennis. "Introduction." In H. Rider Haggard, *King Solomon's Mines* vii-xx.

The Cambridge History of American Literature, vol. 1. Gen. Ed. Sacvan Bercovitch. Cambridge: Cambridge U Press, 1994.

Cameron, Kenneth. *Africa on Film: Beyond Black and White.* New York: Continuum, 1994.

Canby, Vincent. "Toward the Heart of the Sahara: Chic but Lost in Its Vastness." *New York Times* (Dec. 12, 1990) C15.

Cannibalism and the Colonial World. Ed. Francis Barker, Peter Hulme, and Margaret Iversen. Cambridge: Cambridge U Press; 1998.

Carrie Mae Weems (exhibition catalogue). Washington, D.C.: The National Museum of Women in the Arts, 1993.

Carrie Mae Weems: In These Islands, South Carolina-Georgia (exhibition catalogue). University of Alabama, Sarah Moody Gallery of Art, 1995.

Castoriadis, Cornelius. *The Imaginary Institution of Society* (1975). Tr. Kathleen Blamey. Cambridge: Cambridge U Press, 1987.

Cawelti, John G. *Adventure, Mystery, and Romance: Formula Stories as Art and Popular Culture.* Chicago: U of Chicago Press, 1976.

Challenging Boundaries: Global Flows, Territorial Identities. Ed. Michael J. Shapiro and Hayward R. Alker. Minneapolis: U of Minnesota Press, 1996.

Chatman, Seymour. "2 1/2 Film Versions of *Heart of Darkness.*" In *Conrad on Film* 207-223.

Cheyfitz, Eric. *The Poetics of Imperialism: Translation and Colonization from The Tempest to Tarzan.* New York: Oxford U Press, 1991.

Chrisman, Laura. "The Imperial Unconscious? Representations of Imperial Discourse." *Critical Quarterly* 32:3 (Autumn 1990) 38–80.

The Cinematic Apparatus. Ed. Teresa de Lauretis and Stephen Heath. Houndsmills: Macmillan Press, 1980.

Clifford, James. *The Predicament of Culture: Twentieth-Century Ethnography, Literature, and Art.* Cambridge, Mass.: Harvard U Press, 1988.

Cole, Sarah. "Conradian Alienation and Imperial Intimacy. *Modern Fiction Studies* 44:2 (Summer 1998) 251–281.

Colonial Discourse and Postcolonial Theory. Ed. Laura Chrisman and Patrick Williams. Hempstead: Harvester Wheatsheaf, 1993.

Colonial Discourse, Postcolonial Theory. Ed. Francis Barker, Peter Hulme, and Margaret Iversen. Manchester: Manchester U Press, 1994.

Comaroff, Jean and John Comaroff. *Of Revelation and Revolution: Christianity, Colonialism, and Consciousness in South Africa,* vol. 1. Chicago: U of Chicago Press, 1991.

Combs, Richard. "Do the Wrong Thing: *White Hunter, Black Heart.*" *Sight & Sound* 59:4 (Autumn 1990) 278–279.

Conrad, Joseph. *Heart of Darkness* (1902). Harmondsworth: Penguin, 1973.

Conrad on Film. Ed. Gene M. Moore. Cambridge: Cambridge U Press, 1997.

Constructing Masculinity. Ed. Maurice Berger, Brian Wallis, and Simon Watson. New York: Routledge, 1995.

Coombes, Annie E. *Reinventing Africa: Museums, Material Culture, and Popular Imagination in Late Victorian and Edwardian England.* New Haven: Yale U Press, 1994.

Corbett, John. *Extended Play: Sounding off from John Cage to Dr. Funkenstein.* Durham: Duke U Press, 1994.

Cosmopolitics: Thinking and Feeling beyond the Nation. Ed. Pheng Cheah and Bruce Robbins. Minneapolis: U of Minnesota Press, 1998.

Coupland, Douglas. *Generation X: Tales for an Accelerated Culture.* New York: St. Martin's Press, 1991.

Cover, Robert. *Justice Accused: Antislavery and the Judicial Process.* New Haven: Yale U Press, 1975.

Crary, Jonathan. "Eclipse of the Spectacle." In *Art after Modernism* 283–294.

Crichton, Michael. *Congo* (1980). New York: Ballantine, 1993.

Critical Essays on Herman Melville's "Benito Cereno." Ed. Robert E. Burkholder. New York: G. K. Hall, 1992.

Csicsery-Ronay, Istvan. "Cyberpunk and Neuromanticism." *Mississipi Review* 16:2/3 (1988) 266–278.

Cultural Encounters: American Studies in the Age of Multiculturalism. Ed. Mario Klarer and Sonja Bahn. Tübingen: Stauffenberg Verlag, 2000.

Cultural Readings of Imperialism: Edward Said and the Gravity of History. Ed. Keith Ansell Pearson, Benita Parry, and Judith Squires. New York: St. Martin's Press, 1997.

The Cultural Studies Reader. Ed. Simon During. London: Routledge, 1993.

The Culture of Sentiment: Race, Gender, and Sentimentality in Nineteenth-Century America. Ed. Shirley Samuels. New York: Oxford U Press, 1992.

Culture on the Brink: Ideologies of Technology. Ed. Gretchen Bender and Timothy Druckrey. Seattle: Bay Press, 1994.

The Cultures of Globalization. Ed. Fredric Jameson and Masao Miyoshi. Durham: Duke U Press, 1998.

Cultures of United States Imperialism. Ed. Amy Kaplan and Donald Pease. Durham: Duke U Press, 1993.

Curti, Lidia. *Female Stories, Female Bodies: Narrative, Identity, and Representation.* New York: New York U Press, 1998.

Dällenbach, Lucien. *Le récit speculaire: Essai sur la mise en abyme.* Paris: Édition du Seuil, 1977.

David Hammons: Rousing the Rubble (exhibition catalogue). Ed. Tom Finkelpearl et al. New York: The Institute for Contemporary Art, P.S. 1 Museum, 1991.

Davies, Ioan. "Negotiating African Culture: Toward a Decolonization of the Fetish." In *The Cultures of Globalization* 125–145.

Davis, Eric. *TechGnosis: Myth, Magic, and Mysticism in the Age of Information.* New York: Harmony, 1998.

Davis, Mike. *City of Quartz: Excavating the Future in Los Angeles.* New York: Vintage, 1990.

Debord, Guy. *The Society of the Spectacle* (1967). Tr. Donald Nicholson-Smith. New York: Zone Books, 1995.

De Certeau, Michel. *The Practice of Everyday Life* (1984). Tr. Steven Rendall. Berkeley: U of California Press, 1988.

Decker, Christoph. "Interrogations of Cinematic Norms: Avant-Garde Film, History, and Mnemonic Practices." *Amerikastudien* 43:1 (1998) 109–130.

De/colonizing the Subject: The Politics of Gender in Women's Autobiography. Ed. Sidonie Smith and Julia Watson. Minneapolis: U of Minnesota Press, 1992.

Deleuze, Gilles. *Negotiations, 1972–1990.* Tr. Martin Joughin. New York: Columbia U Press, 1995.

De Man, Paul. "Autobiography as De-facement." *Modern Language Notes* 94:5 (Dec. 1979) 919–930.

Dery, Mark. "Black to the Future: Interviews with Samuel R. Delany, Greg Tate, and Tricia Rose." *The South Atlantic Quarterly* 92:4 (Fall 1992) 735–778.

De-Scribing Empire: Post-Colonialism and Textuality. Ed. Chris Tiffin and Alan Lawson. London: Routledge, 1994.

Diawara, Manthia. "Afro-Kitsch." In *Black Popular Culture* 285–291.

———. *In Search of Africa.* Cambridge: Harvard U Press, 1998.

Diederichsen, Diedrich. *Freiheit macht arm.* Köln: Kiepenheuer & Witsch, 1993.

———. "Hören, Wiederhören, Zitieren." *Spex* 1 (Jan. 1997) 43–46.

———. *Politische Korrekturen.* Köln: Kiepenheuer & Witsch, 1996.

———. "Verloren unter Sternen: UFOs, Aliens und das Mothership." In *Globalkolorit* 237–252.

Dinesen, Isak. *Out of Africa* (1938). New York: Vintage Books, 1989.

Displacing Whiteness: Essays in Social and Cultural Criticism. Ed. Ruth Frankenberg. Durham: Duke U Press, 1997.

Doane, Mary Anne. *Femmes Fatales: Feminism, Film Theory, Psychoanalysis.* London: Routledge, 1991.

Dorall, E. N. "Conrad and Coppola: Different Centers of Darkness." In *Joseph Conrad* 303–311.

Douglass, Frederick. *Narrative of the Life of Frederick Douglass* (1845). In *The Classic Slave Narratives.* Ed. Henry Louis Gates, Jr. New York: Penguin, 1987.

Drinnon, Richard. *Facing West: The Metaphysics of Indian-Hating and Empire-Building* (1980). Norman: U of Oklahoma Press, 1997.

Dumont, Georges-Henri. *Léopold II*. Paris: Fayard, 1990.

During, Simon. "Postmodernism or Post-colonialism Today." In *Postmodernism* 448–462.

Dyer, Richard. *The Matter of Images: Essays on Representations*. London: Routledge, 1993.

———. *White*. London: Routledge, 1997.

Early America Re-explored: New Readings in Colonial, Early National, and Antebellum Culture. Ed. Fritz Fleischmann and Klaus H. Schmidt. Frankfurt/Main: Peter Lang, 2000.

Easthope, Antony. *What a Man's Gotta Do: The Masculine Myth in Popular Culture* (1986). Boston: Unwyn Hyman, 1990.

Edwards, Owen. "The Toast of Society Photographs the Death of a World: Peter Beard, Photographer." *Village Voice* (Dec. 29, 1975) 18–19.

Ellwood, Robert S., Jr. *The Sixties Spiritual Awakening*. New Brunswick: Rutgers U Press, 1994.

Elsaesser, Thomas and Michael Wedel. "The Hollow Heart of Hollywood: *Apocalypse Now* and the New Sound Space." In *Conrad on Film* 151–175.

The Empire Writes Back: Theory and Practice in Post-colonial Literatures. London: Routledge, 1989.

Engelhart, Steve (text), Neil Yokes, Jay Geldhof (graphics), et al. *Ape Fear. Congorilla 4*. New York: DC Comics, 1992.

Eshun, Kodwo. "Fear of a Wet Planet." *The Wire* 167 (Jan. 1998) 19–20.

———. *More Brilliant Than the Sun: Adventures in Sonic Fiction*. London: Quartet Books, 1997.

Ethnic Cultures in the 1920s in North America. Ed. Wolfgang Binder. Frankfurt/Main: Peter Lang, 1993.

Fagel, Brian. "Passages from the Middle: Coloniality and Postcoloniality in Charles Johnson's *Middle Passage*." *African American Review* 30:4 (1996) 625–634.

Fanon, Frantz. *Black Skin, White Masks* (1952). Tr. Charles Lam Markmann. New York: Grove, 1967.

Feldmann, Lisa. "Editorial." *Cosmopolitan* 6 (June 1996) 10.

Felman, Shoshana and Dori Laub. *Testimony: Crises of Witnessing in Literature, Psychoanalysis, and History*. New York: Routledge, 1992.

Female Subjects in Black and White: Race, Psychoanalysis, Feminism. Ed. Elizabeth Abel, Barbara Christian, and Helene Moglen. Berkeley: U of California Press, 1997.

Ferguson, Dwayne (text and graphics). *Bite of the Scarab. Captain Africa 3*. Glen Ridge, N.J.: Diehard Studio, 1994.

Fields, Barbara. "Ideology and Race in American History." In *Region, Race, and Reconstruction*, 142–177.

Fields, Karen E. *Revival and Rebellion in Colonial Central Africa*. Princeton: Princeton U Press, 1985.

Fires in the Mirror: Essays and Teaching Strategies. Ed. Pamela Benson. Boston: WGBH Educational Print and Outreach, 1993.

Fischer, Michael J. "Ethnicity and the Post-modern Arts of Memory." In *Writing Culture* 194–233.

Fisher, Philip. *Hard Facts: Setting and Form in the American Novel*. New York: Oxford U Press, 1985.

Fluck, Winfried. *Das kulturelle Imaginäre: Eine Funktionsgeschichte des amerikanischen Romans, 1790-1900.* Frankfurt/Main: Suhrkamp, 1997.

Foner, Eric. "Hollywood Invades the Classroom." *New York Times* (Dec. 20, 1997) A:13.

The Four Voyages of Columbus. Tr. and ed. Cecil Jane. New York: Dover, 1988.

Fox, Robert Elliot. "Blacking the Zero: Toward a Semiotics of Neo-Hoodoo." *Black American Literature Forum* 18 (1984) 95-99.

Frank, Thomas. *The Conquest of Cool: Business Culture, Counterculture, and the Rise of Hip Consumerism.* Chicago: U of Chicago Press, 1997.

Frelik, Pavel. "Return from the Implants: Cyberpunk's Schizophrenic Futures." In *Simulacrum America* 87-94.

Frith, Simon. *Performing Rites: On the Value of Popular Music.* Oxford: Oxford U Press, 1996.

Fuller, Mary. *Voyages in Print: English Travel to America, 1576-1624.* Cambridge: Cambridge U Press, 1995.

Funktionen des Fiktiven. Ed. Dieter Henrich and Wolfgang Iser. *Poetik und Hermeneutik,* vol. 10. Munich: Fink, 1983.

Fury, David. *Kings of the Jungle: An Illustrated Reference to "Tarzan" on Screen and Television.* Jefferson, N.J.: McFarland, 1994.

Gans, Herbert J. "Symbolic Ethnicity: The Future of Ethnic Groups and Cultures in America." In *On the Making of Americans: Essays in Honor of David J. Riesman.* Ed. H. J. Gans et al. Philadelphia: U of Pennsylvania Press, 1979.

Garber, Marjorie. *Vested Interests: Cross-Dressing and Cultural Anxiety* (1992). New York: Routledge, 1997.

Gates, Henry Louis, Jr. "Editor's Introduction: Writing 'Race' and the Difference It Makes." In *"Race," Writing, and Difference* 1-20.

———. *Figures in Black: Words, Signs, and the 'Racial' Self.* New York: Oxford U Press, 1989.

———. *The Signifying Monkey: A Theory of African-American Literary Criticism.* New York: Oxford U Press, 1988.

Gibson, William. *Count Zero* (1987). London: HarperCollins, 1993.

———. *Neuromancer* (1984). London: HarperCollins, 1993.

Giles, Paul. "Virtual Americas: The Internationalization of American Studies and the Ideology of Exchange." *American Quarterly* 50:3 (Sept. 1998) 523-547.

Gilman, Susan. "The Mulatto, Tragic or Triumphant? The Nineteenth-Century Race Melodrama." In *The Culture of Sentiment* 221-243.

Gilroy, Paul. *The Black Atlantic: Modernity and Double Consciousness.* London: Verso, 1993.

Giroux, Henry A. *Fugitive Cultures: Race, Violence, and Youth.* New York: Routledge, 1996.

Givhan, Robin. "The Problem with Ugly Chic." In *No Sweat* 263-274.

Globalkolorit: Multikulturalismus und Populärkultur. Ed. Ruth Mayer and Mark Terkessidis. St. Andrä-Wördern: Hannibal, 1998.

Goldberg, David Theo. "Introduction: Multicultural Conditions." In *Multiculturalism* 1-41.

Green, Martin. *Dreams of Adventure, Deeds of Empire.* New York: Basic, 1979.

Green, Renée. "Leidige Liebe: My Alien/My Self—Readings at Work." In *Loving the Alien* 134-151.

Green, Renée: World Tour (exhibition catalogue). Ed. Russell Ferguson. Los Angeles: Museum of Contemporary Art, 1994.

Greenblatt, Stephen. *Learning to Curse: Essays in Early Modern Culture*. New York: Routledge, 1990.

———. *Marvelous Possessions: The Wonder of the New World*. Oxford: Clarendon Press, 1991.

———. *Shakespearean Negotiations: The Circulation of Social Energy in Renaissance England*. Oxford: Clarendon Press, 1988.

Griffiths, Alison. "'Journeys for Those Who Can Not Travel': Promenade Cinema and the Museum Life Group." *Wide Angle* 18:3 (1996) 53–84.

Grossberg, Lawrence. "The Space of Culture, The Power of Space." In *The Postcolonial Question* 169–188.

———. *"We gotta get out of this place": Popular Conservatism and Postmodern Culture*. New York: Routledge, 1992.

Gruesser, John C. "Afro-American Travel Literature and Africanist Discourse." *Black American Literature Forum* 24 (Spring 1995) 5–20.

Guerrero, Ed. *Framing Blackness: The African American Image in Film*. Philadelphia: Temple U Press, 1993.

Haggard, H. Rider. *King Solomon's Mines* (1885). Ed. and intro. Dennis Butts. Oxford: Oxford U Press, 1989.

Hall, Stuart. "Encoding, Decoding." In *The Cultural Studies Reader* 90–103.

———. "New Ethnicities." In *Stuart Hall* 441–459.

———. "When Was 'the Postcolonial'? Thinking at the Limit." In *The Postcolonial Question* 242–260.

Hansen, Miriam. *Babel and Babylon: Spectatorship in American Silent Film*. Cambridge, Mass.: Harvard U Press, 1991.

Haraway, Donna. *Primate Visions: Gender, Race, and Nature in the World of Modern Science*. New York: Routledge, 1989.

———. *Simians, Cyborgs, and Women: The Reinvention of Nature*. New York: Routledge, 1991.

Harth, Dietrich. "Exotismus." In *Moderne Literatur in Grundbegriffen* 135–138. Ed. D. Borchmeyer. 2nd revised ed. Tübingen: Niemeyer, 1994.

Harvey, David. "What's Green and Makes the Environment Go Round?" In *The Cultures of Globalization* 327–356.

Haselstein, Ulla. *Die Gabe der Zivilisation: Kultureller Austausch und literarische Textpraxis in Amerika, 1682-1861*. München: Wilhelm Fink, 2000.

———. "Stephen Greenblatt's Concept of a Symbolic Economy." *Real: Yearbook of Research in English and American Literature* 11 (1995) 347–370.

Healy, David F. *US Expansionism: The Imperialist Urge in the 1890s*. Madison: U of Wisconsin Press, 1970.

Heath, Stephen. "The Cinematic Apparatus: Technology as Historical and Cultural Form." In *The Cinematic Apparatus* 1–13.

———. "*Jaws*, Ideology, and Film Theory" (1976). In *Movies and Methods* 509–514.

Hebdige, Dick. *Subculture: The Meaning of Style*. London: Methuen, 1979.

Hemingway, Ernest. *Green Hills of Africa* (1935). New York: Simon & Schuster, 1996.

———. "The Short Happy Life of Francis Macomber" (1936). In *The Short Stories*. New York: Simon & Shuster, 1995.

Higham, John. *Send These to Me: Immigrants in Urban America*. Baltimore: Johns Hopkins U Press, 1984.

Hochschild, Adam. *King Leopold's Ghost*. Boston: Houghton Mifflin, 1998.

Hoffman, Donald L. "A Darker Shade of Grail: Questing at the Crossroads in Ishmael Reed's *Mumbo Jumbo*." *Callaloo* 17:4 (1994) 1245–1256.

Holert, Tom. "Mischkalkulationen und Gesichter der Zukunft. Noah Gabriel Becker, Tiger Woods, ein 'bi-rassischer' Androgyn und das 'vibe thing.'" In *Globalkolorit* 25–39.

Holert, Tom, and Mark Terkessidis. "Einführung in den Mainstream der Minderheiten." In *Mainstream der Minderheiten* 5–19.

hooks, bell. *Outlaw Culture: Resisting Representations.* New York: Routledge, 1994.

———. "Representing Whiteness in the Black Imagination." In *Displacing Whiteness* 165–179.

Hulme, Peter. *Colonial Encounters: Europe and the Native Caribbean, 1492–1797.* London: Methuen, 1986.

Hutcheon, Linda. "'Circling the Downspout of Empire': Postcolonialism and Postmodernism." *Ariel: A Review of International English Literature* 20 (1989) 149–175.

Hyde, Lewis. *Trickster Makes This World: Mischief, Myth, and Art.* New York: North Point Press, 1998.

Hyperkultur: Zur Fiktion des Computerzeitalters. Ed. Martin Klepper, Ruth Mayer, and Ernst-Peter Schneck. Berlin: Walter De Gruyter, 1996.

Ickstadt, Heinz. "Masks, Role Play, and Transgression—Crossing Boundaries as Topos and Strategy in American Literary Modernism." In *Crossing Boundaries: Inner- and Intercultural Exchanges in a Multicultural Society.* Frankfurt/Main: Peter Lang, 1997.

Iliffe, John. *Africans: The History of a Continent.* Cambridge: Cambridge U Press, 1995.

The Invention of Ethnicity. Ed. Werner Sollors. New York: Oxford U Press, 1989.

The Invention of Tradition. Ed. Eric Hobsbawm and Terence Ranger. Cambridge: Cambridge U Press, 1983.

Isak Dinesen: Critical Views. Ed. Olga Anastasia Pelensky. Athens: Ohio U Press, 1993.

Iser, Wolfgang. "Akte des Fingierens. Oder: Was ist das Fiktive im fiktionalen Text?" In *Funktionen des Fiktiven* 121–152.

———. *Das Fiktive und das Imaginäre: Perspektiven literarischer Anthropologie.* Frankfurt/Main: Suhrkamp, 1993.

James, Darius. *Negrophobia* (1992). New York: St. Martin's Press, 1993.

Jameson, Fredric. "Class and Allegory in Contemporary Mass Culture: *Dog Day Afternoon* as a Political Film" (1977). In *Movies and Methods*, vol. 2, 715–733.

———. "Foreword." In Jean-François Lyotard, *The Postmodern Condition* vii–xxv.

———. "Notes on Globalization as a Philosophical Issue." In *The Cultures of Globalization* 54–77.

———. *The Political Unconscious: Narrative as a Socially Symbolic Act* (1981). Ithaca: Cornell U Press, 1982.

———. *Postmodernism, or, the Cultural Logic of Late Capitalism.* Durham: Duke U Press, 1991.

JanMohamed, Abdul R. *Manichean Aesthetics: The Politics of Literature in Colonial Africa.* Amherst: U of Massachusetts Press, 1983.

Jeffords, Susan. *Hard Bodies: Hollywood Masculinity in the Reagan Era.* New Brunswick: Rutgers U Press, 1994.

Jehlen, Myra. "The Literature of Colonization." In *The Cambridge History of American Literature,* vol. 1, 11–168.

Johnson, Barbara. "No Short Cuts to Democracy." In *Fires in the Mirror* 9–11.

Johnson, Charles. *Being and Race: Black Writing since 1970.* Bloomington: Indiana U Press, 1990.

———. *Middle Passage* (1990). New York: Plume, 1991.

Jordan, Winthrop D. *White over Black: American Attitudes toward the Negro, 1550–1812* (1968). New York: Norton, 1977.

Joseph Conrad: Heart of Darkness. Ed. R. Kimbrough. New York: Norton, 1988.

Kanneh, Kadiatu. *African Identities: Race, Nation, and Culture in Ethnography, Pan-Africanism, and Black Literature.* London: Routledge, 1998.

Kaplan, Amy. "'Left Alone with America': The Absence of Empire in the Study of American Culture." In *Cultures of United States Imperialism* 3–21.

Karcher, Carolyn L. "The Riddle of the Sphinx: Melville's 'Benito Cereno' and the *Amistad* Case." In *Critical Essays on Herman Melville's "Benito Cereno"* 196–229.

Keith Piper: Relocating the Remains (exhibition catalogue). London: Institute of International Visual Arts, 1997.

Kenner, Hugh. *A Homemade World: The American Modernist Writers.* New York: Alfred A. Knopf, 1975.

Kenney, Catherine McGehee. *Thurber's Anatomy of Confusion.* Hamden: Archon Books, 1984.

Kilgour, Maggie. "The Function of Cannibalism at the Present Time." In *Cannibalism and the Colonial World* 238–259.

Kimmel, Michael S. "Consuming Manhood: The Feminization of American Culture and the Recreation of the Male Body, 1832–1920." In *The Male Body* 12–42.

Kingsolver, Barbara. *The Poisonwood Bible.* New York: HarperFlamingo, 1998.

Kipnis, Laura. "'The Phantom Twitchings of an Amputated Limb': Sexual Spectacle in the Post-colonial Epic." *Wide Angle* 11:4 (Oct. 1989) 42–51.

Die kleinen Unterschiede: Der Cultural Studies-Reader. Ed. Jan Engelmann. Frankfurt/Main: Campus, 1999.

Knapp, Jeffrey. *An Empire Nowhere: England, America, and Literature from Utopia to* The Tempest. Berkeley: U of California Press, 1992.

Knapp, Laurence F. *Directed by Clint Eastwood.* Jefferson: McFarland, 1996.

Krasner, James. "'Ape Ladies' and Cultural Politics: Dian Fossey and Biruté Galdikas." In *Natural Eloquence* 237–251.

Kuczynski, Alex. "Enough about Feminism: Should I Wear Lipstick?" *New York Times* (Mar. 28, 1999) sec. WK, 4.

Kultur und Gedächtnis. Ed. Jan Assmann and Tonio Hölscher. Frankfurt/Main: Suhrkamp, 1988.

Latour, Bruno. *We Have Never Been Modern.* Tr. Carolyn Porter. Cambridge, Mass.: Harvard U Press, 1993.

Lears, T. J. Jackson. *No Place of Grace: Antimodernism and the Transformation of American Culture, 1880–1920.* New York: Pantheon, 1981.

Le Carré, John. *The Constant Gardener.* London: Hodder & Sloughton, 2001.

Lee, Judith. "The Mask of Form in *Out of Africa*" (1985). In *Isak Dinesen* 266–282.

Lemke, Sieglinde. *Primitivist Modernism: Black Culture and the Origins of Transatlantic Modernism*. New York: Oxford U Press, 1998.

Lenz, Günter. "'Making Our Own Future Text': Neo-HooDooism, Postmodernism, and the Novels of Ishmael Reed." In *Theorie und Praxis im Erzählen des 19. und 20. Jahrhunderts* 323–344. Ed. W. Herget, K. P. Jochum and I. Weber. Tübingen: Gunter Narr, 1986.

Levenson, Michael. "The Value of Facts in the *Heart of Darkness*." *Nineteenth-Century Fiction* 40:3 (1985) 261–285.

Levine, Lawrence. *Black Culture and Black Consciousness: Afro-American Folk Thought from Slavery to Freedom*. New York: Oxford U Press, 1977.

Lippard, Lucy. *Mixed Blessings: New Art in a Multicultural America*. New York: Pantheon Books, 1990.

Lipsitz, George. *The Possessive Investment in Whiteness: How White People Profit from Identity Politics*. Philadelphia: Temple U Press, 1998.

Liska, George. *Career of Empire: America and Imperial Expansion over Land and Sea*. Baltimore: Johns Hopkins U Press, 1978.

Lott, Eric. *Love and Theft: Blackface Minstrelsy and the American Working Class*. New York: Oxford U Press, 1993.

———. "White Like Me: Racial Cross-Dressing and the Construction of American Whiteness." In *Cultures of United States Imperialism* 474–495.

Loving the Alien: Science Fiction, Diaspora, Multikultur. Ed. Diedrich Diederichsen. Berlin: ID Verlag, 1998.

Ludwig, Sämi. "Dialogic Possession in Reed's *Mumbo Jumbo*." In *The Black Columbiad* 325–336.

Lueken, Verena. "Weißer Jäger, schwarzes Herz". *epd Film* 7:6 (June 1990) 32.

Lynch, Lisa. "The Neo/bio/colonial Hot Zone: African Viruses, American Fairytales." *The International Journal of Cultural Studies* 1:2 (1998) 233–252.

Lyotard, Jean-François. *The Postmodern Condition* (1979). Tr. G. Bennington and B. Massumi. Manchester: Manchester U Press, 1984.

Mackenthun, Gesa. *Metaphors of Dispossession: American Beginnings and the Translation of Empire, 1492-1637*. Norman: U of Oklahoma Press, 1997.

———. "Postcolonial Masquerade: Antebellum Sea Fiction and the Transatlantic Slave Trade." In *Early America Re-explored* 537–567.

———. "Spectacle as Amnesia: The *Amistad* Case and the Sacrifice of Historical Truth." Paper presented at the EAAS Conference in Lisbon, 1998.

———. "State of the Art: Adding Empire to the Study of American Culture." *Journal of American Studies* 30:2 (1996) 263–269.

Macropolitics of Nineteenth-Century Literature: Nationalism, Exoticism, Imperialism. Ed. J. Arac and H. Ritvo. Durham: Duke U Press, 1991.

Mainstream der Minderheiten: Pop in der Kontrollgesellschaft. Ed. Tom Holert and Mark Terkessidis. Berlin: ID-Archiv, 1996.

The Male Body: Features, Destinies, Exposures. Ed. Laurence Goldstein. Ann Arbor: U of Michigan Press, 1994.

Marchetti, Gina. "Action-Adventure as Ideology." In *Cultural Politics in Contemporary Africa* 182–197. Ed. Jan Angus and Sut Jhally. New York: Routledge, 1989.

Marciano, Francesca. *Rules of the Wild*. New York: Pantheon, 1998.

Martin, Carol. "Bearing Witness: Anna Deavere Smith from Community to Theatre to Mass Media." In *A Sourcebook of Feminist Theatre and Performance* 81–93.

Martin, Emily. *Flexible Bodies: The Role of Immunity in American Culture from the Days of Polio to the Age of AIDS.* Boston, Mass.: Beacon Press, 1994.

Martin, Reginald. *Ishmael Reed and the New Black Aesthetic Critics.* New York: St. Martin's Press, 1988.

Masilela, Ntongela. "The Los Angeles School of Black Filmmakers." In *Black American Cinema* 107–117.

Maslin, Janet. "'Tarzan': Monkey Business—Rewriting the Jungle Book." *New York Times* (June 18, 1999).

Mason, Theodore O., Jr. "Performance, History, and Myth: The Problem of Ishmael Reed's *Mumbo-Jumbo.*" *Modern Fiction Studies* 34:1 (Spring 1988) 97–109.

Mayer, Ruth. "Cosmo-Politisch: Feminismus, Globalisierung und Modemagazine in den Neunzigern." In *Globalkolorit* 163–179.

———. "Cyberpunk: Eine Begriffsbestimmung." In *Hyperkultur* 221–233.

———. "Magical Mystery Tours: Ben Okri, Ishmael Reed and the New Age of Africa." *Zeitschrift für Anglistik und Amerikanistik* 45:3 (1997) 226–235.

———. "Pop as a Difference Engine: Music, Markets, and Marginality." In *Simulacrum America* 149–160.

———. "Schmutzige Fakten: Wie sich Differenz verkauft." In *Mainstream der Minderheiten* 153–168.

———. *Selbsterkenntnis, Körperfühlen: Medizin, Philosophie und die Amerikanische Renaissance.* München: Fink, 1997.

———. "Der Text als Hologramm: Die Cyberpunk-Literatur und die Kultur der Virtualität." In *Hyperkultur* 221–233.

———. "'Ther's somethin' in blood after all': Late Nineteenth-Century Fiction and the Rhetoric of Race." *Real: Yearbook of Research in English and American Literature* 11 (1995) 119–138.

———. "Vielbevölkerte Zone: Kulturwissenschaften zwischen Gutmenschentum und dem Glamour der Rebellion." In *Die kleinen Unterschiede* 231–243.

Mayer, Ruth and Mark Terkessidis. "Retuschierte Bilder: Multikulturalismus, Populärkultur und *Cultural Studies* in Deutschland." In *Globalkolorit* 7–23.

McClintock, Anne. "The Angel of Progress: Pitfalls of the Term 'Postcolonialism.'" In *Colonial Discourse, Postcolonial Theory* 253–266.

———. *Imperial Leather: Race, Gender, and Sexuality in the Colonial Contest.* New York: Routledge, 1995.

McClure, John. *Late Imperial Romance.* London: Verso, 1994.

———. "Postmodern/Post-secular: Contemporary Fiction and Spirituality." *Modern Fiction Studies* 41:1 (1995) 141–163.

Medeiros, Paulo. "Simian Narratives at the Intersection of Science and Literature." *Modern Language Studies* 23:2 (1993) 59–73.

Me Jane: Masculinity, Movies, and Women. Ed. Pat Kirkham and Janet Thumin. New York: St. Martin's Press, 1995.

Melville, Herman. *Benito Cereno* (1855). In *Billy Budd and Other Stories.* Harmondsworth: Penguin, 1986.

Mercer, Kobena. "Black Hair/Style Politics." In *Out There* 247–264.

———. *Welcome to the Jungle: New Positions in Black Cultural Studies.* New York: Routledge, 1994.

———. "Witness at the Crossroads: An Artist's Journey in Post-colonial Space." In *Keith Piper* 13–85.

Messent, Peter. *Ernest Hemingway.* New York: St. Martin's, 1992.

Bibliography 351

Metz, Christian. *The Imaginary Signifier: Psychoanalysis and the Cinema* (1977). Tr. Alfred Guzzetti et al. Bloomington: Indiana U Press, 1982.

Michaels, Walter Benn. *Our America*. Durham: Duke U Press, 1995.

Miller, Christoph. *Blank Darkness: Africanist Discourse in French*. Chicago: U of Chicago Press, 1985.

Mills, Sara. *Discourses of Difference: The Analysis of Women's Travel Writing and Colonialism*. London: Routledge, 1991.

Mitchell, W. J. T. "Foreword." In *On Narrative* vii–x.

———. *Picture Theory: Essays on Verbal and Visual Representation*. Chicago: U of Chicago Press, 1994.

Moddelmog, Debra A. "Re-Placing Africa in 'The Snows of Kilimanjaro': The Intersecting Economies of Capitalist-Imperialism and Hemingway's Biography." In *New Essays on Hemingway's Short Fiction*, 111–136.

Modernity and Its Malcontents: Ritual and Power in Postcolonial Africa. Ed. Jean Comaroff and John Comaroff. Chicago: U of Chicago Press, 1993.

Modleski, Tania. "Doing Justice to the Subjects. Mimetic Art in a Multicultural Society: The Work of Anna Deavere Smith." In *Female Subjects in Black and White* 57–76.

———. *Feminism without Women: Culture and Criticism in a 'Postfeminist' Age*. New York: Routledge, 1991.

Morrison, Toni. *Paradise* (1997). New York: Plume, 1999.

———. *Playing in the Dark: Whiteness and the Literary Imagination*. Cambridge, Mass.: Harvard U Press, 1992.

———.*Song of Solomon* (1977). London: Picador, 1989.

Moses, Wilson J. *The Golden Age of Black Nationalism, 1850–1925*. New York: Oxford U Press, 1978.

Movies and Methods, vol. 2. Ed. Bill Nichols. Berkeley: U of California Press, 1985.

Mudimbe, V. Y. *The Invention of Africa: Gnosis, Philosophy, and the Order of Knowledge*. Bloomington: Indiana U Press, 1988.

Multiculturalism: A Critical Reader. Ed. David Theo Goldberg. Oxford: Blackwell, 1994.

Mulvey, Laura. *Visual Order and Other Pleasures*. London: Macmillan, 1989.

Nagl, Tobias. "'I wonder if heaven's got a ghetto': Aliens, Ethnizität und der SF-Film." In *Loving the Alien* 68–87.

Natural Eloquence: Women Reinscribe Science. Ed. Barbara T. Gates and Ann D. Shteir. Madison: U of Wisconsin Press, 1997.

The New American Studies: Essays from Representations. Ed. Philip Fisher. Berkeley: U of California Press, 1991.

New Critical Approaches to the Short Stories of Ernest Hemingway. Ed. Jackson J. Benson. Durham: Duke U Press, 1990.

New Essays on Hemingway's Short Fiction. Ed. Paul Smith. Cambridge: Cambridge U Press, 1998.

The New Historicism Reader. Ed. H. Aram Veeser. New York: Routledge, 1994.

North, Michael. *The Dialect of Modernism: Race, Language, and Twentieth-Century Literature*. New York: Oxford U Press; 1994.

Norton, Chris. "Black Independent Cinema and the Influence of Neo-Realism" <http:\\imagesjournal.com/issue05/features/black.htm>.

No Sweat: Fashion, Free Trade, and the Rights of Garment Workers. Ed. Andrew Ross. New York: Verso, 1997.

Noyes, John. *Colonial Space: Spatiality in the Discourse of German South West Africa, 1884-1915*. Chur: Harwood, 1992.

On Fashion. Ed. Shari Benstock and Susanne Ferriss. New Brunswick: Rutgers U Press, 1994.

On Narrative. Ed. W. J. T. Mitchell. Chicago: U of Chicago Press, 1981.

Out There: Marginalization and Contemporary Cultures. Ed. Russell Ferguson et al. Cambridge, Mass.: MIT Press, 1990.

Owens, Craig. "Earthwords." *October* 10 (Fall 1979) 121–130.

Pakenham, Thomas. *The Scramble for Africa: White Man's Conquest of the Dark Continent from 1876 to 1912*. New York: Avon Books, 1991.

Paquette, Robert L. "From History to Hollywood: The Voyage of 'La Amistad.'" *The New Criterion* 16 (Mar. 1998) 74–78.

Parry, Benita. *Conrad and Imperialism: Ideological Boundaries and Visionary Frontiers*. London: Macmillan, 1983.

———. "Narrating Imperialism *Nostromo*'s Dystopia." In *Cultural Readings of Imperialism* 227–246.

———. "Resistance Theory/Theorising Resistance, or Two Cheers for Nativism." In *Colonial Discourse, Postcolonial Theory* 172–196.

Pease, Donald. "New Americanists: Revisionist Interventions into the Canon" (199ᴄ). In *The New Historicism Reader* 141–160.

Pedersen, Carl. "Middle Passages: Representation of the Slave Trade in Caribbean and African-American Literature." *Massachusetts Review* 34:2 (1993) 225–239.

Pfeil, Fred. *White Guys: Studies in Postmodern Domination and Difference*. London: Verso, 1995.

Phillips, Richard. *Mapping Men and Empire: A Geography of Adventure*. London: Routledge, 1997.

Pollock, Griselda. "Empire, Identity, and Place: Masculinities in *Greystoke: The Legend of Tarzan*." In *Me Jane* 128–147.

Porges, Irwin. *Edgar Rice Burroughs: The Man Who Created Tarzan*. Provo: Brigham Young U Press, 1975.

The Postcolonial Question: Common Skies, Divided Horizons. Ed. Iain Chambers and Lidia Curti. London: Routledge, 1996.

The Post-colonial Studies Reader. Ed. Bill Ashcroft, Gareth Griffiths, and Helen Tiffin. London: Routledge, 1995.

Postmodernism: A Reader. Ed. Thomas Docherty. New York: Columbia U Press, 1993.

Pratt, Mary Louise. *Imperial Eyes: Travel Writing and Transculturation*. London: Routledge, 1992.

Race, Nation, Class: Ambiguous Identities. Ed. Etienne Balibar and Immanuel Wallerstein. London: Verso, 1991.

"Race," Writing, and Difference. Ed. Henry Louis Gates, Jr. Chicago: U of Chicago Press, 1986.

Radway, Janice. "What's in a Name? Presidential Address to the American Studies Association, 20 November 1998." *American Quarterly* 51:1 (1999) 1–32.

Ranger, Terence. "Invention of Tradition in Colonial Africa." In *The Invention of Tradition* 211–262.

Rawley, James A. *The Transatlantic Slave Trade: A History*. New York: W. W. Norton, 1981.

Reed, Ishmael. *Mumbo Jumbo* (1972). New York: Atheneum, 1988.

Region, Race, and Reconstruction: Essays in Honor of C. Vann Woodward. Ed. J. Morgan Kousser and James M. McPherson. New York: Oxford U Press, 1982.

Reinelt, Janelle. "Performing Race: Anna Deavere Smith's *Fires in the Mirror.*" *Modern Drama* 39 (1996) 609–617.

Reisen im Diskurs: Modelle der literarischen Fremderfahrung von den Pilgerberichten bis zur Postmoderne. Ed. Anne Fuchs and Theo Harden. Heidelberg: Winter, 1995.

Reitberger, Reinhold and Wolfgang Fuchs. *Comics: Anatomy of a Mass-Medium* (1971). London: Studio Vista Publishings, 1972.

Remaking History. Ed. Barbara Kruger and Phil Mariani. Seattle: Bay Press, 1989.

Re-visioning the Past: Historical Self-Reflexivity in American Short Fiction. Ed. Bernd Engler and Oliver Scheiding. Trier: Wissenschaftlicher Verlag Trier, 1998.

Richburg, Keith B. *Out of America: A Black Man Confronts Africa* (1997), with a new afterword. San Diego: Harcourt Brace, 1998.

Robbins, Bruce. "Comparative Cosmopolitanisms." In *Cosmopolitics* 246–264.

Rogin, Michael P. *Blackface, White Noise: Jewish Immigrants in the Hollywood Melting Pot.* Berkeley: U of California Press, 1996.

———. "'Make My Day!' Spectacle as Amnesia in Imperial Politics." In *Cultures of United States Imperialism* 499–534.

———. "Spielberg's List." *New Left Review* 230 (1998) 153–160.

———.*Subversive Genealogy: The Politics and Art of Herman Melville.* Berkeley: U of California Press, 1983.

Root, Deborah. *Cannibal Culture: Art, Appropriation, & the Commodification of Difference.* Boulder, Colo.: Westview Press, 1996.

Rosaldo, Renato. *Culture and Truth: The Remaking of Social Analysis* (1989). Boston: Beacon Press, 1993.

Rose, Tricia. *Black Noise: Rap Music and Black Culture in Contemporary America.* Hanover: Wesleyan U Press, 1994.

———. "Give Me a (Break) Beat! Sampling and Repetition in Rap Production." In *Culture on the Brink* 249–264.

Rosen, Gary. "'Amistad' and the Abuse of History." *Commentary* 105 (Feb. 1998) 46–51.

Ross, Andrew. "The Gangsta and the Diva." In *Black Male* 158–166.

———. "The Great White Dude." In *Constructing Masculinity* 167–175.

———. "Pop-Politik: Schwarze Musik und weiße Identität." Tr. Esther Fritsch. In *Globalkolorit* 59–64.

———. *Strange Weather: Culture, Science, and Technology in the Age of Limits.* London: Verso, 1991.

———. "Tribalism in Effect." In *On Fashion* 284–300.

Rothstein, Edward. "From Darwinian to Disneyesque. In Tarzan's Evolution, a New Theory: The Survival of Nearly Everything." *New York Times* (July 15, 1999) E1, E8.

Rushdie, Ashraf H. A. "The Phenomenology of the Allmuseri: Charles Johnson and the Subject of the Narrative of Slavery." *African American Review* 26:3 (1992) 373–394.

Said, Edward. *Culture and Imperialism* (1993). New York: Vintage, 1994.

———. *Orientalism.* Harmondsworth: Penguin, 1978.

Sale, Maggie Montesinos. *The Slumbering Volcano: American Slave Ship Revolts and the Production of Rebellious Masculinity*. Durham: Duke U Press, 1997.

Sandoval, Chéla. "Theorizing White Consciousness for a Post-empire World: Barthes, Fanon, and the Rhetoric of Love." In *Displacing Whiteness* 86–106.

Sassen, Saskia. *The Global City: New York, London, Tokyo*. Princeton: Princeton U Press, 1991.

———. *Globalization and Its Discontents*. New York: New Press, 1998.

Schell, Heather. "Outburst! A Chilling True Story about Emerging-Virus Narratives and Pandemic Social Change." *Configurations* 5:1 (1997) 93–133.

Schirato, Anthony. "Comic Politics and Politics of the Comic: Walter Abish's *Alphabetical Africa*." *Critique* 33:2 (Winter 1992) 133–144.

Schmidgen, Wolfram. "The Principle of Negative Identity and the Crisis of Relationality in Contemporary Literary Criticism." *Real: Yearbook of Research in English and American Literature* 11 (1995) 371–404.

Schüwer, Martin. "Superhelden in der Krise: Revision eines Pop-Mythos in Alan Moores und Dave Gibbons' *Watchmen*." Master's thesis, U of Cologne, 1998.

Seeßlen, Georg. *Abenteuer: Geschichte und Mythologie des Abenteuerfilms*. Marburg: Schüren, 1996.

Semmler, Iliana Alexandra. "Ebola Goes Pop: The Filovirus from Literature into Film." *Literature and Medicine* 17:1 (1998) 149–174.

Serres, Michel. *The Parasite*. Tr. Lawrence R. Schehr. Baltimore: Johns Hopkins U Press, 1982.

Shohat, Ella, and Robert Stam. *Unthinking Eurocentrism: Multiculturalism and the Media*. London: Routledge, 1994.

Silverman, Kaja. "Fragments of a Fashionable Discourse." In *Studies in Entertainment* 139–152.

Simulacrum America: The USA and the Popular Media. Ed. Carolin Auer and Elisabeth Kraus. Rochester: Camden House, 2000.

Slavery in the Americas. Ed. Wolfgang Binder. Würzburg: Könighausen & Neumann, 1993.

The Slave's Narrative. Ed. C. T. Davis and H. L. Gates, Jr. Oxford: Oxford U Press, 1985.

Slotkin, Richard. *Regeneration through Violence: The Mythology of the American Frontier, 1600–1860* (1973). New York: HarperPerennial, 1996.

Smith, Anna Deavere. *Fires in the Mirror: Crown Heights, Brooklyn, and Other Identities*. New York: Anchor Books, 1993.

Smith, Paul. "Eastwood Bound." In *Constructing Masculinity* 77–97.

———. "Introduction." In *New Essays on Hemingway's Short Fiction* 1–18.

Smith, Sidonie. "The Other Woman and the Racial Politics of Gender: Isak Dinesen and Beryl Markham in Kenya." In *De/colonizing the Subject* 410–435.

Sollors, Werner. *Beyond Ethnicity: Consent and Descent in American Culture*. New York: Oxford U Press, 1986.

Solomon-Godeau, Abigail. "Photography after Art-Photography." In *Art after Modernism* 75–85.

A Sourcebook of Feminist Theatre and Performance: On and beyond the Stage. Ed. Carol Martin. London: Routledge, 1996.

Spillers, Hortense. "Mama's Baby, Papa's Maybe: An American Grammar Book." In *Within the Circle* 454–481.

Spindler, Amy M. "The Splash Heard Round the World." *New York Times* (Sept. 13, 1998) sec. 9, 1.

————. "Taking Stereotyping to a New Level in Fashion." *New York Times* (June 3, 1997) A:21.

Spivak, Gayatri Chakravorty. *A Critique of Postcolonial Reason: Toward a History of the Vanishing Present.* Cambridge, Mass.: Harvard U Press, 1999.

Stange, Maren. "Memory and Form in Recent African American Photography: From *12 Million Black Voices* to Carrie Mae Weems." Paper presented at the EAAS Conference in Lisbon, 1998.

Stanley, Henry Morton. *How I Found Livingstone: Travels, Adventures, and Discoveries in Central Africa.* London: Low, 1872.

Sterling, Bruce. *Islands in the Net* (1988). New York: ACE, 1989.

Sterling, Susan Fisher. "Signifying: Photographs and Texts in the Work of Carrie Mae Weems." In *Carrie Mae Weems* 18–36.

Stuart Hall: Critical Dialogues in Cultural Studies. Ed. David Morley and Kuan-Hsing Chen. London: Routledge, 1996.

Stuckey, Sterling. "'Follow Your Leader': The Theme of Cannibalism in Melville's *Benito Cereno.*" In *Critical Essays on Herman Melville's "Benito Cereno"* 182–195.

Studies in Entertainment: Critical Approaches to Mass Culture. Ed. Tania Modleski. Bloomington: Indiana U Press, 1986.

Sundquist, Eric. *To Wake the Nations: Race in the Making of American Literature.* Cambridge, Mass.: Harvard U Press, 1993.

Tasker, Yvonne. *Spectacular Bodies: Gender, Genre, and the Action Cinema.* London: Routledge, 1993.

————. *Working Girls: Gender and Sexuality in Popular Cinema.* London: Routledge, 1998.

Taussig, Michael. *Mimesis and Alterity: A Particular History of the Senses.* New York: Routledge, 1993.

————. *Shamanism, Colonialism, and the Wild Man: A Study in Terror and Healing.* Chicago: U of Chicago Press, 1987.

Taves, Brian. *The Romance of Adventure. The Genre of Historical Adventure Movies.* Jackson: University of Mississippi Press, 1991.

Terkessidis, Mark. *Psychologie des Rassismus.* Opladen: Westdeutscher Verlag, 1998.

Thomas, Brook. "The Legal Fictions of Herman Melville and Lemuel Shaw." In *Critical Essays on Herman Melville's "Benito Cereno"* 116–126.

Thurber, James. "The Secret Life of Walter Mitty" (1939). In *The Thurber Carnival* 47–51. New York: Harper & Brothers, 1945.

Tibbetts, John. "A New Screen Tarzan." *Films in Review* 35:6 (June/July 1984) 360–364.

Torgovnick, Marianna. *Gone Primitive: Savage Intellects, Modern Lives.* Chicago: U of Chicago Press, 1990.

————. *Primitive Passions: Men, Women, and the Quest for Ecstasy.* New York: Knopf, 1996.

The Traffic in Culture: Refiguring Art and Anthropology. Ed. George E. Marcus and Fred E. Myers. Berkeley: U of California Press, 1995.

Trebay, Guy. "*Tribe.*" *Village Voice Literary Supplement* (July/Aug. 1998) 7.

Treichler, Paula. "AIDS and HIV Infection in the Third World: A First World Chronicle." In *Remaking History* 31–86.

Über Grenzen: Limitation und Transgression in Literatur und Ästhetik. Ed. Claudia Benthien and Irmela M. Krüger-Fürhoff. Stuttgart: Metzler, 1999.

Uncontrollable Bodies: Testimonies of Identity and Culture. Ed. Rodney Sappington and Tyler Stallings. Seattle: Bay Press, 1994.

Vero, Gianpiero de. "Esotismo e dialettica." In *Esotismo e crisi della civiltà* 205–231. Ed. B. Cappelli, E. Cocco. Naples: Tempi moderni, 1979.

Vidal, Gore. "Tarzan Revisited" (introduction). In Edgar Rice Burroughs, *Tarzan of the Apes* 1–14.

Walcott, Derek. "The Sea Is History." In *Poems, 1965-1980* 237–240. London: Jonathan Cape, 1980.

Wallerstein, Immanuel. *The Politics of World-Economy: The States, the Movements, and the Civilization. Essays.* Cambridge: Cambridge U Press, 1984.

Wark, McKenzie. "Fashion as a Culture Industry." In *No Sweat* 227–248.

Warren, Kenneth. "Appeals for (Mis)recognition: Theorizing the Diaspora." In *Cultures of United States Imperialism* 392–406.

Watney, Simon. "Missionary Positions: AIDS, 'Africa,' and Race." In *Out There* 89–103.

Wehler, Hans-Ulrich. *Der Aufstieg des amerikanischen Imperialismus zur Entwicklung des Imperium Americanum, 1865-1900.* Göttingen: Vandenhoeck & Ruprecht, 1974.

Weingart, Brigitte. *Ansteckende Wörter: Repräsentationen von AIDS.* Frankfurt/Main: Suhrkamp, forthcoming 2002.

———. "Parasitäre Praktiken: Zur Topik des Viralen." In *Über Grenzen* 207–230.

Wesseling, Elisabeth. *Writing History as a Prophet: Postmodernist Innovations of the Historical Novel.* Amsterdam: John Benjamins, 1991.

West, Cornel. *Race Matters.* New York: Vintage, 1993.

West, Russell. *Conrad and Gide: Translation, Transference, and Intertextuality.* Amsterdam: Rodopi, 1996.

White, Allon. *The Uses of Obscurity: The Fiction of Early Modernism.* London: Routledge & Kegan Paul, 1981.

White, Andrea. *Joseph Conrad and the Adventure Tradition: Constructing and Deconstructing the Imperial Subject.* Cambridge: Cambridge U Press, 1993.

White, Hayden. "The Value of Narrativity in the Representation of Reality." In *On Narrative* 1–23.

Wideman, John Edgar. *The Cattle Killing.* Boston: Houghton Mifflin, 1996.

———. "Fever." In *Fever* 127–161. New York: Henry Holt, 1989.

Wiener, Jon. "Tall Tales and True." *The Nation* (Jan. 31, 1994) 134.

Wilentz, Gay. "Civilizations Underneath: African Heritage as Cultural Discourse in Toni Morrison's *Song of Solomon.*" *African American Review* 26:1 (1992) 61–76.

Williams, Patricia J. *The Alchemy of Race and Rights.* Cambridge, Mass.: Harvard U Press, 1991.

———. "'In the Times of the Drums'" (book review). *New York Times Book Review* (Aug. 15, 1999) 24.

———. *The Rooster's Egg: On the Persistence of Prejudice.* Cambridge, Mass.: Harvard U Press, 1995.

Williams, Sherley Anne. "Two Words on Music: Black Community." In *Black Popular Culture* 164–172.

Williamson, Judith. "Woman Is an Island: Femininity and Colonization." In *Studies in Entertainment* 99–115.

Within the Circle: An Anthology of African American Literary Criticism from the

Harlem Renaissance to the Present. Ed. Angelyn Mitchell. Durham: Duke U Press, 1994.

Witte, Arndt. "Fremd- und Eigenerfahrung in Westafrika: Am Beispiel von Gertraud Heises *Reise in die schwarze Haut* und T. Coraghessan Boyles *Water Music.*" In *Reisen im Diskurs* 374–390.

Woolf, Marie. "Me Tarzan, You Jane, We PC: Disney Sanitizes Lord of the Jungle's Dark Continent Adventures." *The Guardian* (Nov. 12, 1995) 4.

Writing Culture: The Poetics and Politics of Ethnography. Ed. James Clifford, George E. Marcus. Berkeley: U of California P, 1986.

Young, Robert. *Colonial Desire: Hybridity in Theory, Culture, and Race.* London: Routledge, 1995.

———. *White Mythologies: Writing History and the West.* London: Routledge, 1990.

You Tarzan: Masculinity, Movies, and Men. Ed. Pat Kirkham and Janet Thumim. London: Lawrence & Wishart, 1993.

Yurca, Catherine. "Tarzan, Lord of the Suburbs." *Modern Language Quarterly* 57:3 (Sept. 1996) 479–504.

Zapf, Hubert. "Reflection vs. Daydream: Two Types of the Implied Reader in Hemingway's Fiction." In *New Critical Approaches to the Short Stories of Ernest Hemingway* 96–111.

Filmography

Allan Quatermain and the Lost City of Gold. Dir. Gary Nelson. With Richard Chamberlain, Sharon Stone, and James Earl Jones. Golan-Globus Production, 1986.

Amistad. Dir. Steven Spielberg. With Djimon Houson, Matthew McConaughey, Anthony Hopkins, and Morgan Freeman. Dreamworks, 1997.

Congo. Dir. Frank Marshall. With Laura Linney, Dylan Walsh, and Ernie Hudson. Paramount, 1995.

The English Patient. Dir. Anthony Minghella. With Kristin Scott-Thomas, Ralph Fiennes, Juliette Binoche, and Willem Dafoe. Tiger Moth Productions, 1996.

The Ghost and the Darkness. Dir. Stephen Hopkins. With Michael Douglas, Val Kilmer, and John Kani. Paramount, 1996.

Gorillas in the Mist. Dir. Michael Apted. With Sigourney Weaver, John Omirah Miluwi, and Bryan Brown. Universal City Studios/Warner Bros., 1988.

Greystoke: The Legend of Tarzan, Lord of the Apes. Dir. Hugh Hudson. With Christopher Lambert, Ian Holm, and Andie McDowell. Warner Bros., 1984.

Heart of Darkness. Dir. Nicolas Roeg. With Tim Roth, John Malkovich, and Isaach de Bankole. Turner Network Television, 1994.

Ishtar. Dir. Elaine May. With Dustin Hoffman, Warren Beatty, and Isabelle Adjani. Columbia, 1987.

The Jewel of the Nile. Dir. Lewis Teague. With Michael Douglas and Kathleen Turner. Twentieth Century Fox, 1985.

Khartoum. Dir. Basil Dearden and Eliot Elisofon. With Charlton Heston, Laurence Olivier, and William Blackstone. Cinerama, 1966.

King Solomon's Mines. Dir. J. Lee Thompson. With Richard Chamberlain, Sharon Stone, and Ken Gampu. Golan-Globus Production, 1985.

Last Angel of History. Dir. John Akomfrah. With Edward George. Researchers Kodwo Eshun and Floyd Webb. Death Audio Film Production, 1995.

Live and Let Die. Dir. Guy Hamilton. With Roger Moore, Jane Seymour, and Yaphet Kotto. Eon Productions, 1973.

Out of Africa. Dir. Sydney Pollack. With Meryl Streep and Robert Redford. Universal Pictures, 1985.

Outbreak. Dir. Wolfgang Petersen. With Dustin Hoffmann, Rene Russo, Morgan Freeman, Donald Sutherland, and Cuba Gooding, Jr. Warner Bros., 1995.

Sankofa. Dir. Haile Gerima. With Oyafunmike Ogunlano, Kofi Ghanaba, Alexandra Duah, and Mutabaruka. DiProCi/Ghana National Commission on Culture/Negod-Gwad/NDR, 1993.

The Sheltering Sky. Dir. Bernardo Bertolucci. With John Malkovich, Debra Winger, Campbell Scott, and Eric Vu-An. Warner Bros., 1990.

Tarzan. With Wolf Larson and Lydie Denier. A Franco-Canadian-Mexican coproduction, TF-1/Dune, 1991–1993.

Tarzan. Dir. Kevin Lima and Chris Buck. Art dir. Daniel St. Pierre. Ed. Gregory Perler. Tarzan character animator Glen Keane. With the voices of Tony Goldwyn, Minnie Driver, and Glenn Close. Walt Disney Pictures, 1999.

White Hunter, Black Heart. Dir. Clint Eastwood. With Clint Eastwood, Jeff Fahey, and George Dzundza. Warner Bros., 1990.

White Mischief. Dir. Michael Radford. With Greta Scacchi and Charles Dance. White Umbrella Film, 1987.

The Young Indiana Jones Chronicles. Dir. Dick Maas. With Corey Carrier, Sean Patrick Flanery, and George Hall. Lucasfilms, 30 episodes, 1992.

Index